An Introduction to Music Studies

Why study music? How much practical use is it in the modern world? This introduction proves how studying music is of great value both in its own terms and also in the post-university careers marketplace. The book explains the basic concepts and issues involved in the academic study of music, draws attention to vital connections across the field, and encourages critical thinking over a broad range of music-related issues.

- Covers all main aspects of music studies, including topics such as composition, music theory, opera, popular music, and the economics of music.
- Provides a thorough overview of a hugely diverse subject, from the history of early music to careers in music technology, giving a head-start on the areas covered in a music degree.
- New to "neume"? Need a reminder about "ripping"? Glossaries give clear definitions of key musical terms.
- Chapters are carefully structured and organized enabling easy and quick location of the information needed. Each chapter contains:
  - a chapter preview presenting a clear and concise introduction to the topic
  - a bullet list of key issues, showing at a glance the aims and content of the chapter
  - a chapter summary at the end of the chapter, providing a useful revision tool
  - a list of key discussion topics to help broaden thinking on the subject.

J. P. E. HARPER-SCOTT is Lecturer in Music at Royal Holloway, University of London. He is the author of *Edward Elgar, Modernist* (Cambridge, 2006), *Elgar: An Extraordinary Life* (2007), and co-editor, with Julian Rushton, of *Elgar Studies* (Cambridge, 2007).

JIM SAMSON is Professor of Music at Royal Holloway, University of London. He is the editor of *The Cambridge History of Nineteenth-Century Music* (2002) and the author of *Virtuosity and the Musical Work: The Transcendental Studies of Liszt* (Cambridge, 2003). He is also one of three Series Editors of *The Complete Chopin: A New Critical Edition*.

An Introduction to
MUSIC STUDIES

Edited by

J. P. E. HARPER-SCOTT

and

JIM SAMSON

CAMBRIDGE
UNIVERSITY PRESS

CAMBRIDGE UNIVERSITY PRESS
Cambridge, New York, Melbourne, Madrid, Cape Town, Singapore, São Paulo,
Delhi, Tokyo, Mexico City

Cambridge University Press
The Edinburgh Building, Cambridge CB2 8RU, UK

Published in the United States of America by Cambridge University Press, New York

www.cambridge.org
Information on this title: www.cambridge.org/9780521603805

First published 2009
Reprinted 2011

Printed in the United Kingdom at the University Press, Cambridge

A catalogue record for this publication is available from the British Library

ISBN 978-0-521-84293-8 hardback
ISBN 978-0-521-60380-5 paperback

Contents

Illustrations

Notes on contributors

J. P. E. HARPER-SCOTT has scholarly interests in Elgar, Walton, Britten, Vaughan Williams, Strauss, Wagner, Schenkerian theory, the philosophy of Heidegger, and meaning in music. He is the author of two books, and the co-editor of a third, on Elgar, and is preparing a monograph on Wagner.

JIM SAMSON has published widely (including seven single-authored books, and six edited or co-edited books) on the music of Chopin and on analytical and aesthetic topics in nineteenth- and twentieth-century music.

RACHEL BECKLES WILLSON has research interests that lie primarily in Cold War music politics, twentieth-century music historiography and analysis, and the anthropology of music (particularly in connection with Israel–Palestine). She is the author of *György Kurtág: The Sayings of Péter Bornemisza Op. 7* (Ashgate, 2004) and *Ligeti, Kurtág and Hungarian Music during the Cold War* (Cambridge, 2007).

KATHARINE ELLIS is author of *Music Criticism in Nineteenth-Century France* (Cambridge, 1995) and *Interpreting the Musical Past* (Oxford, 2005). Her work embraces many aspects of the cultural history of music, with a focus on nineteenth-century France.

JOHN RINK has produced three edited books for Cambridge University Press: *Chopin Studies 2* (1994; with Jim Samson), *The Practice of Performance: Studies in Musical Interpretation* (1995), and *Musical Performance: A Guide to Understanding* (2002). He has also published a Cambridge Music Handbook entitled *Chopin: The Piano Concertos* (1997), which draws upon his experience in performing these works.

ANDREW BOWIE has published a number of major books on German philosophy, literature, and music, including *From Romanticism to Critical Theory* (Routledge, 1997) and *Music, Philosophy, and Modernity* (Cambridge, 2007). He is an enthusiastic jazz performer.

HENRY STOBART is the author of *Music and the Poetics of Production in the Bolivian Andes* (Ashgate, 2006) and is co-editor with Patricia Kruth of the interdisciplinary volume *Sound* (Cambridge, 2000) and with Rosaleen Howard of *Knowledge and Learning in the Andes: Ethnographic Perspectives* (Liverpool, 2002).

STEPHEN ROSE has published many articles on German music between 1500 and 1700 in its social, material, and performing contexts, and he is finishing a book on *The Musician-Narratives of the German Baroque*. He is Reviews Editor (Books and Music) of *Early Music* and is active as an organist and keyboard continuo player.

DAVID CHARLTON is the author of *French Opera 1730–1830: Meaning and Media* (Ashgate, 2000), editor of *The Cambridge Companion to Grand Opera* (Cambridge, 2003), and co-editor with Mark Ledbury of *Michel-Jean Sedaine (1719–1797): Theatre, Opera and Art* (Ashgate, 2000). He has also edited the writings of E. T. A. Hoffmann.

ERIK LEVI has interests in both the academic and practical aspects of music. He has published the pioneering book *Music in the Third Reich* (London, 1994) and numerous articles and chapters on aspects of German musical life from the 1920s to the end of World War II, and has also worked as a professional accompanist.

ELIZABETH EVA LEACH is the author of *Sung Birds: Music, Nature, and Poetry in the Later Middle Ages* (Ithaca, 2007), editor of *Machaut's Music: New Interpretations* (Woodbridge, 2003), and co-editor with Suzannah Clark of *Citation and Authority in Medieval and Renaissance Musical Culture: Learning from the Learned* (Woodbridge, 2005). She has also published widely on the music of late medieval secular francophone culture and the analysis of early music, as well as an article on the Spice Girls.

JULIE BROWN has interests in early twentieth-century music, music analysis/criticism, and music and the moving image. She is author of *Bartók and the Grotesque* (Ashgate, 2007), editor of *Western Music and Race* (Cambridge, 2007), and is completing a book on films about music before developing a project about cinema organ culture.

TINA K. RAMNARINE is a musician, anthropologist, and explorer. She is the author of *Creating Their Own Space: The Development of an Indian-Caribbean Musical Tradition* (University of West Indies Press, 2001), *Ilmatar's Inspirations: Nationalism, Globalization, and the Changing Soundscapes of Finnish Folk Music* (Chicago, 2003), and *Beautiful Cosmos: Performance and Belonging in the Caribbean Diaspora* (Pluto Press, 2007), and editor of *Musical Performance in the Diaspora* (Routledge, 2007). A former co-editor of *Ethnomusicology Forum*, she now serves on the journal's editorial board.

JULIAN JOHNSON is the author of *Webern and the Transformation of Nature* (Cambridge, 1999), *Who Needs Classical Music? Cultural Choice and Musical Value* (New York, 2002), and *Mahler's Voices* (New York, 2008). He is also a composer whose music has been professionally performed in Europe and the USA.

BRIAN LOCK is an internationally acclaimed composer specializing in film and multimedia. His movie scores include *The Land Girls*, *Vipère au poing*, *The Gambler*, and *Foreign Moon* and his TV music can be heard on the BBC's *Panorama* and *Coast* as well as CBS's *60 Minutes*. His multimedia work explores the edges between acoustic and technological composition and includes the recently premiered *Concerto for Clarinet, Percussion, Birds and Computers* and the *Sonata for Cello and Mixing Desk*.

NICHOLAS COOK directs the AHRC Research Centre for the History and Analysis of Recorded Music (CHARM). His books, mostly published by Oxford University Press, include *A Guide to Musical Analysis* (1987); *Music, Imagination, and Culture* (1990); *Beethoven: Symphony No. 9* (1993); *Analysis through Composition* (1996); *Analysing Musical Multimedia* (1998); *Music: A Very Short Introduction* (1998); and *The Schenker Project: Culture, Race, and Music Theory in Fin-de-siècle Vienna* (2007).

Preface

This book, written entirely by academic staff at Royal Holloway, University of London, is designed as a companion for music students, and aims to answer the questions "how and why do we study music?" It is targeted at first-year university and college students, non-majors who are considering going on to a music major, and first-year music majors, but is also useful for "A"-level and high-school students who are preparing for a music course and need an overview of the field. It explains the basic concepts and issues involved in the academic study of music, provides an introduction to the principal areas of study, discusses approaches to a wide range of repertoire, and considers important aspects of the practice of music today. In particular, through its cross-references, it draws attention to vital connections across the field. The book is thus designed to be used as a background text and to encourage critical thinking over a broad range of music-related issues.

The editors would like to thank Vicki Cooper and Rebecca Jones at Cambridge University Press for their encouragement of this project and their patience as it was brought together. They are also grateful to Matthew Pritchard for preparing the index.

Nicholas Cook would like to thank David Patmore for his comments on a draft of chapter 16. John Rink would like to thank Eric Clarke and Aaron Williamson for helpful suggestions.

Features of this book: a guide

1 Music history

JIM SAMSON

Chapter preview

This chapter asks what we mean by music history and why we study it. It considers some of the different kinds of history that can be, and have been, written, ranging from the stylistic history of musical works to the social history of how those works came to be written. It looks at the different strategies demanded by the study of music in different periods, in different places, and for different audiences. It looks at some of the tools, methods, and sources historians use to learn about musical practices in the past. considers some of the conventional categories they employ in an order in history. They often refer to musical "traditions," for example, they invoke period terms such as "Baroque" and "Classical." The chapter also addresses some of the overt and hidden agendas found in different types of historical writing, it queries whether some aspects of music history have been neglected in favor of others at different times, and it asks how much we can learn by considering the reception of music through the centuries. It further considers how the study of music history is supported by, and may in turn illuminate, some of the other categories of musical study discussed in this book.

Key issues

- How can we do historical justice to works of music, given that they are part of our present?
- Is music history shaped primarily by composers and scores, or by the cultural conditions which demanded and/or enabled musical performances?
- What kinds of evidence can
- What is a "fact" of music histo create a network of stories aro these so-called facts?
- How useful is it to divide m (including nations) and into te

Chapter previews provide a clear and concise introduction to the topics covered, together with a list of **key issues** to be discussed in each chapter.

or example, the introductory a *raga*, that organizes and governs melody in Indian classical music, involves the improvised exploration of the "personality" of the chosen *raga*. In free time, sometimes lasting up to an hour, the performer will gradually introduce the *raga's* various pitches (*srutis*) and melodic characteristics or gestures (*pakar* or *chalan*). Listeners who are familiar with the style may appreciate and be profoundly moved by the way that a highly skilled and imaginative performer reveals, develops and confers emotional intensity to the various ele ments of a *raga's* to life in performance "Doing music" ized as th pa of the sic lies he sense of well-being ared or individual expression it involves, rather than in its acoustic result. In such musics, people may be

Feature boxes offer illustrative case studies to clarify the meaning of important themes, and to give a taste of the wider contexts you will explore in your degree.

Box 6.2 Raga Yaman

Yaman is one of the first Hindustani ragas taught to students; it is seen to provide a strong foundation from which to learn and understand others – of which there are hundreds. The time traditionally associated with Yaman performance is late evening (9–12 p.m.) and ter is generally categorized as "grand" and d with the idea of a brave and noble-minded hero (dor 1999:164). Like other ragas, the tonal center is Sa (notated here as C), and two other notes are of special importance, the *vadi* ("sonant") and *samvadi* ("consonant"). For Yaman: these are respectively Mi (E) and Ni (B). The notation below shows Yaman's pitches (incorporating Indian *sargam* note names) and its ascending and descending contour, as well as a few of its most characteristic melodic gestures (*pakar* or *chalan*).

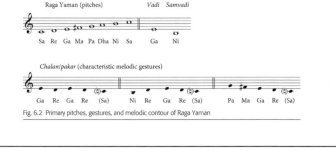

Raga Yaman (pitches)   Vadi Samvadi

Sa Re Ga Ma Pa Dha Ni Sa   Ga   Ni

Chalan/pakar (characteristic melodic gestures)

Ga Re Ga Re (Sa)   Ni Re Ga Re (Sa)   Pa Ma Ga Re (Sa)

Fig. 6.2 Primary pitches, gestures, and melodic contour of Raga Yaman

Annotated lists of **further reading** point you towards essential resources for further research, **references** give a convenient list of the sources referred to in each chapter, and **glossaries** offer accessible definitions of key terms.

Further reading

Lehmann, Andreas C., Sloboda, John A., and Woody, Robert H. (2007), *Psychology for Musicians* (New York: Oxford University Press).
    This "concise, accessible, and up-to-date introduction to psychological research for musicians" is divided into sections on musical skills, and musical roles (including performer, teacher, listener).
Rink, John, ed. (2002), *Musical Performance: A Guide to Understanding* (Cambridge: Cambridge University Press).
    Contains entry-level studies on the psychology of performance, developing the ability to perform, preparing for performance, memorizing music, communicating with the body, ensemble performance, performance anxiety, and listening.
Sloboda, John A. (1985), *The Musical Mind: The Cognitive Psychology of Music* (Oxford: Clarendon Press).
    A classic text, focusing on music as a cognitive skill; music, language, and meaning; performance; composition and improvisation; listening; musical learning and development; and cultural and biological issues.

References

Adler, Guido (1885), "Umfang, Methode und Ziel der Musikwissenschaft," *Vierteljahrsschrift für Musikwissenschaft*, 1, 5–20.
Clarke, Eric (1995), "Expression in perfor[...] semiosis," in John Rink (1995) (ed.), *[...] Interpretation* (Cambridge: Cambri[...]
Clarke, Eric (2002), "Understanding the psyc[...]
Clarke, Eric and Cook, Nicholas (2004) (e[...] *Prospects* (New York: Oxford Unive[...]
Clarke, Eric and Davidson, Jane (1988), "T[...] Thomas (1998) (ed.), *Composition, [...] Process in Music* (Aldershot: Ashgat[...]
Davidson, Jane (2002), "Developing the a[...]
Deliège, Irène and Wiggins, Geraint A. (2[...] *Research in Theory and Practice* (Hov[...]
Deutsch, Diana (1970), "Tones and numb[...] memory," *Science*, 168, 1604–5.
Dixon, Simon, Goebl, Werner and Widm[...] Worm: real time visualization of [...] Loudness Animation," *Proceedings [...] (ICMC2002)* (accessed 30 July 2008[...] dixon02performance.html.

Glossary

Mode	The term has been used in a variety of different contexts, the common core of which is the relationship between notes, whether in terms of duration or pitch. In the context of its discussion in chapter 2, mode refers to a collection of notes with a particular hierarchy of pitch relationships: it can be a scale (i.e., ordered) or a melodic type (i.e., not ordered). The former is used most often for classifying pitch systems; the latter, as a basis for improvisation or composition. Mode is a descriptive term that serves as a translation of non-Western concepts understood to be similar or identical (the *pathet* of Javanese gamelan music, for instance).
Motif	In general terms, a motif is a short musical idea, defined by melody, rhythm, harmony or a combination of all three. Rudolph Réti, whose analyses were based around motifs, defined it as "any musical element, be it a melodic phrase or fragment or even only a rhythmical or dynamic feature which[...] varied throughout a work or a [...]positional design somewhat [...]ne arts."

Chapter summary

- Aesthetics has to do with changing ideas about subjectivity and objectivity.
- Music is produced in terms of rules and yet also has to do with free expression.
- There are differing traditions of aesthetics of music, one of which sees music as an object to be defined, the other of which sees it as a practice connected to other practices.
- The aesthetic need to appreciate music as an art, and [...] to understand how music is linked to political, hist[...] sophical issues play a central role in recent developments [...] understanding of music.

Discussion topics

- Is taste actually subjective, despite all the objective factors which play a role in its formation?
- Can music be true?
- How does one interpret the fact that musical evaluation changes as society changes?
- Does music need philosophy, or does philosophy need music?
- What do we understand when we talk about the meaning of music?

Chapter summaries help you to check that you have understood the main thrust of each chapter, while **discussion topics** help you to broaden your thinking on particular subjects through imaginative speculation.

Introduction

J.P.E. HARPER-SCOTT

Why do you want to study music? Do you perhaps dream of spending three or four years developing advanced performing skills on one or more instruments, learning a little about the history of music and its theory on the side, and emerging from the experience with a degree certificate? That might seem an attractive enough idea, and most university music departments these days will offer you a range of performing possibilities alongside the more traditional academic courses. But as the teaching of humanities (of which academic music is a part) in the modern university becomes less a focus for the rigorous intellectual scrutiny of the history and artefacts of civilizations, and more a site for the development of competencies for the post-university workplace, you (and especially your parents) will rightly ask what practical use such study might be in the contemporary world. Studying the practice and history of music seems on the face of it too narrowly focused to be of much use to anyone but an aspiring school music teacher, an orchestral musician, or a music journalist – and there are far fewer jobs in those areas than there are music graduates. Fortunately, however, a music degree offers a more genuinely useful training for graduate life than might at first be imagined.

Like other humanities disciplines, but perhaps more so than any other, musicology (as study of music is generally called in the UK; the US splits this into "musicology," broadly meaning music's historical and cultural contexts, and "music theory," the study of music's structural and pitch organization) provides a breadth of training in transferable skills that will make you particularly valuable to other professions as a music graduate. The richness of music study is owed to its multidisciplinary focus: that is to say, studying musicology involves learning and applying methods and insights from many distinct disciplines.

Like literature students (in English or foreign languages, ancient or modern, sacred or secular), as a music student you will deal extensively with texts, and develop refined skills in interrogating them. In the case of music the text may be anything from a musical score to critical writings on a composer or musical tradition. Music students learn to establish historical, social, and wide-ranging intellectual contexts for the texts they examine, and to make interpretative decisions about how to evaluate them. They acquire fundamental research skills and learn to maximize our natural tendency to enquire into the unexpected and unknown.

At the same time you will learn, of course, to hone your writing and oral skills to a range of particular applications. All of these tools would serve just as well for further advanced study in any humanities subject, as also for the synthesis and original interpretation of a number of legal documents or government reports. Your contextual understanding (historical, literary, religious, ethnological, etc.) and critical acumen will, therefore, be enlarged not simply for the use they serve in understanding and communicating about music, but for their own sakes.

Work with musical notation lends study of music a distinctive edge over other humanities disciplines. The manipulation of its often complex symbolic systems, together with the elaborate theories that have been developed (over the course of millennia) to enable discussion, will encourage you to develop analytical skills of a kind more often associated with mathematics and the natural sciences – disciplines that indeed exercise a strong influence on parts of the discipline, as some of the following chapters will show.

Experience of ensemble performance, and in some cases fieldwork, most obviously develops social skills, but it also calls on entrepreneurial abilities and effective techniques of time management. It will widen your experience and understanding of other people and other societies, with their protean traditions of intellectual, religious, scientific, and musical life. Other creative work, for instance in compositional technique, will develop your creative potential and further stimulate the intellectual urge – already alive if you are considering or starting a music degree – to explore and originate ideas. Composition in today's musical world ranges from traditional orchestral, instrumental, and vocal composition for public performance through the composition of music for film to the creative synergies of the rock or pop recording studio; it seems so very varied that again you might imagine the skills learned through any aspect of it would be limited in application. Yet common to all these approaches to musical production is their heavy and increasing dependence on technology and on the practicalities of the music business: this makes learning compositional technique yet another way that you will engage with perhaps surprising contemporary issues, in this case technological and economic.

In the chapters that follow, we hope to convey something of this exciting diversity of approaches to a single subject. What follows is a very brief summary of their contents. You may find it useful to browse the "chapter preview" and "key issues" sections of chapters that seem particularly interesting before you plunge into them. Each chapter also has a clear summary at the end, along with some discussion topics for you to think about, and lists of references cited and of further reading, should you want to explore certain aspects in more detail.

Part 1, "Disciplines," will give you an insight into the principal broad approaches to the question of what music is and where it fits in to our common and personal life and history. In chapter 1 Jim Samson explores the question of what is meant by music history, and explains why musicologists study it, before in chapter 2 Rachel Beckles Willson discusses the range of possibilities for analyzing the musical texts themselves; together they will give you a taste of the foundational components of most music degrees. Katharine Ellis's chapter on the sociology of music shifts the emphasis to the social networks surrounding music, and the way that our judgments of musical value reflect social situations, while in chapter 4 John Rink turns the focus back on to the psychological experience of music by individuals, adding a further dimension to the way we construct musical sense and meaning, and giving an insight into the feeling you probably already have that music has a way of getting to you somehow. The more abstract question of what music is, and how it relates to the self and to the world, is given a historical introduction and exploration by Andrew Bowie in chapter 5.

Having introduced you to the ways that musicologists think and write about music, Part 2, "Approaches to repertoire," gets down to what kinds of music are written and thought about. You may be surprised to hear how much academics have learned about some kinds of music. The section begins with an exploration by Henry Stobart of the various musics of the world that are not part of the Western art-music tradition (the music you will find cordoned off in its own section in record shops), showing through case studies how different musical repertoires shape and respond to people's understanding of the world. A similarly "alien" tradition is the focus of chapter 7 by Stephen Rose, which looks at the history of "early music," its relation to established belief systems like Christianity, and the ways in which we try to draw this music into our present, through historically informed performance and other means. Chapters 8 to 12 examine particular genres or styles of musical composition. David Charlton's chapter on opera explores its history and its relevance to today's society, drawing out the ways that music theater can convey political and ethical messages. Erik Levi's chapter on concert music is a guide through the vast repertoire of Western art music that is likely to form the largest component of your degree in one way or another; it examines the complementary roles of musical and social changes in the development of musical institutions and media. In chapter 10, Andrew Bowie considers jazz alongside other forms of music and asks how the style relates to academic disciplines and to the role of technology in modernity. The section closes with two kinds of music that some of you may particularly be wondering about in a university context: popular and film music. In her chapter on popular music, Elizabeth Eva Leach works with the problem of defining popular music and studying it as part of musicology, examining issues in production and reception. Closing the section, Julie Brown's chapter on music in film and television charts the development of music on screen, and explores the expressive effects of music on the total experience of these mixed art forms.

Part 3 concerns "Music in practice," something with which most (but not all) music students are familiar; you may find it stimulating to see how musicologists think about music practice in a more concentrated way than you might have done already. It opens with Tina K. Ramnarine's chapter on musical performance itself, which explores the social contexts and political dimensions of performance, and examines the role of the personal – even the bodily – in aspects of performance. Chapter 14, by Julian Johnson, situates composition in the study of music, emphasizing its practical basis in the imagination, manipulation, and appropriate fashioning of materials for specific ends. The background to modern compositional practice is expanded by Brian Lock in chapter 15 on music technology, which offers an introduction to the technical means by which musicians nowadays produce and disseminate their music: this may be of particular interest if you are drawn to studio recording and the technologies employed in film composition. The book is rounded off by Nicholas Cook's exploration of the economics and business of music, a world you may seek to enter at some stage. It begins by showing how economics and music have traditionally been intertwined before outlining the contemporary music business and assessing the future of the industry in the digital age.

Overall we intend the book to suggest that studying music will encourage you to make interdisciplinary connections and cross-references between these many different approaches. We hope to demonstrate at least some of the richness of this subject of study and the purely intellectual rewards you will gain from being a student within it.

Part 1
Disciplines

1 Music history

JIM SAMSON

Chapter preview

This chapter asks what we mean by music history and why we study it. It considers some of the different kinds of history that can be, and have been, written, ranging from the stylistic history of musical works to the social history of how those works came to be written. It looks at the different strategies demanded by the study of music in different periods, in different places, and for different audiences. It looks at some of the tools, methods, and sources historians use to learn about musical practices in the past, and it considers some of the conventional categories they employ in order to create an order in history. They often refer to musical "traditions," for example, and they invoke period terms such as "Baroque" and "Classical." The chapter also addresses some of the overt and hidden agendas found in different types of historical writing, it queries whether some aspects of music history have been neglected in favor of others at different times, and it asks how much we can learn by considering the reception of music through the centuries. It further considers how the study of music history is supported by, and may in turn illuminate, some of the other categories of musical study discussed in this book.

Key issues

- How can we do historical justice to works of music, given that they are part of our present?
- Is music history shaped primarily by composers and scores, or by the cultural conditions which demanded and/or enabled musical performances?
- What kinds of evidence can we use to construct histories of oral traditions?
- What is a "fact" of music history (Dahlhaus 1983)? How do historians create a network of stories around their particular interpretations of these so-called facts?
- How useful is it to divide music history into geographical regions (including nations) and into temporal periods?

• What do music histories tell us about the time and place of their provenance? How might we rewrite music history for today's world?

Art versus history

Think about the differences between a history of music and a general history: let us say a history of Reformation England, or a history of the American Revolution. We could make a list of such differences, but I just want to draw your attention to one of particular importance. Among the principal objects of study in a music history are musical works. We might take Beethoven's "Eroica" Symphony (No. 3) as our example. Now the "Eroica" was composed at a particular time and in a particular place; we can assign to it a fairly precise completion date (summer of 1803). Despite this, it cannot quite be consigned to "the past." On the contrary, as you surely know from your own experience, the "Eroica" is still very much an active, living part of our present. The same could not be said of political events, nor even of more long-term socio-economic transformations. These have their repercussions, of course, and they often play a major role in shaping later political and social realities, but of themselves they belong clearly to "the past," as "events" of greater or lesser duration.

This difference has major implications for our understanding of music history, or indeed of the history of any art. If the work is really part of our present, it is rather difficult to do historical justice to it; hard, in other words, to see how the work "for today" can be related to the work "in its time." All history is concerned with a dialogue between now (the present) and then (the past). One of the main reasons we study it in the first place is because "then" can maybe inform us about "now." This is a bit more complicated than it might seem. History is written in the present, but even in general histories it is hard to say quite where the past ends and the present begins. I hope you can see that in art histories the dialogue between the two is even more complicated. And actually, if you really are interested in the qualities of the "Eroica" as a work – a work "for today" – you might learn more by examining it analytically rather than historically (see chapter 2 on this). That is the real point of my subtitle "Art *versus* history." It highlights one of the reasons why it is not always very easy to decide how best to make history out of musical works.

On the other hand it is rather easier to see how we can make history out of the **reception** of musical works. Not only is the "Eroica" alive and well amongst us today; it was no less alive and well in early twentieth-century Paris, in mid-nineteenth-century Leipzig, and of course in the Vienna of Beethoven's own lifetime, though, importantly, it tended to mean rather different things in each of these cases. We might say that it exerted a different kind of power in each of those "thens." You can trace how the "Eroica" threaded its way through different social and cultural formations, attaching itself to them in

different ways, adapting its own semblance and in the process changing
theirs. In a word, you can note how it
was heard "with different ears" at
different times and in different
places. In his monograph on the
work, Thomas Sipe outlines some
of the stages in this process of reception (Sipe 1998). I have tried to present these side-by-side (inevitably at
some cost to the subtlety of Sipe's
argument) in Box 1.1, but it is important to realize that responses of this
kind are not created afresh by each
generation; the earlier categories of
response linger on in later periods.

Now there is nothing particularly
new about looking at how music
was received, but modern reception
histories, many of them really quite

> **Box 1.1 Beethoven's "Eroica": some patterns of reception**
>
> - Revolutionary propaganda. The dedication to Napoleon Bonaparte and the subsequent withdrawal of that dedication, together with the association of its finale with Prometheus, inevitably associates the work with an "Age of Revolution"
> - Programmatic interpretations. Growing from the above, we have early nineteenth-century accounts based on battlefield imagery, links with Homeric and Virgilian epic, and portraits of Bonaparte
> - Psychological interpretations. These stem mainly from the later nineteenth century, and are usually biographical readings, stressing Beethoven's putative German nationalism, his "clairvoyant" insight, his victory over adversity (deafness), and so on
> - Structural and historical interpretations. These include twentieth-century analytical approaches designed to demonstrate the "unity" of the work through motive or harmony, as well as accounts that seek to recover its original historical meanings

specialized, do tend to raise some larger questions. They often suggest –
explicitly or implicitly – that contemporary readings (the reception of the
"Eroica" by audiences of Beethoven's time) have no particular privilege, and
that the meaning of the work is something that unfolds and develops throughout its subsequent reception right down to the present. You might want to
think about that issue, as it is rather central to historical study and throws up a
number of related questions that I will just leave hanging. Is a reception history
of the "Eroica" really about changes in musical taste and the social factors that
influence those changes (in which case music history arguably collapses into
social history), or can it reveal something about the work itself? And what is
it, anyway, that elevates a work like the "Eroica" to the status of a masterwork,
a component of the **canon**? Is the answer to this last question to be found
exclusively in qualities of the work itself, to be revealed perhaps by analysis?
Or is it in part ideological? In other words, is the canon largely a construction
by people who exercise cultural power? And if that is the case, do we need
to ask ourselves why certain groups (women, for example) and regions (Greece,
for example) have been excluded from, or marginalized by, music histories?

Stylistic or social history?

Historical questions look very different from the kinds of analytical questions
that will be discussed in chapter 2. Given a common object of study, analysts

might ask: "how does it function in musical terms?," whereas historians would be more likely to ask: "where does it come from?," or "what made it possible?," or perhaps "how did it shape later developments?" If we stick for the time being with musical works as primary documents of a music history, then we might ask those historical questions from two rather different perspectives. The first would address purely musical, or stylistic, influences, while the second would look at the shaping role of social, political, and intellectual contexts.

Let us take a step back in time from our Beethoven example and consider the works of Guillaume Du Fay from the early Renaissance period (in music history, roughly the first half of the fifteenth century) as a collective case study. We might answer our historical questions here by discussing Du Fay's indebtedness to major predecessors and contemporaries. Such historical trajectories might then be extended to embrace evolutionary developments within his output, allowing for differences of idiom between sacred and secular, and between mass and motet, and perhaps also for an individuality of idiom we might not immediately associate with music before Du Fay. And we might go on to note that Du Fay's mature idiom functioned in its turn as a principal model for later fifteenth-century composers. Now all of these answers are based on comparisons of musical **style**. We locate Du Fay within a narrative that reaches back to the fourteenth-century *Ars Nova* and forward to Josquin des Prez (born *c.*1450–5). He becomes a pivotal figure, in other words, in the transition from medieval to Renaissance music, though we need to be rather careful about reading this story as a kind of "progress," and therefore labeling Du Fay as a "progressive" figure. He was that in one sense, but maybe the term "progressive" has taken on some modern meanings that would not have been appropriate in the fifteenth century (we should be careful anyway about assuming that music history describes a progression from simple to complex forms and materials). See Box 1.2 for a very rough indication of the kind of stylistic history I mean here.

Of course we might equally find answers to our questions by considering the context in which Du Fay worked. Many factors would come into play here.

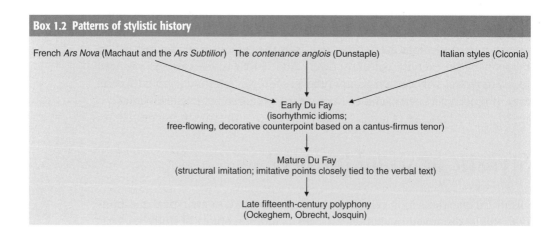

Box 1.2 Patterns of stylistic history

French *Ars Nova* (Machaut and the *Ars Subtilior*)   The *contenance anglois* (Dunstaple)   Italian styles (Ciconia)

Early Du Fay
(isorhythmic idioms;
free-flowing, decorative counterpoint based on a cantus-firmus tenor)

Mature Du Fay
(structural imitation; imitative points closely tied to the verbal text)

Late fifteenth-century polyphony
(Ockeghem, Obrecht, Josquin)

There are the constraints imposed, and the opportunities afforded, by the liturgy (Du Fay was a church composer employed for much of his life as a papal singer: many early "composers" were in fact employed principally as performing musicians). There are the specific demands made by particular patrons (he was also a court composer working at various times at the Savoy court) and particular commemorative occasions (court weddings, deaths, rededications of churches, and ceremonial occasions of other kinds). There are the contrasted ambiences of different cultural centers (Renaissance Florence as against Burgundian Cambrai). And there are the effects of a wider climate of ideas (the strengthening individualism we associate with an age of humanism, for example). This is what I meant when I referred to "the shaping role of social, political, and intellectual contexts" at the beginning of this section. We are evoking here a rather different perspective on Du Fay's music, revealing in effect how musical styles respond to social imperatives. But we should note all the same that this perspective still places musical works right at the center of our story. These days musicologists sometimes speak of a **work concept** to describe this foregrounding of musical works (Goehr 1992), and you will encounter that term elsewhere in this volume. It is discussed in chapter 11, for example, and there is it contrasted with alternative ways of thinking about how we might begin to define what music actually is. These alternative readings naturally have a bearing on how we construe the subject-matter of a music history, and I want to reflect a bit more on them now. Have a look at Dahlhaus's question in the fourth of our key issues above. What, indeed, is a "fact" of music history? There is more than one kind of answer.

It is worth reminding ourselves, obvious though this may seem, that music is a performing art, and that its history includes the history of music-making as a cultural practice. The subject-matter of a music history, then, might include all the many and varied practices involved in making music, promoting music, listening to music, and thinking about music. Performance, teaching, and manufacturing sites and professions would form the heart of this story, but in the later stages of music history, taste-creating institutions such as journals and publishing houses, and eventually broadcasting and recording companies, would enter the narrative as important subplots. This all adds up to what we might call a "social history" of music (see chapter 3 for further commentary on this), as distinct from the stylistic history illustrated in Box 1.2, a move that parallels that found in some general history away from study of kings and queens and towards "ordinary people." The primary concern of a "social history of music" would be with the role that music played in people's lives, so it would not be unduly interested in questions of aesthetic value (Chartier 1988). Contrast that with a history based on musical works, which is more likely to reinforce our sense of that canon of masterpieces I referred to earlier. Indeed these two histories can rather easily tend in opposing directions, separating out the "popular" repertory that engaged most of the people most of the time and the "significant" repertory that catered for the (usually socially privileged) minority. You should note that these days so-called "popular music" is increasingly part of the study of music history at tertiary level, which is why we have devoted a chapter to it in this volume (see chapter 11).

Oral histories

It is obvious that different repertories and periods of music history will respond better to some approaches than to others, and may indeed require different historical tools. In studying what is often called "early music," for instance, we may find that little biographical information is available even for some of the most highly valued composers, and that part of the historian's task is akin to a kind of detective work, combing the archives to establish the authorship or chronology. In such contexts, the study of genre (mass, motet) or medium (choral, keyboard) may well take precedence over the study of individual composers (see chapter 7). And like style, both genre and medium have acted as major controlling concepts in music histories, as a glance at randomly selected book and chapter titles will quickly show you. When we reach late eighteenth- and nineteenth-century music, on the other hand, our approach often becomes more composer- and work-centered. This explains the prominence not just of biography, but of philological approaches. In contrast to early music, there is often a wealth of manuscript and early printed sources available for musical works in these later periods, and this has promoted a whole industry of philological study dedicated to the production of reliable texts. Take Chopin, for example. When you pick one of the Nocturnes off the library shelf you may be quite unaware of the mountain of sources relating to just that one piece. There may be sketches, autograph manuscripts prepared for the engravers (the music was typically published simultaneously in three different countries to avoid piracy), scribal copies, proof copies, the three first editions (which often disagree), later impressions of those editions (that's not the same as later editions), student copies with autograph glosses, and so on. Box 1.3 illustrates a typical source chain, or *stemma*, for a Chopin piece (here the Two Polonaises Op. 40), where **A** = autograph, **C** = a copy made by Julian Fontana.

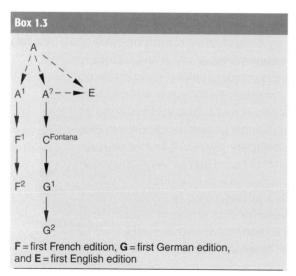

Box 1.3

F = first French edition, **G** = first German edition, and **E** = first English edition

Now we need to remember that all of this concerns only the notated art music of what is usually called the Western tradition, just one corner of the world's music (see chapter 6). How, you might ask, are we to make historical sense of those traditions of art music where there are no scores and where improvisation is an important constituent of music-making? Or for that matter the various kinds of so-called "folk music," these days more often described by the less loaded term "traditional music"? To begin with, we should be wary of making too clean a separation between oral and literate traditions, and in particular of equating the former with simplicity and the latter with complexity. After all, the products of literate traditions, usually associated with composers, works, and complexity, still depend heavily on oral transmission, and on a body of performative insight that is largely unwritten (Treitler 1992). And conversely, the fact that a composition does not exist in notated form, but lives rather in the minds of performers, does not disqualify it as a "work," and as "complex." That said, there are very real difficulties facing historians of oral culture, given that there is often little primary evidence prior to the phonograph. This has the effect of privileging early recordings as documents that are presumed to inscribe some sort of primary state of the music in question rather than a particular stage of its evolution. And it can also encourage the reassuring but questionable belief that prior to the sea-changes of modernity, rural "folk music" (as distinct from urban "popular music") existed in much the same form for centuries. In fact, "folk music," as we normally understand it, is something of a construction, by no means to be equated with ritual song and dance that might be observed or recorded in the field.

So in tracing the history of oral traditions we have to be careful about finding evidence where we can, while at the same time avoiding the temptation to place undue weight on what just happens to have survived. Iconography is one way into reconstructing oral practices, especially of the ancient world. Passing references in histories and chronicles are another. Inventories of musicians and pieces can also be instructive for some practices, as can theoretical treatises. In the case of some Persian and Arabic art music, for instance, scholars have found it helpful to set medieval treatises alongside contemporary practices, allowing history and ethnography to work together to mutual benefit. In the case of Ottoman (Turkish) classical music, where some notations do exist, historical accounts given by travelers both from the east and the west have proved illuminating. And in the case of Roma (gypsy) music from central Europe, we can learn a good deal by studying the appropriation of popular idioms by art music. I will elaborate on this last point by way of a more concrete example. When in early seventeenth-century England music was written (probably by Robert Johnson) for a gypsy dance in Ben Jonson's masque *Gypsies Metamorphosed*, the rhythm was the same 9/8 pattern (2 + 2 + 2 + 3) – needless to say, hardly typical of art music at that time – heard in performances by Roma in Turkey and the Balkans today. In other words, we can learn from this appropriation something of the antiquity of these oral traditions.

In the end, though, we have to accept that with many "non-Western" (note, by the way, how loaded that term is) and traditional repertories, historians quickly come up against what Oliver Strunk once called the "impenetrable barrier of oral tradition." Even with the recorded and transcribed repertories that became available from the early twentieth century onwards, there are challenging questions to ask about practices and products, about stability and change, about the meeting-points between musical styles, and (conversely) about the effects of cultural isolation. There are questions too about how changes of musical idiom map onto underlying social changes, about just when an accumulation of such changes amounts to a break with tradition (many would say that the effect of modernity on traditional music – meaning folk music – constitutes just such a moment), and about how we can (or whether we should) draw what is often an endemic diversity of local styles into anything like a synthesis. And all this before we get to questions of subject position (what ethnomusicologists call "insider/outsider" or "emic/etic" perspectives, as discussed in chapter 6). It is perhaps not so surprising that many students of folk music and popular music choose to deal more with social context than with the music itself.

Narratives in history

In trying to make sense of the past, we sometimes use tactics that are closer to narrative fiction than we might like to think. We create stories about the past, and that means constructing plots that enable us to select and then order what seems important (you will note the inescapable chicken-and-egg dilemma here). Many of these plots are really about place. They focus on geography, and above all on geographical difference: north and south, east and west, and most importantly center and periphery. Historians very often refer to a mainstream **tradition** (it might be Burgundian polyphony, Italian opera, or German symphonism), and then arrange everything else around the edges of these traditions. But we need to bear in mind that traditions are constructed after the event, and that they can function a bit like distorting lenses through which we look back at events and practices. In other words, they carry covert (and often overt) values, and can even encourage a kind of chauvinism. When we construct a genealogy of German symphonists (we are back to the canon), we at the same time push other composers and other places into the margins. The key word here is "other."

You might be familiar with Edward Said's book *Orientalism*, in which he argued that Europe constructed the orient to its (that is to Europe's) own specifications (Said 1979). Well, there is a rather obvious "other" in this case, but arguably the same approach is at work elsewhere. In discussing Russia, for example, Richard Taruskin suggests that European musicians have constructed their own Russia, and he goes on to demonstrate that our evaluations of Russian music are not at all congruent with those of Russian musicians (Taruskin 1984). This has some bearing too (though the issue is less clear-cut) on constructions of eastern Europe, and also of northern Europe. What we often get is a kind of assimilationist history. You might look at two rather specialized commentaries on Sibelius: one by the British writer Tim Howell and the other by the American scholar James Hepokoski (Howell 1989; Hepokoski 1993). They have very different takes on Sibelius, but they both seem agreed that to discuss him as a Finnish or even a Scandanavian musician is to court provincialism. In these analyses Sibelius is claimed, as it were, by a canon of pan-European modernism. He is no more Finnish than Stravinsky is Russian. This is a defensible position, but it may not be the whole story. We can learn a great deal from Hepokoski and Howell, but perhaps we need to read them with Taruskin's cautionary remarks in mind.

All of which brings me to one of the most common plots underlying music histories, the tendency to write them as national narratives. In some European countries, music history courses in academies and universities are cleanly divided into two streams, one focused on the national history and the other on the wider European history. Much of this is a legacy of nineteenth-century **nationalism**. It is undoubtedly true that music played a major propaganda role for political nationalism in the nineteenth century, partly picking up on ideas promoted by the German writer Johann Gottfried Herder (very roughly, Herder took the view that the "spirit of a people" is embodied in its language and culture). So we often find nineteenth- and early twentieth-century composers committing to nationalist agendas by turning to the history and mythology of the nation, and also to its folk music. (We might note here, by the way, that although the folk music in such cases may play a legitimate symbolic role, it is rather doubtful that it can be taken as a real emblem of the nation. Folk culture in general is invariably regional or social rather than national in impulse. It is no respecter of political borders.)

It may be helpful to consider two brief case studies, beginning with Germany. We can trace the gradual forging of German musical nationalism partly through symbols and institutions. Cologne is a good starting point. The completion of the cathedral in the early 1840s inaugurated a powerful musical symbolism centered on the Rhine, leading to a vast outpouring of Rhinelieder ("Rhine songs"), to works like the "Rhenish" symphony by Schumann, and ultimately to Wagner's tetralogy *Der Ring des Nibelungen* (Porter 1996). The folk ethos and nature worship here is central to one strand of German nationalism, particularly when opposed to its "others" (Robertson 1999). If we then move to Leipzig, we encounter a rather different strand. Here, at around the same time (the mid-century), the German canon was steadily consolidated through the Conservatory syllabus, the Gewandhaus concerts, the music journals, and the publishing house Breitkopf and Härtel, which began issuing collected editions of the great German masters. Not long after, in neighboring

Weimar, yet another strand was forming. Here we see the beginnings of a rhetoric of German modernism that was associated with Liszt and his circle, including the critic and historian Franz Brendel. It was Brendel who coined the significant term "Neue Deutsches Schule" (New German School).

Our second short case study takes us to the Czech lands. If we examine music and musical life in Prague, we find a significant change of orientation around the 1860s. Again, this was partly to do with institutions: the Provisional Theatre, dedicated to Czech-language productions, and later the National Theatre (Tyrrell 1988); the Žofín Academy concerts with their modern programs; the choral societies and wind bands promoting popular Czech music. But partly it was a deliberate and sustained attempt by the highly valued composer Bedřich Smetana to build a national music based on an alliance between national images and symbols and the most progressive trends in European music, thus creating a store of devices and associations on which his later compatriots would draw. You may not know his operas, but you will probably be familiar with his tone poem *Vltava*, from the cycle *Má Vlast* ("My Country"). It remains to this day a classic of Czech musical nationalism.

There is, then, some explanatory value in creating national narratives for nineteenth-century music, at least from the mid-century onwards. But when we turn to earlier periods, we can rather easily succumb to what some philosophers have called a retrospective fallacy. By that I mean that we assign national labels to composers and repertories as though present-day political borders had some kind of permanent meaning. Events, people and practices are all claimed for the nation, when in reality they belonged to rather different socio-political structures. We might at this stage turn the pages all the way back to Renaissance music and unpick terms such as "Franco-Flemish," but it will perhaps make more sense to look at the immediate pre-histories of our two case studies. I should probably have placed "Germany" in quotes in my earlier discussion, since it only became a nation state in 1871. Prior to the Congress of Vienna in 1815 "Germany" (known as the "Holy Roman Empire of the German Nation") consisted of numerous small courts and arch-bishoprics, reduced at the Congress to a confederation of thirty-eight and then thirty-nine. Indeed the gradual transformation from court to city to nation is one way to read German music history in the nineteenth century, with the cultural nation preceding the political nation. As to the Czech Republic (as we call it today), this was part of the multinational Habsburg Empire in the eighteenth and early nineteenth centuries, and the musical life of its courts and cultural capitals reflected this. Leading Bohemian composers, such as Dussek, Tomášek and Voříšek, and even Smetana in his early years, were cosmopolitan figures, as much at home in Vienna or London as in Prague.

I want to turn finally to a rationalization of music history that has to do with temporality rather than place. This is the periodization of history. Terms like Baroque, Classical, Romantic, etc. are certainly familiar to you, at least in principle, even if you cannot supply dates! It is easy of course to dismiss periodization as a kind of naive reductionism – or even as a mere strategy of presentation. But think for a moment about your own biographies. Probably you translate your experienced life into constructed history in just this way. You might mark off your elementary school years, for instance, or that part of your life you spent in a particular part of the country, or even a vacation somewhere. In all these cases you are combining classificatory convenience (a well-defined unit) and interpretative coherence (a strongly characterized unit). And this raises just the same questions about continuity and rupture that are raised when we periodize music history.

Consider a term such as "Romanticism." It was only around the mid-nineteenth century that Romanticism in music was first identified as a definable period term in something like our modern sense (by the way, much the same is true of the formal archetype known as "sonata form"). It was in 1848, for instance, that Kahlert defined a modern, "Romantic" music (meaning post-Beethoven, around 1830) through its separation from a Classical golden age (Kahlert 1848). And early in the twentieth century that separation of Classical and Romantic periods was made even cleaner by Guido Adler (Adler 1911).

Yet contemporary (early nineteenth-century) perceptions were really very different, with Beethoven and even Mozart described by writers such as E. T. A. Hoffmann as "Romantic" composers (Hoffmann 1809–13). I will return to the tension between these two perspectives in a moment, but first I will outline in Box 1.4 some of the competing periodizations of Classical and Romantic music. Note, by the way, the congruence with key dates in the political history of the "long nineteenth century," inaugurated by the French Revolution (1789), subdivided by the 1830 and 1848 Revolutions and ending with the outbreak of World War I (1914).

The Kahlert view here suggests that the periodization is applied only when a period-defining theme has been identified. The whole process, then, is developmental or evolutionary, with the climax of the development represented as a kind of ideal, a "point of perfection." This ideal in turn allows us to generate an essence – in

> **Box 1.4 Periodizing Romanticism**
>
> 1. In the early nineteenth century, E. T. A. Hoffmann identified Romantic tendencies in the music of the late eighteenth century. Here Romanticism is a "movement" concurrent with Classicism.
> 2. In the mid-nineteenth century, K. A. Kahlert made a period division between Classicism and Romanticism; here Romanticism meant the post- Beethoven generation. This became the conventional view, confirmed by the stylistic history of Guido Adler in the early twentieth century. The Romantic Age, then, began around 1830 and extended through to the modernism of the late nineteenth and early twentieth centuries.
> 3. In the twentieth century, historians such as Carl Dahlhaus and Peter Rummenhöller located the end point for Romanticism at the middle of the nineteenth century (as in literature and the visual arts), and sometimes coined the term "Neo-Romanticism" as a description of the second half of the century (Dahlhaus 1980; Rummenhöller 1989).
> 4. Also in the twentieth century, Friedrich Blume identified a single Classic-Romantic era reaching back into the eighteenth century and extending well into the twentieth, thus recovering something of the early nineteenth-century sense of the term as a movement or tendency running concurrently with Classicism (Blume 1972).

this case "Romanticism" – that is taken to characterize the period as a whole. Returning to your biography, you might want to ask if something similar happens there. Are the "periods" of your life similarly characterized retrospectively? The other perspective is rather different, focusing more on the moment of change itself, and apparently seeking to recover more directly the experience of that moment. To flog our analogy to death, this latter approach would be concerned with the moments of change in your biography, and on the sense of rupture they created. There is perhaps a debate to be had about these two approaches to historical method, the first focusing on structures (a kind of rationalization after the event), the second on experience and agency (an attempt to recover the historical moment).

Hidden agendas?

You have probably heard of *Grove's Dictionary of Music and Musicians*. Since it first appeared in four volumes in 1879–89, this has been revised roughly every twenty-five years (the latest version, the second edition of *The New Grove*, appeared in 2001 and is effectively the seventh edition). It is remarkably interesting to look at the changes that have taken place over the life of this dictionary. Entirely new terms came into play in the 2001 edition. Some are perhaps not so unexpected: technical terms associated with theory and analysis ("golden number," "deconstruction"); terms concerned with popular music, which had a lower profile in earlier editions ("cantopop," "techno"); and terms reflecting the recent evolution of our discipline in the direction of contextualism ("narratology," "gay and lesbian music"). Others are more surprising. "Canon," in the sense I have used it in this chapter, appeared for the first time in 2001; likewise "genre," and – wait for it! – "music." But even more interesting are the changes that have taken place in the meanings of terms that have been there from the start. It is fascinating to track the shifting meanings of a term such as "analysis," for instance. It has now all but lost touch with the definition attempted by Grove himself way back in 1879. What all this illustrates is that there is nothing absolute about the subject-matter of music history. It is influenced by the climate of ideas in any given era, and it therefore betrays – often unwittingly – the prejudices of its time and place.

This is no less apparent if you look through the various histories of music with a detached and critical eye. One might even write a history of the histories; indeed an early attempt to do just that was W. D. Allen's *Philosophies of Music History* of 1939. Some of the early histories of what we usually call Western Classical Music (Johann Nikolaus Forkel and Charles Burney in the late eighteenth century, François-Joseph Fétis in the mid-nineteenth) do at least pay lip service to the value of music from other cultures, but with Franz

Brendel's late nineteenth-century volumes the typical model of a European canonic history was established, and it lived on right through to well-known later histories such as the much-used, not to say over-used, study by Donald Grout of 1960. Guido Adler challenged Brendel's model when he proposed a history of musical styles rather than of "great composers" in his *Der Stil in der Musik* of 1911 and *Methode der Musikgeschichte* of 1919. So, rather later, did Walter Wiora when he turned to folk music as an important shaping influence on music history (Wiora 1957). And so, in different ways, did twentieth-century historians such as Ernst Bücken and Georg Knepler, both of whom were symptomatic of the swerve towards context, though interestingly they approached their social history from very different political perspectives (of the right and left, respectively; note the dates of their books, and the fact that Knepler was working in Communist East Germany (Bücken 1937; Knepler 1961)). What I am suggesting here is that the histories tell you a great deal about their authors, and, more widely, about the time and place in which they were written. This goes for present-day histories too.

It may be worth ending this chapter by drawing attention, however briefly, to three areas in which the subject-matter of music history seems to be undergoing something of a revision. The first concerns gender, and in particular the coverage of women, which has been found wanting both in its extent and in its depth, notably by commentators such as Marcia Citron (Citron 1993). A variety of perspectives has enriched our understanding of the importance of women in music history in recent years: in-depth historical-biographical work (on Fanny Hensel, for example), detailed music-analytical work (on Josephine Lang), performance history (the activities, creative as well as performative, of singers such as Henrietta Sontag and Maria Malibran), and social-historical research (especially the history of patronage, where the women played a key role, not least through their involvement in that complex and much misunderstood institution, the salon). Such work has gone a long way towards demonstrating just how seriously undervalued women have been in conventional narratives of music history.

I mentioned performance history. Musical performance is the second of my three neglected areas, and actually it is related to the first. If we rewrote music history in such a way that we placed performance closer to center stage, a number of other things, including gender balance, would also shift around a bit. So too would our understanding of the geography of music history. London would emerge as the musical capital of Europe during the age of Beethoven and Schubert, for example. Our instincts as historians (and also as analysts, though that is a different issue) have been by and large to value composers rather than performers, even to the point of disguising the rather basic condition of music as a performing art. To do justice to performance, however, we may first need to emancipate it from the paradigm of interpretation. Musicians often seek to recover original meanings (of the composer) when they perform. Yet it is questionable how far this is really possible. I want to suggest to you that they are more likely to create new meanings. And that simple shift of orientation has the potential to liberate our discussions of performance, as Nicholas Cook and others have recognized. It enables us to speak of "performance in" rather than "performance of" a work. If you go along with that, you will perhaps agree that performers can make an essential claim on our reading of music history (see chapter 13).

My third lacuna returns us to an earlier point about geography. Music histories have tended on the whole to concentrate their discussion in just a handful of locations, most obviously in Italy, Germany, and France. A reasonable question then might be how to give a voice to those regions that have been represented as peripheral, if only by omission. You can, of course, choose your own periphery. But some of my own work at the moment concerns music in the Balkans (south-east Europe), a region that seems to exemplify periphery in an especially interesting way. I will pose directly some of the questions that concern me here. What does a study of music history in the Balkans tell us about the construction of cultural traditions, east and west, and about the consequent relationship between cultural politics and aesthetic value? What is the role of different musics in defining national, regional, social, and cultural identities in the Balkans? How do Balkan "others" illuminate European projects of modernity? And what has been the impact of westernization and modernization (and, conversely, of orientalization) on the Balkans themselves? I will not attempt answers here. But as you can see from the questions, the idea is to investigate how cultural traditions (west European and Ottoman-Turkish) are shaped, supported, and promoted through symbiotic processes of marginalization and canon formation; the two are after all mutually dependent.

As I say, you can choose your own periphery. The Balkan peninsula is hardly prominent in existing narratives of music history. But then, neither are the Baltic States; nor Spain; nor Portugal; nor Sweden. It is at least worth asking if the way we have constructed so-called "mainstream" traditions might not have as much to do with chauvinist politics as with art, and whether this may in turn have colored our view of so-called peripheral cultures. That we have identified little of value in some of these traditions is as often as not because we know little about them. We need to ask, in other words, if the neglect of some of these repertories is attributable to inferior music or ignorant listeners. At least there are plenty of indications these days that we may be ready to recognize chauvinism for what it is.

Chapter summary

- Music histories differ from political and social histories in that works of music still live in our present, creating a tension between art and history.

- Stylistic histories and social histories tend in opposing directions, the former towards an affirmation of the canon, the latter towards its deconstruction.
- Oral repertories can be all too easily misconstrued as "simple" and/or ahistorical, when compared with notated traditions.
- Music historians, like all historians, make sense of the past by constructing narratives based on geographies and temporalities.
- Music histories have covert, or overt, agendas. There is no neutrality in scholarship.

Discussion topics

- This chapter reflected on the difficulty in relating Beethoven "in his time" to Beethoven "for today." Try a similar exercise first with Machaut, then with Debussy.
- Reflect on the challenges of writing a history of either British or American pop music since the 1960s. What approaches would you take? How would the task differ from other forms of music history?
- Consider the usefulness of invoking nationality in writing music history. Does the picture change from one period of history to the next?
- In his history of nineteenth-century music, Carl Dahlhaus set up an opposition between Beethoven and Rossini. These days Beethoven is regarded as the central figure of early nineteenth-century music. Could you make a case for Rossini?

Further reading

Carr, Edward Hallett (1961), *What is History?* (London and New York: Macmillan; St. Martin's Press); revised edition (1986) ed. R. W. Davies (London: Macmillan).

A useful introduction to the philosophy of history, exploring some of the ideological roots of historical inquiry.

Gellner, Ernest (1983), *Nations and Nationalism* (Oxford: Blackwell).

An influential account of the rise of nationalism in Europe, it argues that nationalism was made possible by the homogenizing effects of bourgeois high cultures (resulting, as Gellner sees it, from a strengthening industrial-technological base in European societies).

Hobsbawm, Eric and Terence Ranger (1983) (eds.), *The Invention of Tradition* (Cambridge: Cambridge University Press).

A collection of historical essays, whose larger point is that traditions are created retrospectively and are really about the exercise of political power.

Morgan, Robert P. (1991), *Twentieth-Century Music: A History of Musical Style in Modern Europe and America* (New York: Norton).

A useful overview of the stylistic history of twentieth-century music.

Owens, Jessie Ann (1990–91), "Music historiography and the definition of 'Renaissance.'" *Notes*, xlvii, 305–30.

A challenging essay on the nature of historical writing about Renaissance music, especially good on the changing status of the composer.

Taruskin, Richard (2005), *The Oxford History of Western Music*, 6 volumes (Oxford: Oxford University Press).

An ambitious single-author history of the whole of Western art music, this is ideal as a reference text.

Treitler, Leo (1989), *Music and the Historical Imagination* (Cambridge, MA: Harvard University Press).

An attempt to relate music in its time to music as we hear and understand it today, this book provides stimulating thoughts on the relation between music history and music analysis.

Wölfflin, Heinrich (1950), *Principles of Art History*, trans. M. D. Hottinger (New York: Dover; orig. edn 1917).

An influential attempt to define the relation between individual, national, and period styles in art history, and to arrive at systematic principles underlying these styles.

References

Adler, Guido (1911), *Der Stil in der Musik* (Leipzig: Breitkopf & Härtel).
Adler, Guido (1919), *Methode der Musikgeschichte* (Leipzig: Breitkopf & Härtel).

Allen, Warren Dwight (1939), *Philosophies of Music History: A Study of General Histories of Music, 1600–1900* (New York and Boston: American Book Company).

Blume, Friedrich (1972), *Classic and Romantic Music: A Comprehensive Survey*, trans. Mary Dows Herter Norton (London: Faber).

Brendel, Franz (1852), *Geschichte der Musik in Italien, Deutschland und Frankreich von den ersten christlichen Zeiten bis auf die Gegenwart* (Leipzig: Heinrich Matthes).

Bücken, Ernst (1937), *Die Musik der Nationen, eine Musikgeschichte* (Leipzig: A. Kröner).

Burney, Charles (1776–89), *A General History of Music, from the Earliest Ages to the Present Period* (London: Printed for the author).

Chartier, Roger (1988), *Cultural History: Between Practices and Representations*, trans. Lydia G. Cochrane (Ithaca, NY: Cornell University Press).

Citron, Marcia J. (1993), *Gender and the Musical Canon* (Cambridge and New York: Cambridge University Press).

Dahlhaus, Carl (1980 [1974]), *Between Romanticism and Modernism: Four Studies in the Music of the Later Nineteenth Century*, trans. Mary Whittall (Berkeley and Los Angeles: University of California Press).

Dahlhaus, Carl (1983 [1967]), *Foundations of Music History*, trans. J. B. Robinson (Cambridge and New York: Cambridge University Press).

Dahlhaus, Carl (1989 [1980]), *Nineteenth-Century Music*, trans. J. Bradford Robinson (Berkeley and Los Angeles: University of California Press).

Fétis, François-Joseph (1869–76), *Histoire générale de la musique depuis les temps les plus anciens jusqu'à nos jours* (Paris: Didot).

Forkel, Johann Nikolaus (1788), *Allgemeine Geschichte der Musik* (Leipzig: Schwickertschen).

Goehr, Lydia (1992), *The Imaginary Museum of Musical Works: An Essay in the Philosophy of Music* (Oxford and New York: Clarendon Press).

Grout, Donald Jay (1960), *A History of Western Music* (New York: Norton).

Hepokoski, James A. (1993), *Sibelius Symphony No. 5* (Cambridge: Cambridge University Press).

Hoffmann, E. T. A. (1809–13), Reviews of works by Beethoven, *Allgemeine Musikalische Zeitung*, 12–15; reprinted in H. von Ende (ed.), *E. T. A. Hoffmanns musikalische Schriften* (Cologne: S. Halbleinwand, 1899).

Howell, Tim (1989), *Jean Sibelius: Progressive Techniques in the Symphonies and Tone Poems* (New York: Garland).

Kahlert, Karl August (1848), "Über den Begriff der klassischen und romantischen Musik," *Allgemeine musikalische Zeitung*, 50/18, 289–95.

Knepler, Georg (1961), *Musikgeschichte des 19. Jahrhunderts* (Berlin: Henschelverlag).

Porter, Cecilia Hopkins (1996), *The Rhine as Musical Metaphor: Cultural Identity in German Romantic Music* (Boston: Northeastern University Press).

Robertson, Ritchie (1999), *The "Jewish" Question in German Literature 1749–1939: Emancipation and its Discontents* (Oxford: Oxford University Press).

Rummenhöller, Peter (1989), *Romantik in der Musik: Analysen, Portraits, Reflexionen* (Munich: Deutscher Taschenbuch Verlag).

Said, Edward (1979), *Orientalism* (New York: Pantheon Books).

Sipe, Thomas (1998), *Beethoven: "Eroica" Symphony* (Cambridge and New York: Cambridge University Press).

Taruskin, Richard (1984), "Some thoughts on the history and historiography of Russian music," *The Journal of Musicology*, 3/4, 321–9.

Treitler, Leo (1992), "The 'unwritten' and 'written transmission' of medieval chant and the start-up of musical notation," *Journal of the American Musicological Society* 10/2, 131–91.

Tyrrell, John (1988), *Czech Opera* (Cambridge and New York: Cambridge University Press).

Wiora, Walter (1957), *Europäische Volksmusik und abendländische Tonkunst* (Kassel: J. P. Hinnenthal).

Glossary

Reception	A term applied both to the history of social responses to art, and to an aesthetic which privileges those responses. Reception histories are concerned less with individual responses, which are properly a subject for music psychology, than with collective responses based on determinate groups of listeners, whether these are defined by nationality, social class, cultural milieu, or profession.
Canon	A term used to describe a list of composers or works assigned value and greatness by consensus. It tends to foreground the ahistorical, and essentially disinterested, qualities of musical repertories, as against their more temporal, functional and contingent qualities.
Style	A concept that is defined by processes of selection and negation, but also by processes of standardization. In common usage it can refer to something larger than a tradition (the classical style, for example) or to something smaller than a work (the style of the middle section, for example).
Ars Nova	Literally, "new art," but used to refer to changes in musical style and syntax around the beginning of the fourteenth century, especially in France. It is often used as a blanket term to describe French music of the fourteenth century.
Work concept	A term used to suggest that European musical culture comes to be work-centered (i.e., regulated above all by musical works) around 1800 or so. This thesis was first proposed by German scholars in the 1970s, but it was popularized above all by Lydia Goehr in her book, *The Imaginary Museum of Musical Works*.
Tradition	A corpus of significant works whose shared characteristics have been "handed over" or "handed down" (Latin: *tradere*) from one generation to the next. A tradition is invariably constructed after the event, and often along national (and therefore political) lines.
Nationalism	A term usually used to describe an ideology of nationhood that sprang from eighteenth-century Enlightenment values of popular sovereignty and egalitarianism, and that informed nineteenth-century nation-building projects. Cultural nationalism is premised on the idea that nations have a clear sense of cultural identity.

2 Music theory and analysis

RACHEL BECKLES WILLSON

Chapter preview

This chapter introduces music theory as a practice that has been undertaken in Europe and Asia for many centuries, and defines it as a set of generalizations about musical sound, works, and (occasionally) composition or performance practice. The focus of the chapter is on the theories that have been applied to Western classical music in the twentieth century and beyond, and the way in which they interact with methods of analysis. It shows that a theory may provide a secure framework for analysis, but also that analysis may also be used to test (and ultimately disprove) a theory. This process may lead to the creation of a new theory, and new analytical methods. Both analysis and theory are subject to change, then, and each is further influenced by the purposes for which it is designed. The chapter places theory and analysis within the triangle of composer, performer, and listener, in order to illuminate their flexible practical existence in a range of different contexts.

Key issues

What is analysis for?
- Analysis and the composer.
- Analysis and the performer.
- Analysis and the listener.

What is theory for?
- Theory for analysis.
- Analysis to test theory.
- New theory and new analysis.

Introduction

Music theory tries to tell us what music is by providing a generalized representation of it. But there are a lot of musics, so there are a lot of theories. They vary according to the music they are addressing, who is doing the addressing (and where), and what the theories are for.

Music's most frequently theorized elements are pitch (tuning systems, intervals, and **modes**) and rhythm (in terms of time units and cycles). This has been the case throughout Europe and Asia since the sixth century BCE. But making general statements about even these basic elements has always involved reference to other phenomena. Theories about pitch have referred to entities as diverse as mathematical proportions (as did Plato, drawing on Pythagoras), nature and God (this was typical of German Romantic thought), and the cosmos (a frequent component of Arabic theory, among many others). Also, pitch theories depend on the instruments producing the pitches: early Arabic pitch systems were described with reference to the frets on the lute (*ūd*), for instance. Pitch theories are often interlocked with other systems: in India, for example, art music has long been theorized in the context of theatrical dramaturgy, physical gesture, poetics, and metrics.

This should indicate that theory, however abstract it may seem, is a product of a society, and that social change and patterns of travel may influence it profoundly. When a short-necked Persian lute (*pipa*) was brought into China around the third century, it brought with it a theory according to which there were eighty-four musical modes. Moreover, music theory also tends to absorb and represent the hierarchies in society. The Chinese philosopher Confucius (551–479 BCE) was one of the first to define "proper music" against "vernacular music" and assert the ethical superiority of the former. Imperial China preserved this distinction for centuries, so that theories in the Confucian tradition served to perpetuate the supremacy of the "art" music. This legitimizing role of theory has been important to Indian art music too, just as it has for the separation of "art" and "popular" music in modern Europe and America.

If you look back over this introduction so far, you may already be able to work out one of the relationships between theory and analysis, namely that in order for a theory to come into being, someone has to do a lot of study and – most likely – analysis. That way, analysis helps to generate theory. Theory does not always merely represent music that exists, however. Sometimes it is more speculative, attempting to enlarge the field of possibilities for creative musical practice (this was the case with some early Arabic pitch theorists). It has sometimes attempted to provide practical instruction (the ninth-century *Musica enchiriadis*, for instance, is a manual about how to improvise medieval organum; and C. P. E. Bach wrote a treatise about how to realize figured bass (*Essay on the True Art of Playing Keyboard Instruments*, Part Two, 1762)). Furthermore, theory, as a set of generalizations, can be the basis for further learning: the study of music is based on various general rules or principles (theories). Some of these are used for musical analysis, helping us to separate out various elements of music and consider how those elements work together. This way, theory helps generate analysis.

This chapter focuses on the theories we use for analysis of the Western art-music tradition, which cannot tell us much about what music is in general, though some people combine analysis with philosophy in order to do so (see chapter 5). But these theories try to tell us what musical works are. In other words, they are not concerned with the medium so much as with specific creations using that medium. That is partly because the medium was normalized in the tuning system known as "equal temperament" during the nineteenth century; partly because of the way the Western art tradition is formed around musical works notated in scores; and partly because of our interest in history. There are a lot of different musics in the Western art-music tradition, so there are a lot of different theories through which to analyze them.

What is analysis for?

Analysis and the composer

As you will know from chapter 1, the study of Western art music is very concerned with composers, who have frequently been thought of as the ultimate source of knowledge about their compositions. As a result, many writers have justified their analyses on the grounds that they will demonstrate how a great composer wrote. The theory of Heinrich Schenker (1868–1935), for example, demonstrates how the ornamental aspects of music can be carefully peeled away by an analyst to reveal a basic architectural structure supporting them: he understood the compositional process as being the reverse of this peeling away. In other words, he conceived composers such as Beethoven starting with a basic, universal structure and elaborating it progressively. Another writer, Rudolph Réti (1885–1957), was concerned with small building blocks of a composition, which he called **motifs**. Identifying one or more significant motifs in works by Beethoven (among others), he demonstrated how all (or most) parts of the piece were imbued with their transformations. He argued that the composer himself must have written music with the aim of unifying his pieces architecturally through just this motivic development.

But Schenker and Réti cannot both be right about how Beethoven worked! In fact, they each reveal less about the time of Beethoven than about the preoccupations of their own times (this should remind you of chapter 1 again). Schenker wrote in an era when the construction of critical editions and affirming a canon of "masterworks" was high on the musicological agenda. Establishing criteria for these "great" works with reference to tonality's reflection of nature and the spirit was a way of affirming their value (and dismissing the works that did not conform to his criteria as inferior – notice the parallel with Confucius). Réti's work, on the other hand, is more in line with the early compositional theories and freely developing motivic music of Arnold Schoenberg. Schenker had particular historical grounds for his theories, because he developed them from species counterpoint, which Beethoven and many other composers studied as a compositional principle. But there are distinct limitations to how much score-based analysis can reveal past compositional practice.

There are two other main ways in which we can approach it analytically, although each has its own limitations. One way is through comparison with contemporary theoretical writings. But theoretical writings rarely develop in parallel with compositional practice, because theory is usually based on music that has already been written. Also, composers rarely follow theory and are often determinedly individualistic, which suggests we should look at another way of investigating their processes – analyzing their manuscripts. These might suggest how a composition developed over a period of time. In some cases, alternative versions may have been set aside by the composer, and comparative work can show how the structure of a given piece could have turned out very differently. But much of the compositional process cannot be traced in the manuscript sources, and even what *is* available can only rarely tell us much about a finished piece.

Some composers have been theorists themselves. Jean-Philippe Rameau (1683–1764) is one of the most famous. Since the latter half of the nineteenth century, certain composers have attempted to explain or analyze their own works. This certainly tells us something about how a composer viewed his or her own music, and how they wanted us to view them. In the twentieth century there were composers who constructed extensive theories about their methods. Olivier Messiaen (1908–92) is one example: he published descriptions of the various modes he had used, and what they symbolized for him. These descriptions may have stimulated other composers to write in related ways. But Messiaen's own music does not depend on his descriptions (it would be a very limited music if it did!) and they can only explain some aspects of it. That is almost always true, even in the rather special case of Schoenberg (about whom more below). So it is always a good idea to look beyond a composer's self-analyses. Fundamentally, our analyses are for *our* activities as composers, performers, listeners, or researchers; and, although they can, our analyses *need not* involve the composer of the works we analyze very much at all.

Analysis and the performer

While analysis does not necessarily bring us close to what a composer did, it is often understood as being in the service of the performer. The work of Donald Tovey (1875–1940) is an obvious case, because Tovey wrote descriptions of themes and significant events in pieces in a measure-by-measure narrative that can be followed a bit like a travel guide. His approach was pragmatic, engaging with the aspects of a piece that could be identified readily either by reading the score, while playing, or while listening to a recording. You should find doing this sort of analysis a good way to gain basic familiarity with a piece. But there are more theoretical writers who also considered their work crucial for performers. Schenker was one of them: he thought his theories were ideal pedagogical tools.

You might think that the basic architecture of a piece is too abstract to help at all with the practical business of learning music for performance. But if you analyze a tonal work following his principles, you will gain insights that can help you play it. Inevitably you will know the piece much better by the end of the process; also, you should have a clear sense of a piece's proportions through having grasped the main harmonic shifts, the underlying structures of phrases and movements, and the relative structural significance of passage-work. Just as interesting, and most important to the Schenkerian approach, you will also have analyzed the piece as unfolding in time. You will be able to think of it not just as a collection of "vertical" chords, but as a "horizontal" set of lines, because Schenker encourages us to explore part-writing, or "voice-leading." This temporal dimension of his analysis has led some performer-analysts to combine Schenkerian approaches with commentaries about performance activities, as performers necessarily experience music in a linear way.

Réti, Schenker, and Tovey all analyzed scores, but while they were doing that, un-notated (and un-notatable) musics from other traditions were being collected by ethnomusicologists in sound recordings, and some of these were analyzed as musical sounds. This sort of approach has emerged much later in analysis of the Western art music tradition, because the score was broadly understood to hold all the composer's secrets, and analysis was supposed to lead us to the composer, and to the most authentic performance of the composer's ideas. But the proliferation of recordings can now reveal that performances based on the same score can differ a great deal. Consequently, these days the performer is less often the person for whom analysis is done than the producer of some of the objects that are actually analyzed. This sort of analysis is often comparative: a number of recordings of the same piece can be compared in terms of their use of factors such as time, pitch variation, dynamics, and articulation, for example. And this leads us towards the relationship between analysis and the listener.

Analysis and the listener

You might think that unless analysis tells us about things we *can* hear, then it is not relevant to our understanding of music. On the other hand, you might think that unless it tells us things we *cannot* hear, then it is entirely redundant. Most analysis works between these two positions, modifying each of them in the process. Analysis may offer you ways of conceptualizing what you can already hear. Or it may tell you things you did not hear first of all, but on being told about them you begin to hear them. This second aspect is very important, because it shows that we can hear music in lots of different ways. Analysis can both refine our listening, and provide ways in which we can talk to one another about what we hear and do not hear.

This sort of sharing has often been dogmatic in the past. For Schenker, for example, there was a right way to hear music, and his analyses were intended to propagate that. In a related way, Schoenberg strove to write music that was "comprehensible," and he explained it according to complex pitch structures that listeners should be able to hear. Many later writers were influenced by **structuralism**, which led to the belief that the structures identifiable in the score should be the basis for the listening experience. People are often trained to listen to music in terms of these structures, which can indeed be useful reference points in listening. (You have probably done listening exercises in identifying themes, sections, and harmonic modulations yourself.) At best, listening to structures can guide our hearing and teach us something specific to a piece which will also enable us to compare it with other pieces. But this only represents one way of hearing and comparing. And as studies on large groups of people have shown, many of us do not experience music in these terms. This is the case generally, but is particularly true for non-tonal music, which listeners will rarely understand in terms of its intricate pitch constructions.

There is, after all, much more to music than its structures. It is also about communication. Consequently, some writers have argued that music is better understood as a system of signs and have drawn on **semiotics** to analyze it as such. Just think of "descriptive" music. It can be similar to fog (obscure and cloudy) or sound like a train (imitating the sounds a train makes); it can also symbolize entities such as countries (through a national anthem or folk music, for instance). Some types of music have been associated with something for so long that they carry their own sort of signifying system. These are generally called "topics": marches, dance movements (minuet, sarabande), and fanfares are good examples. One type of semiotic analysis would identify these signs and topics and explore their interaction as part of music's communicative process. Topics also interact with more obviously "structural" music: the music of Haydn, Mozart, and Beethoven in particular rewards study of the interplay between structure and topic; and the ways in which the topics are treated (innocently, ironically, or humorously, for instance), will also tell us things about the piece. The work of Kofi Agawu provides a good example of this approach.

You may be thinking that all this is only available to listeners aware of musical conventions and you will not be far from the truth. That really should not matter too much: after all, nobody is saying that we *must* listen in this way. Other writers have looked beyond musical scores and drawn on psychology to make broader generalizations about how Western art music is heard, however. Leonard Meyer's *Emotion and Meaning in Music* argued that people respond to basic feelings of tension and release in music, and that these feelings are triggered by rising and falling melodies, as well as melodic gaps that – for the listener – "need to be" filled. Fred Lerdahl and Ray Jackendoff's *A Generative Theory of Tonal Music* pushed this sort of approach further by comparing more theoretical analyses of musical scores with listeners' musical intuitions, aiming to provide a sensitive bridge between the two. The problem with both Meyer's and Lerdahl and Jackendoff's approaches was that they never really experimented to see whether people *did* hear the musical structures they identified as important in quite the ways they thought. In other words, they used *structuralist* music theory and theories about psychology to argue about our hearing.

What is theory for?

You might be thinking now that theory has caused a great deal more trouble than it is worth, and that analysis *without* theory would be the safest way forward. Perhaps Tovey's practical approach appeals to you, because it is apparently unburdened with theory. If we look a bit more closely at Tovey, however, we notice he cannot do without the theory about the medium of music. He uses terms such as "tonic" and "dominant," for instance, that stem from the theory of Hugo Riemann (1849–1919) according to which harmony has "function." And he also uses concepts such as "theme" that belong to the basic theoretical vocabulary of musicology. Also, it turns out that he has a very fixed idea that an analysis should be a "story" that unfolds in parallel to the piece of music. That is another covert theory, namely that music is understood as a single line extending in time.

If we look back to the introduction of this chapter and recall that analysis takes music apart and shows how its constituent elements work together, then we will realize that Tovey did not get us very far. He did not break the music down into very small elements, he did not explain why he has written about certain elements and not others, and he did not show us distinctive ways in which his chosen elements interact. He drew on theory without thinking much about it and ended up with a description. Actively thinking about theory can sometimes make us more analytical; and it can also lead us to refine theories. We may even create new ones.

Theory for analysis

Music's apparent affinity with language has influenced theory profoundly. Music can imitate language, has structures that are comparable with those of language, and is a medium of communication. Several of the analytical practices described below are indebted to these thoughts.

Fig. 2.1 Meter in Mozart: Piano Sonata in A K331, first movement, Meyer 1973: 31.

Fig. 2.2 Classical sentence structure. Beethoven, Piano Sonata in F minor, Op. 2 No. 1, first movement

Cooper and Meyer's *The Rhythmic Structure of Music*, for example, drew on analytical techniques applied to poetry and prose since ancient Greece to classify various types of rhythmic pattern encountered in classical music. The theory shows how pulse, meter (number and type of beats in the measure), accent, and duration can be analyzed to identify groupings of notes that are similar to poetic feet known as *iamb*, *anapaest*, and *dactyl*, for instance. Fig. 2.1 shows how the relative emphases of notes in a phrase of Mozart can be grouped into such poetic feet; and how, depending how closely we look at the score, we can regard larger or smaller sections as representing such groupings.

Schoenberg's *Fundamentals of Musical Composition* also drew on linguistic analogy by referring to sections of music with concepts such as "phrase," "theme," and "sentence." Schoenberg's loose definition of a musical "phrase" was a unit of music that could be sung in one breath and implied that a comma should follow it. A "sentence" was a type of theme in which the first part was the same as the second part (although the latter might be in a different key). Fig. 2.2 shows a sentence; each of its two parts could be categorized as a phrase. He contrasted the "sentence" with the "period," which was a theme in which the second part was different from the first. He argued that the vast majority of classical themes were sentences, rather than periods. Schoenberg also drew on traditional theories about how themes were built up into sections, how sections were built up into forms to provide a means through which we can categorize movements into "binary form," "rondo form," and "sonata form," among others. These theoretical representations lead us to analyze music in specified terms.

The semiotic theory discussed above is also indebted to music's linguistic qualities, and specifically to the analysis of language as a communicative sign system. Where Schoenberg's theory teaches us to analyze a theme as a sentence or a period, that of Kofi Agawu might lead us to recognize it as a dance type or a musical "sign" for a fanfare. Semiotic theory does not stop at these identifications, however. It also looks at how units of music can generally be regarded as signs, and how they are distributed in pieces of music. This brings semiotics quite close to motivic analysis and back to thematic analysis, because it involves extracting small sections of music on the basis of their similarities, and identifying how their recurrences shape the music and how they are part of a larger system.

While rhythm and melody can be illuminated with reference to language, harmony has more often been explained with reference to nature. Theorists as recently as the early twentieth century inaccurately claimed that tonal harmony is natural. In fact tuning systems devised by humans divide up the acoustic range in various ways, and tonal music is only one product of such divisions. But even if this sort of theory has lost part of its plausibility today, it retains useful elements. Identifying the relationship between consonance and dissonance (without asserting that one is natural and the other is not) is an important part of tonal analysis, for instance. It enables us to see the basic structures of tonal relations, the way certain harmonies help to articulate musical beginnings, endings, and the time in between.

It is Schenker's tonal theory that has most influenced musical thought in the twentieth and early twenty-first centuries, after it was transformed into an analytical method for university study in the 1950s. At the heart of the theory is the idea that the temporal aspect of tonal music is the "prolongation" of triadic harmony. Fig. 2.3 should give you an idea of how Schenkerian analyses (a) reduce what seems to be complex music to simple two-part counterpoint (which is understood as the skeleton of the harmonies), and (b) suggest that the other notes "prolong" this (they elaborate it, and extend it through time).

Schenkerian thought is most readily conceived as a sort of theme-and-variations idea: just as variations can be "analyzed down" (reduced) to a theme, much tonal music can be reduced to a contrapuntal framework. The point is not so much the reduction itself as the insight we gain when we identify the way the framework supports the elaborations around it. Schenker referred to the framework as "background," and the various degrees of elaborations on it as "middleground" and "foreground." The idea that music is built up in such layers of relative structural significance is a helpful one.

For theorists, one of the most attractive things about Schenkerian analysis is that it seems to represent a complete system, and it can be a useful point of reference between people examining different musics. (This is the value of structuralism: the formal elements of something can be discussed without their specific context.) There is only one equivalent to such a totalizing system for non-tonal music, and rather than being grounded in language or an idea of nature, its closest relative is mathematics.

Bearing this in mind, you may be amused to hear that one of its forerunners, Schoenberg's writings on non-tonal music, justified itself in no other way than

Fig. 2.3 Analysis of Haydn, Piano Sonata Hob. XVI/35, I, mm. 1–8 (from Cadwallader and Gagné, 1998: 112–13)

by making claims for the "naturalness" of dissonances. Once the structuring function of consonance and dissonance was removed from music, then new theories were needed to account for how it worked. Some of these were provided by the music that was constructed according to Schoenberg's method of composing with rows of twelve notes. Although Schoenberg himself did not call his method a "theory," it was adopted by composers and writers who often treated it as one. The pitch organization of a composition was determined by:

(a) the arrangement of the twelve notes into a "row"
(b) generating forty-eight versions of the row through inversion (turning it upside down), retrograde (reversing its order), retrograde inversion, and multiple transpositions
(c) using these rows as building blocks of a composition.

Analysis of its pitch structure could amount to identifying the rows and their arrangements in the piece.

But – remember the section above on "analysis and the composer" – this could only tell us about certain aspects of a composition. Moreover, it could only work for twelve-tone compositions, whereas there were lots of types of non-tonal compositions. So new vocabulary was needed. This grew up in the post-war period, drawing on a cross-fertilization between science and arts, the rise of computer technology, and the prevailing belief that music could be best be explained as a set of abstract relations. The new theory was based around two concepts, "pitch class" and "set."

"C," "C♯," and "D" are all pitch classes. "Class" refers to the type of pitch, without indicating what register it is in. That means that all Cs belong to the same pitch class: the interval of the octave between them does not change their class. Pitch-class "sets" are groups of pitch classes; unlike modes, their order is never specified. As Allen Forte's *The Structure of Atonal Music* demonstrated, there are 220 pitch-class sets (containing from three to nine pitch classes) within the twelve-tone system. Each has its own structure of intervals. Pitch-class set theory enables analysts to find similarities between seemingly diverse sections of music, because once notes are reduced to their pitch class and positioned in groups, they may turn out to be closely related. The groups can be subjected to mathematical operations to discover new relations between them.

Such relationships can be identified most readily when pitch classes and sets are expressed numerically. According to this system, C is 0, C♯ is 1, and B is 11. Fig. 2.4 shows three representations of the same group of notes. A further way of representing it would be to call it the "octatonic scale" or "octatonic collection." This is a name often used for this rather special set. Notice that essentially it divides up the octave space into alternating tones and semitones.

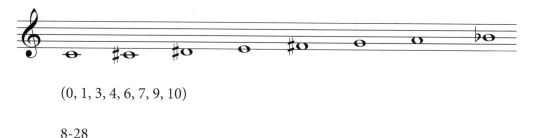

(0, 1, 3, 4, 6, 7, 9, 10)

8-28

Fig. 2.4 The octatonic scale

Other sets that deserve special notice are those that divide up the octave range symmetrically. 4-28 (0, 3, 6, 9) is another example. Can you work out what notes can be in it?

Pitch-class set theory has been criticized from two sides. On the one hand, many find it wildly abstracted from our responses to music. On the other, many people argue that its claims to objectivity collapse when it is used for analysis, because the analyst has to make subjective decisions about which notes to group together into sets. This tension between objectivity and subjectivity is actually at the heart of all music analysis. The best way to work with the tension is to regard analysis as a sort of interpretation. If the interpretation draws intelligently and interestingly on clearly presented principles or established theory, it will be comprehensible – and even plausible – to a significant number of people. It may succeed in persuading them that it is a good analysis.

Analysis to test theory

In the last section we encountered several theories that were invented as tools for analysis. That means that they are less "right" or "wrong," and more "useful" or "useless," depending on what music they are applied to. However, some of them set themselves up as comprehensive, or as "norms" for a particular style of music. If you try to use them to investigate music of that style, but find that the music does not fit, you may start to wonder who is right and who is wrong. Is the piece abnormal within the style? Or is the theory wrong about the style?

One way to resolve these questions is to look closely at the theory's claims. For example, Schoenberg made generalizations about the structures of themes in Classical music. If you encountered a piece that did not begin with a Schoenbergian "sentence" or a "period," you could (1) list which pieces of music he used as examples; (2) ask yourself whether or not these were a representative selection of Classical music; (3) analyze themes from another selection of pieces that you identified as more representative. Your analysis would test his theory. It might also test a new hypothesis, such as:

> If Schoenberg had considered more of Haydn's and Chopin's music when he theorized the thematic structure of Classical music, he would have been led to dramatically different conclusions.

If you discovered that Schoenberg's emphasis on the music of Beethoven had skewed his results, you might end up by proposing a new set of norms for Classical music.

In doing that, you would be using analysis to test (and disprove) theory, and also to create new theory – and possibly even history. For the categorization of styles and historical periods depends on analysis of different works and subsequent generalizations about the analyses. This sort of work is known as style analysis, and Jan LaRue's *Guidelines for Style Analysis* is a sophisticated representative of it, in which complex and nuanced data related to a large number of categories and sub-categories of musical elements are presented in a tabulated form. These days there are computer software packages that can analyze a huge amount of data in this way. This is an excellent way of testing theories, because so much music can be compared (from so many perspectives).

To return to the idea at the beginning of this section, that many theories aren't right or wrong, but useful or useless, one further point to realize is that their usefulness is closely related to their plausibility. By this I mean that Schenker's theory will seem very useful indeed if we believe that it tells us what the composer did, teaches us to perform well, refines our hearing, and reveals the mysterious essence of music's natural, organic processes. Most people do not believe all that nowadays. But that does not mean that Schenker is useless to everyone! Many still find his graphs, and his insight into phrase structure, helpful in learning about a piece, preparing for performance, and thinking about, or imagining, music. Others, however, find their experience of music fundamentally different from Schenkerian ideas, and some of these seek new analytical methods in which they can actually believe. Some of them think the theories described above have become implausible, and that it is time to start asking analytical questions in new ways.

New theory and new analysis

These new analytical approaches can be divided into two broad types, both of which are related to **post-structuralism**. One type has reacted to the elitism of past theory and to the pseudo-scientific quality of past analysis. As a result, there are now approaches (some of them analytical) to musics that were excluded from theoretical scrutiny for a long time (see chapter 10 on jazz, chapter 11 on popular music, and chapter 12 on music in film and television, for instance). Also, there is an interest in incorporating subjectivity in theoretical writing (see chapter 5 on aesthetics and critical theory, in particular the part on post-modernism). So this type is to do with the integration of theory and analysis into related areas.

The other type has responded to some of theory's assumptions about musical structures and the listening experience. As I hinted above, we can learn to listen to music in certain ways, and theory can teach us to do that. But the new approaches are less interested in contributing to that didactic activity than in discovering about listening and sound itself. In other words, they are not so interested in representing what happens in the score as what happens perceptually. They analyze and theorize perception (from a range of perspectives, some psychological (see chapter 4), some neurological); and they also investigate the properties of sound in music.

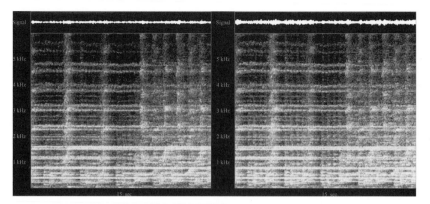

Fig. 2.5 A moment from Wagner's "Ride of the Valkyries"

These analyses of sound do not use the score as their primary basis, so they address the aspects of music that depend on performance: dynamics, vibrato, intonation, and timbre (including the non-pitched aspects of instrumental sound, as well as vocal sounds such as vowels, consonants, and whispering), for example. They can also address density of sonority and how notes are shaped individually. Such analysis can represent, for instance, the fact that we hear a certain piece of music as an increasingly complex textural and dynamic crescendo. Going beyond a verbal description, this analysis can be represented on a computer-generated spectrogram, which captures all the various sonic vibrations graphically. See Fig. 2.5.

As you will notice, in order to connect your hearing mentally with the visual representation that the spectrogram offers, you will need to practice reading spectrograms. This will certainly affect your hearing – in fact, it should refine it. But if this reminds you of Schenker, then remember that this analysis is intended as an open-ended diagnostic tool, not as evidence of the "greatness" of a musical work. Also, the process of generating the spectrogram is merely a first step (unlike a Schenker graph): it enables you to examine certain aspects of music in sound (and in a visual representation of the sound), analyze them, and finally draw an interpretation, or conclusions, from them.

The interpretation might take evidence from the spectrogram about how a singer's manipulation of vowels affected the expressive quality of a performance. Or it might take evidence from the spectrogram to discuss how fluctuations in intonation, as well as instrumentation, explained the ways that very different performances of the same piece functioned. Or it might attempt something more ambitious, such as comparing the following three areas:

(a) psycho-acoustical research into how sound waves enter the ear
(b) compositional principles (such as those related to counterpoint)
(c) musical works (listened to and represented on a spectrogram).

At best, this sort of research combines established research with inventive and open-eared thinking. It may well lead to an enrichment of existing theories of music, as well as new ideas for music analysis.

Chapter summary

In this chapter we clarified that analysis
- can provide a mental representation of music.
- rarely leads us to what composers did in the past.
- may be helpful to performers.
- can develop our listening.

We also established that theory
- is a set of generalizations.
- can provide a framework for analysis.
- can be revised through analysis.

Finally we looked at some types of analysis that aim to make discoveries about music without drawing on conventional theory.

Discussion topics

1. Take a short piece of tonal music you know and try to prove (a) that it is held together by harmony, and then, (b) that it is held together by thematic or motivic repetition. Consider which is the better argument, and ask yourself what it tells you about two different approaches to music.

2. Listen to a piece of music by Steve Reich, such as *Six Pianos*, or *Music for 18 Musicians*. Consider using the analytical methods outlined in the chapter above as a way of learning more about it. Would they be helpful? In what ways? What aspects of the music would they not be able to grasp? Can you think of other analytical ways of approaching this sort of music?

3. "Undergraduate composition students in the UK today write their music without tonality." This is a theory about a certain group of works (it is comparable with any theory generalizing compositional style among composers living in the same place and time). Do you think it is accurate? Think of ways that you might test it using analysis. Consider how you would define "tonality" while you do that. Do you need to replace the theory with another one? What determines the accuracy of a theory like this?

Further reading

Cook, Nicholas (1987), *A Guide to Musical Analysis* (London: Dent).
    A lively introduction to the main methods of tonal and post-tonal analysis,
    with detailed discussion about their relative strengths with reference to case
    studies.
Dunsby, Jonathan and Whittall, Arnold (1988), *Music Analysis in Theory and Practice*
    (London: Faber).
    A book for the advanced student, with more challenging theoretical
    discussion.
Cadwallader, Alan and Gagné, David (1998), *Analysis of Tonal Music: A
    Schenkerian Approach* (New York and Oxford: Oxford University
    Press).
    A very clear step-by-step guide for learning how to do Schenkerian analysis.
    Includes examples for you to work through yourself.
Straus, Joseph N. (1990), *Introduction to Post-Tonal Theory* (Englewood Cliffs, NJ and
    London: Prentice Hall).
    A clear textbook with chapters dedicated to different approaches to
    non-tonal music and theories developed for particular types of music. This
    book also has analysis exercises for the student.
Clarke, Eric and Cook, Nicholas (2004) (eds.), *Empirical Musicology:
    Aims, Methods, Prospects* (New York and Oxford: Oxford University
    Press).
    A collection of essays on recent approaches to music, including the analysis of
    performance, and using computers for music analysis.

References

Agawu, V. Kofi (1991), *Playing with Signs: A Semiotic Interpretation of Classic Music*
    (Princeton, NJ: Princeton University Press).
Cooper, Grosvenor W. and Meyer, Leonard B. (1960), *The Rhythmic Structure of Music*
    (Chicago: University of Chicago Press).
Forte, Allen (1973), *The Structure of Atonal Music* (New Haven and London: Yale
    University Press).
LaRue, Jan (1970), *Guidelines for Style Analysis* (New York: Norton).
Lerdahl, Fred and Jackendoff, Ray (1983), *A Generative Theory of Tonal Music* (Cambridge,
    MA: MIT Press).
Meyer, Leonard B. (1956), *Emotion and Meaning in Music* (Chicago: University of Chicago
    Press).
Schoenberg, Arnold, ed. Gerald Strang (1967), *Fundamentals of Musical Composition*
    (London and Boston: Faber).

Glossary

Mode
: The term has been used in a variety of different contexts, the common core of which is the relationship between notes, whether in terms of duration or pitch. In the context of its discussion in chapter 2, mode refers to a collection of notes with a particular hierarchy of pitch relationships: it can be a scale (i.e., ordered) or a melodic type (i.e., not ordered). The former is used most often for classifying pitch systems; the latter, as a basis for improvisation or composition. Mode is a descriptive term that serves as a translation of non-Western concepts understood to be similar or identical (the *pathet* of Javanese gamelan music, for instance).

Motif
: In general terms, a motif is a short musical idea, defined by melody, rhythm, harmony or a combination of all three. Rudolph Réti, whose analyses were based around motifs, defined it as "any musical element, be it a melodic phrase or fragment or even only a rhythmical or dynamic feature which, by being constantly repeated and varied throughout a work or a section, assumes a role in the compositional design somewhat similar to that of a motif in the fine arts."

Structuralism
: According to structuralist theory, human culture is based on systems that can be analyzed as such. First outlined by Swiss linguist Ferdinand de Saussure (1857–1913) in the early twentieth century, structuralism was a reaction against nineteenth-century historical research and an attempt to make the study of language more scientific. It has been influential in the social sciences (anthropology for instance) as well as in humanities (literature and music, among others), and although its applications vary, the structuralist analytical process is always marked by an attempt to make visible a structure that can be discussed without its particular context or content.

Semiotics
: Semiotics is concerned with the study of signification, that is, the recognition that entities such as language, images, and music can be "signs" for meaning. Ferdinand de Saussure argued that these signs were arbitrary – the word "cat" bears no direct link to an actual cat – and that the structures around and between the various signs generated meaning. In other words, it is only through the system of language that the individual collection of letters C, A, and T, have the meaning of "cat." Another approach to the study of signs was taken by Charles S. Peirce (pronounced "purse"; 1839–1914), who differentiated between three types of sign, "icon," "index," and "symbol."

Post-structuralism   Closely associated with the work of Michel Foucault (1926–84), post-structuralist thought acknowledges that human culture is underpinned by structures, but argues that these both vary across time and space and are inseparable from the things that are said about them. For post-structuralists, "reality" cannot be grasped objectively as a totality, because it is constructed by individuals who are themselves parts of it. Post-structuralist analysis is very varied, but is united in opposition to structuralism: it rejects totalizing structures and resists privileging one analysis over another.

3 The sociology of music

KATHARINE ELLIS

Chapter preview

The relationships between music and the people who produce, perform, and use it are central to the sociology of music. This chapter introduces some of the central ideas of the sociology of music and helps you place it in the context of other approaches. Music is not just the sounds it makes. We like and value some musics and not others, as much because of our social and educational backgrounds, and because of the associations that accompany music, as because of musical style itself. We also include music as part of a wider collection of lifestyle choices. For that reason, the sociological study of music tends to explore the human networks around music, rather than the characteristics of musical style. Nevertheless, it covers contemporary and historical culture from several perspectives, and embraces all types of music. It gives priority to people-centered research methods where possible, to explore music's social meanings; social networks and cultural capital; the shape of the music market; exclusivism and subcultural mentalities; and more general questions about the relationship between music and identity.

Key issues

- Sociologies of music: what are the main questions?
- The problem of "high art."
- Are geniuses constructed, not born?
- "Art worlds" and the music business.
- "Cultural capital," social status, and identity.

Introduction

Imagine that the music business has gone topsy-turvy. You walk towards a CD shop and the first music you hear is a piece of Western classical music blasting out over its entire ground floor. For the sake of argument let us say that it's

43

Mendelssohn's overture to *A Midsummer Night's Dream*. It is No. 1. All your classmates know it and are talking about. It is being played on major radio stations several times a day, and, along with thousands of your peers, you have gone that very week to buy it. It would be uncool not to. Once inside the shop you see other people heading upstairs and downstairs to its darkest corners, where chart pop, film soundtracks, and various kinds of rock music are squeezed into small spaces behind soundproofed doors. By contrast, the space given over to jazz and to world music is huge. You start noticing interesting things about who is browsing where. The three people in the chart pop section are young, white, long-haired men wearing black leathers and chains. The jazz section has a few teenage girls in it, but most of them are queuing up with you for that Mendelssohn. The world music section is crammed with working-class pensioners buying in bulk.

This scenario is as crude as it is unlikely, but its "wrongness" helps us understand how deeply social music is, and how different groups of people tend to identify with different musical genres and styles. It also suggests how a commercial space such as a CD shop can act as a "map" of a subject-area and as an experimental laboratory (even though you will miss out on all those people downloading from the Web). But your own instincts will tell you a lot, even before you start to observe your human subjects, quiz them, and do a statistical analysis of your findings. What are your expectations? How many working-class pensioners have the disposable income to buy a luxury such as recorded music in large quantities? How many teenage girls are jazz fans? Are those men in black leather not more likely to be heading for the heavy metal section? The moment you begin to try to untangle my mismatches of space allocation, social type (age, gender, class, ethnicity), and musical category, you are already thinking about the relationships between individual people, social groups, social structures, and music. And that is what the sociology of music is primarily about.

Sociologies of music

Music is not usually the main focus of the sociology of music. Most of the time its subject is living people, the ways in which they organize their musical experience through institutions, in groups, and via the music market, and the ways in which they affect the ways music is produced, performed, consumed, and understood. For this reason, audiences, their tastes, and their behavior, are central – more so than composers or even performers. So are the people who, while not actually composing pieces of music, help make them happen. Systems of patronage, corporate management, and sponsorship are common subjects of sociological study, and tell us a great deal about how certain types of music are promoted and sustained, by (and for) whom, and why. And the study of group dynamics and power relations within and between musical institutions (bands and record companies, conservatoires, orchestras), gives an insight into the harsh practicalities of a competitive music world in which the agendas of audiences, performers, teachers, conductors, songwriters, and management are often radically different.

All these subjects of study are subjects rooted in today's world, and they bring with them a set of research methods that emphasize direct access to the people being studied. The interview, the questionnaire, and the statistical survey are important tools for sociologists of music, who, like ethnomusicologists, spend much of their time talking to people, noting their responses, and analyzing them as evidence of an attitude, opinion, or taste. Sociology, however, can also be historical, and so can the sociology of music. Here, access to people's opinions and behavior is usually indirect, gleaned for instance via memoirs and letters, family reminiscences, photographs, advertising material, press reports, and old film footage. The questions a sociologist asks are fundamentally the same, though the emphasis tends to shift, and a specific type of music is placed center stage. What did people use this music for? How widely was it known, and among which social groups? What processes were necessary for it to reach the public domain? What did it mean to those who valued (or denigrated) it? How, finally, was it reinvented over time, through different arrangements or covers intended for different types of audience?

Of course, relationships are not just one-way: if, as is often said, dogs look like their owners, then owners must also look like their dogs. Does music, then, "look like" the social groups who identify closely with it? Or those who produced it in the first place? To use a common metaphor, can music "mirror," or "reflect" social structures? One particular branch of the sociology of music, stemming from the work of the German sociologist and philosopher Theodor Adorno (1903–69), explores this idea. For instance, when he wrote that serialism (Schoenberg's twelve-note method) was "totalitarian," Adorno was not commenting on the sound of Schoenberg's music, or analyzing its effect on audiences through surveys. Instead, he was offering his own critique, observing that the technique of serialism tied the composer's hands by effectively prescribing the order in which each pitch should appear. The result could never be "free," since it was not composed freely. Because it appeared to conflict with his own societal ideals, Adorno found serialism problematic as a method in which artists might voluntarily work. Free atonality, of course, was different altogether (see also Chapter 5).

It is worth dwelling a little on this kind of critique, in which aspects of society are seen as embedded within musical structure. This is because it has provided one of the most important recent links between sociology and historical musicology. For instance, when John Shepherd (a sociologist) and Susan McClary (a musicologist) each analyze the ways in which music encodes "male hegemony" (i.e., the domination of men over women in both society and culture), they are working from a similar starting point. They discuss the "ideal" images of masculinity and femininity that surround the music in society, and then

Box 3.1 Vincent D'Indy on sonata form

To the extent that the two ideas exposed and developed in pieces in sonata form perfect themselves, one notices indeed that they really behave like living beings, submitted to the inevitable laws of humanity: liking or antipathy, attraction or repulsion, love or hate. And, in this perpetual conflict, which reflects those in life, each of the two ideas offers qualities comparable to those which have always been attributable respectively to man and woman.

Force and energy, concision and clarity: such are almost invariably the essential *masculine* characteristics belonging to the *first idea*: it imposes itself in *brusque rhythms*, affirming very nobly its tonal ownership, one and definitive.

The *second idea*, in contrast, entirely gentle and of *melodic* grace, is affective almost always by means of its verbosity and modulatory vagueness of the eminently alluring *feminine*: supple and elegant, it spreads out progressively the curve of its ornamented melody; circumscribed more or less clearly in a neighbouring tonality in the course of the exposition, it will always depart from it in the recapitulation, in order to adopt the first tonality occupied from the beginning by the dominant masculine element, alone. It is as if, after the active battle of the development, the being of gentleness and weakness has to submit, whether by violence or by persuasion, to the conquest of the being of force and power.

Such seems to be at least, in sonatas as in life, the communal law …

(Vincent d'Indy, *Cours de composition musicale*, cited and translated in Citron 1993: 136)

analyze the extent to which the music matches, resists, or possibly celebrates that reality. All elements of music are open to analysis from this point of view: harmony, themes, tonality, structure, timbre, instrumentation, and performance. McClary, for instance, has tended to concentrate on nineteenth-century ideas about masculinity, femininity, and sexuality. She has built on a famously graphic description of sonata form by the French composer Vincent d'Indy, dating from around 1898.

Here, a sequence of thematic ideas and tonal areas is described as a battle of the sexes in which the man (first theme/tonal area) conquers the woman (second theme/tonal area). Effectively, McClary asks the question: if this kind of social/musical equivalence is being taught to students (and it was), how deeply embedded must it have been in the music they and their predecessors studied, wrote, and performed?

Shepherd, who in 1990 published a book called *Music as Social Text* (and that tells us a lot in itself), has written about the importance of timbre and voice production. He has identified as "macho" timbres such as those characteristic of Mick Jagger – a rasping sound created mostly in the throat and mouth. By contrast, he has described the idealized sounds of woman-as-carer (common in ballad singing, for instance) as warmer and richer, because its vocal production is more relaxed and comes from the chest. Quoting the blues specialist Paul Oliver, he has noted how certain female blues singers such as Bessie Smith crossed the boundary from the one to the other: "the aggressiveness of the women singers is directly related to their position in Northern black [American] society in the years between the wars. In the main women were more able to get jobs than men, and for this reason found themselves in the position of family 'head'" (cited in Shepherd 1990: 171). The point here is that women felt they had to act like men in their music, since they were taking on a man's role in society. The one paralleled the other.

Many scholars see problems with these kinds of analysis. One is that it lumps all women together and all men together as opposites. There is no middle ground, or flexibility, and no consideration of other factors such as ethnicity, age, religion, or class. The result is a tendency towards what is called **essentialism**, where all people of a particular gender (or ethnicity, or class) are assumed to be the same, or where it is assumed that they *ought* to be the same. Sociology confronts this problem of typecasting all the time because it deals in the classification of types of people (that is what I was doing with my CD shop example). Deciding how complex a form of classification is appropriate is one of the most difficult tasks the sociology of music faces. Its writers generally agree on the importance of social structures such as schools, family life, and the media in the shaping of group tastes (this is called **enculturation** or **socialization**). But they do not agree about how important those structures are and to what extent individuals resist or adapt them, thereby resisting easy pigeonholing. Another objection is that analyses in which music's social meanings are seen as embedded actually give just a single snapshot, because different societies see the same music in different ways. Since societal values and traditions change, so music may be seen from a new angle and given new meanings. It is as though music is not a single, stable thing, but something that is constantly under construction. While new music is being produced all the time, older music also becomes "new." At its most active, this process is known as **appropriation**: the claiming of something for one's own group, possibly through reinterpreting its established social meaning or its symbolism. And that kind of reinterpretation can provoke a strong reaction from other groups who want to hear their music as they always used to, and see such change as an attempt to take it away from them.

The sociology of music, then, is not a single approach to music but a collection of different approaches, some of them conflicting with each other and many of them treading on the toes of other disciplines, including ethnomusicology, psychology, business history, gender studies, and communications research. The range is huge. Sociological method extends from detailed microstudies of human interaction (within a pop band or a string quartet) to macrostudies of mass culture (where the essentialism problem is acute), or models in which the history of Western tonality, dominant from *c*.1580 to *c*.1905, parallels that of Western capitalism, unthreatened in its dominance during the same period. It brings together user surveys and discussions of the ways music is produced in the first place. It also digs deep into questions of money and power. And it deals, in various ways, with music, identity (how we see ourselves, and how others see us), and social meaning. Let us look in more detail at how some of those issues work in practice.

The problem of "high art"

I have deliberately left out one of the defining characteristics of the sociology of culture, music included: its oppositional nature. By this I mean that many sociologists of culture define what they do by actively rejecting methods and attitudes that they see as problematic within the humanities. They see the study of literature, art history, and music history as suffering from the same problem: a tendency to concentrate on works of "high" art ("classical" music comes into this category) and to remove those works from their social context, seeing them simply as the product of genius. Many musicologists would see this description as an unfair caricature of what they do and what they teach. In fact, you can judge for yourself, as you read this book, how far apart you think these two traditions of thinking are. Nevertheless, the sense of high art's "removal from the world" is often intentionally acute. You can feel it if you walk round a museum or sit in a hushed concert hall. There is often only artificial light, there will be as much soundproofing as possible, and minimal distraction from the works you are experiencing (when did you last see patterned wallpaper on a museum wall)?

Most of all, you will be an observer, not a participant. Touch the sculptures and you will be hissed at; sing along with a Mozart concerto and the same thing will happen. The first will come from employees; the second, from your fellow audience members, who now realize that you're not one of them because you either don't know the rules, or you refuse to obey them. There is, then, an etiquette to concert-going or museum-visiting, and it is a quasi-religious one. You are supposed to revere the vast majority of these works even though you might enjoy them, too. The moment you go in you are expected to conform, and if you do not want to conform or if you feel out of place more generally, you may find yourself deciding that the whole set of traditions, the art included, is not for you. (Box 3.2 shows another side of this question).

The reason so many museums and orchestras have outreach programs is to try to break down this kind of barrier. The aim is to reduce what is known as self-censorship – people turning away from an art form they might potentially enjoy because they are intimidated both by its rituals and by the kinds of people who are comfortable with those rituals.

These traditions form part of the cultural baggage of a key concept in the humanities that sociologists have always questioned: the autonomous artwork. This term sounds descriptive (the "independent work of art") but is

---

Box 3.2 "Music that moves the station yobs," by Roger Scott

In 1998 the operators of the Newcastle Metro decided to try a musical deterrent to vandalism that was costing the company £500,000 a year. Instead of continuing to play music by local pop stars – Sting and Jimmy Nail – over the tannoy at the Shiremoor station, they played Delius. Their reasoning had more to do with psychology than sociology (soothing music versus active music), but the results have a distinctly sociological aspect to them:

Vandals and troublemakers who blighted a railway station are being driven away – by the sweet sound of classical music.

The teenage louts, accustomed to the beat of rock and techno, cannot stand the lilting chords of English composer Delius.

In just three weeks, rowdy groups who used to menace passengers, wreck equipment and scrawl graffiti at the Tyneside Metro station of Shiremoor have quietly faded away.

Police and railway officials are delighted. "They just couldn't stand it," said Chief Inspector Allan Curry, of the Northumbria force.

(*Daily Mail*, 30 January 1998, [5])

Fig. 3.1 "Good music unappreciated." From *The History of Music* (1968) by Geoffrey Brace, illustration by Martin Aitchison.

also normative (i.e., it implies a system of values). Simply put, it expresses that idea that a work of art is the purely intellectual product of an unusually creative artistic mind (the genius-composer, for us). The work exists in our world, but its artistic quality makes it somehow other-worldly. It is distant from (and therefore more valuable than) musics that take account of what ordinary people want to buy and to consume. It is unsullied by considerations of commerce, sexuality, or politics and (and here we are back to hermetically sealed concert halls) we are encouraged to value it for those very reasons. We are therefore asked to take it seriously, and to contemplate it. This mode of listening was so ingrained that when BBC public-service radio broadcasting took off in the 1920s, listeners were lectured on precisely how to use the new service. They were not to become passive listeners using music as background distraction, but to select their programs carefully and "to cultivate the art of using their wireless receivers intelligently and artistically" (*BBC Handbook* 1928, cited in Frith 1988: 28). Once freed from sitting in a concert hall, of course, audiences could use broadcast music as they liked (see above, Fig. 3.1): that was what the BBC feared.

Are geniuses made, not born?

At the heart of the idea lies a nineteenth-century concept – that of the genius composer who confounds us all with music we strain to understand, and whose struggles for recognition are successful because the quality of the music wins through in the end. The genius is a heroic figure. But what *is* a genius-composer, from a sociological point of view? Tia DeNora has researched this question in relation to one of the most famous geniuses of Western music: Beethoven. How, she asks, did Beethoven achieve success as a twenty-something composer looking for a freelance career in Vienna? What did it take to get him noticed and (to put it crudely) to set him on the road to superstar composer? Can increasing recognition of the quality of his music be the only, or the main, reason? Her title, *Beethoven and the Construction of Genius*, gives the game away: her answer to that last question is "no." Her subtitle, *Musical Politics in Vienna, 1792–1803* also hints at what she thinks of the idea of "autonomous artwork": it does not exist as something independent of society. Beethoven's works are not free-floating. They exist in the forms they do because they respond to many people's needs, as part of a network of social relationships between Beethoven himself, his aristocratic patrons, publishers, concert promoters and theater directors, and music critics writing reviews for the local papers.

Those people are arranged in a hierarchy, with aristocratic patrons acting as what she calls "gatekeepers for public exposure" (DeNora 1995: 58). Access to good publishing contracts, concert appearances, and bread-and-butter teaching of the right kind of student depended on having one's way "eased" by those in power. Composers who had the right connections did better in their careers and in their reputations after death than those who did not. DeNora is not denying Beethoven's talent here. Nor is she saying that Beethoven acted in a mercenary fashion simply to keep patrons happy. She is simply using historical research to argue that social circumstance worked significantly to his advantage, and that Beethoven saw and successfully negotiated his way through the patronage system then in operation. Nevertheless, lurking beneath her study is another, more profound question, which she illustrates by comparing Beethoven's career with that of a secondary composer whose music was similar in genre and style: Jan Ladislav Dussek. If we were to find an unknown Viennese composer of Beethoven's age and to swap his life story for Beethoven's, would we have heard the name Beethoven at all? And if Beethoven had been female, or black, what then? How secure, then, are those assumptions that the works that get into the museum or the concert hall are the "great" works? Like ethnomusicologists, sociologists of music find these very terms of reference problematic.

"Art worlds" and the music business

DeNora's study has much in common with earlier work on art history. In a pathbreaking text called *Art Worlds* (1982), Howard Becker asked why painters were effectively regarded as the sole authors of their works when what they painted, and how it was received by the public, depended on so many intermediaries who could influence the outcome. Patrons, gallery owners, agents, auctioneers, the commissioners of paintings, and the manufacturers of paints – all were part of a complex production process, responding to and creating demand. Becker also saw those who looked at paintings as important kinds of "author," and tried to strip away the mysterious quality of art, presenting it instead as something normal in which we can all, potentially, be involved. His vision of an "art world" can be applied to many kinds of music. For members of the audience, for instance, the impact of a rock concert is as dependent on the work of technical and lighting staff as it is on the capacities of the musicians themselves as songwriters and performers. And in the case of established bands there is, further "backstage," a similar network of agents, administrators, and record promoters. All have a stake in the image a band presents, from clothing to stage design to the spatial choreography of the musicians themselves as they perform. Musical style is just one component of something much larger. There is more, then, to music, than just music.

Perhaps we think of opera primarily in terms of music; but if so, that is partly because of our enculturation, for exactly the same forces are at work (see chapter 8). We speak of Monteverdi's *Orfeo* and Britten's *Peter Grimes* as though no one else were involved. Even the librettist's name (the person who wrote the text) will not make it onto the DVD front cover. Yet since sociologists see a musical work as taking on a real identity only when it reaches an audience, the number of "authors" expands massively. An operatic cast list begins to resemble a set of film credits. Producers, directors, conductors, translators, designers, and technicians all contribute to the character of the final product. The practical side is no less important. Backstage, the Royal Opera House in London is a major employer of seamstresses, scene-painters, shoemakers, carpenters, rehearsal pianists, and the rest. As successive directors of the ROH have found, organizing the population of this miniature city to common artistic ends, and keeping the Board of Directors happy about the balance sheet, is no joke.

That brings us to money, which is an essential part of the network. Who funds music, and in what ways? What does the music market look like? Studying the financial mechanisms that underpin musical experience and influence choices allows us to see complex value systems at work. Governments, at local and national level, support certain types of music, both within education and beyond it; and not surprisingly, decisions as to how to spend public money are highly politicized. Many composers are supported through being salaried staff in universities. Private trusts and individual donors keep many musical institutions afloat; some are even officially registered as charities. All these modes of funding, however, presuppose the same thing: that music cannot look after itself in a market economy. Crucially for the sociology of music, that is true of some kinds of music but not others.

The recording industry reflects these differences. Within the major companies, a relatively recent trend has been to replace systems of cross-subsidy between divisions with those of individual profit centers. This has left relatively small, or niche, divisions such as jazz and classical music financially exposed: losses that were once cushioned by profits elsewhere become problematic when each and every division has to publish its accounts. One of the results, as Keith Negus explains, is that the shape of classical portfolios has expanded to include seasonal releases, "greatest hits" packages, and crossover (Negus 1999: 49–50), in the hope of attracting a wider audience to a loss-making category of music. The move looks similar to those outreach programs I mentioned earlier, in that part of its aim is to bypass the self-censorship among consumers who would not normally enter the classical section of a CD shop (that is why such CDs are marketed in supermarkets and garages). But it is more immediately dictated by financial, rather than educational, concerns (see also Chapter 16).

"Cultural capital," social status, and identity

Sociological research by Richard Peterson and Albert Simkus dating from 1992 has provided detailed pictures of the relationships in America between class (measured according to nineteen occupational groupings) and musical taste. The results put Western classical music firmly at the top of the status hierarchy (professionals, artists, managers) and country music equally firmly at the bottom (caretakers, transport workers, farm laborers). Within each occupational group, choices are inflected by ethnicity, but not really by gender. Even in a globalized culture and a supposedly classless society, then, musical preference still indicates a lot about social identity and status.

In the light of my previous discussions about the recording industry we might accordingly say that Western classical music lacks economic capital but has plenty of "**cultural capital**." By this I mean, following the French sociologist Pierre Bourdieu, that it is the most closely associated with ideas of quality, refinement, and authority, and indicates a high level of class status. Television advertisers have often used this equivalence to try to impress us or to make us aspire to own a superior car or to choose a classy perfume. Upmarket restaurant owners do it to make sure they attract the right kind of clientele, second-guessing what social messages we are likely to pick up in the music. This provides a more subtle example of the self-censorship I mentioned earlier, since although some people are attracted, others are persuaded to stay away. To a certain extent, one can "buy into" a particular class status by buying into the musical taste that goes with it. A ticket or a donation becomes a cultural investment and an indication of one's place in this particular social group. And the social ladder is often made extraordinarily public, as in the donor lists published in the programs for English National Opera (and other, similar, institutions).

Box 3.3 Two pages of a 2004 English National Opera program listed its supporters under the following categories, in order:	
Corporate supporters	Personal supporters
Season sponsor	Fellow – £3000+
Founders' Circle Partners	Patron – £1200+
Gold Members	Benefactor – £600+
Silver Members	Associate – £300+
Bronze Members	OperaZingers Syndicate – £1000+
Season Ticket Holders	Young Singers Programme – £500+
Sponsors/others	*Ring* Syndicate
	Trojans Syndicate Production Support

All this means, of course, that members of a socially dominant group (white middle-class professionals in particular) are in a unique position to defend the music they value (and which they consider to be a public good), and to insulate it from the demands of the market. Hence, the kind of subsidy given out by the Arts Council and other public bodies.

Statistical studies such as those of Peterson and Simkus can give us a broadbrush view of the shape of the social organization of music. But smaller-scale studies based on interviews and what ethnomusicologists call "participant observation" are becoming increasingly popular as a means to get under the skin of social attitudes. Their authors ask not just what people's views are, but why they hold them. In respect of youth cultures and popular musics, some of the results tell us a great deal about how central musical traditions are in cementing a sense of individual and group identity as children reach adulthood. They also illustrate the appropriation and reappropriation of musical values within different communities, and the power of social construction over social reality. It will be helpful as an example here to define the core musical/lifestyle values (the sub-cultures) of two musical traditions, both of which involve much more than musical sound: heavy metal, and the 1990s clubbing scene.

Demographic research shows that the typical heavy metal fan, almost world-wide, is male, white, aged around twelve to twenty-two, and working-class (or lower-middle class embracing a working-class ethos) (Weinstein 1991: 99, 115). The uniform, alluded to at the start of this chapter, sits between that of the hippie (long hair demonstrating long-term commitment to the cause) and the Hell's Angels biker (black, studded leathers, with gothic logos, and possibly tattoos that must be permanent). It is emblematic of heavy metal's roots in these two strands of 1960s youth culture, and intended to suggest an aggres-sive and even homophobic masculinity, openly admitted to by fans looking for a nostalgic reflection of macho culture in a musical style that celebrates the emotional blood-rush of rebellious power, high volume, technical prowess, and acoustic distortion. Heavy metal fans, like many rock fans, are musically exclusionist and elitist as a matter of honor. Among Weinstein's subjects, chart pop and disco came in for contemptuous denunciation as feminized/ effeminate and gay-influenced forms of music. In addition, given the empha-sis on live performance in heavy metal (no miming allowed) and the overt adaptation of virtuoso techniques from classical music, it is unsurprising to find fans linking chart pop with prefabricated and therefore "inauthentic" bands of no technical or musical merit. Nevertheless, the subculture itself (young, white, heterosexual male) is not entirely essentialist or exclusion-ary. Conformity and commitment count for more. Weinstein tells the story of a black fan "too intimidated" to go to a Rush concert, but who on plucking up the courage to attend a year later, "reported no problems" (Weinstein 1991: 112).

Whatever the real level of social tolerance inside, the sense of social barrier, of course, is as clear to those on the "outside" of heavy metal as it is in many other cases where subcultural membership is at stake. Researching in over two hundred clubs in the UK, Sarah Thornton found similar patterns. Young people from public schools were adopting working-class accents and attitudes in an attempt to enjoy a temporary "authenticity"; the typical age-range was fifteen to twenty-four; most clubbers had no family or financial responsibilities. Unsurprisingly, she also found tightly regulated social codes, a strong streak of exclusionism, and a willingness among many clubbers to be devastatingly frank about musical values they detested (chart pop, disco – also viewed as a feminized "mainstream"). Even within a single club, social fragmentation and self-selection occurred: chart pop drew women out onto the dance floor; acid house produced groups of men trance-dancing in groups. The two, musi-cally and socially, did not mix (Thornton 1995: 106). Getting past bouncers in the first place was a rite of passage dependent on judging dress and behavioral codes correctly; but there was also evidence of covert racism and sexual discrimination. Black boun-cers were sometimes used to imple-ment anti-black "house policies," and some door policies operated on the basis of the assumed sexual prefer-ences of groups turning up at the door.

Most importantly, though, Thornton diagnosed two sets of oppositional stra-tegies at work among clubbers. One provided a reversal of the kind of live-music "authenticity" we saw with heavy metal, and which also exists in rock, jazz, and classical music. Clubbers turned this idea on its head, appropriat-ing the sound of the record, and the artistry of the DJ, as the authentic root

Box 3.4	
US	THEM
Alternative	Mainstream
Hip/cool	Straight/square/stiff
Independent	Commercial
Authentic	False/phoney
Rebellious/radical	Conformist/conservative
Specialist genres	Pop
Insider knowledge	Easily accessible information
Minority	Majority
Heterogeneous	Homogeneous
Youth	Family
Classless	Classed
Masculine culture	Feminine culture

(Thornton 1995: 115)

of the clubbing experience. The other strategy was more common: the opposition of an "us" and "them," of subculture and mainstream.

That mainstream was often dismissed as a form of mass music peddled by the record industry to the credulous. However, Thornton's interviewees never defined it, and it became revealed as a second-hand concept that was, effec-tively, a necessary illusion that made membership of "the club" seem special and exclusive. Just like DeNora's "genius," Thornton's "mainstream" turned out to be a social construction invented from the inside. That does not make it less real as a sociological "fact," because people genuinely believed in it; it simply puts that "fact" into perspective.

Identity politics and the interplay of music and social status are the very stuff of the sociology of music, whatever type of music we study. And whereas music often appears sidelined in other kinds of interdisciplinary work within the arts and the humanities, it is central to sociological analysis because, as Bourdieu put it, it is the most deep-seated kind of taste we know, after that of food. And just as we feel physical revulsion at disgusting food (which others might consider a delicacy), so we react almost physically to music we dislike. It's not a "take it or leave it" art form, and it surrounds and permeates our lives more than ever before. Sociology tries to make sense of what it means to us, and of what it says about us.

Chapter summary

- Human beings invest music with value and meaning and use it as a way of defining themselves socially and binding themselves into groups.

- The sociology of music comprises several different (and sometimes mutually contradictory) ways of thinking about how music "means," establishing who consumes it, and explaining why different groups value different musical genres and styles.
- The sociology of music is often more concerned with people, politics, and social institutions than with the sounds of music itself. However, there is also a scholarly tradition which analyzes the sounds and structures of music in terms of the social elements they embody.
- Historically, the sociology of music has operated as a mode of musical study that opposes the idea – strongly associated with discussion of Western art music – of the autonomous artwork composed by the lone, transcendent, genius.

Discussion topics

- What assumptions about social groups and musical tastes do you think underlie the *Daily Mail* article in Box 3.2? How would you go about testing them out?
- What impressions do you get about musics and gender politics from this chapter? Try to work out why they do or do not surprise you.
- If sociology is able to identify instances of musical/social tension and to diagnose the reasons for them, do you think it should try to resolve them?

Further reading

DeNora, Tia (2000), *Music in Everyday Life* (Cambridge and New York: Cambridge University Press).
>   An analysis, drawing on psychology, sociology, and other disciplines, of the way in which music takes an active role in social and public life in the modern world.

Frith, Simon (1988), *Music for Pleasure: Essays in the Sociology of Pop* (Cambridge: Polity).
>   An essay collection on music videos and television, which traces developments that the use of technology has brought about in rock and pop.

McClary, Susan (1991), *Feminine Endings: Music, Gender, and Sexuality* (Minneapolis: University of Minnesota Press).
>   A classic feminist reading of a wide range of music in the classical and popular traditions.

Martin, Peter J. (2006), *Music and the Sociological Gaze: Art Worlds and Cultural Production* (Manchester and New York: Manchester University Press).
>   An essay collection centering on a comparison of musicological and sociological approaches to the question of music's social meanings. Contains an extended review of McClary (1991).

Negus, Keith (1999), *Music Genres and Corporate Cultures* (London and New York: Routledge).
>   A study of the ways in which individual and corporate identity, creativity and global production, and the propagation of world musics figure in the recording industry.

Small, Christopher (1987), *Music of the Common Tongue: Survival and Celebration in Afro-American Music* (London and New York: J. Calder; Riverrun Press).
>   An important ethnomusicological text examining the history and social contexts of the African-American song tradition, not least as a challenging counterpoint to Western art music.

Straw, Will (2001), "Consumption," in *The Cambridge Companion to Pop and Rock* (Cambridge: Cambridge University Press), 53–73.
>   An examination of how modern consumption of music is shaped by the recording industry and by the tensions between globalized markets and self-defining subcultures.

Weinstein, Deena (1991), *Heavy Metal: a Cultural Sociology* (New York and Oxford: Macmillan).
>   An accessible introduction to the history of the heavy metal genre and its socio-cultural traditions.

Zolberg, Vera L. (1990), *Constructing a Sociology of the Arts* (Cambridge: Cambridge University Press).
>   An examination, via study of institutions, economics and politics, of what might define "art."

References

Bourdieu, Pierre (1986 [1979]), *Distinction: a Social Critique of the Judgement of Taste*, trans. Richard Nice (New York and London: Routledge).

Citron, Marcia (1993), *Gender and the Musical Canon* (Cambridge: Cambridge University Press).

DeNora, Tia (1995), *Beethoven and the Construction of Genius: Musical Politics in Vienna, 1792–1803* (Berkeley, Los Angeles, and London: University of California Press).

Peterson, Richard A. and Simkus, Albert (1992), "How musical tastes mark occupational status groups," in Michèle Lamont and Marcel Fournier (eds.), *Cultivating Difference: Symbolic Boundaries and the Making of Inequality* (Chicago and London: University of Chicago Press), 152–86.

Shepherd, John (1990), *Music as Social Text* (Cambridge: Polity).

Thornton, Sarah (1995), *Club Cultures: Music, Media and Subcultural Capital* (Cambridge: Polity).

Walser, Robert (1993), *Running with the Devil: Power, Gender, and Madness in Heavy Metal Music* (Hannover, NH: University Press of New England).

Glossary

Appropriation	Claiming another group's idea, or music, or style as one's own, by attempting to change the terms of reference associated with it.
Cultural/subcultural capital	The relative power or status associated with a particular cultural idea, style, or artefact, and (by extension) of the people who choose to associate themselves with it.
Essentialism	The idea that a large group of people (defined usually by ethnicity or gender) necessarily displays identical behavioral characteristics and tastes.
Enculturation/socialization	The process by which education and other social structures shape group tastes and behaviors.

4 The psychology of music

JOHN RINK

Chapter preview

This chapter investigates the psychological processes by which human beings make sense of, respond to, and create music. It starts by defining the term "psychology"; it then surveys the history of music psychology, and describes where and how it is currently practiced. A section on the main methods used by music psychologists follows, with numerous case studies drawn from recent literature. This leads to extended consideration of what the "musical mind" entails and how it functions in relation to the body. Further case-study examples are offered here and in the discussion of how we learn music. The section on musical creativity looks in particular at improvisation, while the final part of the chapter considers musical expression and how we perceive it. Topics addressed in the course of the chapter include the "talent myth," sight-reading, and the various types of musical memory and skill as well as the means by which skill and expertise are developed. Emphasis is continually placed on the role of experience and acquired knowledge in interpreting the world around us.

Key issues

- What is psychology?
- What is the psychology of music?
- What do music psychologists do?
- How does "the musical mind" work?
- How do we learn music?
- How do we create music?
- What is expressed in music and how do we perceive it?

What is psychology?

Imagine you are in a crowded classroom. Suddenly, a bell starts ringing. Do you:

1) sit up straight?
2) run to the door?
3) roll your eyes?
4) salivate?

Strange as it may seem, each of these reactions would be justified under certain circumstances – for example, if the bell signaled a teacher's arrival (response 1), fire in the building (response 2), the end of an exam or the beginning of a lunch break (responses 3 and 4 respectively). The most important factor determining your reaction is likely to be your knowledge of what the bell means, based on past experience. Thus, if you have never heard it before, you will probably observe what others do and follow suit.

All of this suggests that sounds have meaning – or rather, *sounds invite our interpretation of and response to their possible meanings*. The same is true of the sounds we construe as music. This process of interpreting and responding on the basis of previous experience and acquired knowledge is partly what defines us as human beings. It is therefore of interest to psychologists, as we shall see throughout this chapter.

But before going further, let us consider what psychology itself means. If someone asked you to define it, you might say "the study of the mind" (or, if you know its etymology, the study of the soul, that is, *psyche* in ancient Greek). This is a useful starting point, but there is more to it than that. First of all, psychology claims to be a science – a term that suggests (but does not guarantee) objectivity, methodological rigor, and systematic explanation. Secondly, psychologists study not only the mind in itself but also its interaction with the physical body. This is a significant point, as you will discover. And thirdly, psychologists study how individuals or groups of people interact with the world around them, in social and other contexts. Some of the most important terms in psychology are therefore mind, body, and environment; others include **cognition**, perception, emotion, and behavior. We shall explore all of these as the chapter progresses, focusing on the key issues outlined above.

What is the psychology of music?

Historical beginnings

The discipline of psychology has evolved over more than 2,000 years and has inspired an immense literature that would take you a lifetime to read. Music has continually attracted the attention of scholars partly because of the effects it has on just about everybody. There is insufficient space here for detailed historical discussion, but I would like to point out the extended debate (over many centuries) between those in the Pythagorean tradition who explained music in terms of its mathematical properties, and those who directly or indirectly adopted the view of Aristoxenus (fourth century BCE) that musical phenomena are perceptual in nature and need to be understood in terms of the perceiver's individual experience – as I have already indicated.

Much ink has been spilt on sound and its perception over the years, but often that ink has been of a philosophical, music-theoretical, physiological, acoustical, or aesthetic hue rather than an explicitly psychological one. On the other hand, in the case of psychology and indeed other disciplines, precise boundaries do not really exist, in that scholars habitually draw from a range of sources and intellectual traditions, thereby enriching their own work and fertilizing the discipline(s) to which they are allied. (See chapter 11 for some examples.) One of the first people to find common ground between the various domains I have referred to was Hermann von Helmholtz (1821–94), whose work paralleled the establishment of psychology as a scientific discipline in its own right. (You will encounter Helmholtz's name when studying music notation, for he invented one of the main systems used to identify register.) Psychology was also acknowledged as a component of the "systematic musicology" (*Musikwissenschaft* – literally "music science" – in German) defined by Guido Adler in 1885. An interesting example in this respect is the **empirical** research of Carl Stumpf (1848–1936), who worked with musicians and drew upon his own practice as a violinist when preparing his pivotal *Tonpsychologie* (psychology of sound). Another pioneer – the American Carl Seashore (1866–1949) – also studied performers, looking in particular at the sources and perception of musical expression, which he measured with specially devised equipment.

The psychology of music today

Many others have contributed to the development of music psychology over the years, to the point that it is now well established throughout the world, with research taking place in the psychology and music departments of innumerable universities, institutes, research centers, and laboratories. Music psychology has its own journals (among them *Psychology of Music*, *Music Perception*, and *Musicae scientiae*), international societies (e.g., European Society for the Cognitive Sciences of Music – ESCOM), and conferences. Echoing my comment above, there is a vast amount of literature specifically on music psychology, much of it written in language that non-specialist readers, including many musicians, sometimes find alienating. One of the tasks of this chapter is to introduce you to key vocabulary, but you will need to read widely to grasp music psychology in its full complexity and to conquer the sometimes opaque terminology used to discuss it. Fortunately, certain recent publications are intended for non-specialists and may be of interest if you are new to the field. These include Sloboda's *The Musical Mind* from 1985, several chapters in

Rink's *Musical Performance* (2002), and the multi-authored *Psychology for Musicians* (Lehmann, Sloboda, and Woody 2007).

I also suggest that you look at "Psychology of music" in *Grove Music Online* (2008), an excellent survey written by leading scholars in the field. You will be impressed (if not overwhelmed) by the range of topics covered there, especially when you consider that in each case the author only scratches the surface.

It will therefore help to bear in mind the four main areas on which much recent research has been focused (Sloboda 2007), which map more or less onto the remaining sections in this chapter:

1) the understanding – or more technically, **cognitive representation** – of pitch and rhythm, and how we construct harmony and melody from them;
2) how musical competence and skill are developed;
3) the processes that underlie musical performance;
4) the emotional responses and similar processes associated with music listening.

Let us briefly consider Sloboda's further observation (2007) that almost all music-psychological work in recent decades "has been directed towards the music of the Western tonal tradition, with particular concentration on the period from Bach onwards." I wonder whether you see this as a limitation and maybe even a deficiency (especially if you have read the chapters in Parts 2 and 3 of this book). Not only might studies in these four areas yield different results when geared toward repertoire outside the tonal tradition, but, as you know, a huge number of musical idioms and practices exist alongside "Western art music," and these warrant equal attention. Given that psychologists look for general mechanisms to explain the cognitive, behavioral, and social processes and characteristics that define us as human, the relatively narrow focus of much music-psychological research may appear self-defeating. In any case, there remains the need for far-reaching synthesis alongside the more focused work that has already been carried out.

What do music psychologists do?

Before delving into the literature on music psychology, you should become familiar with the most common research methods and their potential applications. In due course, you might want to put some of them to use yourself.

Contexts

The starting point for any research initiative involves determining the existing state of knowledge primarily as embodied in the literature. New research is motivated by a wish to answer key questions and fill gaps in the current understanding of a given issue. In music psychology, this might concern whether or not listeners perceive performances differently if musicians play from a score rather than by memory. Research on this very topic is described in Box 4.1.

> **Box 4.1 The value of performing from memory**
>
> Performances of the Preludes from Cello Suites I, II and III by J. S. Bach were recorded on video-tape across five separate conditions, differing with respect to memorisation and the presence of a music stand. Fifty "musicians" and thirty-six "non-musicians" were asked to watch and rate one video-taped performance of each Prelude on four performance aspects: overall quality, musical understanding, technical proficiency and communicative ability. Ratings indicated that (1) performing from memory was superior to playing from the score, (2) visibility of the performer influenced audiences' ratings of performances in a favourable direction, (3) the extra time spent preparing for the memorised performances was beneficial, and (4) musicians seemed biased in favour of performances without a music stand.
>
> (Williamon 1999: 84)

Hypotheses

Having conducted a thorough literature review to establish a context for the study, the psychologist generates a set of *hypotheses*. These are provisional conjectures – educated guesses – based on what is known or what is assumed to be possible; the new investigation attempts to confirm or disprove them.

Hypotheses may be presented not as conjectural statements but as a series of research questions. For example, the research in Box 4.1 focused on four main questions, among them the following:

- Do memorized performances yield the most direct psychological connection with the audience?

As a hypothesis, this would take a different form:

- Memorized performances yield a direct psychological connection with the audience.

Despite its matter-of-fact formulation, do not assume that the statement is true: instead, think of hypotheses as starting with the phrase "It is possible that" and thus as requiring confirmation or inviting disproof.

Methods

After establishing contexts and defining hypotheses, most studies outline the method(s) in use, describing any participants as well as the procedures themselves. Detailed results are then presented, followed by discussion. It is here that the validity of the hypotheses is assessed, leading to final conclusions. In the memorization study, for example, "the results suggest that performing from memory does offer advantages over performing with the music. The evidence points to enhanced communication as a possible advantage of performing from memory" (Williamon 1999: 92).

The principal methods used by music psychologists include, but of course are not limited to, the following:

- experiments
- observation and measurement
- questionnaires, interviews, diaries, etc.
- analysis of other data – e.g., sound recordings, MIDI, videos
- neuropsychological methods.

Sometimes different methods are combined within a single study; also, one or more independent studies may be linked to yield complementary results greater than the sum of their parts. Research may focus on a specific period or take a longitudinal approach – for example, studying how musical skills develop over months or years. It may be empirical or more theoretically driven.

Experiments usually occur under strictly controlled conditions so that extraneous factors do not color the results. Thus the experimental tasks that participants (or "subjects") carry out tend not to conform to their normal behavior. Here are some examples:

- Listeners are tested for their ability to recognize the pitch of a tone played five seconds after they first hear it, but having heard six other "disrupting" tones during that interval. (Deutsch 1970)
- Performers sight-read a score containing deliberate notational errors, to determine whether or not they correct the mistakes despite being told to play exactly what is written. (Sloboda 1976)
- Trained musicians are asked to evaluate expert performances in order to determine the constructs they use to judge expressiveness, as well as the effect of these constructs on their ratings and preferences. (Thompson, Forde, Diamond, and Balkwill 1998)

However elucidatory the findings are with regard to tasks in a controlled environment, certain experimental procedures may produce only limited insight into complex activities such as performing, listening, and composing. That is why some musicians, when reading about such experiments, dismiss them as lacking musical validity. I hope you will not fall into this trap. Instead, try to see beyond the (intentional) limitations of given studies. Even if they do not say all there is to say, such studies may nevertheless extend our understanding of important issues.

The second type of method – observation and measurement – is often used to determine the behavior of performers, listeners, and others. In such cases, the context is more or less natural; participants may even be unaware of the observer's presence. An example is offered in Box 4.2. In different research, Jane Davidson used a tracking technique to study the movement of a pianist. This involved putting reflective strips or spots on his body in order to measure his movements in two dimensions, namely, up/down and forward/backward in relation to the keyboard. The results confirmed "the expected relationship between the movement size and expression – the more intense the expressive intention, the larger the movement" (Clarke and Davidson 1998: 78). But

Davidson did not stop there: she then asked observers to judge the extent to which different parts of the pianist's body conveyed information about his expressive intentions. Interestingly, this showed that listeners could accurately discern the expressive nature of the performance – whether "deadpan," "projected," or "exaggerated" – simply on the basis of the movements of the upper torso and head region, without hearing any sounds at all (Clarke and Davidson 1998: 78).

Davidson's work provides an example of the linked studies I previously referred to. It also makes use of the third kind of research methodology outlined above, which Clarke and Cook (2004) describe as "evaluative and qualitative" techniques. Another example of this is presented in Box 4.3, which, as you will see, involved over 3,500 participants in an ambitious investigation of people's music preferences.

Many other forms of data analysis could be cited, including the different methods of studying sound recordings developed within CHARM (www.charm.rhul.ac.uk) and elsewhere. Typically these focus on changes in timing and/or dynamics, as well as the acoustic properties of the sounds produced by performers, in order to characterize the nature of musical expression. (See the discussion of spectrograms in chapter 2.) For example, Bruno Repp analyzed patterns of timing and dynamics in mm. 1–5 of 115 commercially recorded performances of Chopin's Etude in E major, Op. 10, No. 3. This allowed him to identify four independent "timing strategies" and to observe "a widely shared central norm of expressive dynamics" (Repp 1999: 1972).

Box 4.2 An observational study of classical singers

Unlike instrumentalists, classically trained singers perform words as well as music and must therefore use different memorising strategies. The present study aimed to identify these, to compare the extent to which they were used by singers of varying levels of expertise and to assess which strategies were most likely to be effective. Thirteen participants learned and memorised the same song over the course of six fifteen-minute practice sessions, which were audiotaped. One major finding was that experienced professional singers were not necessarily faster, more accurate memorisers than student and amateur singers, so the strategies they used were not necessarily the most effective. Generally, participants began by practising the music separately from the words and went on to practise words and music together. They began by reading the song from the musical score and went on to practise it from memory once they were confident that they could sing it accurately. Fast, accurate memorisers began memorising earlier and were more likely than slower, less accurate memorisers to count beats aloud during the learning process. This suggests that effective song memorisation requires not only basic musical expertise but also the use of a strategic approach to the memorising task.

(Ginsborg 2002: 58)

Box 4.3 Music preferences and personality

A series of six studies investigated lay beliefs about music, the structure underlying music preferences, and the links between music preferences and personality. The data indicated that people consider music an important aspect of their lives and listening to music an activity they engaged in frequently. Using multiple samples, methods, and geographic regions, analyses of the music preferences of over 3,500 individuals converged to reveal four music-preference dimensions: Reflective and Complex, Intense and Rebellious, Upbeat and Conventional, and Energetic and Rhythmic. Preferences for these music dimensions were related to a wide array of personality dimensions (e.g., Openness), self-views (e.g., political orientation), and cognitive abilities (e.g., verbal IQ).

(Rentfrow and Gosling 2003: 1236)

> **Box 4.4 Singing in the brain: insights from cognitive neuropsychology**
>
> Singing abilities are rarely examined despite the fact that their study represents one of the richest sources of information regarding how music is processed in the brain. In particular, the analysis of singing performance in brain-damaged patients provides key information regarding the autonomy of music processing relative to language processing. Here, we … illustrate how lyrics can be distinguished from melody in singing, in the case of brain damage. We report a new case, G. D., who has a severe speech disorder, marked by phonemic errors and stuttering, without a concomitant musical production disorder. G. D. was found to produce as few intelligible words in speaking as in singing familiar songs. Singing "la, la, la" was intact and hence could not account for the speech deficit observed in singing. The results indicate that verbal production, be it sung or spoken, is mediated by the same (impaired) language output system and that this speech route is distinct from the (spared) melodic route.
>
> (Peretz, Gagnon, Hébert, and Macoir 2004: 373).

The last methodology listed above belongs to "hard science" to a greater extent than the others. Neuropsychological research tries to achieve an understanding of the role of the central nervous system in a range of musical functions. For example, in the case study presented in Box 4.4, psychologists investigated whether a seventy-four-year-old man ("G. D.") who had developed certain speech difficulties could sing the lyrics as well as the melody in some three dozen songs. More often than not G. D. had no problem giving voice to the melody, but only rarely could he articulate the lyrics. The psychologists concluded that his speech difficulties – which were "typical of acquired neurological stuttering disorder" – "affected speaking and singing in a similar fashion," arguing "against the notion that singing enhances speech fluency" while also challenging the claim of previous authors that "stuttering can be alleviated by singing" (Peretz, Gagnon, Hébert, and Macoir 2004: 385).

How does "the musical mind" work?

It goes without saying that "the mind" and the brain have much to do with one another – but they are not the same thing. This distinction is central to the discipline of psychology, which primarily deals with "the organization and use of information" rather than "its representation in organic tissue" (Neisser 1967: 281). On the other hand, it is important to consider the mind holistically and "ecologically," as against the "mind/body dualism" that has dominated much psychological and philosophical thought over centuries. Eric Clarke puts it thus: "the mind is neither divorced from the body nor confined within the skull" (2002: 67–8).

Here is an example drawn from my own experience. I once found myself looking at a score on a train, trying to hear the music in my "mind's ear" – but my aural imagination could not grasp a harmonically complex passage within the piece. I then tried "playing" the passage on the table in front of me, and I found that through the simulated physical enactment of the music – the moving of my fingers as if on a keyboard – I suddenly could hear the sounds in my mind. This breakthrough was attributable to years of training as a pianist, which had created a deep-seated link between physical motion and sound – in this case, between an imaginary performance and imagined sounds.

To fathom "the musical mind," we need to grasp what cognition means. For psychologists, this key concept relates to the processing, structure, and operation of information and knowledge, whether conscious or unconscious. Theoretical explanations of cognition have changed over time. In Ulric Neisser's book *Cognitive Psychology*, "the term 'cognition' refers to all processes by which the sensory input is transformed, reduced, elaborated, stored, recovered, and used" (Neisser 1967: 4). Today, psychologists typically take a much less circumscribed view of what cognition is and how it functions. (For a useful survey of more recent research see Eysenck and Keane 2000; see also Reed 1991.)

When humans first perceive or imagine something, we assign meaning to the object or event while additionally constructing a spatial, temporal, and conceptual framework to explain it in context. Over time, we develop a host of such "frames of reference" to which further phenomena are then related (Neisser 1967: 286). By way of example, consider the ringing bell described at the start of the chapter, which you would interpret by means of these very mechanisms. (Think too of the many other examples presented in chapter 3.)

Music psychology looks among other things at cognitive representations of musical structures comprising pitches, rhythms, timbres, and so on. (Recall the discussion of structure in chapter 2.) Musical memory is closely bound up with these. Whether or not you set out to memorize the pieces you are learning as a singer or instrumentalist, your mind is at work all the time, absorbing and processing the musical stimuli around you. That is also how people without formal musical training can pick up tunes which they later "play" by whistling or singing (as in the case of "G.D."). The complex mechanisms underpinning the assimilation of music in these ways may exploit the following types of musical memory:

- **aural** (i.e. "auditory memory"), which involves music in the "mind's ear"
- **visual**, where images of notated music, physical positions used to play certain configurations, or the look of the configurations themselves (for instance, the layout of a chord on the keyboard) are recorded in the "mind's eye"
- **kinaesthetic** (i.e. physical memory), by means of which particular gestures, distances, speeds of attack, etc. are stored for later use
- **conceptual**, involving harmonic, melodic, formal, and other formulae used to classify individual musical phenomena (see Williamon 2002: 118–19).

Performers and others use different types of memory not just in isolation but in conjunction with one another. Nevertheless, many a concert has been saved by kinaesthetic memory, when a well-rehearsed hand moves "unconsciously"

Box 4.5 An exceptional musical memory

A study investigated an autistic man (NP) with an exceptional aural musical memory, demonstrating that despite having never seen the score, this individual could remember and reproduce a sixty-bar piano piece by Grieg virtually note-perfect after just four hearings, while an equally experienced "control" pianist could manage only a fraction of the piece after equivalent exposure. This apparently remarkable feat depended on stylistic familiarity: a much shorter piece by Bartók, which was stylistically unfamiliar to NP, was remembered dramatically less well, the "control" pianist in this case achieving a far better result. The authors concluded that "the ability [of NP] is structurally based," that he "needs to code material in terms of tonal structures and relations and that his exceptional ability cannot at present survive outside that framework."

(Summary of Sloboda, Hermelin, and Connor 1985, quoted from Clarke 2002: 62–3)

---

to the right notes despite the failure of other forms of memory. This confirms that the psychology of musical performance is not simply about a mind functioning within a skull: it concerns the human being as a whole, acting within particular environments and in response to a range of stimuli, including social ones.

The discussion above reveals the importance of patterning to the musical mind. Consider in this respect the exceptional individual described in Box 4.5. Sight-reading in particular requires the musician to draw quickly from a repertoire of learned patterns and to discern altogether new ones, again responding at high speed. The fact that good eye–hand coordination is critical confirms the need for a holistic understanding of how the mind works. Research on pianists' eye movements when sight-reading similarly suggests that the music's structure influences bodily action: in the case of contrapuntal or polyphonic repertoire, the eyes tend to scan the score in predominantly horizontal spans, taking in a line at a time, whereas in homophonic repertoire a more vertical motion is prevalent (see Weaver 1943). The degree of skill on the performer's part influences the nature and efficiency of this process, likewise in determining how far ahead of the hands the eyes may be reading at any given point (Furneaux and Land 1999).

Two points need to be made here. First, as I have noted, this discussion provides but one example of the integral relationship between mind and body. Secondly, diverse skills are required to carry out difficult tasks like sight-reading. How such skills develop is the topic of the next section.

How do we learn music?

Some of our first interactions with other humans have a decidedly musical character. Psychologists refer to the tuneful, accentuated form of speech that adults use conversationally with babies as **motherese** (also known as "parentese"). Research indicates that motherese tends to be similar across diverse cultures, even those in which fundamentally distinct languages are spoken (see, e.g., Box 4.6). It appears to play an important role in the development of general cognitive abilities, likewise the gestural communication that occurs from early on.

Abilities of a specifically musical kind also develop out of these initial interactions with parents and other care-givers, who can play a pivotal role in providing opportunities for informal and formal engagement with music as a child grows older. The environment in which one develops is of pivotal importance – much more so, psychologists believe, than what is popularly described as "talent," i.e., the seemingly innate ability or predisposition to perform a task well. Without denying the potential advantages of certain physical and intellectual attributes, researchers nowadays tend to regard talent as a red herring, instead claiming that everybody possesses more or less the same potential to become musically accomplished. What is most critical is the availability of resources to support the acquisition of skills, and also the degree to which the individual is motivated to do what is necessary to acquire those skills (with motivation arising from a desire to do well, the prospect of external rewards, and a wish to fit in with others, possibly more than from intrinsic pleasure in performing a given task). (See Davidson 2002.)

> **Box 4.6 Maternal speech to infants**
>
> The prosodic features of maternal speech addressed to two-month-old infants were measured quantitatively in a tonal language, Mandarin Chinese, to determine whether the features are similar to those observed in nontonal languages such as English and German. Speech samples were recorded when eight Mandarin-speaking mothers addressed an adult and their own infants. Eight prosodic features were measured by computer: fundamental frequency (pitch), frequency range per sample, frequency range per phrase, phrase duration, pause duration, number of phrases per sample, number of syllables per phrase, and the proportion of phrase time as opposed to pause time per sample... [The] pattern of results for Mandarin motherese is similar to that reported in other languages and suggests that motherese may exhibit universal prosodic features.
>
> (Grieser and Kuhl 1988)

Another essential factor is the amount of time devoted to acquiring the skill, likewise the nature of the effort that one invests. It would overstate the case to say that practice always makes perfect; on the other hand, there is a correlation between the total amount of *quality* practice time put in and the emerging degree of expertise. The term "quality" must be stressed, in that not all practice is effective; in fact, poorly focused, inattentive practicing may be downright counterproductive, grinding in mistakes rather than developing competence. Some psychologists distinguish careless or recreational playing from what they call "deliberate practice," i.e. "a highly structured activity with the explicit goal of improving some aspect of performance" (Krampe and Ericsson 1995: 86). (Chapter 13 talks about the learning of performance.)

According to Paul Fitts and Michael Posner (1967), skills are acquired in three stages:

1) **cognitive stage**: an initial phase requiring conscious attention;
2) **associative stage**: a phase of indeterminate duration, during which the activity is refined and errors are eliminated;
3) **autonomous stage**: an advanced (though not necessarily final) phase when conscious attention is no longer required in that the skill has become "automatic."

"Automaticity" is an important hallmark (though not a guarantor) of expertise in general. For example, the difficult tasks demanded of performers could not be executed at the necessary speed if conscious attention had to be devoted to every aspect thereof. Nevertheless, performing well is a challenge for experts and non-experts alike, as the following must be mastered to varying degrees:

- structure, notation, and reading skills
- aural skills
- technical and **motor** skills
- expressive skills
- presentation skills (see Davidson 2002: 97–8).

How do we create music?

Musical **creativity** is by no means limited to composers. All of us create music each time we listen to it, even if the result remains in our imagination. And of course performers bring music into the world whenever they sing or play their instruments. (See chapters 3 and 13–15.)

Despite its universality and fundamental significance, psychologists have not thoroughly explored creativity until quite recently. Since 1950, however, a good deal of literature has been published on the topic, including an entire book of multidisciplinary research on the theory and practice of musical creativity (Deliège and Wiggins 2006). The constituent essays address creativity with regard to listening to music, education, performance, and music therapy, in addition to presenting neuroscientific work and "computer models of creative behavior." There is also a postlude on compositional creativity, where an intriguing (if contentious) definition appears: "Creativity may be ... thought of as the entire system by which processes operate on structures to produce outcomes that are novel but nevertheless rooted in existing knowledge" (quoted from Ward, Smith and Vaid 1997: 15).

Let us unpack this a bit. The word "processes" is undeniably vague – but then again, any creative activity, including listening, performing, etc., could be involved. As for "structures," think in terms of the cognitive representations – and moreover the frames of reference – that I referred to earlier. "Structures" here simply means the structured knowledge of varying degrees of complexity acquired through past experience and stored for future use. As for the outcomes of creative processes, the point about novelty is significant, but so is the one about "existing knowledge" being the basis of such outcomes. In other words, we as humans create whatever it is we create *against the backdrop of what we already know and have experienced*, drawing upon the latter even as we transcend it.

You will note that I have been stressing this point throughout the chapter, as I consider it critical to your understanding of how human psychology works and more particularly how we as musicians do what we do. Take the case of improvisation. By definition, improvised music is spontaneous – irrespective of the tradition or idiom in which it takes place – though the degree to which it is original varies enormously. (This distinction between creativity and originality is fundamental.) If you were a professional composer-pianist in 1830s Europe, for example, you might improvise for audiences by piecing together bits of musical figuration you had previously practiced – ready-made formulae, if you like. Hence a contemporary critic's complaint that extempore performance was often "little more than playing from memory" (*The Harmonicon*, June 1830). That need not have been the end of the matter, but then again the writer was correct in asserting the fundamental role of memory in improvisation. (See chapter 1 for related historical discussion.)

Some psychologists have studied the means by which musicians improvise in diverse contexts ranging from ornamented melody to free jazz and silent-film accompaniment (see chapters 11 and 16). One of them, Jeff Pressing, describes the use of models or "referents," i.e., "underlying formal scheme[s] or guiding image[s] … used by the improviser to facilitate the generation and editing of improvised behaviour," whether as a provider of material or "as a focus for the production and organization of material from other sources" (Pressing 1984: 346, 347). He notes that improvisers typically practice both "objects" (motives, scales, arpeggios, etc.) and problem-solving processes such as "transitions, development and variation techniques, and methods of combining and juxtaposition" (1984: 355). The fostering of different types of memory is one goal of this sort of practice, likewise that of the performance skills needed to project the ideas in sound.

Improvisation is an especially interesting form of musical creativity, not least because anyone making music engages in it to some extent. That may be why John Sloboda once referred to "a rich untapped vein of data here which urgently awaits psychological attention" (Sloboda 1985: 150). If you start reading the music-psychological literature on improvisation – for example, Large, Palmer, and Pollack 1995 – you might wonder whether some of it is so remote from actual practice as to call its viability into question. You might feel the same about the research on artificial intelligence (AI) that you will encounter in further exploring musical creativity. And of course the above discussion on creativity has a particularly "cognitive" thrust without accounting for the broad range of factors that impinge upon or arise out of creative activity within music.

Once again, do not dismiss work of this sort simply because it does not accord with your experience and understanding or because you find its scientific character incompatible with musical artistry. It goes without saying that human creativity can never be explained in terms of rules and systems alone. On the other hand, the demonstration of gaps between explanatory models and what one perceives to be reality can be as informative as what a given explanation does get right. As with so many things, it is not a question of either/or, but of *both*: of one informing the other, of mutual enlightenment.

What is expressed in music and how do we perceive it?

The same point applies to the extensive research on musical expression that has been carried out from the perspectives of both performers and listeners. The very notion of what constitutes "expression" has excited controversy among psychologists. One of the most enduring, if problematic, definitions is the "generative" one encapsulated by Eric Clarke as follows: "expression comprises systematic patterns of deviation from the 'neutral' information given in a score" (Clarke 1995: 22). A vast amount of psychological work has been based on this premise, even though it fails to explain expressivity in non-notated music, in the perception of music by listeners who may not be able to read a score even if one is available, and so on. (Consider in this respect some of the discussion in chapters 1 and 3.)

The understanding of expression as a departure from structural norms has been challenged by theories of "composer's pulse," "integrated energy flux," and "narration and drama" (see Clarke 1995 for details). A more integrated approach has also been proposed by Patrik Juslin, who sees expression as "a multi-dimensional phenomenon consisting of five primary components":

- **g**enerative rules
- **e**motional expression
- **r**andom variations
- **m**otion principles
- **s**tylistic unexpectedness, which involves "local deviations from performance conventions."

According to Juslin (2003: 273), "an analysis of performance expression in terms of these five components – collectively referred to as the GERMS model – has important implications for research and teaching of music performance."

Computational models for musical expression have been developed by the following:

1) Johan Sundberg and Anders Friberg, who proposed twenty rules relating to timing, dynamics, and articulation "for the conversion of note signs into sounding music" (Sundberg 1988: 54);
2) Neil Todd, whose simpler rule-based system focuses on aspects of phrase structure;
3) Gerhard Widmer and Werner Goebl, who fed "large amounts of empirical data" (i.e. "precisely measured performances by skilled musicians")

into the computer to find "significant regularities" from which general performance rules can be derived for use as "predictive computational models" (Widmer and Goebl 2004: 208, 209).

Similar data have been used to construct animated images of how timing and dynamics change over time (see for example Dixon, Goebl, and Widmer 2002). These live representations – referred to as the Performance Worm – may correspond to a listener's sense of how music moves or what it looks like in the mind's eye, even if that was not the authors' original intention.

Music perception is itself a vast and complex topic, with a correspondingly huge literature spanning such domains as music theory, psychology, linguistics, neurology, neurophysiology, artificial intelligence, physics, and psychophysics. Throughout this chapter I have given hints of the work in this area, starting with Aristoxenus in the fourth century BCE. Here it suffices to note a feature of music perception that we have encountered in other contexts thus far: namely, that although rules, systems, and models help to explain general phenomena, they need to be understood in terms of the experiences of given individuals in given circumstances. In other words, when it comes to perception, as with so many music-psychological phenomena, the general ultimately makes sense only in terms of the particular, just as the particular must be explained with reference to the general.

Chapter summary

- Humans understand the world around them according to past experience and acquired knowledge, both of which are refined and amplified as further experience is gained.
- Music psychology has a long history, and in recent decades the most prominent areas of research include cognition, skills acquisition, performance, expression, and perception.
- The typical approach of music psychologists involves generating hypotheses on the basis of existing knowledge, which are then tested in such procedures as experiments, observational studies, questionnaires, interviews, and neuropsychological investigations.
- The "musical mind" is not simply "confined within the skull": it must instead be holistically and "ecologically" understood.
- Numerous forms of musical memory exist, likewise aspects of musical skill.
- The creation of music takes place in the imagination as well as in sound; this involves the formation of "cognitive representations" starting from one's earliest exposure to other people and the world around one.
- Musical expression is highly complex, as are the means by which it is perceived.

Discussion topics

1. What factors influence whether or not we perceive sounds as music?
2. Can experiments under controlled conditions ever yield insight into the "reality" of musical performance, listening, or composition, and if so how?
3. What is meant by "cognitive representations of musical structures," and how do these function?
4. When might practicing have a harmful effect on the development of musical skill?
5. What defines "expertise" in music?
6. How might the "rules" of musical expression proposed by some psychologists explain what you personally consider to be expressive about a given piece or performance?

Further reading

Lehmann, Andreas C., Sloboda, John A., and Woody, Robert H. (2007), *Psychology for Musicians* (New York: Oxford University Press).
    This "concise, accessible, and up-to-date introduction to psychological research for musicians" is divided into sections on musical learning, musical skills, and musical roles (including performer, teacher, listener, and "user").
Rink, John, ed. (2002), *Musical Performance: A Guide to Understanding* (Cambridge: Cambridge University Press).
    Contains entry-level studies on the psychology of performance, developing the ability to perform, preparing for performance, memorizing music, communicating with the body, ensemble performance, performance anxiety, and listening.
Sloboda, John A. (1985), *The Musical Mind: The Cognitive Psychology of Music* (Oxford: Clarendon Press).
    A classic text, focusing on music as a cognitive skill; music, language, and meaning; performance; composition and improvisation; listening; musical learning and development; and cultural and biological issues.

References

Adler, Guido (1885), "Umfang, Methode und Ziel der Musikwissenschaft," *Vierteljahrsschrift für Musikwissenschaft*, 1, 5–20.
Clarke, Eric (1995), "Expression in performance: generativity, perception and semiosis," in John Rink (1995) (ed.), *The Practice of Performance: Studies in Musical Interpretation* (Cambridge: Cambridge University Press), 21–54.
Clarke, Eric (2002), "Understanding the psychology of performance," in Rink (2002: 59–72).
Clarke, Eric and Cook, Nicholas (2004) (eds.), *Empirical Musicology: Aims, Methods, Prospects* (New York: Oxford University Press).
Clarke, Eric and Davidson, Jane (1998), "The body in performance," in Wyndham Thomas (1998) (ed.), *Composition, Performance, Reception: Studies in the Creative Process in Music* (Aldershot: Ashgate), 74–92.
Davidson, Jane (2002), "Developing the ability to perform," in Rink (2002), 89–101.
Deliège, Irène and Wiggins, Geraint A. (2006) (eds.), *Musical Creativity: Multidisciplinary Research in Theory and Practice* (Hove and New York: Psychology Press).
Deutsch, Diana (1970), "Tones and numbers: specificity of interference in immediate memory," *Science*, 168, 1604–5.
Dixon, Simon, Goebl, Werner, and Widmer, Gerhard (2002), "The Performance Worm: real time visualization of expression based on Langner's Tempo-Loudness Animation," *Proceedings of the International Computer Music Conference (ICMC2002)* (accessed 30 July 2008), http://citeseer.ist.psu.edu/dixon02performance.html.

Eysenck, Michael W. and Keane, Mark T. (2000), *Cognitive Psychology: A Student's Handbook*, 4th edn (Hove and New York: Psychology Press).

Fitts, Paul M. and Posner, Michael I. (1967), *Human Performance* (Belmont, California: Brooks/Cole).

Furneaux, S. and Land, M. F. (1999), "The effects of skill on the eye–hand span during musical sight-reading," *Proceedings of the Royal Society*, 266, 2435–40.

Ginsborg, Jane (2002), "Classical singers learning and memorizing a new song: an observational study," *Psychology of Music*, 30/1, 58–101.

Grieser, DiAnne L. and Kuhl, Patricia K. (1988), "Maternal speech to infants in a tonal language: support for universal prosodic features in motherese," *Developmental Psychology*, 24/1, 14–20.

Grove 2008. 'Psychology of music', *Grove Music Online*, ed. L. Macy (accessed 30 July 2008), http://www.grovemusic.com

Helmholtz, Hermann von (1863), *Die Lehre von den Tonempfindungen als physiologische Grundlage für die Theorie der Musik* (Braunschweig: Friedrich Vieweg und Sohn).

Juslin, Patrik (2003), "Five facets of musical expression: a psychologist's perspective on music performance," *Psychology of Music*, 31/3, 273–302.

Krampe, Ralf and Ericsson, K. Anders (1995), "Deliberate practice and elite musical performance," in John Rink (ed.), *The Practice of Performance: Studies in Musical Interpretation* (Cambridge: Cambridge University Press), 84–102.

Large, Edward W., Palmer, Caroline and Pollack, Jordan B. (1995), "Reduced memory representations for music," *Cognitive Science*, 19/1, 53–96.

Lehmann, Andreas C., Sloboda, John A., and Woody, Robert H. (2007), *Psychology for Musicians* (New York: Oxford University Press).

Neisser, Ulric (1967), *Cognitive Psychology* (New York: Appleton-Century-Crofts).

Peretz, Isabelle, Gagnon, Lise, Hébert, Sylvie and Macoir, Joël (2004), "Singing in the brain: insights from cognitive neuropsychology," *Music Perception*, 21/3, 373–90.

Pressing, Jeff (1984), "Cognitive processes in improvisation," in W. R. Crozier and A. J. Chapman (eds.), *Cognitive Processes in the Perception of Art* (Amsterdam: Elsevier), 345–63.

Reed, Edward S. (1991), "James Gibson's ecological approach to cognition," in Arthur Still and Alan Costall (eds.), *Against Cognitivism: Alternative Foundations for Cognitive Psychology* (Hemel Hempstead: Harvester Wheatsheaf), 171–97.

Rentfrow, P. J. and Gosling, S. D. (2003), "The Do Re Mi's of everyday life: the structure and personality correlates of music preferences," *Journal of Personality and Social Psychology*, 84/6, 1236–56.

Repp, Bruno H. (1998), "A microcosm of musical expression: I. Quantitative analysis of pianists' timing in the initial measures of Chopin's Etude in E major," *Journal of the Acoustical Society of America*, 104, 1085–1100.

Repp, Bruno H. (1999), "A microcosm of musical expression: II. Quantitative analysis of pianists' dynamics in the initial measures of Chopin's Etude in E major," *Journal of the Acoustical Society of America*, 105, 1972–88.

Rink, John (2002) (ed.), *Musical Performance: A Guide to Understanding* (Cambridge: Cambridge University Press).

Seashore, Carl E. (1938), *Psychology of Music* (New York and London: McGraw-Hill).

Sloboda, John A. (1976), "The effect of item position on the likelihood of identification by inference in prose reading and music reading," *Canadian Journal of Psychology*, 30, 228–36.

Sloboda, John A. (1985), *The Musical Mind: The Cognitive Psychology of Music* (Oxford: Clarendon Press).

Sloboda, John A. (2007), "History. The late 20th century," section I, 3 in "Psychology of music," *Grove Music Online*, ed. L. Macy (accessed 30 July 2008), http://www.grovemusic.com.

Sloboda, John A., Hermelin, Beate, and O'Connor, Neil (1985), "An exceptional musical memory," *Music Perception*, 3/2, 155–70.

Stumpf, Carl (1883, 1890), *Tonpsychologie*, 2 vols. (Leipzig: S. Hirzel).

Sundberg, Johan (1988), "Computer synthesis of music performance," in John A. Sloboda (ed.), *Generative Processes in Music: The Psychology of Performance, Improvisation, and Composition* (Oxford: Clarendon Press), 52–69.

Thompson, William, Forde, C. T., Diamond, Patrick, and Balkwill, Laura-Lee (1998), "The adjudication of six performances of a Chopin Etude: a study of expert knowledge," *Psychology of Music*, 26, 154–74.

Ward, Thomas B., Smith, Steven M., and Vaid, Jyotsna (1997) (eds.), *Creative Thought: An Investigation of Conceptual Structures and Processes* (Washington, DC and London: American Psychological Association).

Weaver, H. E. (1943), "A study of visual processes in reading differently constructed musical selections," *Psychological Monographs*, 55, 1–30.

Widmer, Gerhard and Goebl, Werner (2004), "Computational models of expressive music performance: the state of the art," *Journal of New Music Research*, 33/3, 203–16.

Williamon, Aaron (1999), "The value of performing from memory," *Psychology of Music*, 27/1, 84–95.

Williamon, Aaron (2002), "Memorizing music," in Rink (2002), 113–26.

Glossary

Cognition	The processing, structure, and operation of information and knowledge, whether conscious or unconscious. This may involve both "bottom-up or stimulus-driven processing ... directly affected by stimulus input," and "top-down or conceptually driven processing ... affected by what the individual contributes" (Eysenck and Keane 2000: 2, 3).
Cognitive representation	"A nonspecific but organized representation of prior experience" (Neisser 1967: 287).

Creativity	"The product of a thinking process that is, in some sense, novel and productive, in that it goes beyond what has been previously known by an individual or group of people" (Eysenck and Keane 2000: 529–30).
Empirical	In general, "pertaining to, or derived from, experience" (*Oxford English Dictionary*); in psychological contexts, a type of investigation involving observation, experiment, or similar modes of discovery.
Motor	Involving or relating to muscular movement acting in conjunction with the nervous system. "Motor programs" are series of actions with specific goals, made up of single movements combined into identifiable sequences.
Motherese	"A simplified form of language used (especially by mothers) in speaking to babies and young children, characterized by repetition, simple sentence structure, limited vocabulary, onomatopoeia, and expressive intonation; child-directed speech; 'baby talk'" (*Oxford English Dictionary*).

5 Music aesthetics and critical theory

ANDREW BOWIE

Chapter preview

This chapter demonstrates why aesthetics, the branch of philosophy concerned with art and beauty, should be a part of the study of music. It outlines the emergence of aesthetics from the eighteenth century onwards in terms of the changing relationship between what is considered to be "subjective" and what is considered to be "objective." This relationship has important implications for both the historical and the analytical study of music. In the modern period, ideas about objectivity are changed by the growing sense in many areas of Western society that there is no divine order of things, and that objectivity is therefore in some way dependent upon human subjectivity. Music is a form of art that is both objective, in the sense that it relies on rules of harmony, acoustics, etc., some of which can be formulated mathematically, and subjective, because it addresses human feelings and is judged in part on the basis of feelings. Music becomes important in the modern period because its meaning can be interpreted in very different ways, which are often influenced by issues in the society in which it is located. Aesthetic questions lie at the heart of debates in the contemporary study of music over whether music should be looked at in formal, analytical terms, or whether it should be connected to social and political issues.

Key issues

- What is music aesthetics?
- Is aesthetic evaluation merely subjective, or can it be objective?
- Are aesthetic problems purely philosophical, or are they also historical?
- What does music mean?
- How does music relate to philosophy?
- What role should aesthetic questions play in the study of music?

Introduction

Aesthetics is the branch of philosophy concerned with art and natural beauty. Why, though, should philosophy play a role in the study of music at all? Is it not enough to learn one's instrument(s), and learn the theory, analysis, and history of music? Until fairly recently many musicologists would have been suspicious of the incursion of philosophy into the study of music, and some still are. However, aesthetic questions are now seen to affect many aspects of the study of music. This change has to do with the historical role philosophy plays in relation to other subjects. Beginning with the ancient Greeks, philosophy had the **metaphysical** task of establishing ideas about the world as a whole, and of accounting for what made these ideas true. These tasks were often very closely linked to the idea that philosophy was describing a world made by God. That there really was a true world was therefore not doubted, even if human fallibility meant that we might not be able to give true descriptions of it. In this conception music was often seen as a reflection of the divine harmony of the cosmos.

However, from around the eighteenth century onwards, religious ideas are increasingly put into question, and the natural sciences succeed in explaining and predicting more and more of the behavior of natural phenomena, without relying on the idea of God. Systematic philosophical and theological accounts of the world consequently look less convincing, because they are not based on specific experimental and observational evidence. The emergence of the subject of aesthetics in the second half of the eighteenth century parallels the beginning of this process, as does the new idea that music is more important than the other arts, rather than less, as was previously believed. All these factors are part of what is often termed "modernity," where traditional beliefs, traditional forms of authority, traditional moral precepts, and traditional forms of art all become open to questions as to their legitimacy.

Analytical and Continental aesthetics

Differing modern philosophical approaches lead to very different approaches to music aesthetics. In the Western world there is now a perceived divide between two traditions of philosophy, the **Analytical**, and the **Continental** or **European**. "Analytical philosophy" developed after World War I, and still dominates university philosophy in the English-speaking world. It adopts a specific approach to traditional philosophical questions about knowledge, morality, and art, which are primarily to be approached by analyzing the meaning and use of key concepts. The model for reliable truth is argued to be natural science, because it gives explanations of specific phenomena that lead to predictive laws. This leads to a style of philosophy which seeks maximum precision in argument, but it can lead to difficulties with regard to music.

Analytical music aesthetics often goes under the heading of the "philosophy of art" and the "philosophy of music" (though some people wish to make a difference between aesthetics and these subjects). Its main proponents, who include Malcolm Budd, Stephen Davies, Peter Kivy, and Jerrold Levinson, seek answers to questions like "Is a piece of music beautiful because I like it, or do I like it because it is beautiful?"; "Is there an objective standard of musical taste?"; "Does a musical work consist in the score, a performance of the score, or all performances of the score?"; "Is music a language?"; "Is the emotion in music located in the listener, or in the music itself?" The difficulty is that there has so far been no agreement at all on answers to these questions. This situation contrasts sharply with that for questions in the natural sciences, where there are often widely agreed answers. The lack of philosophical answers in relation to music can mean (a) that people have simply failed to find the right answers yet, or (b) that there may be something wrong with how the questions themselves are being asked. Which view of music aesthetics one finds most convincing will largely depend on whether one thinks (a) or (b) is right.

"Continental" or "European" philosophy developed from the mid-eighteenth century onwards, particularly in response to the work of Immanuel Kant (1724–1804) (see below), and still plays a greater role in mainland Europe than in the Anglo-Saxon world. One major strand of European philosophy, which derives in particular from G. W. F. Hegel (1770–1832), concentrates on ways in which philosophical issues are connected to history. Philosophical problems are understood as manifestations of the cultural and ethical concerns of people at a particular time, and these change as society changes. What music *is* may therefore actually change with history. Philosophy should interpret these changes, rather than look for definitive answers to the kind of questions asked in the analytical tradition of philosophy. The very concept of music is, then, itself contested, rather than being something established that can be analyzed.

Subjective and objective

One implication of some Analytical aesthetics is that the term "music" relies upon evaluation, and so is unavoidably subjective, in contrast to objective, "factual" terms used in the sciences. Many people maintain that all evaluations are a merely personal, subjective matter. One of the key issues in aesthetics is, though, whether claims about art are *nothing but* expressions of subjective preference. Even if, as many people do, someone prefers a boy band's music to Beethoven's, are they right to say that it is better music? Moreover, are there not ways of playing music which are objectively wrong, because they make no sense of what is played? Any practicing musician is confronted with decisions on such matters all the time. These are not decisions like that between flavors of ice-cream, which may indeed be merely subjective. There is, though, often a non-subjective aspect, even to those sorts of preferences: think about the extent to which advertising influences what people think are their purely subjective preferences.

How, then, is the division between the subjective and the objective to be made in relation to music? Could music be judged objectively to be music at all, if it did not involve a *subjective* dimension? After all, music is often regarded as an expression of subjective human emotions. At the same time, it is possible to be objectively wrong about the kind of emotion a piece of music conveys. In addition, the emotion expressed by a piece can itself be false, because it is exaggerated or merely clichéd, so this is not a wholly subjective issue either. The history of aesthetics shows that the division between subjective and objective manifests itself in a variety of ways that are connected to how human beings think about who, and what, they are.

Aesthetic considerations are, then, an inherent part of the social *practice* of music. Music can be highly regulated, and therefore more objective, in certain kinds of traditional religious music, for example. Rules can also become more and more optional and subjective, as they are in some kinds of free improvisation. The relationship of music to rules can be linked to other ways in which societies are governed by rules, and this raises vital questions about human freedom and restrictions on that freedom. When studying music in differing social and historical contexts, where differing rules apply both to music and to other practices, one is therefore involved in the questions addressed by aesthetics, which connect to other evaluative questions in society.

Aesthetics and history

Issues in philosophy are often best understood by looking at their history. The rest of this chapter will therefore introduce some major questions in music aesthetics in relation to the contexts in which they became significant. It will look predominantly at the end of the eighteenth century and the nineteenth century, because subsequent aesthetics depends heavily on ideas developed in that period. First, though, let us take a much older example. In *The Republic* Plato argued for the exclusion of many kinds of music from his ideal society. Music could be damaging, because it encouraged the wrong kinds of social attitude. One way of trying to understand Plato's idea is to think of other contexts in which music is regarded as damaging. Is Plato's stance like that of certain religious fundamentalists, such as the Taliban in Afghanistan, who banned most music? Or is it misleading simply to equate crude religious fundamentalism with the reflections of a highly sophisticated ancient Greek philosopher?

It might seem, for example, as though Plato is obviously engaged in music aesthetics. This would, however, not strictly be true. To begin with, what Plato means by "art" has to do with *mimesis* – that is, "imitation" or "representation." When talking of "art" he uses the Greek word "*techne*," which has come down to us in the word "technique," and which can be seen as having to do with what we call "craft." Since the Romantic period in particular, art has often been explicitly differentiated from craft, being seen, for example, as a revelation of new aspects of the world. We must also now include non-representational kinds of art, such as "conceptual art," in the scope of the term, whereas Plato even sees music as a kind of representation. Furthermore, although the word "aesthetics" has ancient Greek roots, it only comes to refer to questions of art and beauty towards the end of the eighteenth century.

The term "aesthetics" came into wider use via the German philosopher Alexander Baumgarten's *Aesthetica*, whose first volume was published in 1750. Baumgarten's book, which took up the Greek meaning of aesthetics, which has to do with perception by the senses, was a result of a conflict in modern thought, which becomes linked to music. Music has two contrasting aspects, one of which is non-perceptual, the other of which is perceptual: it both involves mathematical proportions which we cannot hear, and can be heard. In the seventeenth and eighteenth centuries, Western philosophy was mainly divided into **rationalism**, which argued that mathematics was the basis of true explanation, and **empiricism**, which argued that observation of the perceptible world was the main foundation of knowledge. Rationalism was backed up by the success of mathematically based theories, like Isaac Newton's theory of gravity. It was, though, also argued by the Scottish empiricist philosopher, David Hume, for example, that this success relied upon empirical observation. The worry about the rationalist view was that it excluded so many of people's everyday ways of dealing with the world by reducing things to general abstractions. Baumgarten wanted to revalue what *appeared* to the senses to be true, such as a specific empirical image of something, although what it revealed could not be given scientific status. Even before it becomes directly concerned with art, then, aesthetics has to do with how different kinds of relationship to the world in modernity can be made to cohere.

Judgment

Music can easily be related to Baumgarten's concerns. What would music be if it were reduced to the numerical description of the relationships between pitches, durations, and intensities? Although at least some of these objective factors are necessary for something to be music, none of them is sufficient to make it music. Another way of judging is needed, which takes into account other aspects of music. Are these other aspects all "subjective"? The tension here between what can be analyzed in non-perceptual terms, and what we actually perceive, relates to continuing disagreements in musicology. Should music be objectively analyzed, or should it be interpreted in terms of what it expresses, its historical implications, what it evokes in the listener, etc.? The conflict between what is "scientific," and what has to be interpreted in ways which involve subjective judgment is, then, not just a musicological one, but an aesthetic one as well. The contrasts between the descriptions of the opening phrase of Beethoven's Fifth Symphony, as frequencies measured by an oscilloscope, as a descending major third, or as "Fate knocking at the door," illustrate what is at issue here. Deciding which description is more apt forces one to think about the norms one considers to be important in music. This is a key aesthetic problem. There is no norm that can be used to adjudicate between these competing norms, because this would then require the norm for that norm, and so on, to infinity.

A decisive moment in the emergence of aesthetics occurs when Kant, who was a pupil of Baumgarten, makes the topic of natural and artistic beauty part of his new philosophy in the *Critique of Judgment* of 1790. Kant's philosophy aims to build a bridge between the empiricist and the rationalist approaches to the world. The important point here is Kant's insistence on the active role of the subjective mind in generating *objective* knowledge from our perceptions. Judging is not simply passive: it is something we *do* both in the sciences and in the arts. Kant plays a vital role in the genesis of new Romantic ideas about subjectivity and objectivity that develop from the 1790s onwards. They do so in the wake of, among others, the philosopher and composer Jean-Jacques Rousseau, who made exploration of the self and its relationship to nature central to his work. Think of how important mood and feeling later become in Romantic music by Schumann, Chopin, or Weber. This is a good example of the problem of what is subjective and what is objective. When music evokes, say, the mood of a twilight scene, it seems invidious to say that what is evoked is solely in the people who experience the mood. Would we have such experiences at all without what evokes them? Nature often appears as wholly opposed to us, but we ourselves are also natural organisms who can respond to the natural world in emotional terms, and these are closely linked to music.

To what extent can our objective scientific knowledge of what we are account for our subjective relationships to things? Such relationships are apparent when we judge something in nature or a work of art to be beautiful. Even though these judgments are essentially subjective, Kant insists that there is a crucial difference between them, and judgments about what we find more agreeable, such as one flavor of ice-cream rather than another. Judgments of beauty involve the demand that others should assent to the judgment. Although aesthetic judgments are not the same as judgments in the sciences, they are not merely subjective either, and we try to get others to share them as an important part of social life. Such judgments point for Kant to what joins us together as human beings, which he terms a "common sense." This idea suggests ways in which human beings can transcend the differences that arise from the loss of traditional norms in modern societies. From the beginning of the nineteenth century the aim of social unification starts to play a new role in music. Whereas for Mozart music was still largely attached to patronage, and any political aims in his music had to be indirect, for Beethoven even wordless music, like the Fifth and Seventh Symphonies, can communicate the spirit of the French Revolution, and Richard Wagner thinks of music drama as a way of forming a new kind of community in the modern world. Can music, though, really bring people together, or does it create a mere semblance of harmony which the real social world lacks? If the latter is the case music would be a form of deception that conceals real conflicts, which in the nineteenth century comes to be called **ideology**. This contrast becomes vital in later music aesthetics, when the connection between music and politics becomes most explicit.

Absolute music

Kant's influence on philosophical thinking about music has mainly to do with his idea that art offers a way of relating to the world which is not "conceptual." Concepts are rules for identifying one thing as the same as another. With regard to our understanding of art Kant talks, in contrast, about "aesthetic ideas." These are ideas that enliven the imagination so that it can find new ways of looking at things, rather than identify them as an instance of a concept. German Romantic writers, like W. H. Wackenroder and Ludwig Tieck, claim that music in particular cannot be reduced to concepts, because it speaks to our feelings in an immediate, individual way. During the same period the poet and philosopher, Friedrich Schlegel, refers to "musical ideas." Music is able to "say" something that no other art can because it is the least conceptual and least representational form of art.

The German musicologist, Carl Dahlhaus, has referred to this conception as the "idea of absolute music." The philosopher Arthur Schopenhauer exemplifies the idea in his *The World as Will and Representation* of 1816, which presents music as the basis of his main metaphysical theory. Music gives access to the forces that drive nature inside and outside us, which underlie the objective world that science can describe in concepts, but which science cannot describe. Schopenhauer sees these forces as part of what he terms the "Will." His idea is close to Freud's later notion of the unconscious nature of the drives that motivate us. The striving of a melody to resolve to the tonic is the most direct image of the constant pattern of desire and merely provisional fulfillment of desire in which life, for Schopenhauer, essentially consists. At the same time, music allows us to escape what it represents, giving us temporary respite from the dissatisfactions of real life.

Schopenhauer is involved in one of the most celebrated cases of the important interaction between the effects of aesthetic and other philosophical thinking on music, and the effects of music on aesthetic thinking. His work was initially ignored, but in the 1850s was read by Wagner and brings about a profound reorientation in Wagner's thinking. From being a political revolutionary, Wagner becomes persuaded that political and social action is ultimately futile, given the underlying nature of reality described by Schopenhauer. This attitude finds expression in Wagner's later works, like *Tristan and Isolde*, where the highest form of fulfillment only takes place when the conscious, individual self is annihilated, either in sexual ecstasy or death (the two being closely related). Wagner's music helps to bring Schopenhauer's work to public attention. It also inspires Friedrich Nietzsche (1844–1900), in *The Birth of Tragedy from the Spirit of Music* (1871), to present music as a means of renewing the sense of the tragic nature of human life, in opposition to the widespread optimism associated with scientific progress in the later nineteenth century.

Nietzsche himself comes to question his earlier assessment of music in his work from the later 1870s onwards. There he regards music with metaphysical resonances, like that of Wagner, as offering an illusory renewal of traditional metaphysical and religious ideas. Such ideas will distract us from facing up to the real challenges of this life, in the name of a non-existent "other life." The ideas that develop from Romanticism to Nietzsche represent the high point of the elevation of music to philosophical significance. This elevation relates to the need for new sources of meaning and inspiration in a world where, as Nietzsche proclaims, God is dead. As science is able to explain more and more of the world, including ourselves, music comes to represent those sides of our existence that are more felt than thought, or that words seem unable to convey.

Form and content

Around the time Wagner composes *Tristan and Isolde*, the Viennese music critic and friend of Brahms, Eduard Hanslick, writes a highly influential text arguing against the idea that music should be understood in extra-musical terms, such as by feelings it evokes or by a "program" of the kind Franz Liszt used for his symphonic poems. If one does not know in words what the symphonic work's program is, there is, after all, little likelihood that one would hear what a *Hamlet* overture, for instance, was about. Hanslick's *On the Musically Beautiful* of 1854 has come to be read as the basis of musical **formalism**. It insists on analysis of the harmonic, melodic, and rhythmic constitution of particular music as the only scientifically valid approach to music. Hanslick's essay has remained a focus for music aesthetics ever since.

Hanslick seeks to establish the "autonomous" status of music, as consisting solely of "sounding moved forms." For him, music "just wants to be grasped as music," though it is also "a language which we speak and understand but cannot *translate*." Whereas words are the means to an end, the musical note is "its *own purpose*." The importance of Hanslick's formalism becomes apparent in the history of twentieth-century music. If strict formalism is correct, music might be regarded as separate from social, political, and cultural issues. It can then function as a kind of respite from the rest of the world. The formalist view might also be used to restrict claims about music to what can be demonstrated by formal analysis. In Romantic aesthetics music had some kind of "content," but the question is what this is, especially if Hanslick is right.

This contrast in attitudes to musical meaning shows how questions in music aesthetics are themselves important for philosophy. Hanslick's objection to program music is apt, insofar as just hearing a moody, dramatic piece will not enable us to know that it is about Hamlet. If meaning is defined in terms of picking out and specifying things in the world, i.e., of the "referential" function of language, music has at best an indirect relationship to meaning. However, meaning is, like music, a contested concept.

Does the gestural aspect of language, apparent in its tone, emphasis, rhythm, and tempo, have nothing to do with the meaning of what is said? Is it possible to get deeper into the world of Hamlet via the "gestures" of a musical piece relating to *Hamlet*? The same piece might admittedly be successfully used in relation to another gloomy play. The referential dimension of music is indeed weak, but, in the right context, music may deepen our understanding of what we experience. Indeed, music can actually change what we experience: an apparently innocuous scene accompanied by sinister music no longer seems innocuous. The very fact of music sounding sinister can be considered to be a fact about its meaning. A vital element of the influence of aesthetics on the study of music is that any decision about the scope of the term "meaning" will affect what we think music is and what interpretative approaches to it are taken to be valid.

Music, politics, and meaning: critical theory

The following two cases illustrate how important the question of meaning and music can be. The Nazis banned music by Jewish composers, like Mendelssohn and Mahler, because of its "Jewishness," and were in general opposed to modernist forms of music and other art. Stalin forced Shostakovich to modify how he composed, so as to escape the charge of "formalism" – i.e., of not contributing to the edification of the Soviet people. Only a racist would claim that the Nazi attitude is a defensible way of regarding music. The whole idea of "Jewishness in music" is a nonsense. However, the very fact that the music was banned suggests that music has a cultural power that is not explained if one adopts purely formalist ideas. On the other hand, the formalist approach could also be seen as a way of defending music against ideological misuse. But then consider Stalin's pressure on Shostakovich. Nearly all of us will have heard music which we consider beyond the pale because we find it uncomfortable to listen to. Part of what makes us think this way is very often that the music challenges our habitual views of what is normal. Stalin's desire to suppress challenging music could consequently be linked to his desire to suppress other things that challenged his authority.

This kind of connection between music and other aspects of modern societies is characteristic of much twentieth-century aesthetics of music. The concern with music and society gives rise to a fundamental dilemma. Some positions in the Marxist tradition, for example, seek to explain the development of music in socio-economic terms. These positions can undoubtedly offer insights into how musical production is affected by society, as the effects on rock music of advertising, marketing, and new forms of communication make clear. On the other hand, the music is likely to be understood solely as a result of the analysis of society, and so has nothing to say which is not already implicit in that analysis. Beethoven, for example, becomes the representative of the heroic period of bourgeois Europe associated with the French Revolution. This kind of analysis was very common in the countries of the former Eastern Bloc.

The West German philosopher, musicologist, and social theorist, T. W. Adorno (1903–69) accepted the Marxist idea that music and society were intertwined, and works towards a **Critical Theory** of society that will include music. Adorno aims to circumvent the trap just outlined. He regards music as a kind of unconscious history of society, whose message resists being converted into what can be said literally. Adorno does not think there is a general answer to the question "what does music mean?," because any answer will depend on the social context in which music is written and performed. The challenge is to be able to analyze the social content of music at the same time as doing justice to its formal aspects. This may sound a rather implausible project. One of Adorno's points is, though, that performance which really reveals the form of a piece is a way of revealing its content. Such performances convey an understanding of the work which had not previously been available. This understanding cannot be encompassed in words. It has to do with the work's relationship to the music to which it reacts, and which it subsequently influences, as well as to issues in society. Think, for example, of the history of performance practice of Bach and what it might reveal about dominant ideas in the societies in which it has taken place, from Mendelssohn's revival of Bach in the nineteenth century to contemporary styles of performance.

Adorno characteristically argues that form is "sedimented content." Much of his thought is based on the idea that oppositions, like that between form and content, are never definitive. Form can become content, and content can become form. The point of this idea is exemplified by the tension in modern music between expression (= content) and convention (= form). The (subjective) desire to express something unique is inseparable from the fact that in order to be understood, one needs to employ musical forms that are to some extent conventional (and thus objective). The worst kinds of modern music, produced by what Adorno calls the "culture industry," are intended to be sellable to the greatest number of people. They appeal to the lowest common denominator by being merely conventional, and Adorno links this to the kind of conformist thinking that allowed the Nazis to come to power. The difficulty for music is to avoid mere convention without losing the ability to express something significant. This is why formal problems can become the social content of music. Adorno concentrates in particular on the radical music of Schoenberg and the other members of the "Second Viennese School." Their refusal to compromise is interpreted as conveying the harsh truths about the period in which they compose. As modern music establishes more new techniques and forms, however, innovation becomes ever more difficult. The same dilemma faces people in modern societies, where the objective pressure of the accepted norms makes critical and innovative activity ever more difficult.

"New musicology"

Adorno's work did not have much influence on English-language musicology until fairly recently. The approach to music he developed does, though, come to play a role in the **new musicology** of Lawrence Kramer, Susan McClary and others. New musicology is also influenced by **post-structuralism** and **post-modernism**. A central idea here is that interpretations of the world cannot be definitive. This is because they often have to do with the exercise of power by the dominant (male) gender, by (white, Western) political and racial groups, by (Christian) ways of controlling sexual and other bodily activity, and by (Western philosophical) ideas of the individual self as the stable basis of human relationships to reality. The history of music is regarded as being the history of a social practice to be understood in relation to other social practices, rather than the history of a series of canonical works. New musicology therefore poses challenges to some established music history and analysis. McClary, for example, notoriously once suggested a link between the violence of the recapitulation of the first movement of Beethoven's Ninth

Symphony and a rape. (This was supposed to refer to the content of the music, not to Beethoven's own sexual life.) It would be unfair to use this example to typify her work, which has raised important questions about gender in relation to music. However, this *kind* of link between music and other aspects of social life does highlight problems in understanding music's relationship to the extra-musical. Adorno interprets the same passage's brutal assertiveness as characteristic of a questionably affirmative attitude to the world, of which Beethoven's other late work is critical. One can list a large number of interpretations of the passage, from those that restrict themselves to motivic, harmonic, rhythmic, and instrumental analysis, to those like McClary's. The decisive aesthetic issue is: what criterion should one use to decide which is correct?

Aesthetic approaches can be crudely divided into those that contract the realm of musical significance, and those that expand it. Each approach has its own dangers. If one sees music as an object, as the analytical tradition largely does, it is assumed to possess certain properties which analysis tries to identify. This generally restricts interpretation to what is acceptable in formalist terms. Even here, however, evaluative judgments concerning which elements are formally important are inevitable. Such judgments can, though, as critical theory and new musicology argue, be expanded to include other kinds of evaluation. This expansion then leads to questions of ideology, for example when some types of formal coherence are regarded as the unquestionable norm against which music should be measured. Such a norm may be seen to have to do with other, perhaps repressive, conceptions of social order. If, on the other hand, music is seen as something that people do, its meaning will be understood in relation to other things they do, and to the world in which music is produced and listened to.

It has become increasingly widely accepted that diversity of interpretations of music, both in the form of performances and of verbal texts, is not something that can ever be eliminated. The study of music is aesthetically important precisely because of music's lack of definitive significance, and aesthetics can influence how those studying music respond to this situation. The challenge is to avoid the dangers in the expansive perspective, which can actually turn into its opposite. Some new musicology tends to contract music into what can be converted into narrative terms. By doing so it loses sight of music's freedom from the limitations imposed by reference to specific aspects of the world. In this way, Elgar's First Symphony can, for instance, become just a piece of English imperialism. Another danger lies in assuming that music's lack of referential meaning allows attempts to understand it to be open to the expansive whim of the interpreter, so that subjectivity excludes objectivity. The value of aesthetics might, therefore, lie in the ways in which it makes us question what we think is subjective and what we think is objective, and this can lead to new forms of performance, as well as to new approaches to analysis and interpretation.

Chapter summary

- Aesthetics has to do with changing ideas about subjectivity and objectivity.
- Music is produced in terms of rules and yet also has to do with free expression.
- There are differing traditions of aesthetics of music, one of which sees music as an object to be defined, the other of which sees it as a practice connected to other practices.
- The aesthetic need to appreciate music as an art, and the critical need to understand how music is linked to political, historical, and philosophical issues play a central role in recent developments in the understanding of music.

Discussion topics

- Is taste actually subjective, despite all the objective factors which play a role in its formation?
- Can music be true?
- How does one interpret the fact that musical evaluation changes as society changes?
- Does music need philosophy, or does philosophy need music?
- What do we understand when we talk about the meaning of music?

Further reading

Bowie, Andrew (2003), *Aesthetics and Subjectivity: From Kant to Nietzsche* (Manchester: Manchester University Press).
> Discusses the philosophical importance of aesthetics particularly in relation to music.

Bowie, Andrew (2007), *Music, Philosophy, and Modernity* (Cambridge: Cambridge University Press).
> Asks whether music can be regarded as a means of questioning the nature of modern philosophy.

Bujic, Bojan (1998) (ed.), *Music in European Thought 1851–1912* (Cambridge: Cambridge University Press).
> A collection of important source materials.

Dahlhaus, Carl (1989), *The Idea of Absolute Music* (Chicago: University of Chicago Press).
> Traces the emergence of the idea of music as the highest of the arts.

Goehr, Lydia (1994), *The Imaginary Museum of Musical Works* (Oxford and New York: Oxford University Press).
> Questions the notion of the musical "work" which underlies so much thinking about music in philosophy.

Kivy, Peter (2002), *Introduction to a Philosophy of Music* (Oxford and New York: Clarendon Press).
> The most concise introduction to the concerns of the analytical philosophy of music.

Kramer, Lawrence (1990), *Music as Cultural Practice* (Berkeley, CA: University of California Press).
> A classic text of the "new musicology," which rejects the idea that music cannot be understood discursively.

Le Huray, Peter, and James Day (1991) (eds.), *Music and Aesthetics in the Eighteenth and Early Nineteenth Centuries* (Cambridge: Cambridge University Press).
> A collection of important source material.

McClary, Susan (2000), *Conventional Wisdom: The Content of Musical Form* (Berkeley, CA: University of California Press).
> A characteristic example of "new musicology" in action.

Ridley, Aaron (2004), *The Philosophy of Music* (Edinburgh: Edinburgh University Press).
> Questions the major assumptions of the analytical philosophy of music.

Scruton, Roger (1997), *The Aesthetics of Music* (Oxford: Clarendon Press).
> An interesting, if flawed, attempt to write a philosophical account of the understanding of music.

Glossary

Metaphysical	Metaphysics is the attempt to give an account of the universal principles of reality.

Analytical philosophy	Philosophy which regards the analysis of the structure and use of language as the basis for dealing with philosophical problems.
Continental or European philosophy	The term "Continental philosophy" is often used to refer to the recent French philosophy of Jacques Derrida, Michel Foucault and others (see post-structuralism and postmodernism). Continental philosophy should really be seen as beginning with Kant's attempt to account for knowledge in terms of the workings of the human mind, which leads to new ideas about subjectivity and objectivity. Continental philosophy is more concerned with the significance of art and of history for philosophy than is analytical philosophy.
Rationalism	In the seventeenth and eighteenth centuries, rationalism refers to the doctrine that the universe has an inherent law-bound structure that is expressible in mathematical terms and is independent of experience.
Empiricism	The doctrine that all knowledge depends on sense-experience, rather than relying on principles that are independent of experience.
Ideology	"Ideology" is first used to refer to a system of ideas. It then often comes to mean a system of ideas that distorts the perception of reality. Ideology is also used to refer to a system of ideas which is based on or is produced by the power of one social group over another.
Formalism	The theory that music should only be interpreted in formal terms, rather than in terms of either its content or of its effects on listeners.
Critical Theory	"Critical Theory" can refer to theory in general in the humanities. It often refers more specifically to the project of the "Frankfurt School" of social theory, founded in 1923, of which Adorno was a member. Its aim was to establish a theory of society which combined social and cultural analysis with criticism of social injustice.
New musicology	The recent direction in musicology which seeks new ways of considering musical meaning by connecting it to issues in society such as gender, power, human subjectivity. It is influenced by Critical Theory, post-structuralism, and postmodernism.
post-structuralism	The direction in French philosophy and American literary theory which derives from Nietzsche's and Heidegger's aim of overcoming metaphysics by showing that it is not possible to establish timeless universal principles of reality. Starting from structuralist

ideas about the linguistic sign, in which each sign is defined by its difference from other signs, Derrida aims to show that that no sign has a fixed meaning because it is dependent on its changing relationships to other signs. This has important consequences for how we think language works.

postmodernism

The general term for a series of ideas about the way the contemporary world has shown that key ideas of the modern period associated, for example, with the notion of progress, or of the identity of the individual human subject, have been revealed as untenable. The French philosopher Jean-François Lyotard's book *The Postmodern Condition* claims that postmodernity involves the end of large-scale narratives that make unified sense of human history in terms of a conception of universal reason. Such ideas are, though, arguably already part of modern thought.

Part 2
Approaches to repertoire

6 World musics

HENRY STOBART

Chapter preview

This chapter explores a range of issues surrounding the study of "world musics." It begins by examining the various uses and histories of the term World Music ("world music"), arguing that this category influences the ways we think about musical repertoires and relate to particular musical cultures. The next section considers a few historical musical encounters, the impact of the concepts of "evolution" and "culture," going on to chart how the study of world music and the discipline of ethnomusicology developed. The role of ethnography and of methods that focus on performance, event, and orality are highlighted as distinctive aspects of the study of world music and ethnomusicology. Drawing on several case studies, the discussion then turns to the relationship between music and place. Both the critical relationship between music and place and the dangers of uncritically mapping music onto place are stressed, leading to a discussion of the relationship between identity, place, and authenticity. The final part of the chapter focuses on issues surrounding the reception of unfamiliar musics. It is an exercise in "ear cleaning," which aims to help us to recognize how power and cultural conditioning shape the ways we hear. It contrasts so-called "listening" and "doing" musics, examines how sounds that might challenge hegemonic modes of hearing are often avoided in the World Music market, and questions our perceptions of rhythm and harmony.

Key issues

- World Music(s): exclusions and inclusions.
- Who studies world musics?
- Does music have a place?
- Can world music be mapped?
- Sounding authentic?
- Can we trust our ears?
- Challenging ears and perceptions.

Introduction. World Music(s): exclusions and inclusions

Why, you might wonder, does a book dedicated to the study of music have a chapter entitled "world musics"? Is all the music of the world not "World Music"? Try finding pieces by the Rolling Stones, Mozart, or Louis Armstrong under the "World Music" section of a CD store – your search may be long and fruitless. Is this because they are excluded from the world of music? Or, alternatively, is it because they can easily be found under well-established categories like "rock," "classical," or "jazz"? So, what is considered "World Music," and why? To start to unravel this we need a little history, but unavoidably we also find ourselves thinking about power and politics.

Our familiarity with the term "World Music" as a marketing category can be traced back to a London pub in the summer of 1987. Representatives of twenty-five small record labels got together to discuss how best to get their releases of African, Latin American, and other international musics onto the shelves of record stores (Taylor 1997, Rice 2000: 224, Feld 2000). They came up with the idea of using "World Music" as an inclusive and appealing marketing term, replacing more problematic and less inclusive ones such as "ethnic," "Non-Western," and even "primitive" music. The term quickly caught on and was further established with the publication of the *Rough Guide to World Music* in 1994, which has now gone through several revised editions.

During the 1980s the term "world music" was also being used as a title for university courses in the USA and increasingly adopted by academics as a means to present the various musics of the world on an equal footing. People also began to talk about "musics" in the plural, even if this plural form was not found in dictionaries, to make the point that the world does not share a single universally comprehensible music any more than it does a language. We talk about "languages," so why not "musics"? World music was also chosen to replace the term "Non-Western music" in the editors' 1988 planning meeting for the *Garland Encyclopedia of World Music*: a ten-volume series that presents the globe as a constellation of world regions without center or periphery. Approaching the world in this way leads the section on "The History of European Art Music" to be allotted fewer than twenty out of the "Europe" volume's 1,144 pages. This is striking when you stop to think that European art music is probably the most extensively studied of all the world's musical traditions and consider how it dominates university music departments and library shelves. In some ways, the notion "world music" can be seen to displace the economic and political dominance of certain traditions and histories, in their place potentially stressing the richness and diversity of the world's musics on their own terms. (Hereafter I will generally distinguish between "World Music" as a marketing category and "world music" as an area of scholarship and study. This contrast is, however, in some ways very unsatisfactory.)

Both the music business and scholars originally used the term World Music as a means to bring under-represented musics to our attention, using it as a catch-all category. But it might be argued that over the years the term has come to mean rather different things, due to fundamental transformations both in the recording industry and in scholarship. In the 1980s record production and distribution was dominated by a handful of multinational companies, but with the advent of digital technologies and the internet a multiplicity of new smaller labels and modes of distribution emerged. Today, typing "world music" into an internet search engine brings up millions more hits than "classical music," "jazz," or even "popular music." This seems to suggest that World Music has gone from being a label applied to under-represented or minority musics to a dominant marketing category. It signals a new plurality in a highly competitive marketplace, evident from for example the *BBC World Music Awards* or the glossy pages of the magazine *Songlines*. The motivations of the music business are clearly to sell and promote, providing consumers (mostly in economically powerful Europe and the US) with a shifting, colorful, fashion-sensitive, and immediately attractive array of artists and musical styles from around the world. This lively diversity, with creative exchanges between the local and global, and where unimaginable economic success has been achieved by certain musicians from poorer parts of the world, such as Cuba's *Buena Vista Social Club*, is seen by many as reason for celebration. Others, however, worry that musicians are exploited by the industry, which is subject to the whims of fashion, and that this global market is leading to greater cultural homogeneity, where everything starts to sound the same (Feld 2000:179–81). What is for sure is that the spread of musics marketed by the World Music business is by no means even. While certain African and Latin American popular musics receive excellent coverage, as do a few European neo-folk styles, many other traditions and parts of the world fare more poorly.

In scholarship since the 1980s the notion of "world music" has also shifted from an almost exclusive focus on what might be called traditional, folk, or indigenous musics linked to specific places to a much broader conception which includes a wide range of popular musics and fusions and takes into account mass migration and globalization. In some ways the label "world music," for the music business and scholarship alike, has become almost so disparate as to be meaningless – so that categorizing a particular performance or artist as World, Popular, Classical, or Folk may seem arbitrary. For example, how would you classify Bluegrass, Scottish fiddle music, Brazilian death metal, Cuban Hiphop, Yo-Yo Ma's Silk Road Project, or Björk?

Nonetheless, within the broader study of music, it remains critically important to carve out a place in which to explore a range of the world's musical traditions. What, then, should an introductory course on world music aim to achieve? Perhaps some of the following:

- Introduce some of the diversity of the world's music and help students appreciate its relationship to their own lives and experience
- Place the music into broader social, political, economic, and environmental contexts so that students appreciate what it might mean to given performers and listeners
- Challenge dominant ("hegemonic") modes of hearing and help appreciate what people find engaging or emotionally powerful
- Consider how the musics of other cultures have been viewed, presented, and studied, and how this shapes the ways we hear and think about them.

Who studies world musics?

Although studies dedicated to the musics of other cultures were rare before the late nineteenth century, the endeavor to comprehend other peoples' music is far from new. The ancient Egyptians and Greeks compared the qualities of exotic foreign musics with those of their own, and European explorers were sometimes deeply impressed by the music they encountered, as in this description of an African arched harp performance from the Congo by Duarte de Lopez dating from the 1500s (in a 1625 English translation):

> Those that play upon this instrument, doe tune the strings in good proportion, and strike them with their fingers, like a Harpe, but without any quill very cunningly: so that they make thereby (I cannot tell whether I should call it a melodie, or no) such a sound as pleaseth and delighteth their senses well enough. Besides all this (which is a thing very admirable) by this Instrument they do utter the conceits of their minds, and doe understand one another so plainly, that everything almost which may be explained with the Tongue, they can declare with their hand in touching and striking this Instrument.
>
> (Samuel Purchas 1625 in Woodfield 1995: 274)

Attitudes to music by settlers and missionaries, who arrived later and tried to govern and impose their values and beliefs, were sometimes much more negative. Music-making was often identified with indigenous resistance or with "pagan" beliefs that were seen to hinder conversion to Christianity. For example, in seventeenth-century Peru Spanish missionaries carefully documented their destruction of musical instruments as part of their "Extirpation of Idolatory" campaign (Arriaga 1621). Yet at the same time musical instruments from other cultures began to be collected and displayed with other exotic objects in private collections – the precursors of today's museums – or illustrated alongside European instruments in treatises such as Michael Praetorius's *Syntagma Musicum* (1619).

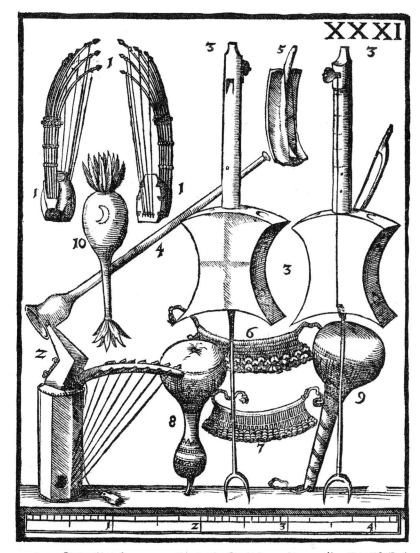

Fig. 6.1 Various "exotic" instruments, from Michael Praetorius's *Syntagma Musicum* (1619)

A few colonial officials took a deep scholarly interest in the music they encountered, including William Jones, a British High Court judge whose *On the Musical Modes of the Hindus* (1792) was the first major study of Indian music in English. But were such scholarly enterprises really just another form of colonial control – a way to classify, contain and dominate, as argued by Edward

Said in his famous book *Orientalism* (1978; see also chapter 1 of this book)? Said makes a similar point about Napoleon's scholarly invasion of Egypt, which led to the publication of *Description de l'Egypte* (1809–29) in twenty-three enormous volumes. Among Napoleon's army of scholars was Guillaume-André Villoteau, who contributed a detailed study of music to the collection (1823). In his introduction he writes:

> we had to put up with the repulsive effects of a music which lacerated the ears with modulations which were forced, harsh and wild, ornaments of extravagant and barbaric taste, and all this executed with unattractive, nasal and unsteady voices, accompanied by instruments whose sounds were either thin and muffled, or harsh and piercing. These were our first impressions of Egyptian music ...
> But like certain drinks which at first we find repugnant, becoming less disagreeable the more we consume them, and sometimes even delicious when completely accustomed to them, the same long habituation with listening to Arab music was able to diminish or dissipate altogether the initial repugnance encountered when listening to this music ... one day might we not find the charms in precisely the things that at first we found most repulsive?
>
> (*Description de l'Égypte: De l'état actual de l'art musical* 1823)

Even if he was a pawn in an imperial project, Villoteau's evocative description of his initial distaste for Egyptian music gradually transforming to intense appreciation suggests the endeavor of an individual to understand the music of others. In his musical transcriptions, he was also probably the first to devise special symbols to notate intervals that could not be expressed in standard Western notation.

Evolutionism, where the world's races were placed on an evolutionary scale with white Caucasians at the top, also critically influenced attitudes to music in the nineteenth century. Reflecting on the indigenous people of Tierra del Fuego he encountered during his voyage to South America, Charles Darwin wrote in his diary: "I believe if the world was searched no lower grade of man could be found" (Desmond and James 1992:133). This same problematic evolutionist perspective was still evident in 1915 when Salvador Daniel wrote that modern Arabic music was still at the level of European troubadour and minstrel music – in other words over five hundred years behind Western art music in its development (Racy 1993:82). Similarly, general histories of music – which almost always meant Western art music, excluding popular, light classical, jazz, and folk musics – published up until even the 1970s usually included a section on "primitive" music which tended to treat indigenous musics from Africa, the Americas, or the Pacific as synonymous with prehistoric forms. The beginnings of the formal study of musics from other parts of the world in the 1880s, so-called "Comparative Musicology," was also largely motivated by a desire to understand the origins of European civilization – viewed as the pinnacle of human achievement.

With the rise of "fieldwork" in anthropology around the 1920s (often identified with Bronisław Malinowski), where researchers began to live with the people they studied over extended periods, came a reaction against evolutionism. It was contested by the concept of "culture": the idea that the world consisted of a variety of different "cultures"; peoples with distinctive values, ways of life and modes of expression. An evolutionist view of the world's peoples, although by no means vanishing entirely, gradually gave way to the idea of a multiplicity of largely independent cultures characterized by difference – a multicultural world.

As Comparative Musicologists set about studying these various musical cultures, attempting to understand and document their distinctive characteristics, they began to feel uneasy about the name of their discipline. Their primary motivation was no longer to create a history of Western art music through comparison with so-called "primitive" musics, but to attempt to understand musical cultures on their own terms. In the 1950s this led to the adoption of a new, if somewhat cumbersome, name for their discipline: "ethnomusicology," often defined as the study of music in society or as culture. You might ask yourself: why not simply call a discipline dedicated to studying the world's music "musicology"? You would not be the first. The principal reason was that "musicology" was already synonymous with the study of Western art music: a canon of perceived "great composers" and their scores.

With its commitment to studying indigenous, folk, or other exotic oral traditions from around the world, ethnomusicology set itself in opposition to musicology's dominance, exclusivity, and elitist object of study. Nonetheless, it could also be argued that these early ethnomusicologists often took an overly Romantic view. They usually avoided urban popular musics or those touched by "Western" influences, and sought out what they then presented as pure, authentic, or uncorrupted traditions. Their published writings and recordings often gave the false impression that, unlike the ongoing developments in Western art and popular music, these musical traditions had somehow remained stable and unchanged over the centuries. But of course they had not; living musical traditions are always transforming and incorporating elements from elsewhere.

Over the past few decades the study of the world's music has transformed in many ways, as have communications, technologies, and the multiplicity of global sounds available. Musicology and ethnomusicology have also put aside some of their differences; some musicologists are adopting more global perspectives and certain ethnomusicologists have applied ethnographic approaches to Western art music (Kingsbury 1988, Nettl 1995). Although ethnomusicology continues to be closely identified with the study of the world's musical diversity, today the discipline is defined less by the kinds of music studied than by its approach. The most distinctive aspect of this approach is the use of ethnography or so-called "fieldwork" (even though much is conducted in major cities or, increasingly, over the internet).

Musical ethnography requires researchers to become familiar with, document, and analyze how people involved in the creation, performance, and reception of music go about their lives, and how they make, talk, and think about music. Ethnomusicologists have often dedicated themselves over extended periods to learning to perform the music, speak the language(s), and participate in other aspects of the lives of the people they study. In other words, they try to experience the musical "culture" from the "inside" or to become "part" of that culture (see chapter 13). This approach is allied to a methodology called "participant observation": an attempt to balance both "insider" and "outsider" perspectives. However, as scholars have stressed over the past few decades, distinctions between notions of "inside" and "outside" are by no means as clear-cut as they might initially seem. Similarly, the notion of "culture," if applied as a kind of definable unit to a group of people or form of musical expression, is deeply problematic. We may share particular cultural resources with certain people, such as knowing how to jive or a sense of the way functional harmony shapes musical experience, but does this make us part of the same culture? While there are undoubtedly cultural resources that are more "typical" of certain groups of people than others, it is important to stress that our individual cultural positions are highly subjective and shift from moment to moment (Turino 1993: 8, Nettl 2005: 215–31, Clayton *et al.* 2003).

In addition to focusing on the social dynamics and processes surrounding music-making, ethnomusicologists have taken a special interest in performance. This concern with performance, performers, the event, and oral dimensions of music-making contrasts with musicology's traditional focus on the composer and score (although maybe this is now a somewhat outdated caricature). Over the years a range of technologies have been used to document performance, ranging from the wax cylinder recorders of the early Comparative Musicologists to today's digital-video and hard-disk recorders. But even the latest technologies can only give a very partial picture of a performance, as do attempts to transcribe world musics into notation. In their analyses, ethnomusicologists draw upon a diverse range of methods and techniques, and continue to explore new approaches.

Does music have a place?

Does place influence the ways we experience and produce music? How much is acoustic, ecological, and social environment likely to shape the ways we make music? Does it make a difference whether we live in a rainforest, high mountain, or urban environment, and how much does it depend on how we engage with the environment? Do we perceive the sounds around us as meaningful spirit or ancestral voices, which inform us about our relationships with the powers that shape our well-being, or do we hear them as annoying background din – as noise pollution?

Firstly, let us turn to a case study from Papua New Guinea by Steven Feld, who demonstrates many intimate connections between the music of the Kaluli and their local rainforest environment (Feld 1990, 1991, 2000). The rainforest's constant hum of insects, birds, flowing water, and other sounds, he argues, is reflected in the way Kaluli sing together. When two people sing, the second voice shadows the first with the same words and melody. Rather than synchronizing, the voices overlap just like the sounds of the rainforest. The Kaluli call this musical mode of interaction *dulugu ganalan* ("lift-up-over-sounding"), which Feld suggests is as critical to Kaluli music aesthetics as "harmony" is to the "West." He also describes how drumming and certain types of song incorporate characteristics from the calls of particular bird species. This brings emotional intensity to musical performance because, following death, the souls of humans are thought to be revealed in the voices of rainforest birds. In other words, to hear a bird cry is to hear the voice of an ancestor; certain bird species being specifically associated with the departed souls of children. Place is also critical to song structure: in *heyalo* songs the refrain (*mo* – "trunk") typically evokes the sounds of a particular local bird, while the verse *(dun* – "branch") maps journeys away from familiar home territory, often provoking a sense of loss or abandonment. In short, connections with place are critical to the aesthetics, structure, and emotional power of Kaluli music.

For our second case study, we move from the rainforest, buzzing with constant sound, to the rural community of Kalankira high in the Bolivian Andes (4,100 m) where the acoustic impression is one of silence (Stobart 2006b). Although we must be wary of environmental determinism, the strident and vibrant music of these rural farmers and herders almost seems to convey the sense that they are compensating for the silence of this open, treeless landscape. The women often sing in high tessitura, panpipes and recorder-like flutes are blown strongly to exploit the upper harmonics, and guitars often favor metal strings for increased volume. A shifting array of musical instruments, genres, and tunings, each invoking different qualities of emotion, is alternated through the course of the year and intimately connected with agricultural production. During feasts it is common to see people playing flutes or panpipes in muddy animal corrals to promote the fertility of their llamas and sheep, at times with nobody else around to listen. People sometimes explain that they are playing to "console" and bring "joy" to the spirits of the landscape that ensure abundant herds and potato harvests. Such ways of organizing and understanding music, which vary from one locality to the next, are intimately connected with particular environments, histories, ways of life, and relationships to place.

In both these case studies, it might be argued that the particularities of place are critical to understanding music. Outsiders, who do not share the same sense of place, might enjoy hearing or attempting to perform these various musics, but presumably the experiences and sentiments provoked will be rather different. Maybe everybody's relationship to place is important, if not critical, to his or her experience of music – whatever its form. How does being in a night club, street parade, church, airport terminal, or at home in your lounge influence your musical experience – its emotional impact and meaning? Would all musics be equally effective, or environmentally "at home," in these places? Also, are there ways in which more urban environments shape musical preferences and creativity? Is it mere coincidence that music with an electronically produced repetitive beat is the product of modern urban environments, where machines and cars are ubiquitous? To argue this in terms of a simple causal relationship would be ridiculously naive, but to entirely discount acoustic ecology would also seem unwise.

Can world music be mapped?

If music can be seen to be so intimately connected with place, is it then possible to create a map of the world's music? Does the world really consist of pockets of music with identifiable characteristics that can be mapped onto the globe? In some ways this is precisely the way that the world's musics have been, and often continue to be, studied and presented. Thus, in the World Music section of most CD stores, recordings are conventionally categorized according to country or region (e.g., Mediterranean, Middle East, Africa) – whereas other genres are placed according to composer or artist. (Internet stores, of course, usually offer a range of search options.) But, are there problems with this approach? Can we really talk about discrete and stable pockets of music with identifiable characteristics, linked to particular cultural groups?

The Suyá people of the Brazilian Amazon, studied by Anthony Seeger, provide an interesting – if not particularly unusual – example of the way in which groups often appropriate musical resources from others. Although they consider certain forms of song to have originated among the Suyá, sometimes acquired from bees, plants, birds, or fish, certain others are claimed to be borrowed from other neighboring groups. Indeed, it is the very association of this music with outsiders which is seen to give the music its power (Seeger 1991, 2004: 58–9). However, whether the supposed creators of such music would still recognize it as "their own," when sung by the Suyá, is another matter. In other words, even at such a local level when music is often closely linked to ecology, attempting to map music on to place becomes challenging. When we start to take into consideration large-scale musical exchanges, migrations, and today's multitude of diasporic and multicultural communities, the notion of mapping becomes even messier and more problematic.

The example of a Surinamese master drummer in Holland is a case in point. The country of Surinam is a former Dutch colony located on the Caribbean

Box 6.1 Acquiring new music in the Indigenous Americas

In many parts of the Americas the acquisition of powerful new songs and music, which were thought to be able to effect transformation or "make things happen," was traditionally connected with sources in the natural world. Among the Flathead of Western Montana in the USA, such songs were acquired through a "vision quest": the individual spending several days alone and without food in the mountains to provoke a trance-like state. The song, which may become the person's song for life, would typically appear in the form of a dream connected with a particular wild animal. In contrast, songs composed by individuals – so-called "make up" songs – were viewed as purely for entertainment, lacking the capability to effect special things (Merriam 1967: 1–19).

The Suyá of the Brazilian Amazon also identified the origin of certain of their songs with particular spirit communities of the natural world, such as animals, bees, fish, birds, plants and trees. Humans gained access to these songs when a person's spirit was caused to leave the body and travel to one of these natural communities; usually the result of an attack by a jealous witch. While often suffering sickness, fever, and convulsions, this "person without a spirit" was seen to become a teacher of new songs, who could transmit the powerful songs of, for example, the birds, bees, or fish to the realm of

humans (Seeger 2004: 53–8). In the Bolivian Andes the *wayñu* melodies of the rainy season, which are closely connected with potato cultivation, are traditionally collected from the *sirinus* ("sirens"). These are enchanting and dangerous spirit beings associated with waterfalls, wild places in the landscape, and the interior of the earth. Traditionally the new melodies required each year were collected in the weeks leading up to Carnival (February/March). Older musicians tell of how the tunes entered their heads, as if in a dream, as they listened to the sound of waterfalls. More recently, as fewer people visit the *sirinus*' waterfalls, commercial artists have begun to produce cassettes and DVDs of new Carnival *wayñus* for the year. Flute players learn the new melodies from these recordings to play during the feast, and – despite the involvement of commerce and new technologies – often maintain that the tunes originate with the *sirinus* (Stobart 2006a: 121, 2006b).

These three examples demonstrate close links between musical creation and the knowledge and powers that are seen to reside in the natural world, even if mediated through technology. Powerful music is not attributed to human creativity or genius, as in some traditions, but is seen to be acquired through entering a close metaphysical relationship with the powerful forces of the natural world on which humans depend.

---

coast of South America. It was previously under British sovereignty, before being exchanged for the Dutch settlement of New Amsterdam (today's New York) in 1667. Surinam's attraction to the Dutch was as a sugar producer, and many slaves were shipped there from Africa to work the plantations. Some slaves escaped down-river to form communities in the remote interior of the country. These communities of so-called *maroons* ("strays") accompanied their ceremonies with West African-derived drum music, developing a range of new elements and styles. When Surinam achieved independence from Holland in 1975, some 50 percent of the country's population chose the option to migrate to Holland. The master drummer André Mosis learnt the polyrhythmic *maroon* drum style in his youth in Surinam, including traditional drum language used to communicate with the spirit world and with dancers in performance. He is deeply committed to maintaining *maroon* traditions, but regularly gives drum workshops for Dutch and Surinamese students on the African

Djembe. Alongside family members and other musician friends he also gives staged performances, including shows representing an imagined Africa. So how do we map his music? Do we place it in Holland where he has made his life since 1990 – seeing his children through university and into high-powered jobs, in Surinam for which he clearly feels a deep sense of nostalgia and commitment, or Africa – a continent he has not visited, but which he imaginatively invokes in his performances and identifies with the roots of his music? We might reasonably argue that each one of these places has shaped his music in particular ways, and that it does not exclusively belong to any one of them.

Sounding authentic?

A few seconds of sound are probably enough for you to immediately connect a number of musics with particular parts of the world. For example, the *sitar*'s evocative slides and sympathetic drone strings with India, the flamenco guitar's Phrygian tonality and descending cadences with Spain, the didgeridoo's rich and vibrant harmonic spectrum with Australia, or Salsa's *clave*-based rhythms and *montuno* piano with Latin America. These sounds and many others permeate our films, TV adverts, and other media and serve to evoke particular parts of the world and associated sentiments. On the one hand they are accepted codes used to invoke distinctiveness, an imagined sense of place, or the exotic, but they are also stereotypes. The above examples all involve an element of "truth" but at the same time are by no means representative of the various musics found in the parts of the world that they purport to signify. Does this make those musics from Africa which do not sound "African" to our globally attuned ears any less African? In turn, might this mean that people wishing to highlight African heritage need to sound "African," by using the sounds that are globally identified as African?

This is precisely what has happened with *Powwow* music in North America. Among the Native American communities of the USA and Canada, asserting indigenous identity has become important as a means to gain visibility as a minority group and to claim rights to land and other benefits. *Powwow* drumming, singing, and dancing is a widely recognized means of expressing and celebrating such identity. Although historically restricted to the plains region, the idea that *Powwow* is authentically Native American became deeply instilled in the popular imagination (Powers 1990: 159–60), in part thanks to Hollywood movies. Circuits of *Powwow* events are now organized in a wide range of locations, including on university campuses, with participants sometimes traveling huge distances to attend. This mode of expressing indigenous identity has become so influential that in some Native American communities *Powwow* has replaced other forms, such as fiddle music, which had been performed since the nineteenth century. In some areas, however, groups are reviving their own local indigenous traditions and discarding what they now identify as a "Hollywood

Indian" image (Miller 1999: 33). Nonetheless, the explosion of the *Powwow* phenomenon highlights the importance of being perceived to look and sound authentic, even if there is little cultural or historical basis for the form this takes.

Perceived authenticity, even if based on shaky or entirely false grounds, confers a form of authority and influences a person's or group's reception. For example, the Hawai'i-based ethnomusicologist, Ricardo Trimillos, is regularly surprised and amused by how he is frequently ascribed Japanese heritage when he dresses in a kimono and kneels to play the Japanese *koto* in concerts. He is Asian in looks, being Filipino with an admixture of Chinese, but he is certainly not Japanese. For his audience, he notes, this (mis-)perceived Japanese ethnicity makes the concert experience more "authentic" and increases his credibility as a practitioner and authority of the *koto* (Trimillos 2004: 37). But even though he is not fluent in Japanese, Ricardo Trimillos probably knows a great deal more about playing the *koto* than the average person in Japan, and regularly teaches students of Japanese heritage. Similar examples abound and can make questions about the location of a particular musical tradition and the authority of an individual to act as culture bearer surprisingly problematic.

Nonetheless, music is also a critical identity marker. When a young man from a rural community in the Bolivian highlands walks into town casually strumming his small mandolin-like *charango*, most locals will immediately recognize his ethnic group and associated territory from the style and rhythm of his strumming. It is also common during Andean feasts to encounter cacophonous musical battles, where bands identified with particular communities or neighborhoods compete to dominate the acoustic space. Each will often play an emblem melody, but even if playing the same tune in the same key (as sometimes happens) the players would not dream of joining forces and playing together in a unified group. This may seem a pretty extreme example, but more generally music is a key means of marking who you are (and who you are not), the people with whom you identify, and where you come from. But, of course, as part of basic social skills we all alternate identity markers – whether dress, music, or language – according to context, often quite unconsciously. In other words, you probably do not share your enthusiasm or distaste for particular musics equally among your various acquaintances.

Can we trust our ears?

> So different is the taste of the several races, that our music gives no pleasure to savages, and their music is to us in most cases hideous and unmeaning.
>
> (Charles Darwin, *The Descent of Man*, 1871)

Darwin is identified with the rise of evolutionary thinking which, as noted earlier, included approaching the world's races as different stages of human development. Maybe you think that the above quotation from *The Descent of Man*, which identifies a mutual failure to understand or appreciate music across different races or peoples, implies a more cultural way of thinking? Or maybe not? Firstly in this quote, Darwin stresses musical "taste" (or "aesthetics") which, as we heard above from Guillaume-André Villoteau, is acquired through extended exposure and familiarity to particular types of music. But taste is also a means of ranking people; we cannot neatly separate discrimination in musical taste from other forms of discrimination. I wonder if Darwin thought that he would come to appreciate the singing of the indigenous people of Tierra del Fuego if he lived there for long enough. Secondly, the above quote refers to intelligibility, where musics might be compared to languages, which are characterized by particular vocabularies and grammars. Darwin is not explicitly saying that "the West is best" when it comes to music, but the superiority of Western art music has been (and probably remains) a "common sense" assumption for a good number of people. This has been justified on the basis that it is built on natural acoustical laws (drawn from science), that it has greater complexity, and that it is more emotionally profound and meaningful (Becker 1986). All these claims quickly lose validity if examined objectively, and begin to look ethnocentric. But, of course, being a bit ethnocentric is unavoidable because our perception of the world is shaped by our experience and its cultural context. That is just as true for unfamiliar cultures, as for those we might think of as "our own." So, one of many good reasons for studying world music is that it helps us to appreciate how our own various musical practices and perceptions are culturally constructed.

Is music just an aural phenomenon? Most definitions of music stress its aural component, but in reality musical performance usually involves many other sensory dimensions. Indeed, viewed from a more global perspective, the insistence on silence and restrictions on movement, food, and drink in the Western classical concert are a striking and fascinating exception. In other contexts movement, especially dance, liberty to make sound, and the consumption of food and drink are often integral to musical experience. For example, in festive contexts, music is often just one in a range of sensory elements which contribute to the event. Also, when we play musical instruments and dance, our primary sensations often involve touch, movement, groove, and interactions with other people, rather than just the sounds. In other words, if we treat music as a purely acoustic phenomenon we will probably miss many of the key reasons why it is so important to people and is such a universal phenomenon. What are the implications for the world's musics of prioritizing the sonic over the social?

You might also ask yourself which aspect of music should be prioritized: making a beautiful sound and performing technically "correctly," or sharing a sense of engagement, well-being or empathy with other people? We might approach this question by distinguishing between what I shall call "listening music" and "doing music," although probably no music is exclusively one or the other. Maybe what should be stressed here are differences in values and status typically ascribed to particular types of musical experience. There is also the tricky issue that we don't always know which aspect is prioritized in unfamiliar musical traditions because we can not always be sure what constitutes "a beautiful sound" or, for that matter, a "meaningful musical experience."

"Listening musics" are likely to include aspects that aim to capture and maintain the listeners' interest and attention, such as narrative-like structures, variation and development, opportunities for contemplation, or impressive technical feats. These elements are also likely to give rise to critical judgments and more intellectualized styles of appreciation. For example, the introductory *alap* section of a *raga*, the framework that organizes and governs melody in North Indian classical music, involves the improvised exploration of the "personality" of the chosen *raga*. In free time, sometimes lasting up to an hour, the performer will gradually introduce the *raga*'s various pitches (*srutis*) and melo-

dic characteristics or gestures (*pakar* or *chalan*). Listeners who are familiar with the style may appreciate and be profoundly moved by the way that a highly skilled and imaginative performer reveals, develops and confers emotional intensity to the various elements of a *raga's* identity, bringing it to life in performance – see Box 6.2.

"Doing musics" might be characterized as those that prioritize participation, where the value of the music lies primarily in the sense of well-being and shared or individual expression it involves, rather than in its acoustic result. In such musics, people may be

> **Box 6.2 Raga Yaman**
>
> Yaman is one of the first Hindustani ragas taught to students; it is seen to provide a strong foundation from which to learn and understand others – of which there are hundreds. The time traditionally associated with Yaman's performance is late evening (9–12 p.m.) and its character is generally categorized as "grand" and linked with the idea of a brave and noble-minded hero (Bor 1999:164). Like other ragas, the tonal center is Sa (notated here as C), and two other notes are of special importance, the *vadi* ("sonant") and *samvadi* ("consonant"). For Yaman: these are respectively Mi (E) and Ni (B). The notation below shows Yaman's pitches (incorporating Indian *sargam* note names) and its ascending and descending contour, as well as a few of its most characteristic melodic gestures (*pakar* or *chalan*).

Raga Yaman (pitches)   *Vadi* *Samvadi*

Sa Re Ga Ma Pa Dha Ni Sa   Ga   Ni

Chalan/pakar (characteristic melodic gestures)

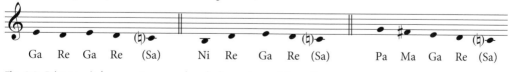

Ga Re Ga Re (Sa)   Ni Re Ga Re (Sa)   Pa Ma Ga Re (Sa)

Fig. 6.2 Primary pitches, gestures, and melodic contour of Raga Yaman

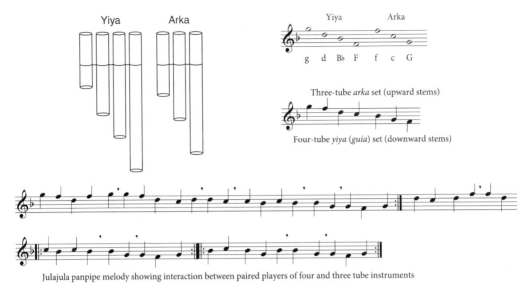

Julajula panpipe melody showing interaction between paired players of four and three tube instruments

Fig. 6.3 Diagram and notation of a jula jula panpipe melody

quite unconcerned by so-called "wrong notes" or "technical inadequacies," or choose temporarily to overlook them in favor of participation. These musics may be characterized by elements that encourage ad hoc participation, such as limited technical requirements, short repetitive musical structures, or concealment of individual contributions in a unified group texture. For example, the *jula jula* panpipes of the Bolivian Andes consist of pairs of four- and three-tube bamboo pipes, made in several sizes which are played using "hocket" techniques between paired players. *Jula julas* are played during feasts lasting several days, which are linked with pilgrimages and ritual battles (Stobart 2006b). As in most other musical traditions in the region, the players dance or walk as they play. It is important that a large number of men participate in the ensemble to give a sense of community solidarity and force when encountering other groups. The simple playing technique and conventional structure of the repeated melody (which must be new for each year's feast), means that so long as a few players can lead the melody others can quickly join in without prior rehearsal, swelling the numbers and sound. While prioritizing participation is vital to the *jula jula* performance, it is also important to note that when encountering other groups or entering the square of a town the acoustic power resulting and its impact on other people is critical.

As the example of the *jula julas* demonstrates, "doing" and "listening" dimensions of music cannot be entirely separated. However, even if people derive great enjoyment from playing this music together during feasts, they are unlikely to put on a recording of it to relax to at home in the evening. The repetitive nature and lack of variety in sound means that recordings of

Fig. 6.4 Jula jula players at the feast of San Francisco in Toracari, Northern Potosi, Bolivia. The photograph features players of the largest paired four-tube *yiya* and three-tube *arka* instruments kneeling to perform a *kulwa* in front of the church door. (Photo: Henry Stobart)

traditional *jula jula* music are very unlikely to become a sustained hit on the World Music market. Does this mean that musics that prioritize participation are in some way "inferior," or that their emotional impact is somehow less potent or profound? The point we need to be wary about is that "doing" musics often provoke negative value judgments in relation to "listening" musics, or are seen to be of lower status and not deserving of serious consideration, despite the powerful experiences they often involve.

Challenging ears and perceptions

As noted for "listening music" above, commercial recordings and staged performances for the World Music market typically include variations in sonority, mood, rhythm, and melody, and incorporate new techniques in order to sustain listener interest. However, sounds that might challenge dominant – or hegemonic – global tastes are also often avoided. For example, New Flamenco often opts for smooth lyrical voices, rather than the rough, impassioned and wailing style of traditional singers, in which for many lies the essence of Flamenco's emotional potency. Similarly, when making recordings of world music in the studio, Zimbabwean *mbira* players have sometimes found engineers sticking tape over the shells and bottle tops on their instruments to stop them buzzing. For the engineers this buzzing quality is seen to distract from the pure sound produced by the metal keys, while for the players it is considered intrinsic to the sound and aesthetic of the music (Berliner 1993: 11; see Box 6.3).

The study of world music encourages us to look beyond the sonic dimensions of music to examine the ideas, relationships, beliefs, and contexts that motivate people to create music in particular ways. It also challenges our ears to explore other ways of hearing. When we listen to a piece of music, are we hearing the same things as other people? Each person's physical faculties to process musical experiences are unique, so perhaps no two people ever experience a given piece of music in precisely the same way. But we also know that there are many aspects of musical experience that we share with others – indeed this is one of the reasons why it is so important to us. But what about musics from less familiar cultures: can we be sure, for example, that we experience the same sense of pulse or that we can distinguish harmony from dissonance?

African musicians playing in European venues are sometimes disorientated to discover a large body of people dancing to a different pulse to the one shaping their performance. This inability for non-Africans to perceive the underlying pulse is quite

Box 6.3 The Soul Mbira (*Mbira Dzavadzimu*)

Although now familiar to the international stage, the roots of the mbira *dzavadzimu* ("soul") lie with the Shona people of Zimbabwe, who played it alongside *hosho* gourd rattles, singing and dancing in possession ceremonies called *bira* (Dutiro 2007). Its music is traditionally used to aid a medium's entry into a state of trance, thereby opening communication with the souls of the ancestors to whom people turn in cases of illness or misfortune. During a *bira* the performers' mbiras are usually placed inside a large gourd, to which are attached many shells or bottle tops, to amplify the sound and provide additional buzzing. Ceremonies tend to feature traditional repertoire; old melodies that the ancestors will recognize and return to hear. The binary interaction between each hand's thumbs or fingers on the mbira's twenty-two metal keys typically produces a polyrhythmic texture against the triple-based rhythms of the dancers and *hosho* rattles, a critical dimension of the music.

(Berliner 1993).

widespread in African polyrhythmic musics. It has even led the world-famous Youssou N'Dour from Senegal to add an extra synthesized drum beat, emphasizing the music's pulse, into his the mix of his *Mblax* recordings for non-African markets.

Notions of dissonance and harmony, and how these are expressed musically, are also brought into question in the rural Andes. In the Bolivian highlands, recorder-like *pinkillu* flutes are associated with producing two forms of sound: *tara*, which is strong, dense, and vibrant, and *q'iwa* which is weaker, thin, and clear. The vibrant quality of *tara* is literally "dissonant" from the perspective of Western acoustics. It results from difference beats, associated in acoustics with two pitches being "out of tune" with one another. *Pinkillu* flutes are constructed so that, when blown strongly, a rich multiphonic texture is produced which includes what players identify as "two voices," approximately one octave apart, which beat against one another. But for the players the concept of *tara* is connected with notions of social harmony, productivity, the circulation of energies to others, or the idea of reciprocity between two people. By contrast, *q'iwa* is a pure flute sound that would seem harmonious from a Western musical perspective, but in the rural Andes the term is also used widely to refer to social dissonance. For example, it is applied to individuals who are mean or miserly, who "do not give," and who are unproductive, lazy, or cowardly. In other words, in this Andean context, harmony is linked with notions of sharing and productivity, expressed musically with strong vibrant flute timbre, whereas dissonance is connected with failure to share and produce, articulated musically as a thin weak sound (Stobart 2006b: 214–17). There is little doubt that the harsh and dissonant flute sounds characteristic of many parts of the Andes convey a joyous sense of harmony and abundance to local people, even if outsiders may initially find them hard to appreciate. Maybe we need to question the cultural limits of our hearing and inform our listening with ethnography.

Chapter summary

- World Music ("world music") means different things according to context and its meaning has shifted over time; power and politics are critical to its meanings.
- Facing the challenges of world music has the potential of opening up a wealth of new perspectives on the world.
- Music might be seen to be a particularly rich area for developing inter-cultural dialogue and understanding.
- In many ways it is hard to study world music without becoming aware of, or concerned about, social inequality and the lives of other people.

- World music confronts you with alternative ways of thinking, hearing, and feeling: if you would rather keep your head and ears firmly buried in the sand, then it is probably not an area of study you should pursue.
- Study of world music will be endlessly fascinating if you are interested in finding out about and learning to appreciate some of the diverse ways in which people around the globe make and experience music, and relish the challenge of reflecting on your own musical experiences in a wider global context.

Discussion topics

- Should the study of world music be concerned with the maintenance and preservation of musical traditions, or should it restrict itself to documenting and analyzing what it encounters?
- What single aspect most characterizes, defines, or identifies a piece of music? (e.g., composers, genre, performer(s), place, etc). Discuss contrasts in the ways that different forms of music are classified in, for example, books, libraries, CD shops, university courses. How might such categorization impact on the way we hear, talk, and think about music?
- The formerly common term "non-Western" is usually carefully avoided by ethnomusicologists today (as it was by the editors of *The Garland Encyclopedia of World Music*). Discuss why the implications surrounding this term might be perceived as problematic.
- Despite its aim to treat the world's musics as equals, ethnomusicology largely and necessarily operates in an "elite" and "intellectual" context. How might this impact on ethnomusicologists' interpretations of musics from the "majority" world?

Further reading

Broughton, Simon, Ellingham, Mark, Muddyman, David, and Trillo, Richard (1994),
World Music: The Rough Guide (London: The Rough Guides).
An accessible introductory guide to a wide range of world musics.

Fletcher, Peter (2001), *World Musics in Context: A Comprehensive Survey of the World's Major Musical Cultures* (Oxford: Oxford University Press).
A very substantial, but still accessible, survey of the development of world musics from antiquity to the present.

Nettl, Bruno (2005), *The Study of Ethnomusicology: Thirty-One Issues and Concepts*, new edition (Urbana, IL: University of Illinois Press).
A landmark study by an influential ethnomusicologist, which provides a broad overview of the discipline.

Nettl, Bruno and Stone, Ruth M. (1998 onwards) (advisory eds.), *The Garland Encyclopedia of World Music*, 10 vols. (New York: Garland).
An essential reference source for conducting research into world musics.

Taylor, Timothy (1997), *Global Pop: World Music, World Markets* (New York: Routledge).
An examination of the politics of commercial music around the world.

References

Becker, Judith (1986), "Is Western art music superior?," *Musical Quarterly*, 72/3: 80–111.

Berliner, Paul (1993), *The Soul of Mbira: Music and Traditions of the Shona People of Zimbabwe* (Chicago and London: University of Chicago Press).

Bor, Joep (1999) (ed.), *The Raga Guide: A Survey of 74 Hindustani Ragas* (book with four audio CDs) (Nimbus Records).

Clayton, Martin, Herbert, Trevor and Middleton, Richard (2003), *The Cultural Study of Music: A Critical Introduction* (New York: Routledge).

Desmond, Adrian and Moore, James (1992), *Darwin* (London: Penguin).

Dutiro, Chartwell (2007), *Zimbabwean Mbira Music on the International Stage* (Aldershot: Ashgate).

Farrell, Gerry (1997), *Indian Music and the West* (Oxford: Oxford University Press).

Feld, Steven (1990), *Sound and Sentiment: Birds, Weeping, Poetics and Song in Kaluli Expression*, 2nd edn (Philadelphia: University of Pennsylvania Press).

Feld, Steven (1991), "Sound as a symbolic system: the Kaluli drum," in David Howes (ed.), *The Variety of Sensory Experience: A Sourcebook in the Anthropology of the Senses* (Toronto: University of Toronto Press), 89–99.

Feld, Steven (2000), "Sound worlds," in Patricia Kruth and Henry Stobart (eds.), *Sound* (Cambridge: Cambridge University Press), 173–200.

Hoefnagels, Anna (2001), "Remembering Canada's forgotten soldiers at contemporary powwows," *Canadian Journal for Traditonal Music*, 28 (http://cjtm.icaap.org/).

Kingsbury, Henry (1988), *Music, Talent and Performance: A Conservatory Cultural System* (Philadelphia: Temple University Press).

Merriam, Alan (1967), *Ethnomusicology of the Flathead Indians* (New York: Wenner-Gren Foundation for Anthropological Research).

Miller, Bruce-Subiyay (1999), "Seeds of our ancestors: growing up in the Skomish song tradition," in Willie Smyth and Esmé Ryan (eds.), *Spirit of the First People: Native American Musical Traditions of Washington State* (Seattle: University of Washington Press), 25–43.

Nettl, Bruno (1995), *Heartland Excursions* (Urbana, IL: University of Illinois Press).

Nettl, Bruno (2005), *The Study of Ethnomusicology: Thirty-One Issues and Concepts*, new edn (Urbana, IL: University of Illinois Press).

Powers, William K. (1990), *War Dance: Plains Indian Musical Performance* (Tucson and London: University of Arizona Press).

Racy, Ali Jihad (1993), "Historical worldviews of early ethnomusicologists: an east-west encounter in Cairo, 1932," in Stephen Blum, Philip Vilas Bohlman and Daniel M. Neuman, *Ethnomusicology and Modern Music History* (Urbana, IL: University of Illinois Press), 68–91.

Rice, Timothy (2000), "World music in Europe," in Timothy Rice, James Porter and Chris Goertzen (eds.), *The Garland Encyclopedia of World Music, vol. 8: Europe* (New York: Garland), 224–30.

Seeger, Anthony (1991), "When music makes history," in Stephen Blum, Philip Vilas Bohlman and Daniel M. Neuman, *Ethnomusicology and Modern Music History* (Urbana, IL: University of Illinois Press), 23–34.

Seeger, Anthony (2004), *Why Suyá Sing: A Musical Anthropology of an Amazonian People* (Urbana, IL and Chicago: University of Illinois Press).

Stobart, Henry (2006a), "Devils, daydreams and desire: siren traditions and musical creation in the central southern Andes," in Linda Phyllis Austern and Inna Naroditskaya (eds.), *Music of the Sirens* (Bloomington, IN: Indiana University Press), 105–39.

Stobart, Henry (2006b), *Music and the Poetics of Production in the Bolivian Andes* (Aldershot: Ashgate).

Taylor, Timothy (1997), *Global Pop: World Music, World Markets* (New York: Routledge).

Trimillos, Ricardo D. (2004), "Subject, object and the ethnomusicology ensemble: the ethnomusicological 'we' and 'them,'" in Ted Solís (2004) (ed.), *Performing Ethnomusicology: Teaching and Representation in World Music Ensembles* (Berkeley, CA: University of California Press), 23–52.

Turino, Thomas (1993), *Moving away from Silence: Music of the Peruvian Altiplano and the Experience of Urban Migration* (Chicago: University of Chicago Press).

Woodfield, Ian (1995), *English Musicians in the Age of Exploration* (Stuyvesant, NY: Pendragon Press).

7 Early music

STEPHEN ROSE

Chapter preview

"Early music" can refer to a particular period (here, repertories before 1750) or a performing approach that revives instruments and styles from the era when a piece was written. This chapter probes the challenges of researching and reviving early music, noting the different approaches taken by scholars and performers; it also outlines the main sacred and secular genres before 1750.

Key issues

- What is "early music"?
- What is "authentic" or "historically informed" performance?
- How far can we recover the sound of early music?
- How did music before 1750 relate to the Christian liturgy?
- Interpreting the notation of early music.

What is early music?

Before the twentieth century, "early music" was defined as music over a certain age. In eighteenth-century London the Academy of Ancient Music defined "ancient music" as being at least 150 years old, although the later Concert of Ancient Music (founded 1776) included works as little as twenty years old.

Since 1950, however, "early music" has increasingly indicated not a particular period but an attitude towards music of the past: namely, the belief that older repertories sound best if performed with instruments and styles of the composer's own era. Often this requires the recovery of lost performing skills (such as Baroque bowing, old keyboard fingerings, and systems of unequal temperament) and the revival of old instruments (such as harpsichord, viola da gamba, and valveless trumpet). With music earlier than 1600, there are also skills required to decipher the notation of the original sources. In the 1970s and 1980s performers promoting such historically aware styles often went under the banner of "authenticity," for they claimed to restore the music to its "original" or "authentic" state. More recently these musicians have adopted the more cautious label of "historically informed performance" (or "HIP"). The revival of period styles has been particularly successful for repertories such as French Baroque music, whose idiom is closely connected to the local performing conventions of the time.

In rejecting the performing techniques of the mainstream, performers in the early music movement reveal a conviction that the past is a strange, distant place. As L. P. Hartley writes in his novel *The Go-Between* (1953): "The past is a foreign country; they do things differently there." To a modern-day European, the medieval world – where feudal princes and the Church were all-powerful, and where electricity and easy travel did not exist – may seem as remote as the lives of tribes in Papua New Guinea. Arguably the medieval Europeans are more distant from us, because there is no way that we can visit their world, even though many relics of medieval buildings and culture still survive today. Applying a similar mindset to music, an emphasis on the sheer strangeness of the past can stimulate research and lead to historical periods being viewed with new intensity. Although some aspects of performances can never be recovered (as will be discussed below), research into period techniques is a good way for performers to gain a fresh interpretation of a piece. The search for novelty and difference is particularly valuable when making recordings, to distinguish a new performance from its competitors. It is no coincidence that historically informed performance boomed during the late 1980s and early 1990s, when the market for recordings expanded with the introduction of CDs.

Since the 1980s the quest to recreate period styles has been applied to more recent repertories. Ensembles that play on period instruments increasingly tackle music of the nineteenth and early twentieth centuries. The current Academy of Ancient Music, established in 1973 by Christopher Hogwood to perform eighteenth-century music, now also performs Mendelssohn, Schumann, and Weber; the Orchestra of the Age of Enlightenment has performed operas by Weber and Verdi; and the New Queen's Hall Orchestra has recorded Gustav Holst's *The Planets* (1914–16) on instruments of the early twentieth century. Thus although the early music movement is most closely associated with repertory before 1750, it is not limited to music of that era.

This chapter, however, does focus on music from before 1750, and in particular on what makes such repertories foreign or strange to present-day ears. It considers the main obstacles to recovering music of the past, probes the historical context of early repertories, and discusses what can be learned from early notation. This chapter recognizes that early music has been researched by both performers and scholars, whose approaches can overlap but whose goals are ultimately different.

How far can we recreate the music of the past?

Despite the enthusiasm of scholars and performers to explore the music of past centuries, there are several obstacles preventing a close understanding of these repertories. Music primarily exists in performance, and before the advent of sound recording in the late nineteenth century, all performances were lost the moment they finished. We cannot board a time machine to find out how music sounded in the eighteenth century or earlier. Instead, scholars and performers must rely on written sources, which inevitably give an incomplete picture.

Many aspects of music before the nineteenth century are little recorded in writing, if at all. These include many of the performing techniques for instruments and voices; the extensive improvised repertories, including much instrumental and dance music; and the popular music of street, tavern, and countryside. Traces of this rich aural culture may sometimes be reconstructed from such sources as illustrations or diaries. Paintings and engravings may show the personnel and seating of instrumental ensembles, while diaries such as that kept by Samuel Pepys in 1660s London describe the music heard on the streets. As for playing and singing techniques, the particular area of interest for historically informed performers, a variable amount of information survives. Although treatises describing performance skills were published from the sixteenth century onwards, they were usually for amateurs and thus cover only basic techniques. Professional musicians tended to keep their skills secret, sharing them only with apprentices in order to protect the status of their profession; indeed, many books of the time said the only way to learn singing or playing properly was to imitate a master. Such advice reinforces the importance of learning by ear in past centuries – an option not available to today's historically informed performers, who will never be able to hear what musicians sounded like before the nineteenth century.

The compositions of the eighteenth century and earlier are preserved in manuscripts and printed editions of the time. Yet the musical notation of the time is far from being an exhaustive record of how the music sounded. To modern eyes the notation of earlier repertories often looks incomplete, and the way that many aspects such as rhythm or scoring are left to the performer's discretion will be explored in the closing part of this chapter.

Moreover, only a fraction of the music that was notated survives. Many manuscripts were eaten by mice and moths, burned by accident or on purpose, or dismembered and used to bind newer books. Before the nineteenth century, music was rarely seen as worth saving once it had served its immediate purpose; one common attitude was that "nothing is more useless than old music" (see Box 7.1). Given such outlooks, it is not surprising that huge

Box 7.1 "For nothing is more useless than old music"

Until the nineteenth century, earlier repertories were rarely seen as worth preserving. In 1477 Johannes Tinctoris declared that "there does not exist a single piece of music composed more than forty years ago that is regarded by the learned as worth hearing." Attitudes had barely changed over 270 years later. In the quotation below, Caspar Ruetz (1708–55), a church musician in Lübeck, describes his attitude to the music of previous generations:

> I inherited a large pile of church music from my late father-in-law Sivers and grandfather-in-law Pagendarm. Of the pieces left by Pagendarm I have been able to use not a single one, and only a few from Sivers. They testify to the enormous diligence and industry of these upright men. Everything that these men wrote with so much trouble and work … has not the slightest value now, although no small amount of capital went into it. This mass of musical paper from many years ago has diminished by about half: much of it has gone into the stove in place of kindling, much has been used around the house, and much has been given to people who can use all sorts of scrap and paper in their shops … But who will give anything for it, other than someone who needs scrap paper, for nothing is more useless than old music.
>
> (Snyder 2007: 316–18)

amounts of music are lost. Some scholars estimate that between 80 and 90 percent of medieval manuscripts are no longer extant. Numerous individual pieces are known to be lost: nothing survives of Claudio Monteverdi's second opera *Arianna* (1608), apart from the famous lament; and about one hundred of the church cantatas of Johann Sebastian Bach are probably lost. Countless other pieces survive incomplete, with one or more voice parts or instrumental lines missing.

Given these gaps in the notated record, musicologists are only too aware of how little is known about music of the past. Studying earlier repertories is like trying to do a jigsaw with half of the pieces missing. Hence scholars and performers alike must take an informed yet creative approach: we must imagine what the past was like, because we can never know it exactly. Many performers, indeed, are attracted to earlier repertories by the challenge of reconstructing them in a convincing way.

Even if it were possible to recreate the past exactly, there are aesthetic and philosophical reasons why such a recreation would be undesirable for historically informed performers. Present-day performances must appeal to present-day tastes. Although today's listeners can educate themselves to change their tastes, they belong in the twenty-first century and hear early repertories against the backdrop of the subsequent centuries of music. Richard Taruskin (1995) has provocatively argued that historically informed performers are not really historical at all, but that they remake the past in the image of the present. The insistence of some historically informed performers on being utterly faithful to the composer's intentions or to the original score is, Taruskin suggests, a very modern mindset, shared by such composers as Igor Stravinsky. Before the nineteenth century there was actually a lot of freedom in how compositions were performed (see the last two sections of this chapter). Taruskin also suggests that the emphasis in the 1980s on light, fast performances of Baroque music reflected a modernist aesthetic, again advocated by Stravinsky among others.

Other interpretations are offered by John Butt (2002), who suggests that the search for historic styles may reflect a lack of confidence and certainty in present-day culture. The use of earlier styles shows that modern performing techniques are no longer seen as automatically superior; rather, different techniques suit different musics. Butt also shows how the twentieth century increasingly valued and preserved the heritage of previous eras, perhaps as a response to the wars and modernization that destroyed many buildings, landscapes and cultural artefacts. Like Taruskin, Butt believes that historically informed performance fills an important need in today's culture.

The relationship between current taste and historically informed performance is also exposed by research into early twentieth-century performing styles as preserved on early recordings. These recordings have been studied by Robert Philip (1992), who identifies such mannerisms as heavy use of portamento (slides between notes of different pitch), sparing use of vibrato, and a rushing of short notes. Such features are not to present-day taste and in general have not been emulated by today's performers of early twentieth-century music, not even by those favoring historically aware styles. The early recordings are evidence not only of how quickly performance styles can change – thus reinforcing the value of research into period styles – but also how some elements of the past remain alien to modern ears.

If we were able to board a time machine to listen to eighteenth-century performances, it is also likely we would find some aspects distasteful to us. Today's performers must respect prevailing taste (although they can also try to influence it) and have conviction in what they do; it would not be authentic or honest to themselves as performers to imitate aspects of the past that they disliked. Here it can be seen that the goals of scholars and historically informed performers are not the same. Scholars admit the uncertainties and gaps in our knowledge of the past. By contrast, performers – as the singer Susan Hellauer puts it – "are forced to make musically viable choices. As I often say, you can't sing a footnote" (quoted in Sherman 1997: 50).

Music for the Church

The majority of notated music from before 1600 was intended for the Christian Church; indeed, the very first notated music was plainchant, to be sung as part of Christian worship. These sacred repertories need to be understood within the context of the Christian liturgy and the cycle of the Church year. Since medieval times, Christian worship in Western Europe has taken two primary forms: the Divine Office (a series of prayers at set times during the day, focusing on the recitation of psalms) and the Mass (which re-enacts the Last Supper). Both types of service include fixed texts (the Ordinary) and those that change with the liturgical calendar (the Proper). The liturgical year begins on the first Sunday in Advent (the Sunday nearest 30 November). The penitential period of Advent precedes the commemoration of Jesus's birth at Christmas,

Box 7.2 The typical structure of the medieval Mass.

Box 7.2 The typical structure of the medieval Mass.

Items in **bold** are sung by the choir; items in SMALL CAPITALS are intoned by the celebrant; items underlined are a dialogue between celebrant and choir. After Harper 1991: 115.

Proper (variable text)	Ordinary (fixed text)
Introit	
	Kyrie
	Gloria
COLLECT	
EPISTLE	
Gradual	
Alleluia	
Sequence	
GOSPEL	
	Credo
Offertory	
SECRET	
	Sursum corda
	PREFACE
	Sanctus/Benedictus
	PATER NOSTER
	Pax domini
	Agnus Dei
Communion	
Postcommunion prayer	
	Ite missa est (or **Benedicamus Domino**)

and the penitential period of Lent prepares for the celebration of his resurrection at Easter. Further feast days mark other events in Christ's life (such as Ascension Day or the Transfiguration); there are also many festivals commemorating saints.

The Divine Office originated in monasteries as a way of offering prayer and praise throughout the day. In monastic life eight Offices were celebrated (Matins, Lauds, Prime, Terce, Sext, None, Vespers, and Compline). Of these eight services, Matins and Vespers were the longest and had a substantial musical portion. Vespers, for instance, begins with the versicle and response *Deus in adjutorium* and always includes the canticle of the *Magnificat*; it also incorporates a set of psalms appropriate for the day.

Box 7.2 shows the structure of the Mass, indicating the interplay of the Ordinary and Proper.

In the medieval Church, most portions of the Mass were sung to plainchant, the official repertory of unison monophony (i.e., an unaccompanied melodic line). Chanting was a way to heighten the words of the liturgy and increase the sense of ritual. As Box 7.2 shows, some chants were assigned to the choir and some to the priest celebrating Mass. The melodic style of the chant depended on who was singing and its place in the worship. The simplest chants were for the celebrant (SMALL CAPITALS in Box 7.2); these were reciting formulae for prayers and Bible readings, mainly on one note, with one or two nearby notes at the end of lines. Similar formulaic "tones" were used for the recitation of psalms in the Divine Office. By contrast, the chants of the Ordinary of the Mass sung by the choir (bold in Box 7.2) tended to be long and carefully constructed, with repeated sections or phrases: the Kyrie and Agnus Dei are prayers of supplication, while the Gloria and Sanctus are acclamations of God's greatness. Of the Proper chants sung by the choir, the Gradual and Alleluia are responsorial chants, i.e., where the choir answers a soloist; the choral refrains are among the most elaborate of all chants, with melismas and melodic repetition.

By the eleventh century plainchant was adorned with the addition of extra voice parts. Often these extra parts were improvised, but some written examples survive. In **discant** the parts move note-against-note, whereas in ***organum purum*** one note of the chant is held below many elaborating notes. These techniques for decorating chant led to the development of a genre called the motet, in which a tenor taken from a section of plainchant was overlaid with one or more parts singing separate texts (which usually glossed or moralized upon the meaning of the tenor's words). Although the motet originated as an adornment of the liturgy, in the thirteenth and fourteenth centuries it was also used recreationally by the clerical elite at churches, cathedrals, universities, and courts.

Whereas most sacred polyphony of the medieval era sets elements of the Proper of the Mass or Office, composers in the fifteenth and sixteenth century preferred to set the Ordinary of the Mass, presumably because the resultant composition could be used on many occasions. 104 Masses survive, for instance, by Giovanni Pierluigi da Palestrina (1525/6–94). By the late fifteenth century, motets were again being used liturgically, but simultaneous texts were generally avoided; instead composers favored texts from the Proper (such as the Gradual or Offertory) and increasingly sought to portray the words in a vivid manner. This desire to depict the text was encouraged by humanism, the movement associated with the Renaissance that involved the revival of rhetorical and linguistic techniques from ancient Greek and Roman civilization.

Although most sacred polyphony before the eighteenth century originated in the Christian liturgy, such pieces tend to be heard in isolation today, within concerts or on CDs. When we encounter a Palestrina Mass on CD – five or six choral movements lasting up to twenty minutes in total – we should not think of it as some kind of sixteenth-century equivalent to a symphony. Rather these movements would originally have been interspersed with chant, readings, prayers, and ritual. Indeed, some broadcasts and CDs seek to reconstruct this liturgical context, framing sacred polyphony with the appropriate chants and often also including processions, organ music, and church bells. It has been popular to reconstruct grand ceremonial services with a particular sense of richness and drama: notable here are the recordings by Paul McCreesh and the Gabrieli Consort and Players for Deutsche Grammophon, with such titles as "Venetian Vespers," a "Venetian Easter Mass," and a "Lutheran Mass for Christmas Morning." Such CDs take historical reconstruction to a new height, although the festal services chosen are hardly typical of everyday worship in the period.

Until the sixteenth century, most of the musical elements of Christian worship were sung by the educated elite, mainly priests and monks. The words were in Latin, legible and comprehensible only to the educated. Polyphony required highly trained singers, able to hold their own parts, and medieval polyphonic genres such as the motet were emphatically for a narrow circle of the elite, particularly in the case of pieces with simultaneous texts that might not be easily audible. Countless sung services took place without a congregation. In England, for instance, there were many chantry chapels, foundations of priests and singers that offered Mass and the Office for the good of the benefactor (or for the soul of a deceased benefactor). Consequently much sacred polyphony could be esoteric or inward-looking, for the ears of the musicians and God alone.

The notion that church music should be intelligible to the laity – or be sung by the congregation – took root only in the sixteenth century as part of the Protestant Reformation. The newly established Protestant denominations wanted to involve the laity in worship, and were also influenced by humanist ideals about music clearly delivering a text. In German lands, the Lutheran Church pioneered the chorale (a vernacular hymn for the congregation to sing, or at least to be understood by all the congregation); Calvinists, by contrast, eliminated all music except for simple metrical psalms that anyone could sing. In England, the Anglican Church introduced anthems, short syllabic settings of English texts for the choir. But even in these Protestant denominations, many elements of the Catholic liturgy remained. The Anglican Church kept many aspects of the Divine Office to create its services of Matins and Evensong; even today in most English-speaking countries, the musical focus of Anglican cathedrals is the service of Evensong. The Lutheran Church retained a strong awareness of the liturgical calendar: the sacred cantatas of J. S. Bach, for instance, are each assigned to a particular Sunday and refer to the set scriptural readings.

In later centuries the Church preserved or revived several repertories of early music, often for ideological reasons. The compositions of the papal musician Palestrina have been performed more or less continuously by the Sistine Chapel in Rome since his lifetime, because they represent an ideal of Catholic choral music. In England, the Anglican Church was re-established in 1660 and immediately revived its repertory of sixteenth-century music, to stress the continuity with its original state. Other pioneering revivals of earlier repertories and performance techniques also took place within the Church. In the mid-nineteenth century, the Benedictine abbey of Solesmes led a revival of plainchant, with the monks promoting the then-revolutionary attitude that the most authentic melodies are found in the oldest surviving sources. And around 1900, the center of English Catholicism – Westminster Cathedral in London – spearheaded a revival of pieces written for the Latin liturgy by early English composers, as a way to assert the Catholic musical heritage in a predominantly Protestant country.

Secular music

Because of the power and omnipresence of the Church in medieval Europe, it can be hard to draw a strict line between secular and sacred music. Pieces with religious texts were performed outside church services, for private devotion or during mealtimes; we have already seen how the motet was used to entertain clerics. Furthermore, the courts of monarchs and aristocrats rarely tried to rival the power of the Church, but instead used religion as an integral part of their rule; hence most courts included a chapel of musicians who sang at regular services.

Much secular music from before the fifteenth century is lost. One reason for this is that outside the Church, musicians did not necessarily have the education to notate their repertory, and they did not share the Church's enthusiasm for writing as a way to ensure liturgical uniformity. Virtually no instrumental music survives in written form from the Middle Ages, with the exception of a few dance tunes in manuscript, but there is plenty of evidence in illustrations, sculptures, letters, and poems that instrumental music was an important source of entertainment during banquets and festivals, in taverns and on the streets.

There is much more evidence of the monophonic songs performed with vernacular words in different parts of Europe. Some of these songs were devotional, but the bulk consisted of love songs. In France during the eleventh and twelfth centuries, the singer-songwriters known as troubadours and trouvères created a large body of songs on the theme of courtly love (where a knight pledges his love and loyalty to a noble lady). In German-speaking lands, a similar repertory existed known as *Minnesang* (love song), some of which are on earthly topics, while others address moralistic or satirical subjects. By the fourteenth century the polyphonic song increasingly occupied the energies of elite musicians. Initially the genres of polyphonic songs were named after poetic forms – the **ballade**, **rondeau**, **virelai** – but by the middle of the fifteenth century, song-types such as the **chanson** or **frottola** used a variety of poetic forms.

Around 1600 the solo song returned again to dominance, this time for singer with continuo accompaniment supplied by a chordal instrument such as lute or keyboard. The new style was brought to prominence by Giulio Caccini's collection *Le nuove musiche* (1602); it was influenced by a Florentine desire to recapture the emotional effect of ancient Greek music, but also incorporated melodic and harmonic formulae from Neapolitan and Roman traditions of unnotated popular songs.

In the seventeenth century the importance of secular music was reinforced by the rise of instrumental genres independent of the voice. Previously much instrumental music had been transcribed from vocal pieces. By contrast, the new genres such as the sonata and concerto were conceived separate from the voice and thus rarely had a link with sacred words. Yet some instrumental pieces originated in or were associated with the Church. Arcangelo Corelli (1653–1713) wrote church sonatas and also chamber sonatas, the latter being characterized by their use of dance movements that would be inappropriate in church. The concertos of Giuseppe Torelli (1658–1709) developed from experiments with different groupings of instrumentalists in the echoing acoustics of the Church of San Petronio, Bologna. Several of the violin concertos by Antonio Vivaldi (1678–1741) – such as his Concerto in F major "Per la Solennità di S. Lorenzo," RV 286 or his Concerto in D major "Per la Solennità della santa Lingua di S. Antonio" RV 212 – bear titles indicating that they were used in religious services. Such close connections remained between secular and sacred music until the middle of the eighteenth century.

Notation and the role of the performer

The main evidence of early music is the notated record; yet to modern eyes this early notation can be hard to interpret. Many of its symbols are enigmatic to modern musicians and need to be learned using handbooks such as Willi Apel's *The Notation of Polyphonic Music* (1961). Early notation may also seem incomplete at first sight, leaving much freedom to the performer. Yet this is no deficiency in the notation; it rather reflects the balance between the responsibilities of the composer and the performer in earlier periods. Performers were guided partly by the notation and partly by conventions learned orally. In general, notation became more specific over the course of the centuries, although there were many exceptions to the trend.

By the ninth century, plainchant was being notated with symbols that look like small pen-strokes (lines, curves, and hooks) above the words of the chant. These so-called **neumes** indicate the direction of melodic movement; pitch and rhythm are not specified. Such notation may have been intended as an aide-memoire for singers who had already learned the chants by ear; in some cases it may have reminded them of particular features in performance.

In the eleventh century the staff was introduced, allowing the neumes to indicate specific pitches. Rhythm, however, still went unnotated. Consequently there has been widespread debate about how to sing the rhythm in plainchant. In the early nineteenth century it was common to sing chant in strict rhythm, as if it had bar-lines; but the monks of Solesmes (see above) promoted a free, declamatory performance that followed the syntax and rhythm of the Latin words. By the twentieth century this Solesmes style was adopted in most Catholic performances of chant.

In the early thirteenth century a major notational innovation occurred in France. The scribes of the polyphony of Notre Dame, Paris, began to indicate rhythm by the groupings of two or three notes in ligatures. The sequence of ligatures denotes the underlying rhythmic pattern (or **rhythmic mode**). Because rhythm is indicated by the context of a note, this system of notation can be ambiguous: more than one rhythmic interpretation can be possible when pitches are repeated or when the rhythm is irregular. There is also ambiguity about the polyphonic sections known as *organum purum* where an upper voice moves over held notes in the tenor. Here the note-lengths in the upper voice should reflect their relationship with the lower voice: if the upper note is dissonant, it should be short; if it is consonant (an octave, fifth or fourth), it should be long. But it is unclear how free the rhythms should be in the upper voice, and modern editors of Notre Dame polyphony have chosen different solutions. In the recent L'Oiseau-Lyre edition of the *Magnus liber organi* (Monaco, 1996–2003), for instance, Thomas Payne chooses to notate the *organum purum* in exact modern rhythm; whereas in other volumes of the series, Mark Everist notates the upper voice in unstemmed black notes like those used for modern transcriptions of plainchant.

There has also been scholarly debate over whether the rhythmic modes should be applied retrospectively to the unmeasured songs of the troubadours and trouvères. Some late manuscripts of trouvère songs use mensural notation, and in the early twentieth century several transcribers claimed to detect an underlying rhythm in troubadour songs, usually by relating the poetic meter to the rhythmic modes. More recently, editors and singers have preferred a flexible, unmeasured performance that follows the declamation of the poetry. Scholars will probably never know the exact rhythms used by trouvères and troubadours; most likely there was a mix of practices in different places and periods. Modern performers must decide which rhythmic interpretation is most convincing for themselves and their audience.

Between 1600 and 1750 musical notation again left considerable freedom to the performer. Many Baroque pieces are written in a shorthand that must be read according to the performing conventions of the period. The situation is analogous to jazz, where the lead-sheet usually shows only the melody and the basic harmonies, and players are expected to improvise over chordal formulae. Of the types of notational shorthand in the Baroque, the best known is figured bass, whereby a chordal accompaniment is indicated by numerals over the bassline. The numerals specify the harmonic structure, but leave considerable freedom in the spacing of chords, their ornamentation, and their scoring. Another example is the melodic lines in the slow movements of Corelli's Op. 5 violin sonatas. These were originally written as unadorned half notes and quarter notes; but the 1710 edition published by Estienne Roger claims to include Corelli's own ornaments, shrouding the plain tune with roulades of thirty-second notes.

Improvisatory freedom was particularly common in keyboard genres. In most European countries until the early eighteenth century, keyboardists were expected to be able to improvise a complete piece; this was a requirement, for instance, in auditions for organists in German cities such as Hamburg and Lüneburg. The role of improvisation can also be seen in notated keyboard music. Louis Couperin (*c*.1626–61) notated his keyboard preludes as unmeasured works, simply indicating the pitches and leaving the performer to decide how to time the elaborate rolled chords.

George Frideric Handel's Op. 4 organ concertos have many "ad lib" markings in the solo part (which was originally played by the composer), inviting extensive ornamentation. His Op. 7 organ concertos go even further, omitting whole movements which the organist is supposed to improvise. In other movements of Op. 7 (for instance, the second movement of Concerto No. 4 in D, or the finale of Concerto No. 6 in B flat), the orchestral parts are supplied complete but only fragments of the solo part are notated. The fragmentary solo parts may reflect the fact that when Handel wrote and performed the concertos, his eyesight was deteriorating and it was easier for him to improvise rather than play from a solo part. Moreover, the concertos were published after Handel's death, so the composer could not be asked to supply more detail for the printed solo part. But the fragmentary state of the concertos also indicates the importance of improvisation by Handel as organ soloist. Indeed it may have been in Handel's interest to notate only the bare minimum, so that some of his tricks as a soloist would remain secret.

The examples of notation described above possess a subtle mix of precision and freedom, often because the composer was very close to (or was the same person as) the performer. It can be hard to retain this subtle balance when an early piece is transcribed in a modern edition, because modern notation often imposes an inappropriate degree of precision. We have already discussed the modern editions of Notre Dame polyphony, where the nature of modern rhythmic notation requires an editor to stipulate a single rhythmic solution in passages where originally the performers might have made the decision. In the case of Louis Couperin's unmeasured keyboard preludes, the original notation is the only way to capture the rhythmic fluidity desired in performance.

Hence notation is not merely a set of symbols that can be deciphered to find the essence of a composition; often the original notation is part of that essence. This is why it can be so enlightening to examine facsimiles of original sources, using anthologies such as that edited by Nicolas Bell (2001). Not just the notation but also the format of the source may be significant. The page size (ranging from the tiny size of sextodecimo to the sumptuousness of folio) suggests whether a music-book is for carrying in a pocket or for placing reverently on a lectern. Most polyphonic music before 1600 was notated in separate parts rather than the score that is the norm in modern editions; this promoted a horizontal understanding of how individual voices interlock, rather than the awareness of vertical sonorities gained when examining a modern edition in score. The format and notation of sources are thus major factors controlling our perception of early music; there is an element of truth in Marshall McLuhan's adage that "the medium is the message."

The changing status of the composer

The overview of notation (above) shows how compositions often circulated in a form that gave considerable discretion to performers. In most repertories before 1750, the boundary between performer and composer was fluid. Often the performer and composer were the same person, as with the troubadours and trouvères who wrote and sang their own poetry. Even when the performer and composer were different people, the singers and players had considerable control over the shape and ornamentation of a piece. Composers, by contrast with the concert culture of the nineteenth and twentieth centuries, had a relatively low profile.

The earliest notated music is generally preserved with no details of the composer. Indeed, in the music that survives from before 1750, compositions by anonymous figures outnumber those by any known composer. In the case of plainchant, the exact origins of the older melodies are obscure, given that they were transmitted orally for centuries before the invention of musical notation. It is likely that improvised chants slowly gained fixed forms, reinforced by the Church's desire for liturgical standardization. By the ninth century the tradition had arisen that the melodies had been dictated to Pope Gregory the Great (pope from 590 to 604) by the Holy Spirit in the form of a dove (hence the name "Gregorian chant"). This story of divine inspiration reflected medieval views of music as a gift of God; according to such a mindset, God was the ultimate creator of all compositions.

Until the fourteenth century, plainchant was the basis of most polyphonic compositions. Polyphony was a gloss on sacred tunes, in much the same way as manuscripts of scripture might add explanatory commentaries and illustrations. The composer's role was to adorn existing material, rather than create something afresh (a task that only God was believed to be capable of). Such a tradition persisted into the sixteenth century, when many Masses were based on the themes and structure of existing polyphonic works. This so-called parody procedure was used extensively by Palestrina (who wrote, for instance, a Mass on his motet "Assumpta est Maria"); as late as 1610 Monteverdi based a Mass on Nicolas Gombert's motet "In illo tempore."

As music was notated in more detail and as more pieces were circulated beyond the immediate circle of the composer, there was a corresponding increase in the status of the composer (see also chapter 1). Guillaume de Machaut (c.1300–77), the leading musician-poet of the fourteenth century, was aware of his own creative status, disseminating his songs and sacred music in manuscripts that contain exclusively his own works. One of the first musicians to achieve wider recognition as a composer, rather than as a performer or music director, was Henricus Isaac (c.1450–55 to 1517); in 1497 he was employed as "court composer" (not as a singer or instrumentalist, as earlier composers had been) by the Holy Roman Emperor, Maximilian I. Also achieving renown in the same generation was Josquin des Prez (1450–55 to 1521). Josquin's fame largely rested on his compositions, which were widely disseminated in copies produced by the newly invented technique of music printing. Editors and publishers realized that Josquin's name sold copies, so much so that they falsely attributed works to him. In 1540 the German musician Georg Forster wryly observed: "I remember a certain eminent man saying that, now that Josquin is dead, he is putting out more works than when he was alive." Another indication of the rising recognition of composers was the composition competition run by a confraternity in Evreux, Normandy between 1575 and 1589: this awarded a prize to the best composition submitted each year, suggesting how the focus of interest was shifting away from performers.

Yet the status of composers did not strengthen consistently. In the seventeenth century the emphasis on instrumental and vocal virtuosity could reduce the recognition given to composers. During this period it was unlikely that the audience at an opera would know the name of the composer, although they would probably be aware of the name of the librettist and certainly the names of any star singers in the show. Well into the eighteenth century, performers continued to defend parameters that they saw as their prerogative. In 1737 Johann Sebastian Bach was criticized by Johann Adolph Scheibe for prescribing small details of performance in his music: "Every ornament, every little grace and everything that one thinks of as belonging to the method of playing, he expresses completely in notes: and this not only takes away from his pieces the beauty of harmony but completely covers the melody throughout" (David and Mendel 1998: 338).

Chapter summary

- Studying early music is a reminder of how the past is strange and different to us.
- The function of early repertories, their notation and the relationship between composer and performer are likely to confound present-day expectations and hence require careful research.
- Performers and scholars respond in different ways to the strangeness of the past: performers need to make early repertories relevant to their present-day audiences, whereas scholars need to admit the uncertainties and gaps in our historical knowledge.

Discussion topics

- How faithful should performers of early music be to original styles of playing/singing?
- Should we attempt to hear music of previous centuries as the original listeners heard it?

- If you were making an edition of a piece of early music, what would your aims be?
- How important is the religious context to an understanding of a piece of sacred music?
- If you were able to get into a time machine and meet a musician from a past century, what would you ask her/him?

Further reading

Bent, Margaret (1994), "Editing early music: the dilemma of translation," *Early Music*, 22, 373–92.
> An important essay which addresses the problem of "translating" elements of early notation into modern equivalents.

Bergeron, Katherine (1998), *Decadent Enchantments: the Revival of Gregorian Chant at Solesmes* (Berkeley, CA: University of California Press).
> Narrates the nineteenth-century revival of Gregorian chant by monks at the Benedictine abbey at Solesmes, which laid the foundation for certain editorial methodologies in modern musicology.

Kenyon, Nicholas (1988) (ed.), *Authenticity And Early Music: A Symposium* (Oxford: Oxford University Press).
> A collection of important articles on historically informed performance.

'Listening practice," special 25th anniversary issue of *Early Music*, 25 (November 1997).
> A collection of articles exploring who listened to music, and in what ways, in various eras before the nineteenth century. Shows the gap between our experiences of earlier repertories and how they might have originally been heard.

Owens, Jessie Ann (1997), *Composers at Work: The Craft of Musical Composition 1450–1600* (New York: Oxford University Press).
> Offers invaluable insights into the nature of the compositional process in the fifteenth and sixteenth centuries.

References

Apel, Willi (1961), *The Notation of Polyphonic Music, 900–1600*, 5th edition (Cambridge, MA: Mediaeval Academy of America).

Bell, Nicolas (2001) (ed.), *Music in Medieval Manuscripts* (London: British Library).

Butt, John (2002), *Playing With History: The Historical Approach to Musical Performance* (Cambridge: Cambridge University Press).

David, Hans T. and Mendel, Arthur (1998) (eds.), *The New Bach Reader*, revised by Christoph Wolff (New York: Norton).

Harper, John (1991), *The Forms And Orders Of Western Liturgy From The Tenth To The Eighteenth Century* (Oxford: Clarendon Press).

Philip, Robert (1992), *Early Recording And Musical Style: Changing Tastes in Instrumental Performance, 1900–1950* (Cambridge: Cambridge University Press).

Sherman, Bernard D. (1997) (ed.), *Inside Early Music: Conversations with Performers* (New York: Oxford University Press).

Snyder, Kerala J. (2007), *Dieterich Buxtehude: Organist in Lübeck*, 2nd edition (Rochester, NY: University of Rochester Press).

Taruskin, Richard (1995), *Text and Act: Essays on music and Performance* (New York: Oxford University Press).

Glossary

organum (discant and *organum purum*)	Polyphony made by placing an additional voice or voices against a pre-existing chant melody, either melismatically (*organum purum*) or in a measured note-against-note style (discant).
ballade, rondeau, and virelai (*formes fixes*)	The formes fixes were standard forms in French-texted song of the fourteenth and fifteenth centuries. The ballade is usually in three stanzas, each ending with a refrain (a repeated segment of text and music). The rondeau typically has the musical form ABaAabAB (with upper-case letters representing a repeat of the original text of these sections; lower-case represents new text). The virelai includes a refrain before, between, and after the verses, and hence typically has the musical form A(bbaA), with the section in brackets able to accommodate additional stanzas of text (usually three).
chanson	A French-texted song with no fixed form.
frottola	A secular Italian song of the fifteenth and sixteenth centuries, an important precursor of the madrigal.
neume	An early kind of notation: written as pen strokes above a text, neumes may or may not be on lines, and indicate single pitches or groups of pitches to be sung.
rhythmic modes	The usual description of various rhythmic patterns (combining long and short notes) in which early polyphony was performed and notated.

8 Opera

DAVID CHARLTON

Chapter preview

Whatever one's prejudices about "opera," there is only one way to categorize it: as a branch of lyric drama, or music theater. This is a huge and interesting subject, whether as entertainment, as study, or as material to perform. Many students will get the chance to sing, or play in, or direct, musicals and operas. Others will perhaps help back-stage or front-of-house. Theaters demand many different activities, as we saw in chapter 3. Studying opera also exists as part of music history; equally, writing music theater is still a flourishing activity, and thus part of the composer's curriculum. Performing and writing about opera often entails what W. B. Yeats (in a poem about staging drama) called "the fascination of what's difficult." There is no universal theory; opera studies borrow methods from whichever discipline is useful. This is seen as we progress through the sections below, each of which explores a separate area. Perhaps because of its obvious challenges, opera studies (within "musicology") is a relative newcomer.

Key issues

- How do opera and music theater fit into history?
- How far is opera relevant to society now?
- What systems are there for analyzing music theater?
- How did opera cope with the twentieth century?
- Singing as a means of persuasion.
- Some ways that music theater conveys morals and messages.
- Production issues: interpreting musical stage works.

Opera as entertainment and ritual

Opera today can still be thought of like a ritual, a human activity bringing people together for a common cultural purpose. An anthropology of opera would note its similarity to religious rituals involving music and organized movement. A book by John Drummond (1980: 15, 21) has explored its various links to pre-history, because if "We do not know when music-drama began," equally "we do not know of a time when man had no music-drama." He points, for example, to cave-paintings representing the buffalo-dance of Blackfoot legend, dating from around 30,000 BCE.

In fact the club of well-born Renaissance men in Florence who created modern opera out of existing forms (e.g., the pastoral and the intermedio) themselves took ancient Greek drama as conscious inspiration. The first, experimental example of opera dates from 1597/98: *Dafne*, by Jacopo Peri, words by Ottavio Rinuccini. If its obscure pre-history is significant, opera itself is already over four hundred years old.

Opera is a mixed-media form of art (see next section for some details), and involves actor-singers, musicians, often dancers, scenery, lighting, props, production staff, and assorted paraphernalia. These were also found four hundred years ago: so in a way, there is a continuity of purpose and tradition that allows us to relate to older works, maybe put them on, record them, or discover forgotten or lost ones. The early-music revival starting in the 1960s helped create a demand for operas by Monteverdi, Cavalli, Handel, and others, which has had an enduring effect (see chapter 16). The spin-offs include a burgeoning repertory of recordings, recently given a new lease of life through the advent of DVDs. Opera students have been fortunate since videotape started; and today's viewers of recorded opera will be tomorrow's experts on the evolution of stage production. It is possible that recording companies will collaborate with opera companies to save on costs, and result in further choice of recorded DVD repertory.

Public opera, for a paying audience, started in 1637 in Venice; but its origins were princely, and its audience privileged. The large costs of putting it on stage have constantly kept opera's finances in the public eye, mainly because of its demands on subsidy. Since it is a performance art *par excellence*, the debate over its future is crucially affected by the supply/demand equation. On one hand we have a theater form that combines skills, energies, and experience in drama, acting, music, and so on, which its supporters consider is unique, valuable, and prestigious. Its cultural capital stands very high in certain sectors. Other sectors decry its perceived extravagance and its artificial conventions, so they exercise self-censorship. As a business and as an entertainment, opera competes against TV, film, and sport, so promoters exploit the more popular appeal of the musical.

Actually, the death of opera has regularly been pronounced. T. W. Adorno's 1955 lecture, "Bourgeois opera," began by claiming that, since the 1920s, "opera's place and function [have] become questionable in today's society," indeed have "come to seem peripheral and indifferent," not least because the bourgeois audience "always wants to hear the same thing" (Adorno 1993: 41). In 1967 Pierre Boulez (in an interview for *Der Spiegel*) suggested blowing up existing opera

CHRISTOPH SCHLINGENSIEF, the *agent provocateur* of German theatre who will direct the new production of *Parsifal* at this year's Bayreuth Festival, set out to bring Wagner to the masses in a unique combination of opera and motor rally recently.

As part of the Ruhr Festival Recklinghausen, Schlingensief staged a 'Wagner-Rallye' in which 10 rally cars sped around the heavily-industrialised Ruhr region of Germany with snippets of Wagner operas blaring from their roofs.'I want to liberate opera from its elitist trappings and bring it to the streets,' Schlingensief said.

The two-member teams were required to solve puzzles and perform tasks en route, with the winning team getting tickets to see *Parsifal* in Bayreuth. *Simon Morgan*

Fig. 8.1 Wagner through a giant horn

Fig. 8.2 BIFF cartoon

houses, in order to construct new ones better suited to the needs of music of our own time. (He has not so far written any operas.) And in a survey of post-1945 opera Paul Griffiths in 1994 argued that the perpetual search for "new kinds of musical-dramatic expression" among avant-garde opera composers "had resulted in the disintegration of opera as a genre" by the mid-1970s (Griffiths 1994: 336). Nonetheless, the show has gone on; important works have continued to be written; and in a much-remarked move, tented audiences were entertained in 2004 at the UK's Glastonbury pop festival by English National Opera, giving (in English) the last act of Wagner's *Die Walküre* (see Fig. 8.2 and Box 8.3).

Writing anti-traditional new works and promoting outreach performances are part of operatic change away from the "bourgeois opera" label. But "bourgeois opera" itself is interesting as a particular "mode of interaction," as Tina K. Ramnarine calls it (chapter 13), which satisfied particular classes of people through ritual and entertainment as a group – an activity that had strong social and political functions designed to exclude outsiders, and reinforce bonds on the personal, professional, and political levels. We see this alive today in the corporate sponsorship of opera, whether directly funding a production (see chapter 3) or funding expensive seats for executives. When opera first admitted the public in 1637, the theater's finances were guaranteed by private capital, and financial stability was attempted by a system of subscriptions: you leased a box for a period of time and used it as though it were part of your own home. This did not exclude people who paid at the theater door, but it emphasized social rituals that had no necessary connection with music or opera at all. These are functions of opera that seem to relate to its origins as a courtly entertainment designed to put wealth on display. Bourgeois society simply borrowed that idea, often in association with aristocratic preferences.

Yet every country has different ceremonies; therefore opera, whatever its relation to a privileged class, has a different flavor in different societies. This process of appropriating opera started early, and is still much to be enjoyed. If you go to Italy in the summer and find yourself near Verona, you will probably end up joining in the ritual of lighting a small candle as darkness falls, an awed semi-silence descending over you and some twenty thousand other spectators gathered for an open-air opera in the Roman arena. Such a performance is never to be forgotten.

However, the importing of opera, normally from Italy, has continually caused complaint because it is often given in the language of its origin. This is not done simply as convention, but because the original composer will have written-in the sounds of his own language to the sung melodies, and every language has different phonetic properties. So the music actually sounds different when sung in a different language.

Moreover different societies and languages possess different kinds of voices and voice-production techniques, so that in spite of globalization and jet-setting soloists, opera still retains a measure of national difference.

In different world cities there is often a visible sign of the fault-line observed in Fanny Burney's *Evelina* (see Box 8.1) over two centuries ago. They are local resolutions of the tension felt by Mr Branghton, and represent a partial step to democratization

---

Box 8.1

A view of opera from eighteenth-century England:

"What a jabbering they make!" cried Mr Branghton ...

"Pray what's the reason they can't as well sing in English? – but I suppose the fine folks would not like it, if they could understand it."

"How unnatural their action is!," said the son; "why now who ever saw an Englishman put himself in such out-of-the-way postures?"

"So, Miss," said Mr Branghton, "you're quite in the fashion, I see; – so you like Operas? Well, I'm not so polite; I can't like nonsense, let it be never so much the taste."

(Quoted from the novel *Evelina* by Fanny Burney (1778) in Brophy (1964: 287)

of opera (moving it closer to ordinary people): one finds pairs of buildings for performing music theater. The larger will often specialize in operatic genres somehow more associated with its privileged history (e.g., tragedy; Wagnerian music-drama; international mainstream works), whereas the other will tend to specialize in comedy, and more locally oriented works (e.g., operetta; works by local composers; those using spoken dialogue instead of recitative). Various names attach to all these genres; today we don't much bother with such "generic labels," because the concept of genre has been succeeded by (a) the substitution of an international core repertory, (b) the broad division between "operas" and "musicals," and (c) the systematic desire of many composers and librettists to do away with old forms and thinking on principle. Yet the old association between a social context (e.g., elite, bourgeois, or working-class) and a certain *place* of music-theater entertainment is still around. And in days gone by these associations – what Henry Stobart calls "the marking of territory" (chapter 6) – went additionally with a system of genres appropriate to that "territory." In effect, it is always wrong to think of opera as an autonomous product, even if exportable. Local performance automatically changes many matters; and "bourgeois opera" meant one thing in 1920s Germany, but a different thing in 1980s Russia, or in 1680s France.

Comedy, it seems, is always vital to the future of musical theater, whether American musicals, Viennese operetta, or London's "Gilbert and Sullivan" variety. Musicals may stress entertainment at the expense of pretension, but now their index of ambition is so wide that the best constitute a canonic mainstream. Writing music theater for profit without subsidy is a venerable practice. Yet another way of escaping "bourgeois opera" is – as Glastonbury suggests – by simply taking it away from older privileged territory. The student theater, the arts center, the school, park, or traveling wagon have all been used for opera performance; much research remains to be done on the role of travelling opera troupes in the past. Modern technology can help to erase some of the acoustic difficulties, but miking-up the voice or adopting a synthesizer is also a cultural marker here: the traditionally oriented audience at the Holland Park opera season (in London) would never stand for less than natural sound, even though it be disturbed by the raucous protests of local peacocks.

And the comic spirit is still regularly used in opera criticism. As weapons against dubious practice or taste, pretension or ignorance, irony and burlesque constitute an old tradition. But they still do the trick, as Andrew Clements showed recently when reviewing Verdi's *La forza del destino* at Covent Garden. He began by noting sarcastically that "the cheers on opening night showed that some opera-goers, at least, were delighted to find the art of coarse opera alive and well," and continued:

> This is the kind of evening that gives Italian opera a bad name, with dramatically implausible performers shouting at the tops of their voices while acting as if trying to get the attention of an audience somewhere in the next county … [Verdi's] great

crowd scenes are arranged with all the dramatic flair of a school photograph. To their credit, the Royal Opera Chorus look as embarrassed about what they are doing as the rest of us are to witness it.

Technology has quite recently made opera more intelligible, as well as more audible: we now see a choice of language subtitles to opera DVDs. And local-language surtitles solve Mr Branghton's problem in the theater, being added on a screen above the stage. We once struggled to remember Italian-language jokes to get the best out of Mozart's *Il nozze di Figaro* sung at the Met or the Staatsoper or Covent Garden. Now the appropriate translation, which appears on cue, has taken away that need. The jury is still out in the debate over what the possible losses might be. It is hard to argue against surtitles on historical grounds, because in the eighteenth century the house lights remained suffi-ciently bright during the show for people to read the words – and a translation if necessary – in their own copy of the libretto (that is, the word-book). In effect, surtitles achieve the same end in a parallel way.

Analyzing the workings of opera

The camel

In a way, operas can be compared to camels, i.e., the animal proverbially designed by a committee. There exist thousands of defunct operas and musi-cals, and most of them became defunct precisely because the different parts contributed by separate people failed to work properly together, and in good proportion. To have a good working musical drama (strong enough to with-stand future performances) one needs every element to work convincingly alongside the others. It is difficult to achieve this, partly because there is no rule. Each new work is a separate mixture of elements; the danger is either that the forms might not suit the subject, or the vocal solos might distract from the action, or the music might be uninspiring, or the story not communicated effectively. All that is without considering the contingent difficulties of staging and singing. Each person in the auditorium is liable to have, in addition, a different perception (mental as well as physical) of the activity in progress. One will privilege the singer's tone, another the spectacle, another the score. (Anton Bruckner, the symphonic composer, is rumored to have sat through Wagner's *Tristan und Isolde* with his eyes closed. This of course remains a valuable option to anyone wishing to relieve either bore-dom or disgust.)

Creators of opera are normally too busy to write systematically about their art. So we glean what we can from their letters, prefaces, or program notes.

Other writers have supplied frameworks for discussion: Pierluigi Petrobelli, for example, has put forward (1994: 127) the notion of three "systems" which, in musical theater, "act simultaneously, each operating in accordance with its own nature and laws," to combine in creating "something more than their sum total": *action* on stage, *verbal expression* of dialogue within the libretto or book, and *music*, played as well as sung. "The function of the music is twofold," he says; "it establishes the temporal dimension of the dramatic events, and it characterizes them through its own means." So the music sets the pace of events seen, but also comments upon these events. Petrobelli often draws attention to the structure of the poetry (incidentally, it *was* always poetry; prose only came in during the late nineteenth century): he shows that the librettist's internal forms interact with the composer's decisions as to how to overlay the poetry with music. These will be highly sensitive decisions; in any show, we presume that the words must be valued as carriers of information (e.g., motivation, tone, character). Although the singer-actor can vary the dynamics, shading, and tempo, s/he is constrained regarding the pitch, local rhythms, and duration of syllables. The composer fixes all these, plus the harmony and accompaniment, choosing how to group the words relative to the information needed for the narrative, at that point. As soon as s/he composes a vocal line, some distortion of spoken and poetic values sets in.

Box 8.2

Petrobelli's "Three systems"

1. *The dramatic action*, in which the events on stage unfold
2. *The verbal organization* of the dialogue which embodies the way the characters interact on stage
3. *The music*, including the instrumental accompaniment, which establishes the "temporal dimension" of events, but also characterizes them as well

From Petrobelli (1994: 127).

A more ambitious attempt at defining similar "systems," by Ulrich Weisstein (1982), accounts for basic operations of the operatic "camel" across four hundred years of time. He discusses a spectrum of views, which will also give us an opportunity to take in a little opera history as we go. One end of Weisstein's spectrum acknowledges those who have denied opera any true dramatic validity at all; similar views are held by some today. On the other hand there are those who, like Richard Wagner, believe that "opera is a veritable symbiosis in which sense and sound unite as equals" (Weisstein 1982: 25).

In Peri's *Dafne* and *Euridice* and Monteverdi's *Orfeo*, the literary element – the poetic values – were strongly reflected in the musical shaping. Here, and at many later junctures (Weisstein says), opera has been regarded as "essentially a literary genre," involving the perception of dramatic poetry rendered through music. A strong indication of this long-held view rests in the fact that reviews of opera in the past (as well as now) will often hardly discuss the music at all. They discuss the plot, give opinions on it, mention the singers, but little more. Whereas we say "Verdi's" or "Handel's" work, the past might have referred to an opera title as a signifier of an entity differently balanced.

In the later Baroque period, and at any time up to the present, another view has been that opera "is primarily spectacle" (Weisstein 1982: 25), entertainment for the senses above all. A separate category contains those views of opera where music's influence is weighted the more heavily. Weisstein quotes Mozart's letter of 13 October 1781 during the production of *Die Entführung aus dem Serail*: "an opera that is well designed must, therefore, please all the more; where words are written expressly for the Music and not merely to suit some miserable rhyme here and there." However, the same letter makes it clear that Mozart's music will be tailored to the drama: "if we composers always just follow our rules [he means, purely musical ones] … we would come up with a kind of music that is just as useless as their librettos" (Spaethling 2004: 289). Whether the fault of untalented poets or unresponsive composers, the specter of the operatic camel was what Mozart had in mind here, the danger of a lack of proper function and proportion.

Weisstein's "pro-music" category in fact better suits operas of the Italian High Baroque, the age of Mozart's parents and grandparents. In its so-called opera seria style, the musical value of solo arias dictated the entire design of the work itself. The outward action almost stops during the arias, which are mostly of the same pattern ABA′ (called the da capo form). They usually end with a vocal cadenza and the singer always goes off-stage afterwards, making the arrangement of the plot highly artificial. Today we have a quite different concept of dramatic realism. But there was no necessary contradiction felt at the time between a succession of gorgeous arias, and a dramatic representation of a historical plot. Some audience members focused on the singing, some on the poetry, some on playing cards, drinking or talking to their neighbor.

Wagner is famed for his totalizing word *Gesamtkunstwerk*, that is, a work of dramatic art in which every ingredient should somehow fuse together (*gesamt*). To arrive at this personal and influential position, Wagner first deconstructed existing operatic practice of his time in essay form, thinking each element through and rebuilding the framework together on new principles. The practical result was first seen in the *Ring* cycle, conceived in the late 1840s but not completed or performed until 1876. In four linked operatic works, lasting some seventeen hours, the composer attempted successfully to control all aspects of the event by writing his own texts (libretto and music), designing his own theater, and producing his operas on stage. It was natural that this achievement should have dominated thinking about opera – and composing it – for decades afterwards. One of Wagner's ways of imposing coherence across the operas was to make musical cross-reference using Leitmotivs (i.e., "leading motives"). Because these were made to be flexible and easy to remember, he could develop them along with the developing situations. They certainly "characterize stage events" in Petrobelli's terms, but they also do so in a way that emphasizes the "psychology" of characters by taking us into their (imagined) minds, "recalling" (as we suppose that they do) past events which bear on future actions.

Box 8.3

Wagner's operatic cycle *Der Ring des Nibelungen* (The Ring of the Nibelung)
1. *Das Rheingold* (The Gold of the River Rhine) in one act (set out in four scenes). Music composed in 1853–4.
2. *Die Walküre* (The Valkyrie) in three acts. Music composed in 1854–6.
3. *Siegfried* in three acts. Music composed in 1856–7 and 1864–71.
4. *Götterdämmerung* (The Twilight of the Gods) in a Prologue and three acts. Music composed in 1869–74.

Weisstein's final category is most important both for some twentieth-century types of modernism, and for the many genres of opera using spoken dialogue. "Text and music enjoy equal rights and privileges but must retain their independence" (Weisstein 1982: 25). He labels it the "anti-Wagnerian" type, relating it to the theater of Bertolt Brecht, namely "alienation," the conscious avoidance of stage illusion. Brecht demanded that the audience bring its brains to the opera; his poem "The Songs" (from which the following is an extract) explains the system at work in pieces such as *The Threepenny Opera*, or *The Rise and Fall of the City of Mahagonny* (both with Kurt Weill's music), or Stravinsky's *The Soldier's Tale*.

> Mark off clearly the songs from the rest.
> Make it clearer that this is where
> The sister art enters the play.
> Announce it by some emblem summoning music,
> By a shift of lighting
> By a caption
> By a picture.
> The actors having made themselves singers
> Will address the audience in a different tone.

(Brecht 1961: 13)

Writing in the present

If it is true that opera and musical belong as part of theater history, then they will relate to spoken theater, whenever written. For example, one can see "operatic" gestures in English Jacobean tragedy (earlier seventeenth century) even though opera did not yet exist in England: there are common dramatic tropes across European drama at the time, e.g., disguises; the theme of corruption; reversals of fortune; use of fanciful events.

Modern opera inevitably reflects the movement of twentieth-century drama in all its diversity. At one extreme there is always kitsch, defined by Milan Kundera as based on "a categorical agreement with being," and denying "the existence of anything it dislikes" (Kundera, in Peter 1988: 351). Some way away we find a huge mass of lyric dramas which explore the dramatic values and methods of earlier times. These often use the systems more or less established by Alban Berg's influential operas, *Wozzeck* (1925) and *Lulu* (orchestration left incomplete at his death in 1935; premiere of completed score given in 1979). Berg, writing his own texts, updated the Wagner legacy and ideal of fusing the words, traditional narrative values, and continuous musical fabric. His blend of twelve-tone technique with bittersweet lyricism, and his choice of dramas of what would now be dubbed "social exclusion," have inspired many followers. Berg's systematic use of objectified musical forms from the past (e.g., sonata, rondo, variations) responded to calls for a return to pre-Romantic text-music balances. But the seeds of still more radical operatic modernism came from the composer and pianist Busoni in 1916. In *Sketch of a New Aesthetic of Music* he proposed that future operas change orientation to use "pronounced dissimulation"; to use "the joke and … unreality as opposites of the seriousness and reality of life," and also "the supernatural or unnatural" in order to reflect life "in either a magic or a distorting mirror" (Busoni 2002: 276–78). This view presciently anticipated the Theatre of the Absurd, by which we mean a basically post-1945 avant-garde movement critically engaged with "the human situation in a world of shattered beliefs," in Martin Esslin's words. Esslin's (1968) subsequent discussion of the novelist-playwright Albert Camus tracks down the moral foundation of this theater to the experience of man "in a universe that is suddenly deprived of illusions and of light," as well as of reason: it portrays "a divorce between man and his life, the actor and his setting." The fact that the term "absurd" signified originally "out of harmony" in a *musical* sense is richly suggestive for opera in the present age. Post-1945 evolution of musical languages made possible the use of extremes of all elements: dissonance, tessitura, volume. It also invited plurality of vocal and instrumental techniques, including especially vocal techniques associated with jagged, expressionistic utterance; and offered a ready-made link between experimental use of music and experimental modes of dramatic expression and metaphor: as Esslin defines it, "a psychological reality expressed in images that are the outward projection of states of mind, fears, dreams, nightmares and conflicts within the personality of the author" (Esslin 1968: 23, 405). In Britain, Harrison Birtwistle's opera *The Mask of Orpheus* (1986) remains the largest-scale response to Absurdist theater, one controlled by Birtwistle's overarching sense of ritual as something inherently capable of fusing the most challenging music with new forms of theater. His subsequent *Gawain* (1991) quintessentially fuses ritual impulses with an English poetic masterpiece from the time of Richard II – one that is itself dominated by cycles of repetition, as well as visceral emotions. The result was an opera in which all constituents seemed mutually heightened in a common endeavor.

If it was complicated to prevent an opera from being like a camel in the past, it is even harder to get the necessary training nowadays. Easier, in an age of commercial trivialization and seeming material wealth, to appeal to the middle-ground audience. Easier that way for theater accountants to present a clean "bill of health" to their boards. One recent phenomenon stands as an answer to those pressures: minimalism in operatic music, applied wholesale to dramatic canvases lasting a complete evening. Famously, Philip Glass's operas have sought open and collaborative solutions to opera's postmodern identity. The challenge involves radically new organization of musical time and space; and yet Glass renews the old tradition of blending sung drama with dance (an operatic ingredient which lack of space forbids us to discuss in this chapter). *Einstein on the Beach* (1976) proved the most anti-traditional of his works, being over four hours long and abandoning sequential narrative. *Akhnaten* (1984) reflected a more traditional narrative scheme but exploded linguistic unity by using fragments from Egyptian and Hebrew texts as well as English. Many other projects followed, testing out a variety of sources including science-fiction collaborations with Doris Lessing, plus a range of multimedia projects, some using Cocteau's films shown against new Glass-originated soundtracks.

With John Adams's *Nixon in China* (1987) the new wave produced a successful and saleable opera, relying on a recognizable mixing of systems from Petrobelli's analysis above: action, verbal organization, and music. Alice Goodman's libretto artfully renewed opera as genre by rethinking its inherited relations with real politics and power. The instruments of media (news, publicity, etc.) themselves became orchestrated into the score and the modalities of the action.

Opera's messages

In Samuel Beckett's play *Endgame* (1957) the character Hamm questions the audience's existential consciousness: "We're not beginning to ... to ... mean something?" Artistic meaning, up to our period, rested on the assumption that sense could be made of the world and that a particular moral purpose be necessarily found within the text (whether poem, play, picture, or opera). Indeed, a specific homily might be sung at the end of an opera: after the death of Don Giovanni (demons having dragged him down to hell), the other characters in Mozart's (and Da Ponte's) *Don Giovanni* sing, as an ensemble, "the ancient moral": "Sinners finally meet their just reward and always will" (Da Ponte 1971: 103). But no chorus condemns Nero and Poppea in Monteverdi's (and Busenello's) opera *L'incoronazione di Poppea* ("The Coronation of Poppea"), where the emperor and his replacement wife conclude events in a duet expressing the triumph of happiness and sexual politics. This is because Busenello knew that audiences would remember that, three years later, Nero kills Poppea anyway. John Adams's (and Alice Goodman's) *Nixon in China* offers a number of morals, sung by different characters, offering plurality rather than certainty: "The revolution must not end" (Chiang Ch'ing); "Speak softly and don't show your hand" (Nixon). A sense of numinous awareness reaches the ageing Chou En-lai, in the opera's last lines: "Outside this room the chill of grace / Lies heavy on the morning grass."

In the last part of this chapter we outline a few topics concerning particular ways that musical drama today is studied from the perspective of its "messages," for opera's artistic power has always been given responsibility for articulating them.

Singing as persuasion

Some of the best epigrams on the unique ways of opera have been written by the poet W. H. Auden (himself the librettist of operas as diverse as Britten's *Paul Bunyan*, Hans Werner Henze's *The Bassarids*, and Stravinsky's *The Rake's Progress*). Consider, for example, the dictum, "its pure artifice renders opera the ideal medium for tragic myth." Auden (1963) argues that musical power, rendered by the human voice, showed him that, in seeing Wagner's *Tristan und Isolde*, "two souls, weighing over two hundred pounds apiece, were transfigured by a transcendent power." He contrasts his satisfying visit to this opera with an unsuccessful filmic treatment of the Tristan theme by Jean Cocteau, *L'Eternel retour*, which he saw during the same week. Cocteau used young, attractive actors, but the effect of the mythic power of the tale was lost precisely because it was *too* natural: the cause of their love seemed merely "a consequence of their beauty."

But singing is not just a means to a beautiful sound: it is also an existential statement of one's condition. We sing for exaltation, or in a group, or in sorrow, or to children, but not normally in discourse to each other. That is why Auden felt that "No good opera plot can be sensible," "sensible" meaning in this case subject more to reasoning and logic than to discovery of something (e.g., a truth, a secret, a person). But he allowed that operas can and must impart information and use logical statements in articulating a personal aim. Although singing in opera suits what Auden calls "passionate and wilful" characters, that is not the whole story. Most operas make use of recitative or spoken dialogue, and there are countless operas that portray ordinary, or comic, or uneducated characters. Opera, for Auden, can demonstrate that "joy, tenderness and nobility" are not the preserve of one class, "but are experienced by everybody," and this transformative power is "one of the glories of opera" (Auden 1963: 465–74).

Characters in spoken drama cannot be made to speak simultaneously for more than a brief and exceptional moment. But of course in opera – as done from the earliest times – two or more characters can be made to sing together. A good librettist and composer may heighten a situation of joy, perplexity, sorrow, or exultation with simultaneous emotions expressed in an ensemble. Though he was sparing of writing them himself, Auden even considered that "the crowning glory of opera is the big ensemble."

Opera houses normally employ singers purely in order to participate in choral music. This is no casual expenditure. The fact is, that groups, crowds, processions, and ceremonials have always formed part of Western drama; the invention of opera meant that such groups could be made to participate in the action as never before. They can also act in real opposition to a solo character, challenging that character's identity or position or choice of action. In an opera like Britten's *Peter Grimes* or Musorgsky's *Boris Godunov* the chorus can legitimately be spoken of as a main character in itself, standing for a specific community within the action, and their *beliefs*. As a result, their emotions or desires are as explicitly dealt with as their actions. To discuss such techniques is also to discuss the portrayal of power relations in lyric drama. It has sometimes been remarked that, as James Parakilas (2003: 83) puts it, "grand opera was born … in the era of electoral politics, and its choral forces dramatize the political order of that era."

From semiotics to process

If theater (also TV today) presents an imaginative health-check of a society's state of mind, then opera's messages will reflect the moral preoccupations of its age. Opera can easily show power relations in force at any one time, via music as well as costume or scenery. Musical elements often act as carriers of meaning in a semiotic sense here. For example, a composer will use a melody or motif or rhythm or instrument (or several of these at once) which cultural training has taught the audience to identify with an extra-musical quality, e.g., "royalty," "thoughtfulness," "death," "the erotic." Those theorists who, like Nattiez (1990), have sought to codify such possibilities across the ages, have found that "these horizons [evoked by music] are immense, numerous and heterogeneous" because "music [is] an essential part of man's anthropological aspect." Thus music can pick up "the play of the swords in Act I [of *Don Giovanni*]" by means of "rising violin scales." Such representation obviously extends to dimensions of distance, space, heaviness, slowness, quickness, etc. But there can never be a "one-to-one correspondence among a musical signifier, the movement aroused, and the feeling evoked" (Nattiez 1990: 102, 119–20). It seems to be agreed, above all, that such musical messages are based on convention, are acquired by experience and education.

Schoenberg's observation that rhythmic identity is a primary resource for musical recognition works very well in opera. It can be related both to universals (like the "musical figure of death" discussed by Frits Noske (1977)) and to the specifics of class and societal divisions. W. J. Allanbrook's study (1983) of Mozart showed that "rhythmic gesture" was a principle that the composer embedded within the fabric of his operatic technique. Because such elements rely on the musical accompaniment for their communication, it might be thought that "rhythmic gesture" was used only in the age of the modern orchestra, e.g., as applied by Wagner in his Leitmotivs. But 140 years before Mozart, Monteverdi also used it brilliantly in the small ensemble that accompanies Poppea's nurse (sung by a man – but that is another story) when s/he sings a lullaby-aria. The audience interprets the occasion as a lullaby, because

Poppea falls asleep in the languorous afternoon air. While the Nurse's melody soothes Poppea, however, the ensemble's rhythm and rocking motif seem rather to represent the breathing pattern of the sleeper, and so to become a metaphor for sleep itself. Indeed we may well become drowsy ourselves, so hypnotic is the effect; and yet we know – if we have read the story – that danger lies just ahead. Therein lies part of opera's power: in a spoken drama a sung lullaby would represent itself, and we would understand its association with fragility and chance and childlike vulnerability. But in the opera we *feel* that vulnerability ourselves, beneath the skin.

A different strand of thought links the persuasiveness of operatic singing with another sort of power: the specifically gendered power of the female opera singer. Forty years ago, a pathbreaking book on Mozart opera by the writer Brigid Brophy (1964: 37) asserted that opera "not merely drew attention to women but pointed up the injustice of assuming that nature made them in every respect inferior to men"; indeed one of her arguments was that "liberal sympathy was drawn to women as a long oppressed class" at the very historical moment when Mozart composed. But if opera was first written around 1600, it may also be argued that the question should be put more perceptually: "What happens when we watch and *hear* a female performer?" asked Carolyn Abbate in 1993. "We are observing her, yet we are also doing something for which there's no word: the aural version of staring." Abbate links this observation with a long-standing interest in the scrutiny of operatic process itself, and concludes that "a singer, more than any other musical performer … stands before us having wrested the composing voice away from the librettist and composer who wrote the score" (Abbate 1993: 254). In other words, there is a sense in which the actors can seem to be making up the music as they go, immersed in the medium of musical sound.

This whole question – plus the question of opera as genre, as well as the female voice in opera – was tabled with supreme acuity by Judith Weir: in 1979 she composed *King Harald's Saga*, a "grand opera in 3 acts," written for unaccompanied female voice and lasting a total of about ten minutes. In narrating the Norwegian saga's story, the singer takes on eight solo roles. It seems impossible; but the opera's success in performance (appealing to the audience's brain as well as heart) shows that we should continue to demand the totally unexpected when considering the future of opera.

The question of novelty, of pushing a message, actually dominates conventional opera production now; but this is more thanks to directors rehashing older works than engaging new commissions. The recent influx of directors from "straight" theater has been very beneficial overall, also resulting in an experimental fringe of work. From this we can take as example the *Don Giovanni* conceived by the Spaniard Calixto Bieito for London, Hanover, and Barcelona in 2001. His stage set becomes a palimpsest of filth in the course of the opera: rubbish from successive scenes remains in place. There is no stone statue, or graveyard scene, or divine retribution. The moral (see earlier quotation) is therefore put aside, because Bieito wants to create only a partial interpretation of the drama as given. Mozart's score is obediently performed, but the characters act and dress in ways inspired by films directed by Scorsese, Kubrick, and Almodovar, or Inglesia's *The Day of the Beast*. The repeated use of simulated violence and sexual acts is intended (according to the program note (Walling 2004)) to impose an interpretation of Don Giovanni as an anarchic force, whose fascistic abdication of social codes somehow infects all the other characters. They, in the end, stab Giovanni to death. He laughs at them, dying in the chair to which they have bound him.

Productions cannot be right or wrong: only (as Oscar Wilde said of literature) either well done or badly done. Opera is a multimedia genre which lives by renewal and rethinking. Its power may reside in one female singer, evoking the futility of ancient battles. Opera can also resemble the proverbial camel, even if Mozart's name is on the program.

Chapter summary

This chapter has discussed the following points:

- Opera is a multimedia performance art, a type of music theater.
- Although it connects with the musical, it must also be considered as a branch of theater in the wider sense.
- It has ancient roots in human society, and is studied partly because it is valued as an ongoing cultural activity.
- This activity includes the composition of new types of operas.
- Music in opera is studied alongside text, drama, staging and performance, though it can be classed as part of musicology.
- Change in operatic style and form mirrors change in society and in the wider theater.
- Singing in opera is studied by non-singers.
- Opera has unique ways of representing characters and their relationships.
- The moral purposes of opera are often explicit, and can be studied in relation to past and present.
- As a performance art, opera is permanently subject to changing interpretation.

Discussion topics

1. Compare the merits of performing an opera in (i) the audience's own language or (ii) a foreign language.

2. What might Judith Weir's purpose have been in writing *King Harald's Saga*?
3. Would you have invited the English National Opera to Glastonbury?
4. Does the director have the right to change the ending of an opera?
5. Is minimalism the right way forward for opera?
6. Is opera dead yet?

Further reading

Abbate, Carolyn (2001), *In Search of Opera* (Princeton, NJ: Princeton University Press).
A philosophical journey into music and singing, using selected operas to connect with spectral and mechanistic images.

Dahlhaus, Carl (1979), *Richard Wagner's Music Dramas*, trans. Mary Whittall (Cambridge: Cambridge University Press).
The most concise and holistic introduction to Wagner, by the most influential scholar of his day.

Holden, Amanda (2001) (ed.), *The New Penguin Opera Guide* (London: Penguin) [an earlier edition was called *The Viking Opera Guide*].
Reference book with over eight hundred opera summaries, and a quick way into opera facts and polemics. See Rodney Milnes's Introduction for a blistering attack on modern trends including electronic surtitles.

John, Nicholas (Series Editor): English National Opera Guides (London: Calder Publications; New York, Riverrun Press).
An excellent ongoing series of some fifty guides each devoted to one or two works, including essays by specialists, with music-thematic guides, and complete librettos in translation.

Miller, Jonathan (1990) (ed.), *The Don Giovanni Book: Myths of Seduction and Betrayal* (London: Faber).
Brief essays inspired by Mozart's opera, written on sex and society by authorities on eighteenth-century culture, and edited by a famous opera director.

Parker, Roger (1994) (ed.), *The Oxford Illustrated History of Opera* (Oxford: Oxford University Press).
Readable essays designed as a complete coverage of opera history up to the late twentieth century, and as an introduction to the social role of opera in past centuries.

References

Abbate, Carolyn (1993), "Opera; or, the envoicing of women," in *Musicology and Difference: Gender and Sexuality in Music Scholarship*, ed. Ruth A. Solie (Berkeley: University of California Press), 225–58.

Adorno, Theodor W. (1993), "Bourgeois opera" in *Opera Through Other Eyes*, ed. and trans. David J. Levin (Stanford, CA: Stanford University Press), 25–43.

Allanbrook, W. J. (1983), *Rhythmic Gesture in Mozart: "Le nozze di Figaro" and "Don Giovanni"* (Chicago: Chicago University Press).

Auden, W. H. (1963), "Notes on music and opera," in *The Dyer's Hand and Other Essays* (London: Faber), 465–74.

Beckett, Samuel (1964), *Endgame* (London: Faber).

Brecht, Bertolt (1961), "The songs," in *Poems on the Theatre*, trans. by John Berger and
    Anna Bostock (Northwood: Scorpion Press).

Brophy, Brigid (1964), *Mozart the Dramatist: A New View of Mozart, his Operas and his Age*
    (London: Faber).

Busoni, Ferruccio (2002), "Sketch of a new aesthetic of music" (excerpt) trans. and
    ed. in Piero Weiss, *Opera: A History in Documents* (New York: Oxford University
    Press), 276–78.

Clements, Andrew (2004), "*La Forza del Destino*," *The Guardian* (18 October).

Da Ponte, Lorenzo (1971), *Don Giovanni*, trans. by Lionel Salter, in *W. A. Mozart: Don
    Giovanni, Idomeneo* (Cassell Opera Guides) (London: Cassell).

Drummond, John D. (1980), *Opera in Perspective* (London: Dent).

Esslin, Martin (1968), *The Theatre of the Absurd* (rev. ed.: Harmondsworth: Penguin).

Griffiths, Paul (1994), "The twentieth century: 1945 to the present day," in Parker,
    Roger (ed.), *The Oxford Illustrated History of Opera*, 317–49.

Kundera, Milan, *The Unbearable Lightness of Being*, as discussed in John Peter (1988),
    Vladimir's Carrot: Modern Drama and the Modern Imagination (London: Methuen).

Mozart's Letters, Mozart's Life (2004), ed. and trans. Robert Spaethling (London: Faber).

Nattiez, Jean-Jacques (1990), *Music and Discourse: Toward a Semiology of Music*, trans. by
    Carolyn Abbate (Princeton, NJ: Princeton University Press).

Noske, Frits (1977), *The Signifier and the Signified: Studies in the Operas of Mozart and Verdi*
    (The Hague: Martinus Nijhoff), 171–214.

Parakilas, James (2003), "The chorus," in *The Cambridge Companion to Grand Opera*,
    ed. David Charlton (Cambridge: Cambridge University Press), 76–92.

Petrobelli, Pierluigi (1994), *Music in the Theater. Essays on Verdi and Other Composers*
    (Princeton, NJ: Princeton University Press), 127–140.

Walling, Michael (2004), "*Don Giovanni*: myth and modernity," in English National
    Opera program-book.

Weisstein, Ulrich (1982), "Librettology: the fine art of coping with a Chinese twin,"
    Komparatistische Hefte, 5–6, 23–42.

9 Concert music

ERIK LEVI

Chapter preview

This chapter suggests various ways in which one might approach the vast repertory of concert music, extending from compositions written for the secular courts of the seventeenth and eighteenth centuries to those of the present day. It attempts to explain why such music was written, to which audiences it was targeted, and to what extent the evolution and growing popularity of the concert changed both the practices of the composers and the expectations of the public. Alongside this discussion is an examination of the ways in which the forms and functions of concert music have been transformed over time from its origins in sacred and courtly life to the explosion of activity in the urban centers of Europe during the nineteenth century. Against this background, specific genres were established, some continuing to hold sway up to the present day. At the same time, technological developments during the twentieth century engendered the current crisis where the "museum culture" of classical music leads an uneasy co-existence with the competing claims of contemporary concert repertoire on the one hand and the commercial "culture industry" on the other.

Key issues

- How does music influence the reaction of critics and audiences?
- The "canon" and its formation.
- Nationalism in music.
- The notion of musical style periods.
- Genres of concert music: concerto, symphony, sonata.
- The avant-garde, modernism, and postmodernism.

Introduction

The repertory explored in this chapter encompasses a wide variety of music that has become part and parcel of the concert repertory, extending from the intimate genres of song, piano music, and chamber music through to the more public arenas of concerto, symphony, and oratorio. The evolution of this repertory from the eighteenth to the twenty-first centuries is closely allied to the shifting political and economic circumstances in which concert music was produced, and to technological changes which in the twenty-first century enabled it to be disseminated to a much larger public than ever before. At the same time, such developments served to hasten a growing rift between a museum culture of classical music and a world where populism and commercialism are frequently valued more highly than aesthetic beauty and technical mastery.

Patronage and funding

On the face of it, the term concert music seems rather loose. Is it simply a convenient umbrella that can cover any music not intended for performance in the opera house? If so, how do we make sense of the very different types of music that are associated with the term? Is it possible to draw any tangible connections between the concert music composed for different functions and performing venues and addressed to different audiences? To what extent has the public concert changed in character from its earliest manifestations at the end of the eighteenth century to that of the present day?

What is a concert?

You will be familiar with the shape of modern concert performances. Public concerts in the early nineteenth century were very different, however. In all likelihood, the program would have been much more extended in duration, and would have embraced a much greater range of musical genres. A lengthy multi-movement work like a symphony might not have been performed in its entirety, and if it was, the audience may well have clapped between movements. In some cases audience demand may have prompted the performers to repeat a particularly crowd-pleasing movement, thus disrupting the natural sequence of the work. Occasionally a work may have been performed complete but interspersed with musical material with which it had no direct connection. This happened, for example, at the first performance of Beethoven's Violin Concerto in Vienna in 1806, when after playing the first movement the soloist Franz Clement gave a rendition of one of his own works which he executed on one string and with the violin held upside down. After this he returned to perform the second and third movements.

   That such antics could have taken place at a public concert seems incomprehensible to us, not least because the work in question is now widely recognized as one of the great masterpieces of Western music. But this episode also reminds us that no matter how such music might have been served up to earlier audiences, one of the prime functions of a concert has always been to entertain. Moreover, since a concert requires considerable sums of financial investment, particularly if a large number of performers is involved, it follows that the driving force behind the repertory that has found favor in different eras is inextricably linked with the specific economic and social conditions that were predominant at any one time. In essence concert music could never have survived without the necessary patronage and funding. Charting its history over a period of three centuries reflects a response to the requirements of different paymasters.

Aristocrats as paymasters

Following the divisions between sacred and secular music outlined in the chapter on early music, the paymasters for concert music in the seventeenth and eighteenth centuries would have been drawn almost exclusively from the aristocracy. Concert music was therefore the province of the court. Composers were given the responsibility to provide concert music for the entertainment and pleasure of the aristocracy. Their work could also serve propaganda purposes in symbolizing and glorifying the relative well-being of a particular province or country. Composers were made fully aware of their responsibilities in this regard, recognizing clear designations in terms of the function and purpose of the concert music they were providing. They also acknowledged that their music had to remain within recognized stylistic boundaries that were often determined by current fashions.

One might imagine that the clearly designated function, purpose, and style of concert music during this period acted as a severe limitation. Although demonstrating technical competence in the handling of melody, harmony, and instrumentation, composers working under such circumstances would surely have been hampered in their ability to provide anything of lasting artistic value. But while few composers would have bothered themselves as to whether their music might outlive its original function, the opportunity to effect creative freedom was by no means denied. Take Joseph Haydn for example. Throughout most of his adult life Haydn was employed at the court of Esterházy to provide both sacred and secular concert music. His patrons proved to be extremely enlightened, attracting some of the finest instrumentalists in Europe to play in Haydn's court orchestra. Working under conditions that allowed him a modicum of artistic freedom that may have been denied to colleagues in other European courts, Haydn was able to use these instrumentalists as his laboratory for compositional experiment. Choosing to focus his creative energies on the burgeoning genres of the symphony and string quartet, Haydn sought increasingly ingenious ways of manipulating his material without ever transgressing accepted norms.

Haydn's career spanned the latter half of the eighteenth century – a period of considerable turmoil that culminated in the destruction of the old social order through the French Revolution and technological change as a result of the Industrial Revolution. Such cataclysmic developments inevitably affected the evolution of concert music, which could no longer be regarded as the exclusive property of the aristocracy. With an emerging middle class eager to establish its own modes of cultural identity, not to mention the vast movements of population away from the countryside to the growing industrial centers of England, France, and Germany, came a demand for different and more varied types of concert music.

The middle class as paymasters

As already mentioned the French Revolution had profound repercussions in undermining the role and status of the aristocracy throughout Europe at the close of the eighteenth century. With the decline of the courts, the middle classes began to take their place as patrons of the arts, empowered by increasing financial wealth that accrued from the increasing industrialization of urban centers.

The emerging middle-class audiences of the early nineteenth century looked to concert music as a means of escaping the drudgery of industrial and metropolitan life. Defining their own specific cultural roots, they demanded music that provided not only entertainment and excitement, but also intellectual and spiritual edification. Given such requirements it is hardly surprising that it was the middle class that established and reinforced the idea of the canon – that concert music could transcend the period in which it was written, attain long-lasting popularity, and be cherished over generations.

There is not space here to detail all the consequences that resulted from middle-class appropriation of concert music, but some general points can be drawn. One particularly germane issue is the growing division that was to develop between so-called "serious" and "light" music. Although Mozart and Beethoven may have expended most of their creative energy on composing overtures, symphonies, and concertos, they were sufficiently versatile to turn their hand occasionally to the more functional area of dance music. Yet by the end of the nineteenth century, few composers were prepared to encompass such a wide creative spectrum, preferring to create a specific niche for themselves. In Vienna, for example, Johann Strauss established an exclusive reputation as the composer of waltzes and polkas, never entertaining the thought of attempting a symphony or large-scale orchestral work. Likewise, his exact contemporary Anton Bruckner focused most of his attention on composing lengthy symphonies, resisting the lure of greater financial security that might have followed had he chosen to write dances. The divisions between different categories of concert music intensified during the twentieth century with the advent of the avant-garde, as we shall see later in this chapter.

Paralleling the divisions that emerged between different categories of concert music were sharp distinctions in the role and status of its practitioners. At the upper echelons were the virtuoso performer and professional musician. The virtuosi toured the metropolitan centers of Europe astounding audiences with performances of their own music that stretched the technical capabilities of their chosen instrument to its very limits. Often they would accept teaching posts in one of the new educational establishments that sprang up in the nineteenth century to offer professional musical training. At the same time, the demands of the amateur musician could not be ignored, particularly as industrialization enabled the production of instruments on a much greater and more affordable scale than ever before. Consequently, concert music embraced not only highly specialized technically demanding compositions, but also works designed for amateur performance and enjoyment in the home.

In essence, concert music in the nineteenth century generated a vast network of spin-offs. For instance, the wider dissemination and greater accessibility of concert music would be immeasurably enhanced by the unprecedented growth of music publishing in European metropolitan centers. Music publishers could act as patrons of certain composers, but they also had to protect their businesses. As a result they sought novel ways of making concert music available to the widest possible public. For evidence of their enterprise, you need only look at a copy of music published in the nineteenth century. If you take a brief glance at the advertisements on the front or back cover of an early Simrock edition of the music of Brahms, for example, you will notice that his output was not merely published in its original instrumentation, but also appeared in various unexpected arrangements. The most obvious examples of this practice were the two-piano, piano-duet, and solo-piano transcriptions of his four symphonies. Before the era of recording in the twentieth century, such transcriptions were commonplace, and in many cases enjoyed the imprimatur of the composer.

Another aspect of patronage that served to institutionalize concert music was journalism. From the nineteenth century onwards, the music critic became a spokesperson for the middle class, acting as an arbiter of taste and determinant of cultural standards. In such circumstances, a critic had the potential to wield great power and influence, as happened in late nineteenth-century Vienna, where Eduard Hanslick mounted a staunch campaign of vitriolic opposition to the "progressive" music of Liszt and Wagner and support for the more traditional principles adopted by Brahms.

Power and status

The great metropolitan centers of nineteenth-century Europe viewed the development of a vibrant musical life as an important status symbol and as an extremely effective vehicle for demonstrating cultural and municipal prestige. Yet to sustain such highly privileged art forms required considerable financial investment. We should remember that many of the great orchestras that tour the world these days were founded in the nineteenth century. Almost certainly their performances took place in halls that were specially built at the time by the city authorities for this purpose.

Although critics and concert managers played no small part in influencing the repertory that would be offered to audiences, far greater power rested with the conductors who were appointed to direct the municipal orchestras. Of course, conductors often acted as exclusive promoters of their own music. But if they were required to devise an entire season of programs, they would also have to engage with other repertory. Given such responsibilities, they were able to shape public taste in profound ways. Consider for example Mendelssohn's role in the revival of interest in the music of Bach. Had the composer not taken upon himself to organize the first public performance of Bach's *St Matthew Passion* in Berlin in 1830, over a hundred years after its premiere (1727), it is questionable whether Bach's music would have exercised such a strong influence on early Romantic music. Likewise, Liszt used his position as music director in Weimar and organizer of the Allgemeine Deutsche Musikverein to conduct the works of many unknown composers, thereby helping to enhance their status with the general public.

Not all conductors succeeded in persuading the public to accept their own music. Indeed, the tendency for conductors to double up as active and successful composers tended to recede by the end of the nineteenth century. This did not, however, mean that a conductor could no longer exercise any creative ingenuity. On the contrary, conductors sought to develop individualistic and often idiosyncratic interpretations of the standard orchestral repertory. Using autocratic methods of rehearsal, they were able to impose their own larger-than-life personalities on the music of others, and to marshal the orchestras they controlled to produce a very distinctive sonority and style of playing.

But some conductors also saw themselves as enlightened educators. Realizing the danger of concert music becoming the exclusive province of the middle-class intelligentsia, they sought ways of bringing it to a wider public. The popular concert series devised in London's Crystal Palace by Sir August Manns and in the suburbs of Paris by Jules Pasdeloup were two such ventures that proved to be extremely successful. The programs presented by these conductors reflected a clever balance between "popular" and "serious" music and managed to attract extremely large audiences. Fortunately such idealism did not founder after the deaths of these two conductors. The spirit of Manns and Pasdeloup is enshrined in the Henry Wood Promenade Concerts founded at the end of the nineteenth century along similar lines, and still going strong.

> **Box 9.1 Comparison of Couperin's Concerts Royaux with Beethoven Piano Concerto No. 5 "Emperor"**
>
> One effective way of illustrating the different system of patronage and function of concert music of the early eighteenth and early nineteenth century is to examine two works with similar titles.
>
> The French composer François Couperin (1688–1733) was appointed one of the organists at the Chapelle du roi. As its title suggests, he composed his set of four Concerts Royaux in 1722 for the regular Sunday concerts organized at the court of Louis XIV. One might expect such a work to follow the conventions of a concerto in placing a solo instrument or group of instruments against a larger ensemble. Yet Couperin's Concerts Royaux are in fact chamber works of great structural ingenuity, scored for a small ensemble of wind and string instruments with harpsichord, and would have been performed in a small intimate auditorium.
>
> Beethoven composed the last of his five piano concertos in 1809. The work was written primarily to demonstrate Beethoven's prowess as a virtuoso of the fortepiano, an instrument that was gaining widespread popularity during the composer's lifetime. The huge dimensions of the work, the enormous technical difficulty of the solo part and the sense of drama and conflict that is unleashed as piano and orchestra vie with each other in unfolding the musical argument make it a landmark in the development of the genre. Although there are moments of intimacy in this long work, its essential quality is heroic.

Concert repertory in the nineteenth century

Having discussed some of the background issues that determined the evolution of concert music, it is appropriate to look in more detail at the genres that were firmly established during the nineteenth century. Broadly speaking, concert music can be divided into two very broad categories, public and intimate. The public genres include oratorio, symphony, orchestral program music, and concerto, while the intimate genres embrace chamber and piano music as well as song.

Both categories experienced transformations in popularity and character during this period. Burdened by adherence to the conventions of the Baroque and Classical eras the oratorio, most favored in England, largely fell out of fashion by the end of the century, being most closely associated with composers who promoted a conservative musical language. In contrast the symphony, although not so prolifically cultivated as at the end of the eighteenth century, emerged as the major genre of orchestral music, generating a flexibility of utterance that could embrace indigenous national styles and make reference to extra-musical elements.

Transferring the intimate genres of string quartet, piano music, and song from the drawing room to the concert hall inevitably resulted in changes of emphasis. By the end of the century, for example, it was more customary for some composers to write songs with orchestral accompaniment rather than with piano. Late nineteenth-century string quartets were richer and more orchestral in texture than ones composed earlier in the century, while piano compositions exploiting brilliance and virtuosity were deemed more suitable and compositionally significant than character pieces intended for the salon.

The public genres

1. Oratorio

Arguably the most public concert genre of the nineteenth century was the oratorio, not least because it constituted the most effective forum for bringing together performers of amateur status (choirs) and professionals (vocal soloists and orchestra). The religious message contained in the oratorio enabled communities in metropolitan centers to engage with spiritual matters outside the realms of the Church. Given a suitably dramatic libretto, the oratorio could also transfer some of the theatrical excitement of the opera house into the concert hall.

As a genre, the oratorio had enjoyed a long and distinguished history which stretched back to the seventeenth century. Handel remained the most successful exponent of the genre, the finest of his oratorios enjoying regular revivals particularly in England many years after his death. In view of Handel's continued popularity, it is not surprising that nineteenth-century composers of oratorio sought to emulate him, to the extent of imitating some of the stylistic features that were associated with the Baroque era. Consider, for example, Mendelssohn's *St. Paul* (1839) and *Elijah* (1846), two of the most durable oratorios of the period. Compared to most of the rest of Mendelssohn's output, it is noticeable that the composer consciously applied more "old-fashioned" gestures (Bachian chorales in *St. Paul*, Handelian recitative and dramatic choruses in *Elijah*) to the musical argument. No doubt, these allusions to a much venerated tradition proved comforting especially to English audiences who were so familiar with the work of Handel. Of course, such reliance on music of the past raises the interesting question as to why a work like *Elijah* enjoyed such sustained popularity, particularly in Victorian England, where it was never dismissed out of hand as being stylistically moribund.

2. Symphony

Compared to the oratorio, the symphony appeared, at least on the surface, to be less weighed down with responsibilities to the distant past. Firmly established by Haydn and Mozart at the end of the eighteenth century as the most technically and musically challenging of orchestral genres, it was subsequently transformed into a confessional statement of artistic intent which can be equated with the novel. Without doubt Beethoven played the major role in effecting this transformation, expanding its structure, orchestration, and levels of expression, and even sanctioning the addition of a chorus in the finale of the Ninth Symphony (1824).

Because Beethoven's achievement was so wide-ranging, few of his successors could withstand his influence. Such influence could be stimulating in that it opened up further possibilities for intensifying the dramatic argument of a symphony, especially given the increased power and expression of orchestral instruments as they became more technologically sophisticated. At the same time, Beethoven's example could also be deemed intimidating. Once the master's symphonies had entered the canon and received regular performance in concerts throughout Europe, any budding composer that presented a symphony in front of the public was burdened by an unusually high level of expectation. Inevitably, the musical worth of a new symphony would be measured against that of Beethoven. Not surprisingly, some composers were extremely wary of such comparisons, and in the case of Brahms, for example, waited many years before committing themselves to such an ordeal.

3. Overture and program music

One path opened up by Beethoven in his "Pastoral" Symphony (1808) was the potential for orchestral music to express extra-musical ideas. In this work, Beethoven attempts an imitation of the sounds of nature, including bird song and the rippling of a brook. The most ambitious and dramatic effects appear in the fourth movement, which depicts the sound and fury of a raging storm. Of course, programmatic instrumental music had been composed well before the nineteenth century. Some notable examples included *Battalia* by the seventeenth-century Baroque composer Heinrich Biber, the *Biblical Sonatas* of Johann Kuhnau, and perhaps most famously of all, the *Four Seasons* by Antonio Vivaldi. But the orchestra afforded composers far greater possibilities for graphic representation through exploiting a much wider range of colors and timbres.

As Hector Berlioz's *Treatise on Instrumentation* (1843/4, revised 1855) demonstrates, some of the most striking orchestral effects that attracted composers originated in the opera house. Given their obvious effectiveness, it is not surprising that they should find their way into the concert hall. The first route in this process was via the overtures that preceded the opera. The slow introductions to Mozart's overtures to *Don Giovanni* and *Die Zauberflöte* provided audiences with a brief musical snapshot of the ensuing drama. Although Mozart may not have intended his overtures to be performed as separate pieces outside the opera house, by the beginning of the nineteenth century they had achieved considerable popularity as effective curtain-raisers to public concerts.

Mozart's successors seized on the potential of the operatic overture to transcend its initial function as a short piece designed to quieten audiences before the curtain is raised. Bringing extra-musical and structural significance to the overture allowed composers more opportunity to present the essence of the drama in purely orchestral terms. In this context it is not surprising that composers resorted to offering listeners tantalizing anticipations of the musical substance of the opera, presenting its most memorable themes and orchestral effects.

Some opera overtures, such as those to Weber's *Der Freischütz* and Rossini's *Guillaume Tell*, became successful concert items in their own right, their popularity exceeding that of the operas themselves. That such music could easily survive outside its original context acted as a spur to other composers to appropriate the genre for the concert hall, writing works of a dramatic and programmatic nature which were totally independent of an opera. In its earliest manifestation, the concert overture, which was to be superseded to a certain extent by the symphonic poem in the latter half of the nineteenth century, afforded the opportunity for composers to attempt a musical representation of a wide variety of literary and dramatic works.

Despite objections from conservative critics such as Hanslick that orchestral program music reflected a debasement of musical values in comparison with the perceived abstract purity of the symphony, concert overtures by Mendelssohn, Berlioz, and Tchaikovsky quickly established themselves as part of the canon, as did a limited number of symphonic poems by Liszt and Richard Strauss. Obviously the lasting success of these works rested primarily with the strength and quality of their musical ideas and the brilliance of their orchestration. But it should also be remembered that the audiences who heard this music for the first time would have been well versed in the literary and visual arts, and would therefore identify more readily with the subject-matter the composers had chosen for their works.

Orchestral program music also served an important function in establishing the musical credentials of an emerging nation. Given that the structural demands of an overture or symphonic poem, not to mention the burden of tradition, were far more flexible than those of the symphony, composers found it easier to give vent to feelings of strong identification with their cultural heritage. Amongst the most obvious musical tools they could use for this purpose were the appropriation of indigenous folk melodies and dance rhythms. Such elements, combined with a program that was inspired by national legends or made reference to critical historical events in a nation's history, could attain an artistic and political significance that extended well beyond the concert hall, as happened after the first performances of Smetana's cycle of symphonic poems, *Má Vlast*.

4. Concerto

Although orchestral program music of the nineteenth century abounds in musical gestures that derive from the opera house, the most overtly operatic of all the public concert-music genres was undoubtedly the concerto. The notion of a soloist playing an extended piece of music against the background of a larger body of orchestral players provided audiences with potentially exciting visual and theatrical spectacle. Some composers exploited the possibilities for musical dialogue and discourse in the most imaginative ways. The slow movement of Beethoven's Fourth Piano Concerto, for example, presents the two protagonists of soloist and orchestra in direct opposition to each other. They argue with and cajole each other as if engaged in a heated conversation, only reluctantly resolving their differences in a final cadence.

Few nineteenth-century composers of concertos attained such levels of musical sophistication, the prime motivation for writing such works being the display of technical virtuosity on the part of the soloist. In the piano concertos of Hummel and Chopin and the violin concertos of Paganini and Wieniawski, the orchestra assumes an entirely subsidiary role in the musical proceedings. But this unbalanced relationship was by no means accepted by all composers. In his two piano concertos Brahms attempted a synthesis between symphonic and concertante elements. The sheer structural dimension and gloomy dramatic tension of the First Piano Concerto baffled conservative audiences at its first performance in Leipzig in 1859. They had probably expected to hear a work of brilliant display and lyrical beauty in the manner of Mendelssohn's two essays in the genre. Instead the work assumes the intellectual weight and grand proportions of a symphony for piano and orchestra. Interestingly, the technical challenges of the solo piano part are no less fearsome than those of the concertos of Liszt, but the element of display is cleverly subsumed into the musical fabric, a practice that is continued on an even grander scale in the Second Piano Concerto, where Brahms dispenses with the customary three-movement structure, adding a Scherzo to make the symphonic connection even more palpable.

Intimate genres

By its very nature, music composed for a small group of instruments, and commonly termed chamber music, serves a somewhat different function to that of orchestral music. On the most obvious level, it would be heard to its best advantage in a much smaller auditorium than the conventional large-scale concert hall. There is plenty of evidence to suggest that much chamber music was originally written for performance in a small drawing room. In some cases, the question of addressing an audience was less important than giving pleasure to instrumentalists who enjoyed the challenges of playing music together.

1. String quartet

By the end of the eighteenth century, the string quartet came to be regarded as the most important of the chamber-music genres. Largely through the efforts of Haydn and Mozart, it had been transformed from a divertimento, essentially a light-hearted work designed for entertainment, into a multi-movement structure of much greater scale and substance on a par with the symphony. Both composers invested the string quartet with intellectual qualities that were designed to appeal to a musically educated audience. Many of their works abound in intricate contrapuntal writing, the most obvious examples being the fugal finales to Haydn's Op. 20 set or the last movement of Mozart's G major Quartet K387. Yet at the same time as emphasizing the esoteric aspects of the string quartet, neither composer overlooked the opportunities that the medium afforded for instrumental virtuosity, as is evident from the enormously taxing first violin writing that Haydn composed for Johann Tost, or the stratospherically high cello parts that Mozart devised in the three quartets he dedicated to King Frederick William of Prussia, a keen amateur cellist.

Several factors determined the gravitation of the string quartet, and other established chamber-music genres such as the piano trio, from the drawing room of the eighteenth century to the concert hall of the nineteenth. Amongst the most important were the increased tonal power and expressive potential of the newer instruments. The development of the Tourte bow allowed string players to exercise much greater variety of tone; the strings themselves were set up with greater tension and used steel-covered gut to increase volume. The professionalization of musical life in the great metropolitan centers also played a role. By the end of the nineteenth century, a number of professional string quartets were established, their membership often drawn from the principal desks of the major symphony orchestras. With increased possibilities for traveling between different cities and countries, these ensembles gave regular concerts throughout Europe and the United States.

Alongside this process came a changing conception of the string quartet as a compositional medium. As with the symphony, Beethoven's contribution was vital. The first of his Op. 59 "Razumovsky" Quartets (1806) effected just as radical a reinterpretation of an established form as did the "Eroica" Symphony (1805). Not only was the music conceived on a much grander scale than previous examples by Haydn and Mozart, but also the composer made far greater technical and musical demands, testing the stamina of his players to the very limit. This desire to reinvigorate the medium reached its climax in the sequence of late quartets composed in the 1820s. These works baffled many of Beethoven's contemporaries, not least for their flexibility of structure, which in some works incorporated a distinctly unorthodox sequence and number of movements, and for their complex and emotionally introverted musical language.

Succeeding generations of composers responded to Beethoven's contribution to the string quartet in different ways. Some, like Mendelssohn, tried to return to the solidly Classical principles established by Haydn and Mozart. Such composers viewed the string quartet as essentially a dry and emotionally restrained medium, bereft of the extra-musical implications and brilliance of color that could be applied to the symphony. Not everyone, however, followed this practice. Many aspired to writing for the strings in an almost orchestral manner, a feature that is particularly noticeable in the full-blooded double stops that grace the openings of the quartets by Grieg and César Franck. Others found it much more congenial to apply such rich textures to larger string ensembles (e.g., the string sextets of Brahms and Tchaikovsky), or more frequently by combining the strings with the piano.

2. Piano music and song

> **Box 9.2 Continuities and discontinuities of concert genres: the string quartet**
>
> Interesting questions arise from the background and nature of concert-music repertories. For example, to what extent have long-established genres maintained a specific aura and tradition? Is it helpful to classify such works in terms of a particular style such as Classical, Romantic, and modern, and are national traditions of paramount importance in any discussions of this repertory?
>
> A brief look at two string quartets that emanate from different eras, a string quartet by Haydn (Op. 76 No. 3 in C major, subtitled the Emperor;1797) and one by the Bohemian composer Antonín Dvořák (Op. 51 in E flat major; 1879), is revealing. Both works are conceived in the traditional four-movement structure established in the late eighteenth century, in which the outer movements carry the most intricate musical argument.
>
> Haydn's writing manifests a transparency of texture and balance and proportion of phrase structure that appears typical of the Classical style. In contrast, Dvořák writes in a much more full-blooded manner with frequent recourse to fluctuations in speed. While adhering to certain structural principles established in the Classical era, Romantic elements are predominant, not least in the slow movement.
>
> The question of national traditions is of particular interest in relation to the Dvořák. Although his quartet maintains a strong relationship to the Austro-German traditions of Mozart and Beethoven, the composer superimposes original melodic ideas and dance rhythms that were directly inspired by Bohemian folk music. Nowhere is this more evident than in the second movement, cast in the form of a Dumka, which opens with a drone cello chord over which first violin and viola intone a sad lament. This material is ingeniously contrasted with sections of vigorous rhythms derived from a Bohemian dance entitled the Furiant.

Of all the instruments under discussion in the context of intimate concert genres, the piano undoubtedly experienced the most dramatic changes in power and sonority in the nineteenth century. As is well known the piano, or fortepiano as it was also initially called (and still is, by some scholars and performers who wish to refer to the eighteenth- or early nineteenth-century instrument), evolved out of a necessity to create a keyboard instrument that was capable of emulating the dynamic range and expressive qualities of string instruments or the human voice. Early instruments were fragile and limited in terms of their projection. The manufacture of pianos with iron frames in the 1820s made the instrument far sturdier, with a capacity to fill a much larger performance space.

The enormous popularity that the piano enjoyed as a solo instrument during the nineteenth century generated a vast repertory of new music. On the one hand, composers wrote intimate character pieces designed primarily for domestic use. A similar tendency could be gleaned when composers combined the voice with piano, as in the songs of Schubert, Schumann, and Wolf. The intimacy of expression of the German Lied and for that matter the French chanson were far less suited to the concert hall, and it is noticeable that regular public song recitals evolved relatively late in the nineteenth century.

At the same time as exploiting its commercial potential as a domestic instrument, composers of piano music also wrote ambitious large-scale works that challenged the technical capabilities of the performer. In many instances their writing for the piano aspires to the full-blooded textures of the symphony orchestra. Nowhere is this more effectively realized than in Liszt's piano transcriptions of Beethoven's nine symphonies, or in the appropriately named Symphony and Concerto for solo piano by Alkan.

The twentieth century and beyond

Introduction

Although many of the genres that were firmly established in the nineteenth century continued to be exploited by composers after 1900, the political turmoil of two world wars and the establishment of repressive dictatorships in Germany, Italy, and Russia had profound consequences for the continued vibrancy of concert music, particularly since a number of composers sought to expand musical language to unprecedented levels of complexity, thereby restricting the appeal of their music to connoisseurs rather than to the general public.

Early modernists and concert music

During the first years of the twentieth century, a number of composers began to react against previously held concepts regarding the nature and function of concert music. Not only did they seek to expand tonal and harmonic language well beyond the levels that had been exploited by nineteenth-century progressives such as Wagner and Liszt. They also challenged the validity and durability of genres that had formed the backbone of concert music for over a century. A brief perusal of the early twentieth-century orchestral output of early modernist composers such as Debussy, Schoenberg, and Stravinsky illustrates this point. Let us take Debussy, for example. One question that might be asked is how effectively it is possible to place the composer's *Nocturnes* (1900), *La mer* (1903–5), and orchestral *Images* (1909–12) within the conventional genres of either symphony or programmatic tone-poem. True, Debussy subtitles *La mer* a symphonic sketch, but despite some overt thematic connections between the three movements, there is little to suggest that Debussy is writing a traditional symphonic work. Likewise, one could hardly conceive of either the three *Nocturnes* or the *Images* as being programmatic orchestral music in the manner that was understood in the nineteenth century. No doubt, the titles that are affixed to specific movements (e.g., "Nuages," "Ibéria") provide a helpful reference point for audiences, but they are not programmatic. Debussy's major preoccupation appears to be to create atmosphere rather than to refer either to a detailed set of extra-musical events or to a broader philosophical argument. Rather, he is attracted to the idea of finding innovative elements of color and texture, expanding the orchestral palette so as to incorporate such radical ideas as a wordless women's chorus in "Sirènes," the final piece of the *Nocturnes*.

Debussy's Austrian contemporary Arnold Schoenberg was no less iconoclastic in his approach to the orchestra. Having composed a gargantuan symphonic poem, *Pelleas und Melisande*, in 1902, in which a huge orchestra charts the essential narrative of Maeterlinck's drama in graphic terms following the principles of Liszt and Richard Strauss, he turned his back on convention. As with Debussy, it is difficult to place the orchestral works he composed before World War I into traditional categories. The First Chamber Symphony, for example, manifests all the necessary thematic and structural ingredients for a tightly organized symphonic structure that one would expect from an Austro-German composer. But the orchestration, conceived for fifteen solo instruments, not to mention the densely polyphonic musical argument which stretches conventional tonality almost to breaking point, begs all sorts of questions. Is Schoenberg writing chamber music within an orchestral framework, and if so, what expectations are set up by this work? Is he making a bold statement vis-à-vis the contemporary cultural milieu that expected symphonies to signify large-scale extended works conceived for orchestral forces of ever increasing sizes?

It is perhaps significant that Schoenberg's next major orchestral work, the *Five Pieces for Orchestra*, owes even less to traditional genres. In a sense, Schoenberg appears to follow Debussy in providing atmospheric titles for each piece. But apart from the third piece, "Summer Morning by a Lake," where Schoenberg explores the notion of orchestral color through the changing timbres of a chromatic chord, the music is essentially fragmentary in nature, offering almost nothing in the way of literal repetition or closure.

Stemming from a completely different tradition, the Russian Igor Stravinsky presents yet another radical manifestation of modernism in the early years of the twentieth century. Although Stravinsky made his debut as an orchestral composer with an academically constructed Symphony and a brilliantly coloristic showpiece, *Fireworks*, his collaboration with the great artistic entrepreneur Serge Diaghilev led him away from conventional concert music genres to composing for the ballet, a genre that had previously been regarded as lightweight and insignificant by most Western composers. Ostensibly, Stravinsky's three early ballets (*Firebird*, *Petrushka*, and *Rite of Spring*) were written for the theater, but they soon made their way to the concert hall.

Indeed thanks to the efforts of Stravinsky, and to Diaghilev, ballet came to be recognized as one of the principal musical genres of the early twentieth century, attracting the interest of a whole host of composers from Richard Strauss to Erik Satie.

With the passing of time, audiences eventually absorbed and accepted the innovations of Debussy and Stravinsky, and their major works have maintained a secure place in the standard repertory. Yet concert audiences in general have felt far less inclined to regard other significant modernists such as Schoenberg, Webern, and Varèse in the same favorable light, and even the most highly esteemed of their concert works have failed to enjoy regular performances on a scale comparable to those of Debussy and Stravinsky.

One might well ask why music composed nearly eighty years ago is still regarded as difficult or problematic and strictly off-limits as far as commercial radio stations such as Classic FM (in the UK) are concerned? Is the musical language that was adopted by these composers too abstract and complex to communicate any sort of message, except to the enlightened few? Did composers of avant-garde concert music simply abrogate their responsibilities to reach out to a wider audience?

There are no simple answers to these questions, but one cannot ignore the fact that the modernist ideals of composers such as Schoenberg and his successors managed to prise open an even greater wedge between the three broad categories of music-making (avant-garde, classical, and commercial) than before, and this process continued many years after World War II. Given the desire of the avant-garde not only to pursue unprecedented stylistic and technical innovation, but to dismantle the entire musical apparatus as it had existed in the nineteenth century, it is particularly interesting once again to return to the two most important genres of concert music, the symphony and the string quartet, during this period.

The symphony and string quartet in the twentieth century

One provocative point to make here is that the notion of regarding the symphony and string quartet as purely musical genres is somewhat misleading as far as the twentieth century is concerned. Perhaps a better description would be to suggest that both forms of music-making are essentially "institutions," their prosperity being totally dependent upon a institutionalized framework involving a great deal of organization, finance, commerce, and marketing. Since the symphony orchestra and to a lesser extent the string quartet remained the hub around which musical and commercial circuits in the concert world of classical music revolved, it is hardly surprising that a great deal of energy has been expended to ensure their survival.

An inevitable consequence of the challenges posed by the avant-garde was that institutions such as the symphony orchestra and the string quartet simply perpetuated a museum culture, ignoring most music written in the last hundred years. On the other hand concert life could not really prosper without fresh musical impetus, and audiences on the whole seemed prepared to accept novelties so long as they offered a tangible link between tradition and the modern world. This explains, for example, the phenomenon of the Gustav Mahler revival that began in the 1960s. Mahler's appeal to a contemporary Zeitgeist cannot be underestimated. Although most of his symphonies were composed during the first decade of the twentieth century, their epic scale and expressions of anxiety strongly appealed to modern sensibilities. Not surprisingly, many twentieth-century composers, including Prokofiev, Britten, Copland, and Shostakovich, followed Mahler's example in trying to effect a rapprochement between nineteenth-century traditions and modernity. Perhaps the most commercially successful of Mahler's followers was Shostakovich, who invested particular energy in writing both symphonies and string quartets until his death in 1975. Shostakovich's growing popularity as a composer of concert music continues to be the subject of much heated debate, not least because of the double-edged nature of his musical language, which on the one hand could be interpreted as an endorsement of the official ideology of the Soviet regime while at the same time suggesting strong disaffection.

Nationalism, internationalization and globalization

Mention of the unusual demands that faced composers working in the former Soviet Union leads us on to consider other factors that had a profound impact upon concert music of the twentieth century. To a certain extent, one can glean a semblance of continuity with the nineteenth century, especially in the desire to preserve national identities through such repertory. But nationalism also proved to be a dangerous tool, particularly when repressive political systems sought to manipulate music for propaganda purposes. Any study of concert repertory composed and performed in Nazi Germany, Fascist Italy, or Soviet Russia would have to consider the hugely prescriptive and often arbitrary criteria by which such music was deemed acceptable to the authorities.

Yet despite the attempts of repressive regimes to bolster national identity, two world wars, not to mention the persecution and migration of large populations, effected a reaction against the potentially pernicious impact of nationalism. During the 1920s, for example, a spirit of internationalism was fostered amongst composers, most obviously manifested in the cultural activities of Germany's Weimar Republic, and in particular the work of the International Society for Contemporary Music (ISCM). This organization, founded in 1922, effectively served as a United Nations of concert music activity, presenting annual festivals of new music in different metropolitan centers. The long-term impact of the ISCM would be to loosen previously held notions that the geographical center of concert-music activity had to be confined to Western and/or Central Europe. Particularly after World War II, concert music had to be regarded as a global activity involving composers and performers from all corners of the world.

Technology and concert music

The twentieth century witnessed the most far-reaching developments in technological endeavor, which was celebrated by a musical avant-garde that utilized electronic music as a means of extending the sound-palette that was available to composers. The creation of electronic studios in several European cities during the 1950s offered the opportunity to experiment with sound in a way that was never possible for previous generations. Yet the impact of electronics on concert music remained mixed. In some respects, the use of electronics reflected a further dehumanization and abstraction of musical language, reducing the spontaneity and physical excitement of live performance. Recognizing this problem, the Hungarian composer György Ligeti abandoned his work in the studio and set himself the challenge of trying to recreate electronic sounds in terms of the conventional orchestra – a development that began with his *Atmosphères* of 1961.

While electronic music remains the most obvious manifestation of technological change in the twentieth century, we should also consider the impact of mass media on concert music. It is worth remembering that in 1900, the means of disseminating concert music were far less sophisticated than today. Admittedly one could have traveled vast distances to hear premieres of important concert works, and these may well have been reported extensively in the press. But to insure that such works could be heard more regularly and in different geographical centers was by no means guaranteed, and remained heavily dependent upon the effective publication and distribution of the musical material and the support of influential performers. Of course these conditions continue to play an important role in supporting concert music. But technological developments, particularly in the area of broadcasting and recording, have become even more influential in this respect.

Consider, for example, the impact of broadcasting. The establishment of radio stations throughout Europe and the United States in the 1920s provided unprecedented opportunities for the patronage of concert music. The BBC, for instance, established its own orchestras and choirs, helping to bolster employment within the music profession. As a national organization subsidized by government funds and licence payers, it evolved a very specific and influential music policy that changed the very nature of concert life in Great Britain. Moreover the BBC's patronage extended to the commissioning of new works, some of which were specially designed for the specific sonic requirements of the radio. Perhaps more importantly, however, the BBC served to bring concert music to a much wider public than ever before (see also Chapter 16).

The advent of recording was equally significant in terms of widening the dissemination of concert music. A glance at the current CD catalog demonstrates the popularity of certain icons of "museum culture" repertory, some of which can be heard in over a hundred alternative recordings. At the same time, recording companies have also served the specialized interests of collectors and have sought to explore neglected music from all eras, much of which is rarely performed in a concert environment. Inevitably, a successful recording can help to enhance the reputation of a work that had previously been overlooked. For contemporary composers such an opportunity has actually transformed reputations, as happened in the 1990s when Gorecki's Third Symphony (1976) enjoyed widespread exposure in a performance recorded by the London Sinfonietta.

Postmodernism

Such is the complexity and variety of twentieth-century concert music that it is almost impossible to draw clear lines of development between the different styles that were fashionable at one time or another. Broadly speaking, however, composers were placed in one of two camps, either modernist/avant-garde or conservative/traditional. Such distinctions, however, have been turned on their head in recent years, especially since the prevailing postmodernist aesthetic has largely refuted the Darwinian idea that advances in stylistic complexity should necessarily be equated with compositional progress.

The transformation from modernism to postmodernism was first manifested by composers who had reached a kind of stylistic cul-de-sac with the avant-garde. A good example was the American composer George Rochberg (1918–2005) who initially adhered to a post-Schoenbergian serialist style, but began to regard this idiom as hollow and meaningless. A turning point came with his Third String Quartet (1971–2) which unashamedly evokes the musical language of late Beethoven as seen through the lenses of Bartók, Ives, and Shostakovich. Parallel cases could be found in Eastern Europe where the First Violin Concerto (1976–7) by the Pole Krzysztof Penderecki (b.1933), and *Fratres* (1976) and the *Cantus in memoriam Benjamin Britten* (1977) by the Estonian Arvo Pärt (b.1935), marked a drastic break with the radical experimentation of their earlier works, embracing a less complex musical language that in the case of Pärt alluded to musical traditions that predated the Baroque era. Not surprisingly, this stylistic volte-face by two major figures had a profound impact on younger composers, influenced on the one hand by American minimalism and on the other by a desire to reclaim communication with an audience that had lost faith in contemporary concert music.

The current cultural environment, which sanctions stylistic plurality and does not regard the use of traditional tonalities and harmonies and references to commercial popular music as being necessarily regressive, offers new opportunities for concert music. Above all, it has begun to erode the barriers between so-called "serious" and popular music that had prevailed for so much of the past two centuries.

Chapter summary

- The vast repertoire of Western art music extends from the secular court music of the seventeenth century to the present day.
- It has been influenced through its history by the changing functions of patrons and other forms of funding, with a general "democratization" over the centuries, accelerated by the popularizing endeavors of performers, conductors, and impresarios.
- Despite great internal development its principal genres (oratorio, symphony, overture, concerto, string quartet, and accompanied song) have remained remarkably resilient even through revolutions in musical style and taste and the changes that technology has brought to the dissemination of music – a process that will remain ongoing and unpredictable.

Discussion topics

1. In which ways do changing structures of patronage influence the way that music is written and consumed?
2. How does music's consumption interact with the changing constitution of audiences, and the ways they access music?
3. How have genres such as the symphony or concerto responded to historical developments, and why do you think they seem to have remained viable for so long? What is it about the symphony that makes it a kind of "gold standard" for some critics and listeners?

Further reading

Bianconi, Lorenzo (1987), *Music in the Seventeenth Century*, trans. David Bryant (Cambridge: Cambridge University Press).
> An accessible introduction to the profound musical developments of the century.

Dahlhaus, Carl (1989), *Nineteenth-Century Music*, trans. J. Bradford Robinson (Berkeley: University of California Press; orig. edn 1980).
> An influential study of nineteenth-century music, with a distinctive view of a "double tradition" of composition following Beethoven and Rossini.

Downs, Philip G. (1993), *Classical Music: Era of Haydn, Mozart and Beethoven* (New York and London: Norton).
> A useful study that places the achievements of Haydn, Mozart, and Beethoven in a balanced historical context.

Hill, John Walter (2005), *Baroque Music 1580–1750* (New York: Norton).
> An important recent study which charts developments in Western European music alongside those in the New World, with a particular emphasis on the achivments of women composers.

Morgan, Robert P. (1991), *Twentieth-Century Music: A History of Musical Style in Modern Europe and America* (New York and London: Norton).
> A readable and reliable introduction to the century.

Palisca, Claude V. (1983), *Baroque Music* (Englewood Cliffs, NJ: Prentice Hall).
> A classic textbook on the age of Bach and Handel.

Plantinga, Leon (1988), *Romantic Music: A History of Musical Style in the Nineteenth Century* (New York: Norton).
> An excellent survey highlighting the strong influence of Beethoven on subsequent musical developments in the century.

Rosen, Charles (1988), *Sonata Forms* (New York: Norton 1988).
> Perceptive analysis and stimulating commentary on the central structural principle of late-eighteenth- and nineteenth-century orchestral and instrumental music.

Rosen, Charles (2005), *The Classical Style: Haydn, Beethoven, Mozart*, revised edn (London: Faber).
> Indispensable and illuminating study of the great composers of the First Viennese School written by a great performer and an outstanding scholar.

Samson, Jim (2002) (ed.), *The Cambridge History of Nineteenth-Century Music* (Cambridge: Cambridge University Press).
> A large collection of essays which offers a very wide range of reflections on genres, traditions, and social and nationalist uses of music in the nineteenth century.

Taruskin, Richard (2005), *The Oxford History of Western Music*, 6 vols. (New York and Oxford: Oxford University Press).
> An ambitious study of Western music by one of modern musicology's most controversial and influential figures. It offers a strongly argued but personal

view of developments in the nineteenth and twentieth centuries, with a
particular emphasis on the USA and Russia.

Whittall, Arnold (1999), *Musical Composition in the Twentieth Century* (Oxford: Oxford
University Press).

An essential study which considers developments in twentieth-century music
from the twin points of view of innovation and consolidation, by one of the
most insightful writers on this period.

10 Jazz

ANDREW BOWIE

Chapter preview

This chapter considers what makes the study of jazz different from the study of other kinds of music. It looks at jazz's mixture of assimilation and rejection of other music, and shows how it relates to important political, social, and economic issues. Problems in writing the history of jazz are examined, and the role of recording and transcription in the reception and teaching of jazz are stressed. The nature of improvisation is considered in relation to composition in classical music, and the tension in jazz between the drive for new forms of expression and the desire to appeal to a wider audience is investigated. The question of whether jazz can still remain a "critical" form of music when it is increasingly being formally taught in schools and universities is raised along with the issue of whether jazz should now be concerned with the preservation of its traditions, or with new musical exploration.

Key issues

- Can we define jazz, and does it matter whether we can?
- How does the study of jazz differ from the study of other kinds of music?
- Does jazz present a challenge to the assumptions and procedures of conventional musicology?
- Is there "progress" in jazz?
- How does jazz relate to history, society, and politics?
- What is jazz's status in relation to other developments in modern music?
- How does technology affect jazz?
- Is jazz now becoming as "academic" as other forms of "serious" music?

Introduction

"That's not jazz" has long been one of the most frequent claims made in discussions of jazz. Why should this be the case? From its beginnings, early in the twentieth century, jazz has attracted controversy because of its disputed relationships, not just to other music, but to other aspects of modern culture. The reasons for the disputed nature of these relationships are central to an understanding of jazz. The question of whether something is jazz or not might, of course, be regarded as just a question of definition, on the assumption that if we had the correct definition we could identify what is jazz and what isn't. The first problem here is, though, that it is far from clear where the word "jazz" first emerged, or what it actually meant. Moreover, many ways of defining what constitutes jazz turn out not to help a great deal. Is jazz, for example, improvised music? Much jazz may be improvised, but quite a lot of famous jazz performances involve very little improvisation, and improvisation occurs in many other kinds of music. Is jazz characterized by its extensive use of syncopation? Earlier forms of jazz often were, but much modern jazz uses very little syncopation. Jazz is supposed to "swing," but many performances don't, because the tempo is too slow, or because that is not the aim of the performance. Other descriptions give rise to similar problems, even as they may also help reveal something about what people call jazz.

The fact is that definitions rarely allow one to describe something definitively, especially if what is in question is part of human culture. Given our ability to discuss cultural and other topics despite a lack of agreed definitions, it is perhaps better to think of terms like "jazz" as tools that we use to talk about things that we find significant. The more interesting question, therefore, is why the use of terms like "jazz" generates such controversy. Part of the answer is that disputes about whether something is jazz or not are part of what jazz is. Jazz develops via its assimilation and rejection of other kinds of music, so that its boundaries are always being contested and redrawn. During the history of jazz, musicians have adopted elements of church music, blues, classical music, musicals, and other popular sources, various kinds of Latin-American music, and, more recently, rock music and "world music." At the same time, jazz musicians have also rejected important aspects of other music (including other kinds of jazz), cultivating rhythmic, melodic, harmonic, and other techniques and approaches that often depend on their differences from what was being rejected. Such a stance played a role, for example, in the development of "bebop" in the 1940s. The new melodic, harmonic, and rhythmic demands of bebop were partly intended to exclude musicians used to playing jazz in a more traditional manner.

This kind of oppositional stance illustrates how jazz is embedded in and motivated by social and political issues. Bebop was in part a reaction against "swing" music, which came by the 1940s to be dominated by white musicians, who had commercial success playing a diluted version of what had previously been a mainly black music. Unlike many jazz musicians before them, bebop musicians did not in the main seek commercial success or court popularity by making compromises in order to please their audiences. Music like bebop and the other more experimental kinds of jazz that follow it has, then, in part to do with the need for African-American culture to sustain its identity against a dominant, often racist white culture. Significantly, experimental jazz also became part of the oppositional culture in those Communist countries that sought rigorous state control of musical expression.

Jazz originated among oppressed and disadvantaged parts of the population of the United States, some of whose very recent ancestors had still been slaves. For these people jazz was – and in some places still is – a form of expression that gave them a cultural identity often denied them by the rest of their society. A reminder of how such socio-political issues have not gone away was apparent in the aftermath of Hurricane Katrina in 2005. In New Orleans it was the deprived African-American population, many of whom were still carrying on the jazz traditions of their home city, that bore the brunt of the catastrophe. Many developments in jazz are, then, closely linked to issues in a particular society, such as racial discrimination, or the cultural effects of a rapidly changing capitalist economy. On the one hand, jazz has been a form of resistance to an unjust dominant culture which relegated (and still does relegate) many African Americans to an inferior economic and social status. On the other hand, though, jazz has – in the "Swing Era" from the 1930s onwards, for example – at times been a commercially very successful form of music. The dilemmas of commercially successful jazz are echoed in the situation now familiar in rock and pop music. The quality of the music can be affected by market influences, and any assessment of jazz must take this into account.

Issues like these mean that the academic study of jazz makes special demands. Serious academic writing about jazz was comparatively rare until fairly recently, and many university music departments still do not have staff specializing in jazz. The reasons for this relate closely to the reasons for the contentious status of jazz. The fact that jazz is not primarily notated and so relies a great deal on recordings also, as we shall see, affects these issues. Jazz musicians have always had a complex relationship to "legitimate," "classical" music, both rejecting it for being "square," and yet also drawing on it for all kinds of musical resources. "Classical" composers have in turn drawn on jazz for new approaches, and have also at times regarded it as inferior to the music that they themselves produce. (When they do use jazz, they tend not to assimilate it fully into their style: listen, for instance, to Stravinsky's "jazz-inspired" *Ebony Concerto* (1946), which by no means sounds "like jazz," but does make use of certain of its features.) As the borderlines between most kinds of music have become more porous in recent years, this mixture of rejection and assimilation has come to seem less important in some quarters, and some jazz is now widely regarded as simply a part of serious modern music. Issues in the academic responses to jazz have, then, to do with the evaluation of the relationship between jazz and other kinds of music, and with jazz's relationship to the societies in which it is played.

History and context

"Jazz" is still only around one hundred years old, having emerged towards the end of the nineteenth century, particularly, but not exclusively, in New Orleans, a port city that was ethnically and culturally very diverse. Jazz's development during the 1920s was affected by migration, particularly of African-American workers, from the rural South to the cities of the North, so that, for a time, Chicago became the center of the new music. Since the 1930s it has been New York that has often attracted and produced the most innovative musicians, though Kansas City and other cities have also played a major role. During the 1950s jazz on the West Coast of America became important. Since then jazz has become more and more international, for instance via its incorporation of Latin American styles, like Bossa Nova, so it is now hard to locate where the most important developments are. Because jazz has developed in such a rapid and varied manner, it is inevitable that much writing about it has been concerned to trace and understand its history, from collective improvisation in New Orleans to the ever more virtuosic forms of individual solo playing characteristic of many of the major forms of jazz.

Because of the lack of clear documented evidence and recordings, the "roots" of jazz are an endless topic of discussion. How much was the music that came to be called jazz based on African music, ragtime, popular song, gospel music, marching music, the blues, etc.? How was it that a mixture of influences from a great variety of places coalesced into something so different from what had gone before that it became the basis of a new kind of music that is now played all over the globe? Such questions cannot be answered in solely musical terms, and they require resources from sociology, anthropology, and other subjects if they are to be answered effectively. Given the magnitude of this task it is not surprising that writing about jazz rarely attends to all the dimensions required to do justice to it. Writing on jazz has, for example, tended towards the merely anecdotal, because it is concerned with the often colorful lives of the musicians without revealing much about the music; or towards the merely impressionistic, because it enthuses about the music without explaining what is special about it with any precision. This situation has changed in recent years, and the rigor and range of writing on jazz has substantially improved.

The history of jazz involves the development of the music from what was in effect a kind of (mainly) instrumental folk music with simple, if novel, harmonic, melodic, and rhythmic techniques, very often used as dance music, to the great complexity of some contemporary jazz, which takes up techniques from every conceivable kind of music in the search for new forms of expression. Just tracing such a development in technical terms – via aspects such as the extension of "permissible" notes and chords to include the flattened fifth, ninth, etc., or via the growing complexity of rhythms employed, or via the emergence of the solo as the main core of many forms of jazz – would fail to offer an adequate interpretation of what these extensions of the "language" of jazz meant, both at the time they took place and since.

The extended language of a particular new jazz style may be regarded as unmusical by adherents of an earlier style – this was the attitude to the playing of saxophonist Ornette Coleman of many of the modern jazz players in the 1960s – and, if employed within an earlier style, may indeed sometimes make little musical sense. Is, though, each new development in jazz an advance on what preceded it, as many musicians who play new styles often suggest by criticizing earlier styles as being "corny," "cheesy," etc.? The difficulty in interpreting the attitude of such musicians becomes apparent in the fact that the history of jazz has also frequently involved the return to older styles, such as the revival of traditional New Orleans jazz that took place in the 1940s and 1950s both in Britain and Europe, and, to a lesser extent, in the United States, or the return from "jazz rock" and "fusion" to versions of bebop and other supposedly superseded styles in the 1980s.

These revivals could, on the one hand, be seen as involving a regression to something that had been replaced by more sophisticated or fashionable approaches, but on the other they could also be regarded as enabling the continuation of a unique form of musical expression, which might otherwise have been forgotten. This situation contrasts with what happens in classical music, where music from the past is now generally more important than most contemporary music. Performing older classical music is not usually regarded as involving a regression. Concern with "historically informed" performance practice does, though, introduce something analogous to a concern with regression, when a modern, and therefore anachronistic, style of performing comes to be regarded by some people as no longer valid. In jazz, reviving a style also has different consequences because what is produced is still likely to be improvised (though some revivals have involved note-for-note recreations), and so is new in some measure, even if the style may still be regarded as "old hat" by many musicians and fans. Musicians often mix elements of old and new styles, so that there is no necessary sense of a "linear progression" from one style to another. Indeed, the very notion of jazz "style" is questionable in this respect. The complexities of jazz history are apparent in such phenomena, and it is vital to be aware of how much assumptions about musical "progress," etc., will affect the writing of that history.

Technical descriptions alone evidently fail to do justice to these sorts of questions. An adequate historical account of any aspect of jazz therefore has to see how different assessments of the music relate to cultural, ideological, economic, and political matters. This leads to the following questions. Are changes in jazz styles just secondary signs of the social changes that they accompany? The move from collective improvisation to solo playing can be seen, for instance, as connected to the move from a more traditional, collective local culture to the individualist culture of big-city life. On the other hand, should the most significant forms of jazz be seen as themselves having social and political effects, because they change peoples' attitudes to the culture in which they live, as some avant-garde music did in the 1960s? There is no simple answer to these questions, and a response to them requires specific research in each case because the music and its context are inextricably linked.

Questions about jazz history can highlight vital problems in the wider study of music. One way to approach these problems is to consider them in terms of the idea of competing "norms," i.e., of rules or expectations governing what is appropriate or inappropriate. Doing this allows one to connect historical and social issues to musical ones, by seeing how musical norms relate to social norms. An example of such a connection is how ways of playing jazz that seem closer to some of the norms of classical music, like some of the highly arranged and elegant swing music of the late 1930s, can come to seem too formal and "correct" in some contexts. Bebop reacts to this situation by offering a more aggressive and less "classical" musical alternative that is often linked to a more assertive social stance with regard to issues of racial and cultural injustice. At the same time, bebop can also be seen as relating to the social crises around World War II, which brought about rapid changes in the nature of American society that are echoed in the more intense, yet highly organized, nature of the music. Something analogous can be observed in the emergence of "free jazz" in the 1960s, which connects jazz to the more overtly political stance of the Civil Rights movement of the time by rejecting the musical norms of the "cool jazz" of the 1950s, because they can be associated with forms of social and political constraint.

Jazz that increases its harmonic, melodic, and rhythmic range, in a manner akin to that in which classical music changed from Bach to Schoenberg, is complemented, particularly in post-World War II jazz, by the development of often extreme expressive means – tonal distortion, aggressive dissonance, etc. – of the kind that also play a role in the classical avant-garde. The tensions between expressive intensity in jazz, and jazz's ability to communicate through melody, harmony, and rhythm in a manner akin to more traditional classical and popular music, echo difficulties in contemporary classical music, where the loss of a broader audience is often the price of pursuing the newest expressive approaches. One of the essential questions in the contemporary assessment of jazz history is, then, whether the drive for novelty, which has been the motor of jazz's astonishingly rapid development, should give way, as people like the trumpet player Wynton Marsalis now argue, to a cultivation of jazz's many traditions, or whether jazz should seek to remain the kind of avant-garde music it became when bebop challenged musical and social norms in the 1940s.

Improvisation and performance

The study of jazz should not, however, concentrate just on history. Jazz can be analyzed like any music, although the techniques for doing this can differ from those in some other kinds of music. Much of the recent analysis of jazz is connected to the practice of learning to play jazz, and here some important issues become apparent. If you are studying a piece by Beethoven, the initial material of study is generally the score of the piece in question. This can be analyzed in harmonic, rhythmic, and melodic terms, and the analysis can be informed by comparison of recorded and live performances of the piece. Although there may be disagreements on the detail of the score, its main features will generally be well established, and performances that fail to do justice to those features will be regarded as inadequate. Disputes about historical performance styles have recently made it more apparent just how complex the relationship between score and performance can be, but the score remains the initial basis of interpretation (see chapter 2).

In jazz (and some other improvised forms of music) these relationships appear in a different manner. Even a big band like Duke Ellington's, which played highly arranged music, often did not have fully notated scores, though the majority of big bands do. Such scores are, however, generally only studied in arranging classes. The initial material of study in jazz is most often a recorded performance, or a tune written as melody with chord symbols, rather than a full score. At the same time, learning to play jazz just with aural resources is difficult. Learning generally requires written notation as well. Written "scores" in jazz generally take the form of transcriptions of solos from significant recordings. The point of transcriptions is primarily practical. They are intended to enable players to extend the resources they use in improvisation, transcribing solos or parts of solos being a tried and tested technique for jazz musicians. Such "scores," many of which are now being commercially produced in the manner of traditional musical scores, are evidently secondary to the original performances, as anyone who tries to play them convincingly without having heard the original performance will testify. Much that matters in jazz cannot be adequately notated – the tone and attack of horn players in particular is essential to their music-making – so learning has to rely both on recordings and notation. It is unexceptional that there is a different kind of relationship between sound and score in differing kinds of music, such as folk music and classical music, but what specific consequences does this have with regard to jazz?

Jazz is closely connected to the development of new technologies. Major changes in jazz styles take place with often remarkable rapidity because of the new capacities to broadcast, record, and electronically manipulate music that are characteristic of the twentieth century, which are already taking on new forms in the new millennium. The need to hear an actual performance, rather than just read a transcription, is imperative, because jazz lives from the individuality of its performers. This means that any bibliography for the study of jazz will need to include a discography: recordings are probably more important than books for knowing about jazz. At the same time, the speed and complexity of much jazz improvisation means that learning to use some of the techniques of a major jazz musician depends on the ability to slow the music down with technological means in order to transcribe it. The role of the improvising "composer" in jazz is different from what it is in European classical music. However, the difference between improvised composition and written composition is probably only a relative one, because similar analytical techniques to those applicable to written composition can be applied to improvised jazz once it is transcribed.

Much jazz is still, of course, improvised on the basis of composed pieces, where melody and harmony are to some degree fixed, though they are very often altered by the performers. There is, however, considerable debate about the extent to which improvised performances are really spontaneous "creation," in the sense that something wholly new emerges in the performance. The complexity of some of the melodic phrases encountered through chord-based improvisation in modern jazz in particular is almost impossible to attain wholly from scratch, however skilled the musician. The ability to create new melodic turns of phrase relies on having learned to use a great deal of pre-prepared material beforehand, and on techniques of varying and transforming such material by the use of embellishment, sequencing, etc. The saxophonist Charlie Parker, who sounds remarkably spontaneous in most performances, has been shown to use a number of essential melodic patterns most of the time, many of which he developed quite early in his career. Parker developed some of his material from listening to saxophonists Lester Young, Coleman Hawkins, and others, but his manner of using it makes it sound very different. It is his ability to manipulate and vary this material in his own manner that is remarkable, and this gives his playing its uniquely spontaneous feeling. Some of saxophonist John Coltrane's most virtuosic solos, like the astonishingly fast one on "Countdown" (on the album *Giant Steps* of 1960), consist mainly of pre-practiced sequences of four notes (many of which recur several times), his remarkable achievement lying in the way these are built into a coherent overall solo at very high speed.

One way of assessing the nature of improvisation in this respect is via comparison of different "takes" of the same tune at a recording session. Are the solos played in very similar ways, or is each solo constructed very differently? Some musicians will repeat an idea or ideas each time, because they "work," others will do something new each time. Jazz here poses interesting questions about musical evaluation, because decisions about what matters musically must be made in assessing whether spontaneous novelty can be more important than more traditional musical virtues. Do we, for instance, assess those soloists in Duke Ellington's band who over many years played much the same solo (one sometimes part-composed by Ellington) in a piece less positively than musicians who almost always play something different, even though the Ellington band solos are excellent in musical terms? Louis Armstrong sometimes improvised something new each time, but at other times he had worked out all but the smallest details of a solo and repeated them. If both performances sound equally spontaneous, does it matter that one is more improvised than the other? What of the many kinds of "free jazz," which do not rely on a chordal structure underlying the improvisation? How are performances of this kind to be evaluated?

These questions also have consequences for learning to play jazz. The phenomenon of the technically excellent player who is just playing material learned from transcriptions of the great soloists has become increasingly common, and such players are often criticized. However, jazz has relied enormously on such imitation from the beginning: is it more questionable now because the means that allow imitation are more readily available and more easily used?

This issue has been important in discussions of methods for the teaching of jazz. Playing jazz has to do with "finding your own voice," but is it so problematic to have a voice derived from that of the great players? Is this situation any different from that in classical music, where talented "second-rank" composers have often used many of the means established by their "first-rank" contemporaries? The problem here is how to establish a balance between acquiring the know-how and technical means to express oneself while being able to find a way of playing that is one's own. This problem is common to many kinds of music. However, in jazz, unlike in classical music, it is sometimes the case that technical limitations may actually enable a player to establish their own voice. Musicians such as the clarinetist Pee Wee Russell, or the saxophonist Archie Shepp, who have relatively limited techniques, but play in an intriguingly idiosyncratic manner, illustrate this point. Perhaps most strikingly, trumpeter Miles Davis lacked the virtuoso technique of some of his contemporaries, but had more effect on jazz than they did because of his ability to explore highly diverse kinds of music.

Jazz as "critical music"

The fact that jazz musicians do not necessarily need to possess a command of all the main technical resources available in order to produce something unique might, however, be seen as conflicting with the widespread demand in jazz to "pay one's dues" by going through a difficult apprenticeship in technique and musicianship. The "jam session" and the competitive climate it creates has, after all, been essential in the development of jazz. The tension between musical competence and the desire for individual expression is vital to the understanding of jazz, as the following examples can suggest. During the revival of traditional jazz in Britain in the 1950s, some players prided themselves on their indifference to refined technical skill, regarding it as an obstacle to "authentic" expression of the kind they heard in the simple style of the older, recently rediscovered, jazz musicians from New Orleans, like the clarinetist George Lewis. Jazz was seen here as being critical of a commercialized musical culture by keeping to its "folk" roots, rather than being corrupted by urban sophistication. The danger involved in this stance is of relying on the myth that an authentic, pure state of the music has been sullied by later developments. We never know that we are hearing the original of any kind of music, because it will always be related to something that precedes it.

A less problematic example of the prioritizing of expression over conventional technique is offered by John Coltrane. His music on the album *Giant Steps* reached a level of technical development that threatened to make it hard for all but the most highly trained musicians to play jazz of this kind. However, starting at the same time as *Giant Steps*, Coltrane concentrated less on rapidly changing, complex chord sequences, and instead played often relatively simple "modal" pieces based on a very few scales (though he soon incorporated some of the harmonic complexity of *Giant Steps* into his improvising on these pieces). The resulting music remained very challenging, but musicians more oriented towards "free jazz," like Shepp, and saxophonists Albert Ayler and Pharaoh Sanders, who did not have Coltrane's conventional technical facility on the saxophone, were then able to add new, unconventional approaches to the music, and so influenced Coltrane in turn. Coltrane explicitly connected his music in this period to political issues. Listen to him, for example, on the track "Alabama" (on *Live at Birdland* of 1963), which relates to an appalling racist murder of the time, which is both an anguished protest and a song of great beauty and simplicity, or to the much more dissonant "free" playing of his last recordings, which protest in a much more angry manner.

The conflicting demands on jazz musicians of expression and technique are perhaps best illustrated by the fact that the record that really established the modal approach to jazz, Miles Davis's *Kind of Blue* (1959), on which Coltrane played tenor saxophone, is one of the most commercially successful jazz records of all time. The balance between the simplified framework of the tunes and the challenge of improvising in a new manner that the musicians faced resulted in a record that was both innovative and accessible to a wider audience. Since then jazz has continued to negotiate the tension between innovation and audience appeal, and approaches to the study of jazz need to be aware of the significance of this tension in different contexts.

Jazz and the academy

Musical ideas of considerable sophistication and complexity developed by Coltrane and other leading modern jazz players, like Parker, Davis, trumpeter Dizzy Gillespie, and pianists Bud Powell and Bill Evans, have been adopted by many musicians in their improvisations, and this points to a key contemporary issue. As the resources for transcribing jazz become ever more readily available – computer technology has also made things increasingly easy – the "canon" of great jazz has become more subject to academic treatment. This often leads to methods of teaching jazz which become more like the graded methods employed in teaching classical music. The consequence is a widespread general improvement in technical competence: there are many musicians now able to play at a level previously only attainable by a few stars. However, the changes in academic evaluations of modern music that have led to previously "marginal" forms, like jazz, being taken more seriously in this way can also threaten to defuse their critical potential, by creating norms that may inhibit new ways of playing and lead to conformism. It is vital to remember, though, that jazz, especially in the USA, is no longer a dominant form of popular music, rock and pop having cornered the market. In this respect, the fact that jazz has joined the mainstream of musical studies might also have some advantages, because it enables the art form to survive and develop without being subject to the market pressures that distort the production and reception of much rock music.

Chapter summary

- Jazz both rejects and assimilates other kinds of music.
- Jazz makes different demands from those encountered in the study of other kinds of music, relying heavily on such techniques as transcription of recordings of performances.
- The social and political history of jazz is inseparable from any assessment of the development of the music.
- Jazz can be seen as a critical form of music which challenges questionable social norms, but it can also be very commercially successful, and jazz studies has begun to become a more formalized academic discipline in recent years.

Discussion topics

- Should jazz concentrate on critical opposition to other kinds of music, or should it seek to assimilate other music?
- Is jazz now too concerned with its own history, rather than with its own future?
- Does jazz rely more on innovation than tradition, or vice versa?
- Is the future of jazz as a popular or as a more esoteric form of music?

Further reading

Most of these books include suggestions for listening, as one cannot learn about jazz by reading alone. This list does not include books on discography and concentrates mainly on informative historical accounts which talk about the specifics of the music and on some manuals for learning jazz theory.

Berliner, Paul F. (1994), *Thinking in Jazz: The Infinite Art of Improvisation* (Chicago: Chicago University Press).
> An investigation of the nature of improvisation.

Cooke, Mervyn, and Horn, David (2003) (eds.), *The Cambridge Companion to Jazz* (Cambridge: Cambridge University Press).
> A selection of essays covering the main issues in the study of jazz.

DeVeaux, Scott (1997), *The Birth of Bebop: A Social and Musical History* (Berkeley, CA: University of California Press).
> A detailed musical and social account of the emergence of the music that made jazz a radical form of art.

Gioia, Ted (1999), *The History of Jazz* (Oxford: Oxford University Press).
> A readable account of jazz history.

Levine, Mark (1995), *The Jazz Theory Book* (Petaluma, CA: Sher Music).
> A good practical guide to the rhythmic, harmonic, and melodic techniques of modern jazz.

Gridley, Mark, C. (2003), *Jazz Styles: History and Analysis* (Englewood Cliffs: Prentice Hall).
> A historical and analytical account of jazz; a CD of examples to accompany the book can also be obtained.

Rawlins, Robert, Bahha, Nor Eddine, and Tagliarino, Barrett (2005), *Jazzology: The Encyclopedia of Jazz Theory* (Milwaukee, WI: Hal Leonard).
> A compendium of major elements of jazz theory.

Schuller, Gunther (1986), *Early Jazz: Its Roots and Musical Development* (New York: Oxford University Press).
> A historical and analytical account of early recorded jazz.

Schuller, Gunther (2005), *The Swing Era: The Development of Jazz, 1930–45* (New York: Oxford University Press).
> A historical and analytical account of swing.

Szwed, John F. (2000), *Jazz 101: A Complete Guide to Learning and Loving Jazz* (New York: Hyperion).
> A general history of jazz which links it to developments in society at the same time as conveying the excitement of the music.

11 Popular music

ELIZABETH EVA LEACH

Chapter preview

This chapter examines definitions of popular music and the ways in which popular music has been studied. The various meanings of the adjective "popular" show that particular meanings of both the term and the music it characterizes depend on social and historical factors. Popular music has been studied by academics from a number of different disciplinary perspectives, including sociology, cultural studies, history, media studies, and musicology. These different disciplinary emphases affect the attitude to the material, and they focus variously on the production, reception, and text of popular songs.

Key issues

- What is popular music?
- What is the popular music "text"?
- How do we study popular music?
- What are the relations between its production and reception?
- How has the study of popular music been affected by, and in turn affected, the rest of musicology?

What is popular music?

If someone asked you "what kind of music do you like?" and you were to reply "opera," they might follow up by asking "no, I meant what kind of *pop* music do you like?" In ordinary usage – the everyday conversations that take place orally, outside the classroom or lecture theater – the term "popular music" is often abbreviated, as in this hypothetical question, to "pop" or simply "music." In trying to define what is meant by "popular music," it seems easier to say what popular music is not. The speaker for whom opera does not count as music is making the commonest and most general division – popular music is that which is not the kind of music that might be referred to as serious, "high," art, or classical. By implication, defining popular music negatively in this way (it is *not* art music, *not* classical music, *not* folk music) sets up the other category (art music, classical music, folk music) as the norm, the normal, more highly valued kind of music. The idea that popular music is not classical music replicates an older division between light music and serious music, which originates in the practical categories of radio broadcasting from the early twentieth century. As we shall see below, the value-laden implications of this division had certain consequences for the early study of popular music.

If not defined normatively or negatively, popular music might instead be named after its association with a particular section of society. It is popular because it is produced and/or consumed appreciatively by the general populace – the people. Depending on the political orientation of the commentator, such a feature may make it unpleasantly vulgar or laudably democratic. For academic purposes it makes it impossible to ignore if scholarship is to have any claims to understanding prominent features of the everyday world. However, this socially based definition is not unproblematic: identifying particular sections of society can be rather difficult, especially in societies with a high degree of social mobility. Add to this the wide diffusion of popular music in the mass media, and the idea of limiting particular kinds of popular music within particular sections of the population seems doomed.

> **Box 11.1 Lawrence Grossberg on popular culture**
>
> Popular culture is a significant part of the material reality of history, effectively shaping the possibilities of our existence. It is this challenge – to understand what it means to "live in popular culture" – that confronts contemporary culture analysis.
>
> (Lawrence Grossberg, *We Gotta Get Out of this Place: Popular Conservatism and Postmodern Culture* (London and New York) 1992: 69)

In fact, the mediation of popular music is also another of its features: popular music is a kind of music whose principal means of dissemination is via the mass media, that is, through radio, television, print, and the internet. However, this definition of popular music would not differentiate it from certain pieces of classical music. Many people will not know what music I am referring to when I cite the flower duet from Léo Delibes's opera *Lakmé* (1883) until I mention its use in a television advertisement for British Airways, which has made it instantly recognisable, arguably as a piece of *popular* music. Thus some of the meanings of "popular music" conflict with one another.

From this last point it seems that what defines music as popular music is not a question of what music it is at all. However, this statement itself relies on drawing a rather strong line between what is the music and what is the context for that music. Traditionally, musicology has drawn this line rather more forcefully (and more narrowly) than other disciplines, limiting its concept of music to an idealized sonic work that is manifested completely neither in any particular score copy nor in any single performance. This "work concept" is, however, not a universally valid definition of music. Ethnomusicologists in particular might choose instead to view a whole set of social practices (actions, words) as a real part of "the music itself." So to rephrase the initial sentence of this paragraph, what defines music as popular music is not a question of those factors that traditional musicology has considered as actually part of the music itself (the stylistic features that arise from a particular set of pitches and rhythms). The very definition makes technological production of the music, performers, performance space, listeners, and use within other forms of popular culture (film, music video, TV, advertising) part of the music's definition. This said, however, popular music *does* also signal a kind of musical style, especially in its shortened form "pop," which is a more specific, *generic* term. Pop is therefore typically differentiated from types of music that, in a handy division between popular and classical music, would come *within* the field of popular music. For example, artists or fans of rock music might typically differentiate rock from pop, as might practitioners or fans of heavy metal, country music, jazz, or folk. These generic terms denote certain stylistic qualities of the music (particular types of rhythm, instrumentation, "sound") but also connote certain values, expectations, and uses of the music (for example, whether the music is a dance track or not).

> **Box 11.2 Popular music defined by Simon Frith**
>
> - Music made commercially, in a particular kind of legal (copyright) and economic (market) system.
> - Music made using ever-changing technology, with particular reference to forms of recording or sound storage.
> - Music, which is significantly experienced as mediated, tied up with the twentieth-century mass media of cinema, radio and television.
> - Music which is primarily made for pleasure, with particular importance for the social and bodily pleasures of dance and public entertainment.
> - Music which is formally hybrid, bringing together musical elements which cross social, cultural and geographical boundaries.
>
> (Frith 2004: 3–4)

In the rest of this chapter "popular music" is used to signal the music that is present in popular culture. Thus it can mean all these kinds of music – any music that is considered to merit that label by anyone; the term depends on who is listening to or consuming the music, when, and where. However, we should beware that the adjective "popular" does not always carry all of its many possible meanings and should always explore its potential for hiding value judgments. As the opposite of unpopular, it is a more valued, positive term (but this hides the fact that many songs from the sixties hit-parade are now unplayed and forgotten); as the opposite of classical (or folk) it is a negative or less valued term (classical music being supposed permanent and serious, and folk music being thought the authentic music of the people as opposed to the commercial product of the music industry). Popular music can even participate in the value of the classics, not only (as we saw above) by popularizing the classics, but also by classicizing certain hit songs which may be marked as "classic rock" and used to form a supposedly permanent canon of "greats," analogous to the masterworks of German genius from Bach to Brahms.

In fact it could be argued that the long form of the adjective – *popular* music – is now only used within academic discourse, where it is pretty much the standard term. The non-academic discourse around the different genres that academia denote by the term "popular music" entails a far finer set of generic distinctions. Academic study of these different genres of popular music similarly focuses on the specifics of those particular types of music, the way in which their audiences and producers define and talk about them, the way in which the music is used, listened to, danced to, and not listened to. However, for the purposes of this chapter's general discussion, the broad categorisation will be used as a heuristic – that is, as a convenient but provisional, and not wholly satisfactory – way of gaining access to some of the issues. However, another kind of division may be of use, because it is one that has already tacitly been in play: the focus of the inquiry may be divided into production, text, and reception.

Dividing popular music for study

The three words in bold capitals boxed in Fig. 11.1 schematically represent three semiotic fields or zones of inquiry. As the word "schematically" suggests, and the arrows and other words in lower-case text start to symbolize, all of

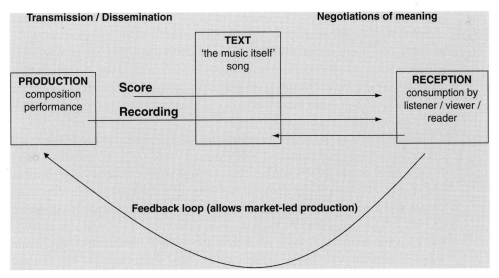

Figure 11.1 Semiotic fields or zones of inquiry in popular music

these fields could be divided further and are complex in their relation to one another.

For example, production has musical, technological, and industrial senses. Production's musical aspect is concerned with the "composition" of this music in the sense of its Latin root "*componere*" – literally, placing or putting together. Such composition could involve improvisation, performance on acoustic instruments, writing (music or lyrics), memorization, recording, and electronic assembly, for example from samples. But production also refers to the industrial aspect of popular music – the music industry or music business – and the ways in which this business functions to disseminate music. Studying this aspect of popular music might entail understanding business theory, economics, law, and technology.

Production and reception are linked by various means of transmission or dissemination – the ways that the music gets "out there" and becomes known. These are not entirely separated from production, they may be viewed as the musical text, and they could include live performance, the use of audio recordings (either as sonic material or within pop-song video), longer music videos, films, television, advertising, the internet, and so on. Studying these aspects may involve understanding the functioning of the media as well as the development of strategies for reading and understanding the products of popular culture. The latter already impinges on the field of reception.

Understanding reception poses questions about the composition of audiences, and their patterns of consumption – for example, which ages, groups, or social classes are buying what kind of music. But equally the use to which music is being put by its audience involves understanding the way the music reaches them – dissemination – which can be as audio (on the radio), as audio-visual (in films, TV, adverts, or pop-song video), or even as purely visual material (easy piano or guitar arrangements in score, cover art, stills, TV in the many places where MTV is showing but the sound system is tuned to a different channel). Reception also involves understanding the meanings that listeners receive or construct from popular music and how these meanings might be used as part of a listener's personal identity and/or in the formation of social groups and subgroups.

Lurking between the zones of production and reception is the elusive product that is being disseminated and received – the text, or "popular music itself." As was alluded to above, this musical object is often described as imaginary, idealized, or transcendent, since it is difficult to pin down. As mentioned above, in classical music it relies on an aesthetic concept in which the work floats somewhere above an individual copy of the score or a single particular performance, both of which are nevertheless judged and made legitimate (or not) by it. In popular music, the "work concept" has limited relevance because of the importance of the performer. In addition there is often no prescriptive score, and the details of the composition are not fixed. In fact, the performer might well be regarded as having the greatest claim to the status of a work, since performances and descriptive scores are judged and legitimated by his or her presence.

Regardless of these problems, however, the "text" of a piece of popular music – whether encompassing the presence of the performer(s) or not – is nevertheless an object that can be open to scholarly scrutiny for its stylistic resonances, its generic characteristics, its musical meanings. The fact that it is not possible to get at any of the aspects of the musical text in a clean, objective way – that is, these readings of the text inevitably involve aspects of production, and may implicate the scholar within the zone of reception because scholarly readings are part, albeit a small part, of the reception history of a popular song – only points to the impossibility of objectively isolating any of the other zones either. Ultimately all scholarly readings can themselves be seen as performances, producing a text that will in turn be consumed (assuming, that is, that anyone reads it).

How do we study popular music?

Studying popular music is part of the larger study of popular culture. Such a study is almost bound to be interdisciplinary in nature and has not yet quite formed a discipline in its own right, partly because it forms a smaller part of a large number of each of the humanities disciplines. Despite their interrelation, the different zones of production, text, and reception tend to hold different levels of attraction for scholars of different disciplines. Although the study of popular music within the academy is relatively new in the field of musicology, which tends to focus on the musical text, scholars from other disciplines have been studying the production and consumption of popular music for longer. Before we see how musicology now approaches this music, it is worth looking at the kinds of approaches that have been pioneered in other disciplinary fields of the modern university.

Approaches from outside musicology

Scholarship has its own history. Some of the earliest attempts to study popular music took place within the discipline of sociology, particularly among scholars interested in youth culture, and later disciplines such as cultural and media studies pursued an ever broader interest in the material from a variety of perspectives. However, one of the ways in which scholarship uses its history is to build on older foundations, utilizing, modifying, refining, or rejecting the way in which previous scholars have approached certain subjects. The scholar who is most frequently mentioned in connection with the study of popular music, especially in its theoretical and sociological aspects, is Theodor Adorno (see also chapter 5).

Adorno (1903–69) is best known to musicologists as a writer on modern music, on Schoenberg and Stravinsky, and on musical aesthetics. Adorno was a member of the "Frankfurt School," a group of scholars working at the University of Frankfurt (Germany), whose understanding of the way in which contemporary society functioned was based on the theories of Karl Marx. We are used nowadays to thinking of Marx's *Communist Manifesto* (1848; co-written with Friedrich Engels) as the intellectual justification behind the communist regimes of the old Soviet Bloc, an association that might lead us to underestimate the contemporary relevance of his thinking. In fact, Marx also wrote a long study of the workings of industrialized society, and his theories continue to provide a compelling analysis of capitalism.

Basing his ideas on the Marxist understanding of exchange value, Adorno viewed the cultural objects of popular culture as commodities rather than artworks because they possess exchange value from which the industry producing them derives a profit. This means that unlike the supposedly transcendent artistic value of, say, a Bach cantata, popular songs are, like cars or T-shirts, mass-produced to a standard mold, and then bought and sold at a profit. For Adorno the industrialized nature of the production process implicates the listener at the reception end, too. As popular songs are more or less standardized, Adorno argues, the details matter less, and the act of listening is therefore far less careful but still gives a sense of pleasure, which in fact comes from the recognition of familiarity in the music. This pleasure allows the controllers of the capital – those who own the record companies – to keep the passive listener happy and unlikely to agitate for more power (control of money) through revolution or other forms of social unrest. In short, Adorno makes two points: popular music exists to make money, rather than for its own sake; more worryingly, it makes money by distracting people from social injustice.

Although he is writing about music between the 1930s and the 1950s, at least half of Adorno's analysis rings true, even half a century later. Popular music's status as a commodity that is bought and sold is self-evident. Its deep penetration into the mass market (from vinyl singles to mp3 downloads) has at least coincided with, if not actually caused, a slump in political engagement in the West, although others would argue that the decline of social injustice during this period might represent a more likely reason for this. And some of the supporting evidence for popular music's commodity status might also have its adherents. For example, popular music is still awash with highly standardized forms – a large number of them, admittedly, but even those in the music business itself have been heard to lament the formulaic nature of certain kinds of songs.

However, is popular music *just* a commodity? Adorno's critique does not sit comfortably with anyone who wants to value popular music, either as a listener or as a scholar (or both), since it implies that it is inferior to some kind of music which is non-standardized, requires attentive listening and bids the listener reflect on the social structures of everyday life by its disruption of them. But what is this complex, socially responsible music? For Adorno it is the music of the Western classical tradition, particularly Beethoven and Schoenberg, significantly the two composers who might be seen to represent the beginning and end of music's Romantic aspiration to transcendence. Had Adorno chosen classical music that was ephemeral, functional-religious, vocal, operatic, or balletic he would have been less able to sustain his argument. One Bach cantata, it could be argued, is much like another. The Church, like the record industry, hires the composer-performer and produces the music to "sell" to its consumers, from whom it makes a profit through the collection of money. Moreover, the pleasure of these familiar tunes and familiar religious truths distracts the listeners from social injustice with the promise of happiness in the next world (after all, as Marx commented, religion is the opiate of the people – and that includes the musical commodities of religion).

On the whole, however, sociologists have accepted Adorno's analytical insights but discarded his attendant value judgment and pessimism about mass culture. In particular, his notion of standardization is now usually viewed as exaggerated – depending on how it is measured, there is as much variation in the forms of a three-minute pop song as there is in the forms of, say, a Classical piano sonata first movement. By abandoning Adorno's hierarchy between popular and classical music, sociologists make possible a more optimistic – or at least more neutral – analysis of the processes by which popular music is produced and commodified, and the kinds of responses that its listeners display.

Scholars in media studies, ethnography, geography, cultural studies, and history have tended to focus in particular on the reception of popular music, on the meanings it holds within people's everyday lives, its use in social group formation and in personal identity. This centers the attention on the meanings that audiences derive from popular music, rejecting a linear model in which the authorial meanings of a text simply emerge self-evidently. Instead the audience members are thus treated as "native witnesses" to the cultural meanings of popular music, some of which may be entirely personal, based on memories of particular life experiences. Potentially this approach opens the door to popular songs having as many meanings as listeners. One of the tasks of scholarship is to make a plausible trade-off between informed scholarly readings of production-based/authorial meanings on the one hand, and the meanings with which cultural products are imbued by their consumers on the other.

Musicological study of popular music

Approaches from other disciplines have tended to focus on either production or reception, or their socio-economic relation. Musicology's more traditional focus on musical works, composers, and the history of musical style means that its starting point is usually the musical text. The criteria by which pieces are deemed musically interesting were developed in connection with a canon of works of central European music from the "long nineteenth century" (roughly 1789–1914). Methods of music analysis – principally dealing with the harmonic interrelation of pitches – were developed to "prove" the fulfillment of these criteria and bolster the place of particular works within the canon. These tools were ill-suited to do anything to popular music other than simply dismissing it (or worse, condemning it, as we have seen with Adorno, who was trained with exactly these tools). The products of popular music are short songs (a form not traditionally central to musicological inquiry even when the songs concerned are art songs), with seemingly banal and/or salacious lyrics, offering pleasurable entertainment in exchange for money. Studies of popular music in other disciplines had ironically underscored this judgment by focusing on those things (production and reception) that, as far as musicology's tools were concerned, were not part of "the music itself." This allowed musicology to conclude that the proper study of popular music was not a musicological one, since its important features were not its musical features.

In the 1980s, several things happened that changed this picture. The presuppositions of certain methods of music analysis were challenged by outlining analysis's role in the formation of the classical canon. There appeared to be a clear parallel between the exclusion of certain classical genres, works, or composers from the classical canon on the one hand and the exclusion of popular music from musicological writing on the other. Both were excluded because they did not meet certain analytical standards. Yet just as methods of music analysis have been modified to deal with these previously marginalized musics "on their own terms," so these methods have been applied to popular music. Musicology's sharp line between music and context was erased and redrawn in very light pencil. Sociological perspectives and methodologies from literary theory were more regularly used in approaching the music of the Western art tradition. While production – at the level of interest in the composer at least – had always been a focus of musicological study, musicological approaches that focused on the musical text tended to adopt many of the same "readerly" approaches from literary and cultural studies as a way of discussing reception. By examining these texts and/or interpretations of them by performers or readers (reading itself being viewed as a kind of performance) scholars could read them for their construction of gender, sexuality, race, social class, and so on.

The regular inclusion of popular music within musicology also dates from this period, with the founding of the journal *Popular Music* and the International Association for the Study of Popular Music (IASPM) in 1981. Popular songs tend now to be discussed by musicologists specifically as "texts" that are strongly anchored in their contemporary social and discursive settings. Exegetical – that is, interpretative – readings of popular songs may thus draw on the way in which these songs circulate within society – as sonic material (listened to, danced to, or background), as videos in various spaces, as part of film tracks, as textualized merchandise (sheet music, fan materials). Treating popular music as a series of texts has the added advantage of allowing for historical musicological perspectives as well as analytical ones. Most sociological and anthropological approaches have relied on the observation of contemporary traditions – even if that contemporaneity is the afterlife of the continued availability of recordings or the continuation of fan culture after the death of an artist. However, popular music exists from before the existence of sound recording. Music not documented in sound is very literally a text, and can be treated in much the same way as the similarly under-notated performance-centered repertories of, for example, the Middle Ages (see Chapter 7).

The benefits of interdisciplinary study

It could therefore be argued that there has been mutual benefit from the incorporation of the study of popular music within musicology by university-based scholars. On one hand the study of popular music has benefited from the insights of scholars equipped to deal with the musical materials, especially if these scholars have been able to adapt their technical expertise in an open-minded way (as opposed to trying to make popular music fit classical harmony and disregarding its performative aspects). These adaptations have benefited the music previously marginalized and non-canonical in musicological study (such as song, opera, non-Western musics, and musical ephemera) in similar ways. On the other hand, the removal of privileged and transcendent status from traditional objects of musicological study has benefited musicology by offering new more historically detached insights on the sociological, cultural, and historical situation of canonical Western art music. In particular, the fact that popular music is seldom prescriptively notated has drawn attention to the importance of recordings and performance for all musicological study.

Popular music studies is now thoroughly institutionalized within the academy and has become an industry in its own right. Popular music now features in course units within traditional music degrees, and as entire programs; there are lectureships and chairs specifically in the subject, and university presses publish books and scholarly journals dedicated to the subject. And if, as Richard Middleton has commented, Pseuds' Corner still beckons for those who apply elite intellectual capital to the raw stuff of the vernacular, this says more about a press for whom the word "academic" is a synonym for irrelevant (as in the phrase "well, that's a bit of an academic issue, really") than about the academic study of popular music. Whether you ignore popular music entirely or subject it to your own form of intellectual inquiry, studying at university requires you to take an intellectual view of non-intellectual, and even anti-intellectual material. Only by thinking about popular music can we understand its manifold roles as a source of revenue, meaning, memory, identity, and pleasure.

Chapter summary

This chapter has discussed the following points:

- Popular music is a broad term whose exact application usually depends on the context within which it is used.
- Popular music has been studied as an aspect of the society of which it is part, by looking at the way in which it reflects and forms the ideas of that particular society.
- The inclusion of popular music as an object of musicological interest both reflects and drives musicologists' understanding of the ways in which musical values they formerly accepted as universal and transcendent are in fact dependent on historical and social factors.

Discussion topics

1. Think of a pop song that has been especially important to you, trying to understand the meanings you ascribe to it and how these have been generated. Are there moments in its history when the song's meaning has been changed, and, if so, how have these changes come about?
2. Follow a local (perhaps campus-based) band or DJ for a defined period of time, making an ethnographic micro-study. How is this kind of popular music funded? Does it make a profit? How are the songs composed? What kind of relationship exists between production and reception? What pleasures do listeners derive from these songs, and what meanings do they construct with them?

3. Hold a class discussion about whether reality TV talent game shows like *American Idol* (or the British original of this format, *Pop Idol*) are a gain or a loss for popular music as a cultural form: "Is *American Idol* (or *Pop Idol*) the end of good pop music?" Then reflect on the ways in which the answers to this question provide evidence for the kinds of values that individuals desire or imagine to be present in popular music. How have these value judgments been informed or created?

Further reading

Connell, John and Gibson, Chris (2003), *Sound Tracks: Popular Music, Identity and Place* (London: Routledge).

Written by two geographers, this reflects on music's ability to construct and define personal identity and a sense of place. The book explores the tension between globalization and music's marketable ability to project local spaces, tradition, authenticity, and originality. It offers an interesting global perspective on the production, diffusion, and reception of popular music.

Frith, Simon (2004) (ed.), *Popular Music: Critical Concepts in Media and Cultural Studies*, 4 vols (London: Routledge).

A four-volume collection, which reprints 77 of the most useful and interesting essays on specific aspects of popular music study. It also has a useful introduction.

Longhurst, Brian (1995), *Popular Music and Society* (Cambridge: Polity).

A clearly written introduction to many of the main issues surrounding the production, text, and audience of popular music. Designed as a classroom textbook for use by students in sociology, cultural studies, media studies and communications, it offers students in musicology a clear guide to popular music's broader context.

Middleton, Richard (1990), *Studying Popular Music* (Milton Keynes: Open University Press).

Uses popular music as a way of critiquing traditional musical histories. It examines theories of production, notably that of Adorno, as well as offering a wide range of analytical approaches.

Shuker, Roy (1998), *Key Concepts in Popular Music* (London: Routledge).

A dictionary of terms associated with studying popular music. It provides useful short definitions, is cross-referenced to related concepts, and makes suggestions for further reading and has a full bibliography.

The main academic journal, *Popular Music*, published by CUP, is worth browsing in hard copy or electronically if your library subscribes (full contents listing is available on-line without subscription from http://journals.cambridge.org/action/displayJournal?jid=PMU). Although scholarly articles on popular music are increasingly appearing in general musicological journals and continue to be published in journals of communication, media studies, sociology and cultural studies, *Popular Music* remains a key locus of scholarship.

References

Grossberg, Lawrence (1992) *We Gotta Get Out of this Place: Popular Conservatism and Postmodern Culture* (London and New York: Routledge).

12 Music in film and television

JULIE BROWN

Chapter preview

Music is an essential part of film and television, and yet it always competes for its place in the "soundtrack" with other sonic elements. What many would describe as the "soundtrack" in television and film therefore makes a slippery object of musicological study. Should we think of the music as functioning separately from sound effects and dialogue? If so, is this really justified by our twenty-first-century understanding of music? How does the sound element of sound cinema or screen-based multimedia fit into the history of nineteenth- and twentieth-century music? This chapter traces some of the issues that film and television present to musicologists.

Key issues

- What is music's role in film and television?
- Has it changed over the history of sound cinema and other screen forms?
- Does the relationship depend on the moving image practice involved?
- What approaches to the study of music in film and television have been adopted?

Case study

Let us start with a short sequence about an hour into *Blade Runner: Director's Cut* (1982), directed by Ridley Scott, with music by Vangelis.

It is Los Angeles in 2019; former "blade runner" (policeman/assassin) Rick Deckard (Harrison Ford) has been re-engaged to retire outlaw replicants (androids). Cut to Deckard's dark and dreary apartment: Deckard and Rachael (Sean Young) are present. Deckard's near-musical "roomtone" is established as a faint, low hum with a detectable pitch – a trilling motion from B to C. When Rachael reveals that she is herself a replicant, this is a cue for music – that is, "pit," or **nondiegetic** music (Box 12.1). It is synthesized rather than orchestral: "dark" C minor string sounds, which lend the moment an uncertainty, a potentially ominous ring. These shuddering sounds suggest shivering (anxiety? fear?), pulsating beats, the quickening of a heart. The sense of a distinction between sound and music begins to dissolve.

Deckard moves to his bathroom and the roomtone becomes more prominent, assuming the status of an ominous pedal note and, according to narrative film-music conventions, increasing our expectation that something might happen. As he takes off his shirt, we hear the chord change (from E♭ minor to A♭ major), more electroacoustic shuddering effects, and the beginnings of some conventionalized computer-sounds ("peep peep peep"). Whether this is **diegetic** sound for the computer on the wall or replicant Rachael thinking remains unclear. As Rachael approaches Deckard, the synth string sonority grows louder and louder, encouraging us to think that she might attack him.

Suddenly the ominous music dissolves. Deckard is safe; Rachael merely asks whether he will chase her if she heads north (he won't). Descending flutters of computer "peeping" once more seem attached both to the computer screen flickering on the wall and to Rachael, whose face we cut to in close-up. Rachael's eyes are down, contemplative; Deckard is now behind her. He says: "But somebody would." A tritone lends the melodic punctuation an interrogative turn: A♮ to E♭ and more computer "peeping." Now, with a close-up of Rachael, the peeping seems to attach quite distinctly to her replicant thought processes, and to this extent amplify her deliberate visual framing as replicant. Now when she speaks to him against the ominous underscore, her voice seems too controlled, too sweet. Fake. Dangerous. Cut to her creeping in towards him, and another melodic punctuation from C to E♭.

Once she enters Deckard's room, the suggestion of a saxophone in the preceding music is confirmed. Deckard is asleep, bare-chested on the sofa, and the saxophone's languid line, identified as the "Love Theme" on the released CD soundtrack, immediately starts up. The alternating chords G♭7 to Fm7 and cool, lounge-lizard jazz inflections absorb both the sleeping and erotic connotations of the image, also perhaps the film's "noir" genre associations. This audio-visual combination creates for us an eroticized point of view, which, because of the camera angle, is unmistakably Rachael's. She approaches a piano and starts to take off her jacket. The vaguely sexual connotations of the music now equally aptly underscore her own undressing, and soon her erotically slow letting down of her hair. When the saxophone phrase ends, Rachael starts to play the piano – her music being at first "source" or "diegetic" music, but soon combining seamlessly with the synth strings and saxophone. A plagal gesture in the music, D♭ to G♭, emphasizes the lullaby dimension of the music, which brings to the scene connotations of slumber (because of Deckard's nap), dreams (as Rachael surveys photos on the piano), and perhaps even innocence after the previous scenes. Taken together, the sound world of this scene and the conventional shot of woman at a domestic piano seem to narrate something of her character's progression from replicant to feeling- and memory-filled human(oid). She and the scene as a whole are filled with humanity, even nostalgia.

Deckard soon sits with her at the piano, and then moves to kiss her. She looks puzzled, wooden. The music starts to take another ominous turn … We now begin to wonder whether she feels anything after all. Has the music been misleading us?

Dividing film music for study

What are our sources?

The sequence above brings into focus many of the issues likely to confront a student of film music and soundtracks. First: like me here, he or she often has only, or mainly, the film as released to go on. While it is easy to buy certain of the better-known *Blade Runner* cues in popular arrangements, it is not possible to get hold of a written score, if indeed such a thing exists for this largely electronic soundtrack. There are commercial editions of some other canonized orchestral film scores; the option in "film music" that the Edexcel board offers for the British A-level examination in Music is based almost entirely around the analysis of written scores, which are made available for close analysis alongside other orchestral works in a course booklet. Published concert-suite versions of film scores sometimes also exist and can prove useful resources. For historical research it might also be possible to consult original source material in film-music archives. The University of California, Los Angeles, has a large collection of this sort; the British Library has a more limited selection of film-score materials, by Vaughan Williams, John Ireland, and others; the British Film Institute (BFI) and the Royal College of Music both hold small eclectic collections of mainly donated scores; the BFI also holds a large collection of music cue sheets – that is, indications of when music appeared in a given "silent" film and who composed it, but not the music itself. These archives are still quite partial, however, and it is still the case that for most analytical and critical work on film and television music our main source is the audio-visual text itself as commercially released. Even this is complicated by the issuing of directors' cuts (as in *Blade Runner*) and the inclusion of out-takes on DVD packages.

We face additional source problems with films of the so-called "silent film" era inasmuch as commercially available prints of such films might themselves be pieced together from old prints, rather than from the original reels. These films were often re-edited for specific exhibition circumstances. Moreover, when music is synchronized with "silent" films for a commercial re-release, the actual synchronization may only be an approximation of what was originally intended, even if both the film stock and the music are "correct" according to available documentary evidence. This is almost as true of thoughtful and scholarly re-issuings as it is of obviously poor examples. The re-issue of Cecil B. DeMille's *Carmen* (1915) with Hugo Riesenfeld's arrangement of Bizet's score finally gives us a print of the film with the original music that was located and recorded by Gillian B. Anderson; the synchronization produced under Anderson's supervision is nevertheless only her best guess. Martin Marks's piano accompaniments for the silent-film collection *Treasures from American Film Archives*, issued on DVD by the National Film Preservation Foundation (San Francisco, 2000), are thoughtful and pedagogically useful examples of their kind, drawing on Movie Mood books and popular songs of the day, and yet Marks's music likely reflects only the most informed and sophisticated approaches to silent-film accompaniment of the time; we know from contemporary accounts that approaches to silent-film accompaniment were quite diverse, and often quite playful, as one would expect from a musical practice entirely dependent upon available local talent and for a long time subject to little guidance. He also makes use of Erno Rapée's *Motion Picture Moods for Pianists and Organists* (1924) for films produced twenty years earlier. For all these reasons, one might argue that the early history of film music is as much a topic of concern for those in Performance Studies. The music accompanying film was often performed live, often improvised, was subject to both historically and locally specific practices, and music was performed as frequently between film showings as during them.

Television raises different questions. Of its nature, television is more ephemeral than film; in the early days of the medium, stocks of film were often disposed of or reused immediately after being broadcast, with the consequence that archival resources can be patchy indeed. Related to this is the fact that turnover pressures and limited budgets mean that television – like radio – has also made considerable use of music libraries – that is, recorded collections of music types (happy music, sad music, etc.). The sources for a student of television music might be collections of library music, their concern the circulation and cross-use of particular library music collections, as much as it is television-specific formal or generic concerns. The pressure of (post-) production schedules in both television and film, coupled with advances in technology, may also mean that more recent "scores" have been composed directly into a computer. There may be very little available beyond the finished synchronized audio-visual text itself. *Blade Runner*'s score was created by Greek composer Vangelis largely in an electronic studio, for instance – and that was as long ago as 1982. Indeed, a scholar of Vangelis's films not only has no readily available score to consult, but little from the composer himself; the Greek composer is famously reluctant to speak about his approach and method. Analysis and criticism of film music often, therefore, demands that we make our own transcriptions. To limit oneself to studying films for which a score is readily available would be to restrict the critical field impossibly.

What is our object of study?

For many, the object of study is the music alone, which is extracted from the film and treated as concert music; orchestral concert programs increasingly include cues from classic film scores which are reified in this way and per-formed as if they were pieces of "purely" symphonic music. Implicit in this approach is an attempt to recuperate a music not previously taken seriously, or seriously enough. In classic Hollywood films music does often appear in discrete sections relatively unencumbered by dialogue and other sounds (see principle 2 in Box 12.1: Gorbman's Seven Principles, which includes the fact that music generally gives way to the dialogue, to which it is secondary), and to a certain extent is therefore susceptible to this sort of isolation. It is not the case in all films, however, especially Hollywood films of the last twenty years or so. The way music functions in *Blade Runner* suggests a different object of study. Though more and more music accompanies the above scene as it unfolds, it is difficult to separate that music from other sounds. When, for instance, do the "peeping" computer sounds stop being simply sound effects and come to be perceived as high-pitched synthesized musical notes which are part of the electronic underscore? Does it matter? The answer to this last question must be "yes" if one is approaching this scene as a critic/analyst. The progression of the "peeping" from ambiguous sound effect (computer screen? or Rachael?) to clear sound effect (definitely Rachael thinking) to music (apparently part of a complex soundscape helping to figure her cinema-tically) is a feature of the scene. The fact that the film's music is largely synthesized and many of its sound effects reflect the sci-fi story's preoccupa-tion with technology means that music and sound effects easily mutate one into the other – and do so apparently deliberately here. Transmuted into a quasi-vibes sound the computer "peeping" ultimately becomes part of a complex of musical sounds associated with Rachael. This progression from "underscoring" with computer "peeping" to saxophone melody, to self-expression at the piano (or is it the expression of Tyrell's niece, whose memories have been implanted in Rachael?) is part of her characterization as replicant becoming human-like, and of the film's engagement with the nature of memory.

Given that cinematic sound and musical practices developed in the twentieth century in parallel with a profound questioning by "art music" composers of the very nature of music, its composition and performance (the Futurists, John Cage, composers of *musique concrète*, and many others), it would be eccentric to ignore the fact that in almost all contemporary commercial films it can be hard to decide where music leaves off and sound effects, ambient noise, and even dialogue begin. Sound has long been an important expressive dimension of film. There was the sound effects person behind the screen in the silent era. There are also directors, such as Alfred Hitchcock, whose *The Birds* (1963), like *Secret Agent* (1936) and *Rear Window* (1954), has no "pit" or nondiegetic music, but relies almost exclusively on sounds – above all, bird sounds – for its sonic effects (Weis 1982). These bird sounds were only partly realistic; they were also significantly enhanced (or "rendered," to use Michel Chion's terminology) by constructed electronic effects by Remmi Gassman and Oskar Sala. Bernard Herrman, a founding and by then veteran composer of classic Hollywood film music, and a long-term collaborator of Hitchcock's (he composed the music to both *Psycho* and *Vertigo*), served as sound consultant.

But sounds can also be created from scratch. What is the sound of a light saber? What sound does a head make when it is violently smashed in? Either the sound is imaginary and needs inventing, or no one tasked with the job knows (fortunately). Creating these is the job of sound effects specialists who closely mike, for instance, a watermelon being smashed by way of legal substitute for a head being smashed, or blend the sound of a TV set and an old 35 mm projector to create the hum created by a light saber, as Ben Burtt, sound editor of *Star Wars*, did. To these are added the subtler sounds of the "foley artist" (named after Jack Foley, a sound editor at Universal Studios), the person who in post-production (re)creates the subtle synchronous sounds that production mikes often miss, such as footsteps, the sound of clothes brushing past furniture, the tapping of fingers at a keyboard, etc. Narrative film demands it: if the camera moves from pointed close-up to pointed close-up, narrative meaning asks that we hear these scenes as well. These are all positioned, in turn, within what might be an equally constructed "atmosphere" or "room tone." Sound effects and ambient soundscapes are not always heavily constructed; outside the Hollywood tradition there is more of a tendency to use location sounds; however, even location sound has an expressive quality warranting careful reading.

The soundtrack also includes dialogue. Dialogue might be parodically inflected to the point of musicality, as happens in cartoons: listen to an episode of *The Simpsons* to verify this proposition. In "Snow Woman" of Masaki Kobayashi's *Kwaidan* (1964), the ghost's words create rich sonic effects as breathy voiceover, then extremely "grainy," closely miked vocal presence, against Tōru Takemitsu's eerie electronic soundscape – this latter, a cross between expressive cinematic music exploiting many narrative film-music ploys, and an asynchronous electronic score. Yet voice doesn't have to be obviously rhythmic, specifically musical, especially breathy and "grainy," or extremely closely miked to form an important part of cinematic soundscapes. The contribution made by dialogue can also be of historical and/or generic interest in the overall construction of the soundscape: accents used in 1930s Hollywood vary considerably from those used today and arguably strike our ears as having a peculiarly alien, quasi-musical quality to them; the verbal constructedness of cowboys with stock dialogue such as "Howdy pardner!" and mobsters with the accents and vocabulary used in *The Sopranos* seems clear (Kozloff 1999). Voice might be justified by an onscreen source or not; it might also be a voiceover. All of these vocal types and cinematic placements create different effects within a multilayered soundscape and serve different roles as part of the film's textuality as a whole.

As we have seen, in our *Blade Runner* sequence expressive use is made of the move from outside atmosphere to inside space, and also in the interaction between sound and musical elements. Voices are also important. Inside, both voices sound closely miked; Rachael's also seems a little too calm, occasionally almost detached from her bodily presence, an effect that might be an accidental by-product of Sean Young's post-production studio re-recording of her dialogue – a common enough procedure, especially in commercial film, referred to as ADR (automated dialogue replacement) – or equally a deliberate directorial strategy to emphasize her half-human, half-robot status. It doesn't really matter which; the effect is what's important. Her voice is both intimate, as a result of being closely miked and placed high in the mix, and strangely removed from her physical presence. Given her bodily absence and the effect of the underscore, it sounds *too* innocent. By contrast, Deckard's dialogue in this scene is choked, obstructed by his bloody, swollen mouth and the water he had used to wash it out. Chiming with the rain sounds of the bleak futuristic cityscape, and with even the "peeping" computer sounds, its sonic qualities contribute to the film's construction of a dystopian atmosphere.

Long an implicit strategy in some directors' work, and even traceable to the cinema organist's job of integrating sound effects with music on the cinema organ, "sound design" is now often an aspect of film-making credited formally. The term was Walter Murch's way of describing his work on *Apocalypse Now* (Francis Ford Coppola, 1979), for which he won an Oscar. Murch – considered the "great" of sound design – has argued that this sort of careful layering of the three sonic elements (sound, dialogue, and music), the quadraphonic mixing, and the three-dimensional placement of the resultant "soundtrack" in cinematic space is a sonic equivalent to interior design (Murch/Cousins 1996). It is not only because of such developments as these that Rick Altman *et al.*'s concept of mise-en-bande seems perfectly justified, indeed a very useful equivalent of mise-en-scène for describing the nature and placement of all sonic elements within the soundtrack (Altman *et al.* 2000). Since film and sound were first synchronized, sound, dialogue and silence have all been part of the film soundtrack; however, as sound production and reproduction have improved – since the 1960s, say – the importance of sound effects and voice as elements of film's expressive language has increased and become more complex. Sound design is far less useful a notion to bring to television, however; the smaller-scale medium, the tighter budgets, the tendency to use less music and more location sound, and the commercially driven need to turn products around much more quickly means that less time and resource tends to be devoted to this side of television, even television dramas.

Approaches to textual study

Though of necessity my analysis of the *Blade Runner* sequence involves more description than one might normally include in an analysis, it is effectively the beginnings of a close textual study of that section of the film. This is a quite different exercise to excerpting the music from the film and analyzing it alone. There is nothing to stop one doing the latter; however to aestheticize the music is to miss its functional point. Since the advent of the talkies, film music's very existence has been subject to its electronically mediated, mechanical synchronization with moving images.

Various approaches to textual study have developed, some quite traditional. For instance, despite the fact that the musicological academy was opened to film-music studies as a result of a paradigm shift in musicology, a book series published by Greenwood Press takes a "monuments of music" approach, for instance, much along the lines of the Cambridge University Press Handbook and Music in Context series, considering the music's genesis, existing archival materials, and including a textual analysis: at the time of going to print, major studies had been published of Bernard Herrmann's music for Alfred Hitchcock's *Vertigo* (1958) and Max Steiner's music for Irving Rapper's *Now, Voyager* (1942). Film-music and soundtrack studies nevertheless generates its own theory apace. Because Hollywood and commercial film-scoring practice has long been conducted according to a reasonably fixed syntax and semiotics, it has been possible to identify a type of grammar of classic narrative film scoring (see the work of Adorno and Eisler 1947/1994; Gorbman 1987; Kalinak 1992; and Kassabian 2001).

From this work we have a now standard vocabulary to describe recurring features of narrative film scoring. Distinctions between "diegetic," "non-diegetic," and "metadiegetic" music remain useful for explanation even when problematized by such genres as the film musical, and such techniques as the move of Rachael's piano music from diegetic to nondiegetic spheres in *Blade Runner*. (Robynn Stilwell describes this phenomenon as the "fantastical gap.") Gorbman's list of Seven Key Principles of Composition, Mixing and Editing in classic Hollywood practice also remain useful (see Box 12.1), as do Gorbman's and others' accounts of classic film scoring's contribution to our situatedness as audio-viewers of a film; that is, narrative film's ability to encourage us to assume particular positions in relation to what we are seeing unfold onscreen. In Adorno and Eisler's book *Composing for the Films*, this critique is rooted in Marxist thought and stems from their observation of artistic practices under totalitarianism. Though they have purely aesthetic objections to (narrative) film music (arguing that it trivializes aspects of musical form such as leitmotif, etc.) their key concern is that it transforms an "object event" into an affect-object event, and undermines the ability of the audio-viewer to retain a critical distance from the events represented onscreen. Though ideological critique is sidelined in Gorbman's account, she adds a psychoanalytical gloss to the **"suturing"** process by which music contributes to cinema's becoming an affect-object event, and we are rendered slightly more malleable. These clear "positioning" effects are used to quite manipulative ends in our *Blade Runner* scene, partly, it seems, to assist in the film's creation of thriller-style genre effects; in this scene the music leads us to think (fear?) that Rachael might do something to hurt Deckard, only for her not to; it leads us to believe that she humanizes, only to undermine this when Deckard kisses her. The music is pulling us into specific positions vis-à-vis what we see on screen, helping to create and resolve fears and beliefs. It does so because of the power of narrative underscoring to do so; it does so in this particularly manipulative way, I would suggest, because of genre norms.

Approaching film from the perspective of a more inclusive soundscape, rather than from the music alone, will benefit from Michel Chion's attempt to theorize **"audio-vision"** more generally. Chion describes and creates a theoretical vocabulary for a range of film sound events, and yet his underlying argument is that "there is no soundtrack," that "the different sounds which are present in a film (words, noises, diverse musics and sounds) and contribute to its meaning, its shape and its effects do not by themselves, by the sheer virtue of their all being sound elements, make up a comprehensive entity that is interdependent and homogenous" (see Box 12.2). For him, "in the cinema the relations of meaning, contrast, concordance or divergence that words, noises and musical elements are likely to entertain with one another are much weaker, even non-existent, in comparison with the relations each of the sound elements, on its own, has with a given visual or narrative element present simultaneously in the image." Well, yes. Cinematic music and sound are both dependent on, and interact with, the visual domain. However, one might want to agree with Nicholas Cook (1998) that the balance in this relationship is capable of being turned upside down. (Though Cook privileges music among the sonic elements, and considers film and television more exclusively

Box 12.2 Chion on the soundtrack

The absence of a sound frame is one of the main reasons which, for a long time, has led me to assert that there is no soundtrack. By this I mean that the different sounds which are present in a film (words, noises, diverse musics and sounds) and contribute to its meaning, its shape and its effects do not by themselves, by the sheer virtue of their all being sound elements, make up a comprehensive entity that is interdependent and homogenous. In other words, in the cinema the relations of meaning, contrast, concordance or divergence that words, noises and musical elements are likely to entertain with one another are much weaker, even non-existent, in comparison with the relations each of the sound elements, on its own, has with a given visual or narrative element present simultaneously in the image.

(Chion 2000: 204)

as "musical multimedia," and comparable in this respect to other musical multimedia such as the more simple song genre.) Moreover, because sound design is increasingly complex, it is still revealing to contemplate this "soundtrack," this comprehensive multi-dimensional entity, by itself – especially if one wants to include film in the history of music.

Semiotics has much to offer students of film music. As Phil Tagg, Anahid Kassabian, and others have spelled out, there are quite high levels of inter-subjective agreement about the meanings routinely created by film and television music, especially in commercial film and television. The musical semantics exploited range from the conventional to the historical, and even to the bioacoustic – namely my readings of certain musical gestures in *Blade Runner* as musical analogs to "heart beating" and "shivering." My suggestion that both the saxophone and piano melodies carry meanings associated with their genre reference – lullaby – depends on an ability to hear and articulate that association; my suggestion that the jazz also links with "film noir," on a knowledge of film history and music's deployment as part of that history. Its semantics retain a certain ambiguity, however, and remain interdependent on other visual and spoken meanings: the lullaby signifies in various directions, for instance, towards Deckard's actual sleep, towards Rachael's exploration of an almost dreamlike past, and even towards the marked innocence of this scene compared to many in the film. Even the most conventional of musical gestures still begs analysis. However, if recognizing the general expressive intention of Hollywood music is quite easy – it is arguably the musical *lingua franca* of our time – analyzing how and why it expresses depends on a knowledge of musical genres, the conventions of nineteenth-century operatic and program music, and an enormous number of conventions and clichés that have developed in film itself: atonality is routinely associated with horror or extreme danger; jazz with eroticism; funk with urban streetscapes; the swelling of volume, especially when the musical device is already creating tension, with a sense of imminent danger (the equivalent of gradually raising your voice at someone to underline a point), etc. These, in turn, might be analyzed for their ability to construct a film's ideological position. When John Williams repeatedly draws on Aaron Copland-esque clichés to depict Americana, what might the ideological fall-out be? How does it position us as audio-viewers of the opening sequences of *Saving Private Ryan* (Steven Spielberg, 1998) and *JFK* (Oliver Stone, 1991)?

Ultimately, critical approaches to film and television music can draw on as many critical techniques as we can muster! In order to be able to say anything about the music itself, we need to draw on our entire musical knowledge – including our knowledge of popular music, given the prevalence of composite pop-music soundtracks. And not only do we need to be able to discuss what we hear (articulate perspectives on musical style, genre, form, motivic and harmonic language, historical context, etc.), we also need a critical vocabulary for analyzing what we see on screen. We therefore need to have a working understanding of filming techniques, to know what establishing shots, point-of-view shots, shot reverse-shots, tracking shots, etc. are; we need to develop a critical eye for reading mise-en-scène and framing, and also for the ways in which narrative and character develop; we need an overall sense of genre and international film styles. In analyzing the role music plays in screen multimedia, we can also potentially draw on any aspect of cultural and literary theory, including gender and postcolonial theory. In approaching music on television, we might be especially keen to delve into cultural, critical, and postmodern theory, given their special pertinence to television as a cultural form. Television's twenty-four-hour presence in the family home, its smaller-scale screen, its tradition of variety formats including music performances in front of a live studio audience, its frequent structuring around commercial breaks, and since the early 1980s its use for the marketing of popular sound recordings via music videos, also suggests that television music studies benefit from close engagement with both performance and popular music studies. My own study of music's role in *Ally McBeal* is one such attempt to marry a range of theoretical and critical approaches. Music's role in computer and video games is dependent on all of the other genres, but raises additional questions as a result of user inter-activity and, if one takes into account game avatars and internet sites such as Second Life, the nature of our (virtual) subject position in relation to what we audio-view. Scholarship has barely even begun to address these questions.

How does it fit into the history of music?

... melodrama, opera, classic Hollywood

To move beyond textual criticism and on to history, it might be argued that reflecting on film and television music opens up important questions about existing accounts of twentieth-century music history (see chapter 1 on center, periphery, and the canon). A typical historical perspective on film music from within film-music studies demonstrates the debts that classic Hollywood film-music practices owe to opera, melodrama, and late-nineteenth-century program music in general. This approach can be supplemented, however, by related histories, such as one identifying twentieth-century Austro-German music bifurcated after its turn-of-the-century post-Wagnerian phase, and proceeding down the atonal route (via Schoenberg), or down the Hollywood route (via Korngold). Another might notice the reciprocal relationship between the two cultural spheres. For instance, those in the film business recognized quite early the prestige that opera could bring to what had been a somewhat disreputable cultural form; de Mille's *Carmen*, starring opera singer Geraldine Farrar, was an overt attempt to borrow some of opera's prestige, as was the building of lavish picture palaces. The production of instructions for adding music to silent films borrowed from stage melodrama practices. Hollywood film music, with its ability to add epic grandeur to film, its use of a broadly late nineteenth-century musical language, and exploitation of leitmotifs becomes a kind of people's opera. The intertwining of film, melodrama, and opera is a multilayered one.

... vaudeville, film musicals, music video, music television

From yet another perspective, film and television music is deeply embedded in a history of relationships with popular music and popular stage performance, and in this connection might be approached more from a cultural studies perspective, or informed by work going on in popular music studies (see chapter 11). As Rick Altman has shown, the early history of the relationship between film and music was more unruly than the opera–melodrama–film-music narrative suggests. Live music was sometimes provided as entertainment between genuinely silent film showings; films were sometimes effectively illustrations of gramophone records, and even earlier popular songs were marketed in sheet-music form alongside live performances of the songs accompanied by lantern slides. If we look at the history of film music from this perspective, we can see continuities across the century between synergetic marketing strategies involving popular music (from sheet music through to pop music on records and CDs), and from vaudeville stage performances of popular songs, via various musical practices during the "silent film" era, through Hollywood film musicals (remembering that the first commercially successful "talkies" were film musicals of a quite vaudevillean type), through the development of a distinctly cinematic form of film musical, to cinematic exploitations of stage musicals, to rock 'n' roll musicals, to music video, whose aesthetics have fed back into mainstream cinema in a particularly MTV style of shooting and use of pop and rock song soundtracks. Perhaps unlikely film genres such as the romantic comedy seem to owe much to this specific history; despite the recent revival of screen musicals, the romantic comedy is arguably the film musical *de nos jours*, having very similar narrative structures to classic film musicals of the 1930s and 40s and pop songs serving a similar function to songs that were originally diegetically performed numbers (see Garwood 2003).

It is important to factor television music into this particular historical perspective on the twentieth century. Both radio and television were also outgrowths of vaudeville, though in a different way to film: both have long involved live variety formats, and live musical performance as part of this. Though the traditional variety format has now largely disappeared from television schedules, we find traces of it in situation comedies (with Frasier occasionally playing at the piano in the sitcom of the same name, and *Ally McBeal*'s deeply playful appropriation of a variety of musical styles), and new versions of it in the various *Pop Idol*-style formats. Approaches to music's role in these areas might be interested as much by socio-economic and cultural critical questions as with aesthetic ones.

... *mise-en-bande*, sound design, *musique concrète*

To approach a film in such a way as to consider music as only one of several sound elements positions the soundtrack phenomenon at the heart of one of the major trends in twentieth-century "art music": *musique concrète* and electro-acoustic music. The theoretical writings of Michel Chion manifest this connection most obviously – above all through his use of technical categories coined by Pierre Schaeffer for describing electroacoustic music; the need for a theoretical category such as "acousmatic music," that is, music without a visible source, is as great for "art music" coming through loudspeakers, as it is for cinematic music without an onscreen source. Chion, himself also an electroacoustic composer, has extended this vocabulary to include such terms as "acousmêtre," which conflates "acousmatic" with the French word "être" ("to be," or "being") for the purposes of describing a cinematic vocal presence without visual justification. (The wizard in *The Wizard of Oz*, Hal in *2001: A Space Odyssey*, voices coming down a telephone line without specific visual justification, much beloved of horror films ...) Whatever you think about individual terms from Chion's exhaustive theoretical vocabulary for sound events and modes of cinematic listening, you cannot reproach him for not taking seriously the complexity of the soundtrack as a phenomenon. His theory gestures towards the inclusion of the cinematic soundtrack within an art-historical perspective on music as organized sound, despite his statement that "there is no soundtrack." There is, in fact, very little conceptual space between a soundtrack considered in this way and *musique concrète*, or John Cage's theories of music, sound, and silence, or even such collage works involving voice, sung and spoken, taped, and orchestral elements as Luciano Berio's *Sinfonia* (1968–9). Notwithstanding the musical language employed by the traditionally understood musical element in film, when such music is combined with sound, voice, and silence in the soundtrack it can be positioned within this trend of progressive twentieth-century composition. Indeed, the compositional trend in "art music" might just as easily be understood as an adjunct to the cinematic phenomena. We know that reception of some modernist music of the mid-twentieth-century came to be judged against cinematic music; Messiaen's *Turangalîla Symphony* was felt by some critics to be too much like film music, an observation that was not meant as a compliment.

The moving image could easily be at the center of our understanding of twentieth-century music. Given concert audiences' increasing alienation from the concert halls and opera houses, more people in the twentieth century are likely to have heard symphonic music, the development of increasingly complex sound designs, and the unfolding of dramas with a musical dimension – in the cinema than ever went to a concert of twentieth-century "art" music or electroacoustic music, or attended an operatic or theatrical performance. Taking film and television music seriously as part of the last hundred years of musical culture immediately begins to question our "modernist greats" approach to twentieth-century music history (Schoenberg, Stravinsky, etc.). Cinema and television become parallel laboratories for musical development.

Chapter summary

- In the twentieth century film music has arguably become the *lingua franca* of music.
- Our experience of music is now mediated both electronically and through screen images.
- Study of screen music is, however, relatively new to musicology, and there is disagreement as to how it should be analyzed (as self-supporting music like concert music? like opera? in conjunction with the screen image? alongside other sound elements in the film, television show, or video?).
- The field of study is difficult to name: "film-music studies" would exclude television, as well as sound effects and dialogue; "screen-music studies" would exclude sound; "musical multimedia" is so inclusive that it goes beyond the screen; "soundtrack studies" implies study of CD compilations.
- Ultimately the field promises to turn long-held historical accounts of twentieth-century music on their head, and to become an area in which students of music can bring together all their musical and intellectual skills.

Discussion topics

- Think of a film you love. Could you say anything specific about the music without watching it again? If so, how would you go about explaining doing so? If not, equally, how might you account for this?
- What impressions do you get about the relationship between film music and film sound from this chapter? Did they surprise you? If so, why?
- If most people in the twentieth century really did experience music rooted in the orchestral tradition via film, what does this have to say for dominant histories of twentieth-century music?

Further reading

Donnelly, K. J. (ed.) (2001), *Film Music: Critical Approaches* (New York: The Continuum International Publishing Group).

> This is an edited collection of individually authored chapters, which I include here principally because the initial two chapters provide an excellent introduction to approaching film music and sound: David Neumeyer and James Buhler, "Analytical and interpretive approaches to film music (I): analyzing the music," and James Buhler, "Analytical and interpretive approaches to film music (II): analyzing interactions of music and film."

Dickinson, Kay (ed.) (2003), *Movie Music: The Film Reader* (London: Routledge).

> A handy collection of book excerpts and essays published elsewhere offering a sampling of many useful analytical and critical approaches to particular genres and screen music contexts.

Gorbman, Claudia (1987), *Unheard Melodies: Narrative Film Music* (Bloomington and London: Indiana University Press).

> This was one of the first major books of film-music studies and remains the classic statement about of how film music works in the narrative film tradition.

Brown, Royal S. (1994), *Overtones and Undertones: Reading Film Music* (Berkeley, Los Angeles, and London: University of California Press).

> Engaging expertly with both Hollywood and European film traditions, this eclectic book provides both historical and theoretical perspectives on film music.

Whittington, William (2007), *Sound Design and Science Fiction* (Austin, TX: University of Texas Press).

> This provides a historical and critical account of the concept of sound design, placing special emphasis on science fiction.

Chion, Michel, *Audio-Vision: Sound on Screen* (1994), trans. Claudia Gorbman (New York: Columbia University Press).

> This is one of many books written by France's foremost film-music and sound theorist, who is gradually assuming significance in English-language scholarship. Written by someone who is also an electroacoustic composer, it provides a theoretical vocabulary for all manner of sound phenomena and functions. It has a handy glossary of terms at the back.

Cook, Nicholas (1998), *Analyzing Musical Multimedia* (Oxford: Oxford University Press).

> This book proposes a general theory of musical multimedia of which film and music video stand alongside Lieder and opera.

Monaco, James (2000), *How to Read a Film: Movies, Media, Multimedia*, 3rd edn (New York and Oxford: Oxford University Press).

> An excellent introduction to the techniques and key terminology of film-making.

www.imdb.com is an essential resource for anyone interest in films. It is a huge searchable database which lists full production credits – including composer and sound designer – for an enormous number of English and foreign-language films. www.filmsound.org is an essential portal for anyone interested in film music and sound. The site houses extensive bibliographies, links to on-line articles and chapters from key books, links to sound effects, and is enthusiastically kept up to date by its author Sven E. Carlsson.

References

Altman, Rick, Jones, McGraw, and Tatroe, Sonia (2000), "Inventing the cinema soundtrack: Hollywood's multiplane sound system," in James Buhler, Caryl Flinn, and David Neumeyer (eds.), *Music and Cinema* (Hanover, NH: University Press of New England), 339–59.

Brown, Julie (2001), "*Ally McBeal*'s postmodern soundtrack," *Journal of the Royal Musical Association*, 126, 275–303.

Chion, Michel (2000), "Audio-vision and sound," in Patricia Kruth and Henry Stobart (eds.), *Sound* (Cambridge: Cambridge University Press), 201–21.

Cousins, Mark (1996), "Walter Murch: designing sound for *Apocalypse Now*," in John Boorman and Walter Donohue (eds.), *Projections. 6: Filmmakers on Film Making* (London: Faber), 124–53.

Eisler, Hanns and Adorno, Theodor W. (1994), *Composing for the Films* (London and Atlantic Highlands, NJ: Athlone Press).

Garwood, Ian (2003), "Must you remember this: orchestrating the "standard" pop song in *Sleepless in Seattle*," in Kay Dickinson (ed.), *Movie Music: The Film Reader* (London: Routledge), 109–17.

Kalinak, Kathryn (1992), *Settling the Score: Music and the Classical Hollywood Film* (Madison, WI: University of Wisconsin Press).

Kassabian, Anahid (2001), *Hearing Film: Tracking Identifications in Contemporary Hollywood Film Music* (London: Routledge).

Kozloff, Sarah (1999), "Genre talk," in Philip Brophy (ed.), *Cinesonic: The World of Sound in Film* (North Ryde, Aust.: AFTRS, 1999), 108–28.

Marks, Martin Miller (1997), *Music and the Silent Film: Contexts and Case Studies 1895–1924* (Oxford: Oxford University Press).

Stilwell, Robynn J. (2007), "The fantastical gap between diegetic and nondiegetic," in Daniel Goldmark, Lawrence Kramer, and Richard Leppert (eds.), *Beyond the Soundtrack: Representing Music in Cinema* (Berkeley: University of California Press), 184–202.

Weis, Elisabeth (1982), *The Silent Scream: Alfred Hitchcock's Sound Track* (Rutherford Fairleigh: Dickinson University Press).

Glossary

Diegetic music ("source music")	Music that apparently issues from a source within the narrative (or diegesis – the story world or place of action).
Nondiegetic music ("pit music")	Music that issues from outside the world of the narrative.

Metadiegetic music	Music that acts as a type of secondary narrator, such as a nondiegetic pop song.
Suture effect	(From the idea of "stitching together") the process by which the elements of the cinematic apparatus are sutured, or stitched, together and the cinematic audience drawn into its conceits in such a way as to make us forget that the camera is doing the looking – "turning enunciation into fiction, lessening awareness of the technological nature of film discourse" (Gorbman 1987: 5)
Audio-vision	(From Chion) what the cinematic audience has, rather than simply "vision." Likewise, we might talk about "audio-viewing" a scene, as opposed to simply "viewing" it.

Part 3

Music in practice

13 Musical performance

TINA K. RAMNARINE

Chapter preview

Music exists in performance. It may seem obvious to say this, but it is not. To say that music exists in performance is to focus on a particular way of thinking about what music is: i.e., that it is a *practice*. Viewing music as a performing art emphasizes the experiential dimensions of music, and its immediacy. Experiencing music in performance highlights music as an interactive process. People respond to musical performances emotionally, bodily, and critically. They may dance to music, fall into trance, or feel a sense of community. This chapter asks questions such as "What are the meanings of musical performances?" and "What are their ritual, social, or political significances?" Music is performed in a wide variety of contexts including concert settings, family celebrations, healing ceremonies, rituals, and competitions. Musical performance features in the realms of everyday experience, from singing lullabies to listening to music while you shop. Yet there is also something special about performance: it is often understood as standing apart from everyday life and it involves presentation to an "audience." Performers may display virtuosic musical skills or they may take on important social roles, for example, commenting on socio-political trends or mediating between supernatural and natural forces. This chapter explores musical performances from a global perspective, addressing questions about the nature, function, and processes of performance, as well as about the social roles and training of performers. Through ethnographic case studies, the chapter considers the ways in which musical performances take place in a network of aesthetic demands and social relationships.

Key issues

- What is musical performance?
- Viewing performance as experience, process, and embodied practice.
- Viewing performance as a mode of interaction.
- Who performs?
- Learning musical performance.

- The contexts and functions of musical performance.
- The social and political dimensions of musical performance.

What is musical performance?

Musical performance has recently come to the forefront of many branches of academic study, but it is viewed and analyzed in different ways. An influential perspective in traditional musicology has been to view performance as the reproduction or realization of scores. From this perspective the performer's task is to communicate the work from its notated state. Understood this way, the best that an individual performer can do is to interpret a score, thereby yielding and communicating insights into the work. At worst, the performer has been seen as offering merely an imperfect attempt toward a perfect rendition of the work. Musicology has recently broken away from this focus on musical texts, and in doing so has further developed an interest in the performer and moved closer toward ethnomusicological modes of perceiving performance as a process rather than as a product. "Music" depends on a performer bringing it "to life" and performances are never exactly the same as previous ones. Some musical traditions are entirely dependent on oral transmission, and in such cases the idea that music exists in performance seems obvious. Even in musical traditions that are also notated, performers listen to other performances, as well as studying scores, such that one can think about performances as oral texts. This allows notation, as Stanley Boorman (1999) has noted, to become a performance opportunity, to become imbued with the additional interpretative qualities that arise in performance, and performers are thus recognized as being integrally involved in the creative process. Recording technologies also play a critical role in helping performers to interpret and re-interpret familiar works.

While performers shape their interpretations in relation to recent performance traditions, the study of older recordings, often available in archives and library sound collections, can provide startling alternative presentations. These include the recorded examples of performances by composer-performers. Examples such as the recordings of Debussy and Schoenberg reveal the extent to which composer-performers depart from their own scores. Even when performers have depended on various kinds of texts (on treatises about performance practice as well as notated scores), aiming to produce "historically informed performances," as in the case of the early-music movement, their interpretations have been understood as being as much a response to modern-day aesthetics as to the results of insights into past performance practices. For Richard Taruskin (1995), understanding historically informed performance as a modern phenomenon is not a criticism of the current practice of "authenticity" (as it has often been perceived by other commentators). Rather, it is a way of bridging the creative and the recreative, the text and the performance.

Musical performance as experience, process, and embodied practice

Ethnomusicologists have long been attentive to performance, in part because their insistence on spending time observing musical traditions in context has led them to focus on the performance event as a way of finding out about many of the world's musical traditions (see chapter 6). Such a focus has led to greater understandings of the place of musical performance in social, ritual, and political life. While some ethnomusicologists and musicologists have been concerned with demonstrating a strong connection between music and society (i.e., music reflects social processes or holds social meanings and vice versa), others have argued that music and society help to form each other. In other words, musical performances do not merely reflect social life. Musical performances shape it.

As well as observing and documenting performances, learning to perform has been one of the central methods of ethnomusicology since the 1960s. Beginning with the experiences of learning music and of being present in "the field" (the musical context under study), ethnomusicologists have reflected on the ways that the writings they produce as a result of their research represent an attempt to translate experience into text. Taking as their starting point the idea that knowledge about music is grounded in the experience of music, several ethnographic texts from the late 1990s on have started to turn the focus increasingly back onto the scholar, who is also an actor within the musical context under study – a realization that broadens the concept of "performance." This trend is in part a response to a theoretical debate of the 1980s dealing with uncovering the motivations and assumptions of researchers that underlie ethnographic texts (the so-called "crisis of representation"). Consideration of the researcher as being a part of the tradition he or she is studying has posed a challenge to the scholar's traditionally objective and authoritative perspective. The researcher becomes one voice among many possible ones. This trend has also been a response to critical thinking about what happens after the fieldwork experience, how knowledge generated in the field features in subsequent research and teaching projects, and how the field experience impacts on the scholar's life experience. Fieldwork itself has begun to be understood as performance, a way of interpreting experience, a way not only of increasing cultural and musical understanding but also of integrating scholarship and life.

Learning to play in a new musical tradition has also shifted academic attention to the "body," to the ways in which people fit into different kinds of grooves and to an emphasis on self-awareness. Musical performance is thus seen as being an "embodied practice," that is, a way of training the body to behave in particular, musically appropriate ways. Scholars interested in understanding the psychology of musical performance have similarly studied the physical and mental skills required, exploring biology in relation to performance abilities and issues such as coordination, timing, gesture, human movement, and the physiological effects of performance anxiety (see chapter 4).

Musical performance as a mode of interaction

Theoretical trends exploring the processes, experiences, and embodied aspects of musical practices present us with richer conceptions of "performance." Simply playing or practicing music, however, is not usually considered to be a musical performance. What marks out a performance from a rehearsal? For the folklorist Richard Bauman (1992) there is a distinction between casual renditions and creative performances because the latter often involve some kind of judgment. The performer expects to present something to an audience and the performance context is marked in some way. For example, if you attend a performance of Brahms's Symphony No. 1 given by the London Symphony Orchestra, you might go to a specific performance space such as the Barbican Centre. You might expect to see the musicians observing a particular dress code, and the audience obeying a kind of etiquette by clapping. For the Temiar of the Malaysian rainforest, singing/trance-dancing ceremonies are distinguished from other ritual singing sessions by the presence of flowers and by the times in which songs are performed. The singing/trance-dancing ceremonies are held at night and take place within a covered structure. To perform these at other times and in open spaces would be to risk illness.

Performers prepare for performances. They have rehearsed the actions that they present in performance, practiced them over and over again, and made conscious efforts to learn them. The performance studies theorist Richard Schechner (2002) calls this "restored behaviour," a concept that can be applied to the analysis of human action in everyday life as well as in marked performance contexts. Performers can reflect on restored behavior in performance: "me behaving as I have practiced," becoming aware of multiple selves – "me" and the "performing me" – and reaching heightened psychological states. But if performances are made of restored behaviors they are nevertheless unique. No two performances will be exactly the same. This is also applicable to recorded performances because not every aspect of a musical event can be replicated. This way of understanding performance emphasizes the interactivity of performance rather than the materials being performed.

Thus what might mark out the uniqueness of the LSO's performance of Brahms's Symphony No. 1 mentioned above is not just the presentation of the work itself but also all the details in the production and reception of the performance, which vary from one performance to another. Such a perspective points to musical performances occurring in webs of social relationships between performers and audiences. To look at the musical performance is thus to be attentive to the listener as well as to the performer. Sometimes music is performed for non-human audiences. Musical performance is often an inherent part of spiritual beliefs and is a way of communicating with deities (for example the Sufi tradition of *qawwali*) or of maintaining human environments and their cosmological significances (as in the cases of traditional music of Australian Aboriginal peoples and of the Saami: see case study in Box 13.1). The interactive aspects of musical performance are also clear in the relation of music to other performing arts such as theater, dance, and film and through technological mediations: performances through radio, TV, internet, recordings, etc.

Box 13.1   Case study
Interactivity: The traditional song genre of the Saami (once known as nomadic pastoralists in the north of Europe) is the *joik*. To *joik* is to sing something rather than to sing *about* something and people have *joik*s in the same way that they have names. Given that a performer *joik*s someone or something it is impossible to think about *joik* in relation to subject and object; the *joik*er can be considered an integral part of the *joik*. *Joik*s are performed for animals and land as well as people. These concepts point to a complex set of relationships between music, personhood, and environment. *Joik*ing has been associated with shamanism and under Church guidelines it was a forbidden performance practice as recently as the 1970s. *Joik* song texts often explicitly deal with themes of "Saaminess," commenting on nature, environmental issues, and the supernatural. In capturing Saami sonic environments, modern *joik* recordings include bird song and reindeer sounds. While these modern recordings are held up as representations of distinctive Saami identity they are also located in a network of musical exchanges, collaborations, and global markets. Contemporary *joik* is produced and disseminated through mass media systems and shaped by technological advances, and institutional, state, and commercial bodies have recently supported some Saami musicians. The *joik* singer Wimme, for example, has produced several recordings in which he engages with heavy metal.

Approaches from performance studies as well as from ethnomusicology present us with broad views of musical performance as symbolic and social action. The paradox in this broad view of performance is that even if everyday life is a performance, musical performances are nevertheless often marked out as being "special," as having communicative and transformative properties. And *what* is being performed is vital to a proper appreciation of the performance event. While academic discourses conceptualize and discuss musical performances in various ways – from an emphasis on performance as the realization of a text (the composition) to performance as social action, patterns of behavior, or embodied practices – they are a fundamental aspect of human experience.

Who performs?

In some musical contexts, like karaoke, anyone can be a performer. Yet even though performance is part of everyday experience, there are several factors shaping who takes on the role of performer. One factor is gender. How many renowned female conductors spring to mind? The gendered dimensions of performance are similarly apparent in the worlds of popular and rock music. Few women, for example, find success as electric guitarists. In north Indian classical music, women are more likely to be vocalists than instrumentalists. In Albanian Prespa wedding celebrations, men and women sing in separate groups using different vocal techniques. Women sing softly; men sing loudly. Another factor determining who performs is that in some traditions being a musician is a hereditary occupation, such as the *klezmorim* (professional folk instrumentalists amongst the eastern European Ashkenazi Jews) who performed at events like weddings. For the Venda of South Africa, people who are born into certain families or social groups and demonstrate exceptional musical abilities often become key performers in important rituals such as those featured in the practices of possession cults. Although amongst the Venda everyone demonstrates musical capabilities and participates in musical life, an outstanding musical performer is often considered to be one who is able to get in touch with spiritual forces.

The idea that musicianship and being a medium are interconnected is apparent in a range of performance traditions. For the Temiar of the Malaysian rainforest, the performer receives compositions or learns songs from a spirit guide, who might be the soul of the flower that he or she tends. These songs are received through dreams and might be performed in healing ceremonies. The performer in this example is also a composer, medium, and healer, holding social and ritual as well as musical roles. Performers may be composers and improvisers as well as interpreters, or they may hold additional social roles that require a range of extra-musical skills, being articulators of political or social discourses (see case study in Box 13.2), mediators, mediums, healers,

---

Box 13.2 Case study

Social roles of performers: Calypso is a song genre associated in particular with the Caribbean islands of Trinidad and Tobago. The song texts play an important role in calypso aesthetics and they are often satirical, critical, humorous, and multi-referential. Texts were subject to colonial censorship during the 1930s but during this period calypsonians became important figures in promoting nationalist causes against the censure of colonial authorities. Calypsonians are political commentators and educators as well as entertainers. Calypso virtuosi extemporize during performance and demonstrate their verbal dexterity, sometimes through the exchange of insults. The Mighty Sparrow is perhaps the most well-known calypsonian. In his 1956 award-winning calypso ("Jean and Dinah"), he commented on the American departure from Trinidad and some of the socio-economic consequences of the American presence. His 1961 calypso addressed the Caribbean Federation and the political drive towards postcolonial states:

> Federation boil down to simply this,
> is dog eat dog and survival of the fittest,
> everybody fighting for independence, singularly,
> Trinidad for instance, but we go get it don't bother,
> but ah find we should all be together …

educators, and entertainers. Performers may hold ritual, cosmological, and environmental knowledge (such as Australian Aborigines) or be the narrators of historical knowledge (like the griots of West Africa).

Notions of musicality also determine who performs. "Talented" individuals are often selected through audition processes as being suitable recipients for further training and professional performance opportunities. This principle applies to popular music training through public media spectacles such as *Fame Academy* and *The X-Factor* as well as to entry into conservatoires, orchestral trials, and concerto performance engagements.

> **Box 13.3**
>
> Some factors determining who performs:
> - Gender
> - Inheritance
> - Social and/or ritual status
> - The ascription of talent

Learning musical performance

Musical performance is learned in diverse ways, from the non-systematized approaches of learning in everyday environments to the special skills that are acquired through formal training systems such as the conservatoire in the Western art-music tradition. In the former context, learning tends to be a social activity. Bulgarian *gaida* (bagpipe) players, for instance, learn tunes from older players through a combination of aural, visual, and tactile information, establishing networks to gain access to the social and public contexts in which *gaida* skills can be practiced, such as village fairs, evening dance parties, and weddings. The Western art music context, by contrast, is characterized by hours of practice (often undertaken as a solitary activity), formal assessments of ability through examinations and auditions, and development of methods to attain high levels of performance achievement (see case study in Box 13.4). Sufficient skill is usually required before participating in orchestral or chamber music contexts.

> **Box 13.4 Case study**
>
> "Zoning In: Motivating the Musical Mind" was a project undertaken at the Royal College of Music in London (1999–2002) to help develop mental and physical skills for performance. Teaching and research methods included neurofeedback (viewing one's brain activity during performance) to achieve psychological states that promote focused attention; mental skills training of the kind used in sports, such as mental rehearsal and imagery; exercise and lifestyle training, involving aerobic exercises to improve cardiovascular efficiency; and Alexander Technique training to develop somatic (i.e., bodily) awareness.

The systematic training of professional performers in the Western art music tradition was shaped by the development of conservatoires from the end of the sixteenth century onwards. Pedagogic practice at institutions in cities such as Venice, Paris, Vienna, London, and Moscow has exerted considerable influence on performance practice and on shaping standard instrumental repertoires.

A demand for method books was met by teacher-performers such as Kreutzer (violin) and Czerny (piano). Shifting aesthetics around the mid-nineteenth century also influenced performance teaching. Performers were increasingly regarded as recreators or interpreters of works, who should adhere to the demands of the text, rather than co-creators, a trend that intensified during the twentieth century. If you have taken instrumental lessons in the Western art musical tradition you may well be familiar with the injunctions to "just play the notes," "follow the score," or "play what is on the page."

Yet performance practice is consistently subject to change. Current historical, global, aesthetic, and analytic research insights have paralleled the increasingly diverse range of performance skills that are encompassed by contemporary conservatoire training systems, informing and challenging performers to adopt new perspectives. Thus many conservatoires offer training not only in Western art music but also in jazz (for example the Royal Academy of Music in London), and in popular and folk music (the Sibelius Academy in Helsinki – see case study in Box 13.5). Some conservatoires hold collections of instruments from around the world (for example, the Royal College of Music in London has a gamelan). Higher education music programs at universities have also increasingly promoted these broader perspectives, and the teaching of performance can include various "world music ensembles" (see Fig. 13.1) as well as orchestras and choirs. The practice of some of today's leading performers exemplifies these trends. While Yehudi Menuhin explored north Indian classical music earlier in the twentieth century, famously collaborating with the sitar maestro Ravi Shankar, musicians today continue to develop these global exchanges. The violinist Itzhak Perlman, for example, has experimented with *klezmer*, and the cellist Yo-Yo Ma has explored musical traditions along the Silk Route (through Central Asia) and of the Kalahari people (South Africa).

> **Box 13.5 Case study**
>
> The Sibelius Academy, established in 1882, began to offer folk music teaching in 1975, setting up a department for folk music in 1983. Overturning models of folk teaching as rural, village-based, and informal aural practice, the folk music program at this conservatoire emphasizes recreating and reinterpreting tradition. With specialized training (including conservatoire-model instrumental lessons, lectures, examinations, and the use of notated sources), performances in the world music circuit and the production of recordings, these folk musicians are seen as "professionals," marking out their practice as being "new folk music." They interact with and are influenced by musicians trained in various musical traditions, including other folk styles, and Western art and popular music.
>
> (Ramnarine 2003).

The rigor of musical training characterizing the conservatoire is also a feature of systematized training in other traditions, such as the *gharana* in north Indian classical music, or "new folk music" in Finland. Some stylistic and technical aspects identify musicians as belonging to specific *gharanas*, which are defined in terms of social as well as musical components. A *gharana* is basically a group of musicians linked through familial relationships or discipular lineages, who share particular approaches to performance practice. For example, the musicians who share Ravi Shankar's tradition identify

Fig. 13.1 RHUL's Gamelan Puloganti, South Bank Centre, London, June 2007 (Photo: Tina K. Ramnarine)

themselves as the Maihar Gharana and their approach to performance is eclectic (following the learning processes and achievements of Shankar's guru, Allaudin Khan). By naming his *gharana*, a north Indian musician indicates the stylistic school of which he is a member. In the learning process, the guru (teacher) is a dynamic figure in north Indian classical music, looking after the daily regimen of practice and overseeing the musical growth of a student. Most training would take place through oral repetition and musicians are expected to practice exercises and scales in developing technical skills. Such practice is sometimes called "*riaz*" (which also means "to sit") and years of *riaz* add up to "*sadhana*," which is "spiritual practice," as well as the ability to bring feeling and life into music. Many musicians use verbal syllables as rhythmic *jatis* (types) to construct the rhythmic patterns familiar to musicians and dancers. Ragas are the melodic frameworks that musicians learn, enabling them to compose, improvise and create moods (*rasa*) in performance.

With regard to preparing for performance, several studies have pointed to a correlation between time spent in practicing and skills acquired. Performers learn to perform by performing, often under the guidance of gurus who may supervise which professional engagements are accepted in the early stages of developing a performance career. In north Indian classical music, students begin to learn performance in performance contexts by appearing on stage with their gurus, providing the drone for an ensemble performance. Preparation can include ritual observances before a performance (e.g., to ward off stage fright, or in worship). In some cases, tuning or "warming up" on stage are preparatory features of musical performances.

The contexts and functions of music

Why do people organize musical performances? When is music performed? Where is it performed? In the section above we began to consider responses to these questions. Various functions of musical performance are summarized in Box 13.6.

Taking a more detailed look at the contexts and functions of musical performance, the following two case studies focus on:

> **Box 13.6 Functions of musical performance**
>
> to mark life events; entertain; educate; transmit knowledge (musical, aesthetic, social, historical); mediate between supernatural and natural worlds; heal; mark identities; transform identities (e.g., through initiation rituals); alter psychological states; establish communities; express human creativity and emotion; express self; bring landscapes into being; demonstrate power.

1. *Music in ritual contexts*: Anthropological perspectives on performance have focused on ritual contexts (initiation rituals, religious rituals, healing rituals and so on), dealing with the transformation of persons (changing who people are) and exploring how performances are both effective and entertaining. Partly drawing on anthropological theory, but presenting more finely nuanced analyses of performances, ethnomusicologists have described musical performance as the primary medium for organizing ritual activity in diverse geographic locations. Box 13.7 looks at one of these examples, outlining musical performance in the healing rituals of the Tumbuka.

2. *Musical conventions*: Musical performances can take place in formal or informal contexts. Performances take place in formal settings such as the concert stage or the ritual space. There are also street performances given by buskers, and festive occasions involving most participants such as parties, weddings, and other celebrations. While these events involve a performer–audience interaction, the musical convention emphasizes the processes of musical transmission and features a performer–performer exchange. It is a somewhat more formally organized version of the everyday interactions that take place between performers. It involves performers "showing performing"

Box 13.7 Case study

Musical performance as healing: In many different geographical contexts, musical performance is an aspect of medical practice. In Britain, the profession of music therapist began to emerge from the mid-twentieth century, although there were turn-of-the-century antecedents, for example the Guild of St Cecilia, which was founded in 1891 to play sedative music to patients in London hospitals. Music therapy has moved from boosting morale to the clinical applications of music, assessing the physiological impact of music, theoretical work, and the training of practitioners in conservatoires such as the Guildhall School of Music and Drama, which began teaching music therapy in 1968.

A variation on the clinical applications of musical performance is found in the example of the Tumbuka of Northern Malawi, for whom musical practice *is* medical practice. Drumming is foregrounded in the Tumbuka experience of clinical reality, highlighting the positive role of drums in several African healing systems. Disease is danced and diagnoses are drummed. The causes of illness are attributed to God (a theory of natural causation), to humans (who perform witchcraft and cause illness through human jealousies), and to spirits (in cases where humans fail to fulfil the requirements of the spirit world). Dancing prophets called *nchimi* fall into a divination trance through dancing to music, which will enable them to see what illness a patient is suffering from. They dance to "X-ray the patients." These prophets are often identified through falling ill themselves: disease thus produces a highly valued member of Tumbuka society. During treatment, patients might sing and dance and they may be positioned very closely to the drummers. The *nchimi* dance *vimbuza* (a term encompassing spirits, the illnesses they cause and the treatment of dance and music) to "heat" the spirits. Music becomes the transformer of spiritual heat, the means by which worlds are mediated, revealed, and constituted. The kinds of perceptual shifts needed to perceive both the spirit and non-spirit worlds are paralleled in the core *vimbuza* drumming pattern, which features threeness and twoness simultaneously. For the Tumbuka, music is used as a medical practice: acting as a source of energy and as a communication technology. Healing takes place through ritual musical performances.

(Friedson 1996)

to other performers. Box 13.8 discusses transmission and interpretation issues in relation to a musical convention held in 1999, "Fiddles of the World."

Social and political dimensions of musical performance

Musical performances often hold a social and political significance, reinforcing, challenging, or rendering "natural" different kinds of political ideologies. These performances include carnivals (see Box 13.9), parades, and competitions. Competitions, in which competing evaluative notions of effective performance, expression, aesthetics, and interpretation come to the forefront, may determine musical career paths, identifying future virtuosi such as in the Tchaikovsky Piano Competition. They may have a more explicitly political content such as the Eurovision Song Contest, displaying national

Box 13.8 Case study

Musical conventions: A musical convention called "Fiddles of the World" took place in 1999 overlooking the Great Harbour in Nova Scotia, Canada, which the Mi'qmaq call Kjipuktuk. Ivan Hicks, a fiddler from New Brunswick, planned the event. He wanted to bring together fiddlers and fiddling styles to share experiences and exchange tunes. "Fiddles of the World" provided opportunities for reflecting on the trajectory of the fiddle as a cultural product and as a marker of identity; and on fiddle repertoires as sites of cultural and musical memory. Fiddlers wanted to learn from other fiddlers about technical approaches to the instrument and about different renditions of familiar tunes. They exchanged knowledge about aspects of musical style. Some of the fiddlers, such as a James Bay Cree fiddler, James Cheechoo, were promoted as being cultural repositories. His performances and workshops highlighted a less well-known aspect of fiddle lore relating to the ways in which native Canadian peoples adopted the violin after contact with Irish, Scottish, and English traders from the 1600s onwards. Cheechoo retains "old tunes" for square and step dances, which were accompanied by a two-sided skin drum played with two sticks until the 1940s. If Cheechoo's practice provided a moment of historical curiosity, the link between Cape Breton and Scottish fiddlers was more fully explored in this convention. Cape Breton became a stronghold of Scottish Gaelic culture in the early nineteenth century with the arrival of around thirty thousand Scots during the time of the Highland clearances. Cape Bretoners trace the origins of what is now a distinct fiddling style featuring bow and fingered ornaments to a Golden Age of fiddling in Scotland (late eighteenth and early nineteenth centuries). Two key features of this style were explained by the fiddler Natalie MacMaster and relate to an emphasis on rhythmic interpretations being derived from dance and ornaments. Bowing ornaments are often a means of creating rhythmic variation and emphasis. The basic principles include adding open string drones, pushing the bow to play an accented note (a "dig"), whip-bow technique (changing the pressure to add an accent within a certain pitch) and cuts (very short bow strokes). The fiddle styles represented at this convention (Cape Breton, Scottish, Irish, Texan, Cajun, and Quebec fiddling) were seen as being broadly linked to but distinct from each other. As one source for a more "authentic" playing style, now lost but in the process of being reclaimed in other parts of the Celtic music world, the local representatives, the Cape Bretoners, provided an important model. The vigor of this style attracted other players who felt that it speaks effectively to modern-day audiences. This was in contrast to Cheechoo's practice, which was interesting because it provided another aural dimension through a historical window but which remained an example of past practice with little modern relevance. This case study thus parallels Richard Taruskin's point about the modern-day aesthetics of historically informed performance. It also highlights another key to understanding musical performance. As well as focusing on *what* is being performed (the tune or the "work") and situating musical performances within the total music event (performance as a process), we have to consider the *how* of musical performances – the stylistic and interpretative dimensions that help us to shift our attention to the performers. Just as how Beethoven's Fifth Symphony is performed might be identified as an interpretation of the Berlin Philharmonic Orchestra under Herbert von Karajan, how fiddlers play a tune identifies them as Cape Breton or Cajun performers and sets up hierarchies of "Celticness." The stylistic and technical details of playing offer a route to a proper emphasis on the "sounds of music" in analyzing the politics of performance practice.

and political allegiances. Musical performances often serve to foster a feeling of community, a sense that this is "our music," to the extent that musical performances play vital roles in marking identities. Folk music in European contexts, for example, has often been referred to in the articulation of national sensibilities, such that we routinely speak about "Bulgarian folk music," "Scottish folk music," or "Hungarian folk music." The intersubjective and critical aspects of musical performance are revealed when music is presented not just as aesthetic but also as political action.

> **Box 13.9 Case study**
>
> *Musical performance as politics*: The pre-Lenten Carnival of Trinidad and Tobago has become one of the Caribbean's major musical events. Calypsonians and costumed bands contribute to Carnival, providing a forum for some of the most intense scrutiny of and commentary on island politics. From resistance to colonial attempts to ban Carnival practices in the mid-nineteenth century to contemporary cultural policy discussions about the development and financing of the Carnival arts in education and ecotourism initiatives, Carnival can be seen as performance that reveals a lot about postcolonial national politics in these island spaces.

Studying performance in higher education

As we have seen in this chapter, various approaches have been taken in exploring musical performance. These include approaches from the psychology of performance, research into historical performance practice, insights from cognate disciplines – drama studies in particular – and interdisciplinary ethnographic studies that help us to take global and comparative perspectives. Studying musical performance in higher education often involves a balance between the practical (continuing to develop instrumental or vocal skills) and the conceptual (thinking about musical performance). Higher education courses may reflect the diverse approaches that have been pursued in seeking to understand musical performance, including opportunities to read a range of literature on performance, participate in different kinds of performance projects, learn from one's peers, and practically engage with various world music traditions.

Chapter summary

- Different thinkers have approached musical performance from diverse perspectives. While some thinkers emphasize what is being performed (i.e., the "work"), others highlight performance as an event, investigate the processes involved in producing a performance, or focus on issues of interpretation.

- Musical performance is often characterized by its evaluative and inter-active dimensions (through the involvement of audiences), as well as by performance markers, behaviors, and codes that set it apart from everyday life or from rehearsal.
- Performers may be subject to selection criteria. There may be gen-dered, hereditary, and hierarchical dimensions to selection, just as there may be evaluations of ability in performance training.
- Musical performance is essentially an interactive aesthetic and social practice. Musical performance can be viewed as a way of knowing and being, as a method of critical and intersubjective inquiry, and as social, political, and aesthetic action.

Discussion topics

1. When does musical practice (in the sense of rehearsal) become musi-cal performance? To what extent can practice be distinguished from performance?
2. Assess the impact of technology on musical performances.
3. Why has the analysis of social meanings and significances in musical performances been so compelling?
4. How relevant are the concepts of the "creative" and the "recreative" to understanding musical performance?
5. Compare the roles of performers and performance events in different performance contexts. What might this comparative perspective tell us about the nature of musical performance?

Further reading

Rink, John (2002) (ed.), *Musical Performance: A Guide to Understanding* (Cambridge: Cambridge University Press).
Outlines themes in the study of performance ranging from practice to psychological concepts.
Solís, Ted (2004), *Performing Ethnomusicology: Teaching and Representation in World Music Ensembles* (Berkeley and Los Angeles: University of California Press).
Explores the ethics and practices of applying what has been learned in a "field" context to the teaching of world music ensembles.
Williamon, Aaron (2004) (ed.), *Musical Excellence: Strategies and Techniques to Enhance Performance* (Oxford: Oxford University Press).
Introduces practical research to help performers develop skills.

References

Bauman, Richard (1992), "Performance," in *Folklore, Cultural Performance and Popular Entertainments* (New York and Oxford: Oxford University Press).
Boorman, Stanley (1999), "The musical text," in Nicholas Cook and Mark Everist (eds.), *Rethinking Music* (New York and Oxford: Oxford University Press).
Friedson, Steven (1996), *Dancing Prophets: Musical Experience in Tumbuka Healing* (Chicago and London: University of Chicago Press).
Ramnarine, Tina K. (2003), *Ilmatar's Inspirations: Nationalism, Globalization, and the Changing Soundscapes of Finnish Folk Music* (Chicago and London: University of Chicago Press).
Schechner, Richard (2002), *Performance Studies: An Introduction* (London and New York: Routledge).
Taruskin, Richard (1995), *Text and Act: Essays on Music and Performance* (New York and Oxford: Oxford University Press).

14 Composition

JULIAN JOHNSON

Chapter preview

This chapter considers the value of studying composition and looks at how it can be taught and assessed. Concentrating on the idea that composition is a practical, constructive activity, it introduces some possible working methods used by different composers, starting with the very different kinds of first thoughts with which composers begin, from personal experiences to a fascination with technical problems or the relation of music to other art forms. It goes on to consider how one moves from initial ideas to concrete sounds, discussing the role of notation, the value of sketches, and the process of learning from performances. The final section considers the relation of composers, performers, and audiences, discussing the idea of originality and the different expectations of different genres of music and their audiences. The question of style became highly contentious in the twentieth century but, at the same time, fragmented and plural. Does this mean that, today, anything goes? The chapter concludes with the suggestion that composers today have to negotiate a difficult path to ensure that their music will communicate with an audience while at the same time, not restricting the freedom of invention that is the legacy of the art-music tradition.

Key issues

- Composition reminds us that musical works are the result of a process of making that might have turned out quite differently.
- Composition involves the presentation and exploration of clear ideas, no matter what the musical style.
- Notation is neither just a way of "recording" musical ideas nor of "instructing" performers, but also an invaluable medium for reworking ideas.
- Musical materials and musical forms are mutually shaped by one another.
- Contemporary composers need to be aware of compositional techniques from both the recent and more distant musical past.

- Composers need to find a balance between the freedom of their own musical imagination and the audience for whom their music is intended.

Studying composition

Composing is a kind of making. That might seem rather obvious, but it is easily forgotten in a musical culture that still sees the composer as a mystical figure, producing music out of thin air. One of the benefits of studying composition – whether you think of yourself as a composer or not – is that you are reminded at once that musical works don't just appear ready-formed in the composer's imagination, but have to be worked at, planned, rethought, corrected, and rewritten, just as much as a good essay. Without denying the power of what we call "inspiration," we can still acknowledge that music is the result of a process of building, construction, or assembly. This aspect of music is often downplayed or forgotten entirely in some approaches to studying it. In music analysis, the score is treated as a self-contained and complete musical object, as if it were a natural phenomenon, rather than the product of human choices that could have turned out quite differently (as composers' sketches often suggest).

Aside from developing your own powers of invention and sharpening your critical faculties, one of the most valuable gains of studying composition is the insight it gives into music itself. To know what a thing is, to understand how it works, involves a sense of how it is made. In this sense, composition is the flipside of analysis; both disciplines are concerned with how music is made, with what its materials are, with its processes and form, with how it hangs together and makes sense. The two things complement each other in the sense that to know how to make something you might often find yourself taking other things apart – like an old-style inventor. That said, composition is not analysis in reverse – nor vice versa. You cannot compose "by numbers." No amount of technical know-how will guarantee that you write an interesting piece. Without the imaginative trip, technique comes to nothing.

There is often some skepticism about whether composition can be taught and assessed. In fact, you can usefully compare the skills required to compose with those skills that all students need to demonstrate in their essay work. Just as an essay needs to present clear ideas and expand upon them in a coherent and connected argument, so do compositions. A piece of music needs to engage its listener just as an essay needs to engage its reader. Both have to "make sense" by avoiding arbitrary or irrelevant detours. Both have to be "well written." Teaching composition thus shares many of the same goals as teaching good academic writing; it seeks to develop in the student an ability to present and develop ideas as clearly as possible, but also to explore the rich potential and imaginative possibilities of those ideas.

It is precisely those kinds of skills that form the basis for the assessment of composition. Just as in assessing essay work or performance, the question is rarely about individual questions of "taste" or preference and much more about criteria such as technique, clarity of presentation, communication, projection of clear ideas. Assessing composition can be hard and takes time – it takes much longer to "hear" a piece from a score alone than it does to read an essay or listen to a performance. For this reason, recordings of composers' work are often invaluable in communicating a sense of the piece though, if the recording is inadequate, it may not do the piece justice. Though most people agree that the score is not the music it is imperative that the page communicates as much detail as is needed to allow the "reader" to hear the piece clearly.

A certain aura of mystique still surrounds composition, despite the fact that it has been central to the school music syllabus for many years. Studying composition can be a good way of demystifying it, of making music your own and coming closer to the concrete problems and solutions that all composers have had to face. That said, composition has meant very different things at different times and places. The Romantic idea of the individual genius inventing music out of nothing is actually rather odd. At different times in European music history and in different world music cultures, "making" a piece has often meant reworking familiar and common musical materials, often collectively and often through performance rather than being "written." Studying composition today necessarily involves reflecting on our assumptions about the composer – about the idea of a solitary individual designing a whole work in advance of performance, about the role of notation, and about the whole idea of concert performance in which the performer acts as intermediary between the composer and a passive audience.

> **Box 14.1 Morton Feldman on composition**
>
> If a man teaches composition in a university, how can he not be a composer? He has worked hard, learned his craft. Ergo, he is a composer. A professional. Like a doctor. But there is that doctor who opens you up, does exactly the right thing, closes you up – and you die. He failed to take the chance that might have saved you. Art is a crucial, dangerous operation we perform on ourselves. Unless we take a chance, we die in art.
>
> Morton Feldman, *Essays*.

Working methods

But if composing is first and foremost about making then it is, primarily, a practical activity – a kind of doing. Like performance, it involves actively engaging with musical materials rather than considering them from a distance as one might in more academic study. And like performance, composition tends to work best when it is approached as a skill to be worked at rather than something that happens only when you feel sufficiently inspired to create "great" music. If you confine yourself to those rare moments you will quickly find that you have a few fleeting musical ideas, none of which gets beyond a few seconds long. Writing at white heat late at night might make you feel like Beethoven but, nine times out of ten, what you put down will look rather different in the cold light of day.

Like all kinds of making, composing is in large part a slow and laborious process requiring patient hard work. Without a good working routine and some useful habits and methods, you will find it very hard to sustain any real progress. It is a good idea therefore to treat composing rather like you might treat music practice – not something you do when the mood takes you, but something timetabled into the day and stuck at even when you are not feeling especially motivated. Whether you work in the studio, in your bedroom, a practice room or the library, whether you work at night or first thing in the morning, give yourself the framework of some regular time and space for composition. Find what works best for you and stick to it.

First thoughts

Different composers begin a new piece in very different ways, but most would agree that the worst thing you can do is sit down on Monday morning with a blank sheet of paper and wait for an idea to come. Equally, you won't get very far if you emulate the cliché of the writer typing late into the night (aided by a whisky and a cigarette), tearing off each half-written page and screwing it up into a ball before hurling it into the waste-paper basket.

Some people begin with improvisation – either alone or with fellow musicians. The musical mind invents spontaneously much quicker than you can write things down. It is a great way to loosen up your inventing muscles and allow ideas to flow, unrestricted by anxiety about whether they are any good or not. Often, in an improvisation, you try the same idea out in countless ways, testing its possibilities. It is a good way of getting certain sounds, motifs or rhythms into your system and there is a good chance they develop in the mind without you being very aware of it.

Some people begin from an extra-musical source. Composers today are not so ready to point to autobiographical origins for their pieces as Berlioz or Mahler might have been, but it is a fair bet that most music with any sense of intensity or urgency is partly fuelled by personal experience. If it helps shape your piece to dwell on a failed love affair, fine. It worked for Mahler. Perhaps a particular striking experience of an aspect of nature, or something you read, or a picture, or simply an idea or a memory. We don't talk about these things very much and perhaps quite rightly, because what matters for your composing is not so much the experience or idea that might have shaped its beginning, but what you do with that musically. The worst thing you can do is to allow the free elaboration of the musical material to be confined and restricted by something extra-musical. Explaining that the onset of a new section in your piece is there because that is the part where the boat capsized (in your private storyline) is worthless if the piece does not make musical sense at that point.

Other composers begin from a technical problem or question. A piece might start from a "purely musical" fascination with the way in which one kind of rhythmic process might develop into another, or with the permutational possibilities of building chords on certain intervals, or with the idea of using an ensemble to amplify the timbral possibilities of a solo instrument. This kind of approach might lend itself to thinking quite analytically about your musical material, rather than "poetically," but many composers find it useful to move between the two. You may be fascinated by the technical questions of electronic transformations of marimba sounds, but still be guided instinctively by the imagery of, say, the refraction of light on the surface of water. What the imagination throws up as a gesture or sound or image, the conscious mind quickly follows in an attempt to find its technical correlate.

Rather than wrestling unproductively with inventing a beginning, some people start by using some pre-existing material as the basis for their own invention. There is a long tradition for this. In the Renaissance period, composers such as Lassus, Victoria, and Palestrina frequently based their settings of the Mass on pre-existing material (the so-called "parody mass"). Sets of variations are perhaps the most familiar example of working in this way, where the richness of the composition lies, in part, in demonstrating imaginative possibilities that seem to transcend the often ordinary melody or ground bass with which the piece began. Works like Bach's *Goldberg Variations* or Beethoven's *Diabelli Variations* are good examples of how composition is far more about what you do with an idea than the initial idea itself. Much jazz is based on exactly that idea – that compositional skill lies in the quality of invention that one draws out of familiar and shared materials, of producing something new in relation to something already given, rather than inventing "out of thin air" (see chapter 10).

Some composers have shaped their own work very productively in relation to other art forms. Debussy's *Prelude à l'après-midi d'un faune* takes its title from a poem by Mallarmé and it has been suggested that the music follows the poem in some quite specific ways, while nevertheless being a wordless orchestral work. The correspondence between Schoenberg and the painter Wassily Kandinsky offers fascinating insight into how ideas of color, line, and form might usefully be exchanged between a composer and a visual artist. Dramatic overtures are often "inspired" by plays or novels whose name they take: Beethoven's *Coriolan* overture, Berlioz's *Rob Roy*, Schumann's *Manfred*, for example. Richard Strauss's orchestral tone-poem *Also sprach Zarathustra* purportedly relates to Nietzsche's philosophical tale of the same title. In all these examples, and countless others, the starting point is often one of atmosphere or character rather than of detailed plot or musical form. The musical imagination, once kick-started by the fascination with drama or color or mood, is usually best left to invent freely thereafter.

From idea to sound

However you begin composing, at some point you will need to think in terms of musical notation unless you are working entirely electronically (and even here, you will need to think of how to jot down ideas, if only as an aid to memory). It is essential that you constantly test that you are content with the way you have notated your musical ideas. So much can be lost between having a brilliant musical idea and a lazy or inaccurate notation. Tell-tale signs of the latter are insufficient detail on the page. Listen inwardly to your imagination and think carefully – what instrument plays those sounds, what is the dynamic shape of the phrase? How is it articulated? Is it in the right register? Did you really hear such a "square" rhythm?

That is the first part of the process – as if you were trying to transcribe the idea dictated by your imagination. But composition is not transcription of some divine dictation. Look at what you have written down. Even if it is what you imagined, does it work? Is it interesting enough? Would it be more dramatic if you altered that rhythm, gave it to a different instrument, tweaked the end of the phrase harmonically? So the next stage is to review what you have, to be self-critical until you're happy with it, until you're satisfied that it's a strong idea – that it works, even if you don't know where it goes next. You have created a character, or set a scene, even if, as yet, you have no idea what the story will be.

If you are working directly with computer software like Sibelius, then what you have notated is basically what you have just played in. But similar questions arise here too – is what you played exactly what you intended? Is the musical idea adequately represented by the information on the screen or do you need to qualify and add further things?

Notation works in two ways therefore. You might think of it as a way of "recording" what you've already invented, but it's also a tool for "working" material. Once you have got some ideas in notated form you can start trying them out and experimenting with them. Arguably, paper and pencil still offer you more flexibility for this than the computer, though of course the latter will play back your experiments as you work. This has an obvious advantage, as does composing at the piano, but both these "hands on" ways of working can sometimes constrict the imagination. As John Cage once remarked about improvisation, there's an inbuilt tendency of your hands to repeat the patterns they already know, which is good in that what they do will probably "work," but bad in the sense that it means you keep writing the same thing over and again. Another problem is that if you are always working "at the wet edge of the paint" you lose sight of the larger shape of the composition. A balance might be struck between hands-on working in this way and deliberately giving yourself time away from the keyboard, to imagine your material and the larger shape of the piece – to make sure you can see the wood for the trees.

Perhaps you can get down a few minutes of your piece, perhaps only a few seconds, before the initial energy of invention seems to run out. What you have written may be what actually stands as the start of the piece in its final form – as if you had written the first few pages of your novel. More likely perhaps, is that you have actually jotted down several different ideas – as if you had sketched out the characters for a novel (or even a painting) but without yet knowing how they will relate to each other or how the plot will unfold. At this point it is invaluable to step back and reflect on what you have so far. Chances are, you actually have all the material you will need to build a piece – even a very large one. What you need to do now is to interrogate your own material. What is it? What is it made of? What does it suggest? Where might it go? What can you do with it? This is a sort of analysis – considering the potential of the musical ideas you have got down. And in that respect, the composition of your piece is a kind of realization of that potential. That does not mean, of course, that the ideas you have initially notated need appear at the start of the piece. They may not appear in that form for some time – or even at all!

Sketching is hugely important but also a very personal thing. Some composers sketch for weeks or even months before committing themselves to the actual piece, trying out endless permutations of some melodic shape, some harmonic system, or some contrapuntal texture. Others scribble an outline on the back of an envelope and set off. There is no right way, but not to sketch at all is very rare. In the end, sketching can save a lot of time and make working much less painful, because it allows you to be much more at home with your material and see the possibilities in a way that you often lose sight of when you have your head down composing. Sketches can also take many forms. They might be incredibly detailed, as with setting out various permutations of a melodic phrase or the possible inversions of a complex chord, and you might find that this produces a "store" from which you can draw materials while leaving plenty of forms unused. But you might also find it useful to sketch the larger shape of the piece – what painters would call the "composition" of the piece.

It is usually best to think about this relatively early on in the compositional process, perhaps soon after your sketch of some initial ideas for the work. What larger shape is suggested by your materials? A gradual and seamless process, by which A is transformed imperceptibly into B? Or something more dramatic perhaps, in which alternating kinds of material interrupt each other? And what are the proportions of the different sections? How long does this middle section need to be compared to the outer sections? Why does the material come back, and how different does it need to be when it does?

One of the things you often have to juggle as a composer is keeping one eye on the moment-to-moment detail of your material and another on the larger form of the whole piece. At any one moment you need to know where you're going, but at the same time you don't want the whole thing to be predetermined or it will feel (and sound) as if you're just filling a musical jelly mould. Keep testing your idea of the larger structure against where the material wants to go, and be prepared to revise it. It is a bit like starting to build a model with a set of instructions but then, as you proceed from one stage to the next, you find you are actually building something rather different and have to revise the instructions as you go!

Composing is hard work: it is time-consuming, intellectually demanding and emotionally exhausting. When you are satisfied that you have reached the end of a piece (whether at the end of a single sitting, a few weeks, or a year) it is tempting to think that is the end of the process. All you need do now is print it out and give it to the performers. Not so. Firstly, the presentation of your work to performers is hugely important for communicating your musical idea. You may be a musical genius, but if the performing parts are full of errors and are hard to read, and the score is too small and has no rehearsal numbers, nobody will want to perform your music. Secondly, you may well want to think of the process of rehearsal and performance as part of the compositional process. Typically at a university or conservatoire, your individual composition lessons will be augmented by workshops and performances. If you can, attend some rehearsals of your piece. There is a huge amount you can learn from these – from technical observations made by performers, but also by using your ears self-critically to reflect on what you hear. Do not rush to think something is your fault (the players need time to master something new) but consider, for example, whether the fact that the melody is inaudible has to do with your over-scoring, or writing in the wrong register for that instrument. Hearing your piece in concert, perhaps that middle section is simply too long, or the ending too abrupt?

> **Box 14.2 Brian Ferneyhough on composition**
>
> European composers have absorbed naturally much of the historic background of Western music before they start being composers ... The assumption is that it's sort of like a pyramid. History is the lower echelons of the pyramid and you then arrive at the point where, having learned everything else, you can move on. I find that a very questionable sort of assumption. My approach is much more what I would call problem-oriented: One thinks of an issue, one tries to formulate a question about possible musical styles, events, processes, and then you look for means of answering that particular question. And that doesn't require any sort of predisposition regarding nationality or stylistic pertinence, or really anything else other than your own inventive powers.
>
> Brian Ferneyhough, interviewed in *New Music Box*.

Composers, performers, and audiences

The distinction between "free" or "original" composition and historical pastiche or stylistic composition is not an absolute one, but it remains important. Many university courses make use of an element of pastiche composition as a valuable tool for developing students' understanding of a particular historical style. Writing exercises in the manner of Palestrina or Bach or Debussy is not intended to set you up in a career of historical impersonation but rather to develop your understanding of a musical language. It is very similar to learning a foreign language. You do not study French or Spanish in the abstract, just learning the grammatical rules or analyzing texts. First and foremost, you learn to speak the language yourself.

Many composers believe that the techniques one learns in stylistic composition are useful tools for the contemporary composer too, since composers from one age to the next wrestle with very similar problems, whatever their style – of how to combine horizontal line and vertical harmony, how to balance repetition and change, how to pace and structure a piece, how to balance the disparate sonorities of voices and instruments, and so on. The idea of "free" composition is perhaps rather outdated today. It implies a freedom from the musical forms or rules of an earlier historical style, but one of the paradoxes explored by composition in the twentieth century was that casting off historical constraints can also create something of a vacuum for the composer. Schoenberg and Stravinsky were by no means alone in finding that they needed to find new ways of limiting the possibilities precisely in order to work creatively. Indeed, both testified to the paradox that the more their music was shaped by certain restrictions, the more free they became to invent. One might spend a lifetime's composing exploring that idea. If it sounds unlikely, consider the experience that all writers, painters, and composers have at one time or another – that there is nothing more frightening than a completely blank sheet of paper.

So what do we mean by "original" composition? How original are you expected to be? This idea too is arguably a product of the Romantic age, when the genius of a composer was understood to be linked directly to their capacity to make something that appeared to be beyond the reach of what had gone before, that exceeded what had been conceived of or imagined by earlier composers. This emphasis on an absolute originality was not how a composer in the sixteenth century would have understood his task, and it is certainly at odds with plenty of popular and non-Western traditions. In more recent decades, Western art music also has become more cautious about the idea of absolute originality, and the emphasis today is often more on how one deploys relatively shared, common materials than inventing entirely new ones.

The student composer has to walk a fine line. You have to avoid undermining your own work at every turn by being too self-conscious about whether this passage sounds a little too much like *x*, or this section sounds like *y*. Just write. Afterwards, you might note that there was more borrowing than you had intended, but you can move on to the next piece with greater self-awareness. The real point is that when you compose you try to speak with your own voice rather than someone else's. This might be impossible (in theory!) but it tends to produce more interesting results anyway, so stick at it. Here is an example of what I mean. A student composer brings me the beginning of his new string quartet. It is an Adagio movement and is clearly meant to be rather intensely emotive. The harmony is largely confined to simple, diatonic triads and the instruments rarely move out of first and second positions, as if the piece were written for beginners. My question to him would be: "Is this really what you *mean*?" "Is this really what you *hear*?" Why does the first violin have the melodic line all the way through? Why is it always in four-part texture? Why is the harmony so restricted? Why – in short – is everything so bland? Do you really want to communicate "blandness" in place of intense emotion?

Let me be clear though – the opposite is equally to be avoided. The piece that is full of arbitrary gestures – no matter how much they can be explained by some "system" – is equally questionable. The "original" aspect of composing comes down to the piece having grown out of some necessity. For some composers, this is an expressive one – of having something to say and needing to say it. For others, it is driven more by the fascination of invention – of being caught up in the possibilities of the musical material. For most perhaps, one alternates and overlaps constantly with the other.

Anything goes?

The question of style is always a contentious one. At school level, musical styles and techniques are sometimes presented as if they were all equally valid and equally available options for the contemporary composer – as if choosing to write a "minimalist" piece rather than a "serialist" piece were like choosing to wear a blue shirt today rather than a white one. Musical techniques are poorly understood if they are separated out from the expressive needs that gave rise to them. The idea that composition students should write "in the latest style" is as foolish and outdated as it is impossible. The notion of a "latest style" has always been problematic and is pretty much abandoned today. But, that said, the abandonment of a clear linear progression from one historical style to the other by no means produces a sense of "anything goes." One of the most obvious results of a postmodern culture is certainly its healthy distrust of boundaries between different (musical) cultures, between Western and non-Western, and between "high art" culture and "popular" culture. Contemporary music today is marked by the presence of elements from diverse and eclectic musical sources – from medieval music to pop, from non-Western to folk – all equally "available" as the materials of the Western classical canon.

It would be dangerously prescriptive for any composition tutor to insist upon a "correct" stylistic language, let alone one that was the most "up to date." But – once again – that said, one might reasonably insist that contemporary composition should *show an awareness* of the music of the last century. Stravinsky famously reused elements of much earlier music in his neoclassical works; Britten revisited the music of English composers such as Purcell. All music is written, more or less self-consciously, in relation to earlier music, and music that is written simply in complete ignorance of the past is rarely strong, relevant, or engaging. The question of tonality provides a good example of this. In the middle of the twentieth century many composers took the view that to write in a tonal idiom was simply outdated and no longer relevant to the ongoing development of the art-music tradition. To do so was the equivalent of adopting the clothes or speech of a much earlier age – a refusal of the modern world, if you like. Today, many contemporary composers no longer take such a view. Tonal centers or keynotes, the use of triads and tonal tensions may form part of the thinking of many composers who are also at home with various approaches to an atonal, fully twelve-note music, and may indeed move between the two in the same piece. The point is that while elements of tonality may have returned in some contemporary music, they do not reproduce the state of tonality as before.

> **Box 14.3 Steve Reich on composition**
>
> I think people suffer from a misconception … about music theory and its relation to music practice. Whatever music theory you encounter, certainly including the rules of four-part harmony, was written after a style had been worked out by ear, and by a good musical ear. Of course it is good for a student to learn the rules of four-part harmony, but with the understanding that they are just student exercises and that parallel fifths may be perfect in another context. All music theory refers to something that has already happened, but if it is taken as a prescription, or worse as a manifesto, heaven help you.
>
> Steve Reich in conversation with Rebecca Y. Kim.

The question of style and musical language cannot be discussed meaningfully without reference to the place of music – its audience and the function music is intended to have for that audience. The composer has always had to reflect upon this because music is successful and valued according to how well it serves a particular function – whether that is to heighten a religious liturgy, to accompany dancing or drama, bring together a community in song, entertain, engage us emotionally in a film, and so on. This basic link to musical and social function is obscured in the tradition of instrumental "art music" which goes back at least to the eighteenth century. Classical music is based on the idea of art for its own sake, as self-sufficient, as being inherently valuable, engaging, and fascinating. In this tradition, the development of musical forms and musical language appears to be driven by purely technical concerns – such as sonata form, motivic work, new harmonic approaches. In practice, we understand that music has always been shaped by social functions; even when it appears to be most "autonomous," it is caught up in social, cultural, political, religious, and even philosophical contexts.

It is self-evident that the composer has to give due regard to the context for his or her music. Writing film music is quite different to writing music for the musical theater, which is different again to writing music for a string quartet. Writing music for a youth orchestra is a different task to writing for the BBC Symphony Orchestra. Purists may sniff at Verdi's maxim that he always composed "with one eye on the music and one eye on the audience" and admire Beethoven's apparently more uncompromising attitude ("this music is not for you but for a future generation"). But both attitudes depend upon a certain kind of audience and a certain conception of musical art. Times have changed since the deliberately provocative stance of Milton Babbitt in his essay "Who cares if you listen?" Today is an uncertain time and the contemporary composer is tugged in two different directions. On the one hand, there is a long and rich musical tradition which resists any external limit on the imaginative genius of the composer. From this perspective, composers should be free to follow musical thought wherever it leads, and in doing so they explore the furthest reaches of human experience and understanding (so says a tradition that runs from Beethoven to Schoenberg to the twentieth-century avant-garde). On the other hand, composers have to consider that the audience justly demands that the composer come out to meet them, that new music remains communicative; where it is not, where the audience can find nothing to follow or with which to engage, it has abandoned new music for something easier and more immediate.

It is fair to say that contemporary music today remains caught in this double-bind. To simply pander to the demands of entertainment alone would seem to sell music short, since the tradition of music seems to suggest it is capable of so much more. On the other hand, to insist on the "purity" of musical experiment shaped only by questions of technique and theory, without regard to music's communicative aspect, alienates the audience and drives the composer into a sterile vacuum.

Chapter summary

- Composition reminds us that musical works are the result of a process of making that might have turned out quite differently.
- Composition involves the presentation and exploration of clear ideas, no matter what the musical style.
- Notation is neither just a way of "recording" musical ideas nor of "instructing" performers, but also an invaluable medium for reworking ideas.
- Musical materials and musical forms are mutually shaped by one another.
- Contemporary composers need to be aware of compositional techniques from both the recent and more distant musical past.
- Composers need to find a balance between the freedom of their own musical imagination and the audience for whom their music is intended.

Discussion topics

- How can "old" musical techniques be of relevance to the contemporary composer? Consider some examples of how twentieth-century composers have revisited much older music in order to develop a new musical language.
- Are traditional methods of "writing" music still applicable to the composer who works directly at the computer? Consider the pros and cons of working directly with computer software.
- Many accounts of the twentieth century suggest that tonality "died" around 1908 but tonality has clearly continued in various forms to the present day. How might a composer today deal with this still-contentious aspect of music?

Further reading

Adler, Samuel (1989), *The Study of Orchestration* (New York: Norton).
> A useful practical guide.

Cone, Edward T. (1962–3), "Stravinsky: the progress of a method," *Perspectives of New Music* 1/1, 18–26.
> An example of how analysis might overlap productively with compositional thought.

Feldman, Morton (1985), *Essays* (Kerpen: Beginner Press).
> Quirky but inspiring thoughts on being a composer.

Howat, Roy (1983), *Debussy in Proportion* (Cambridge: Cambridge University Press).
> An approach to Debussy's music that suggests intricate structural thinking beneath the surface.

Johnson, Julian (2003), "Multiple choice? Composing and climate change in the 1990s," in Peter O'Hagan (ed.), *Aspects of British Music of the 1990s* (Aldershot: Ashgate), 29–37.
> A polemical essay that argues contemporary composers should not be sidetracked by what is merely fashionable.

Reich, Steve (2002), *Writings on Music, 1965–2000* (Oxford: Oxford University Press).
> Thoughtful reflections on contemporary music by one of its most accessible practitioners.

Schiff, David (1983), *The Music of Elliott Carter* (London: Eulenberg).
> A detailed study of a complex musical language.

Steinitz, Richard (2003), *Györgi Ligeti: Music of the Imagination* (London: Faber).
> A very different composer to Carter, but one who transcends any narrow idea of "style."

15 Music technology

BRIAN LOCK

Key terms

- Production.
- Composition.
- Recording.
- Post-production.

Chapter preview

This chapter is mainly concerned with what music technology is and will look at the various ways in which it is studied in universities and music colleges. As part of this, the various applications of music technology in composition, recording, and production will be discussed in more detail. This chapter will also take a look at the broader impact of technology on music in general. It will introduce you to the basic technical terminology and give you some idea of the various uses and general possibilities of the combination of technology and music. We will also have a short look at some of the careers open to those with skills in this area.

Key issues

- What is music technology?
- How do we study music technology?
- How do we use music technology?
- How can we compose, record, and produce music using technology?
- Making music at home, multimedia, and the World Wide Web.
- Courses and careers.

Introduction: what is music technology?

This subject-area is most often concerned with the use of electronic equipment for the recording and composition of music. The subject name, with all the scientific implications brought by the term "technology," can sometimes seem disconcerting. In essence, though, the discipline is a thoroughly creative and practical one concerned with the creation and dissemination of music. It is only the tools that are different – sequencers and **samplers** instead of pencils and paper; **sound modules** and **mixing desks** rather than violins and music stands.

Music technology can appear daunting for students who have come from traditional musical backgrounds. The first impression on walking into a professional studio like Abbey Road in London is often that the equipment resembles something like a jet aircraft cockpit. And, of course, just keeping up with changes in technology and the introduction of new equipment can be more than a full-time job. The subject also has elements of maths, physics, and computing in it. So, other than the new tools that music technology gives musicians, what can it really do? The answers are manifest, including many new ways of thinking about music and being creative, but the underlying answer is that technology allows musicians total control over sound.

How is it studied?

Music technology is defined in many different ways, in different situations and institutions, and it means many different things to different people. This is because the subject embraces a vast number of different types of equipment, approaches, and aesthetics. The subject is studied and much research into it is carried out by experts in areas as diverse as computer programming and acoustics. So studying music technology could mean studying very complex scientific fields that have some musical application. Sometimes, because technology is of great use to composers, it is studied as part of composition. Equally, technology is used for the recording of music and is therefore studied as part of sound engineering. Audio and editing software are vital for broadcast and entertainment applications and in these fields many of the people who use the equipment would not even consider themselves musicians, yet they will have some skill in using technology largely developed for music. At the very least, the equipment used in broadcast and entertainment applications has many similarities with that used by musicians. The variety of fields where music technology could be included is therefore large: composition, recording, production, editing, and programming are only a few of the more common and important areas.

In theory the subject divides very neatly with the equipment and science on the one hand, and musical creation and creativity on the other. You can learn the mechanics of computers and microphones. You can learn how to program audio software, and it is perfectly possible to study the principles on which all of this equipment and technology is based and not take account of music at all.

The interesting part, though, is when musicians try to do something with the technology – compose, record, or edit recordings with it, because at that point the equipment, no matter how thoroughly mastered, is only as good as the musical ideas driving it. There is no denying that this is a big and complex subject and very often musicians who become interested in technology stop writing or performing and spend time learning the techniques and skills demanded by the technology. In the end, though, most remember that the reason they wanted to use technology was to create music, and they return to music making good use of their newly found technological skills.

In academic institutions music technology is most often concerned with the creative products generated between the interaction of musician and equipment. The two most popular areas for study are often therefore recording and composition. We are now going to look at some of the main features and principles of these areas. Equipment will vary from one academic institution to another as it does in the professional world from one studio to another. The type of music will vary depending on the interest of the staff: experimental, film, commercial, and electroacoustic are amongst those most commonly found. Music technology also has a reputation for change and development so rapid that it is almost impossible to keep up with them. Although changes are indeed rapid and significant, the subject is based on principles and general skills which – once they have been mastered – enable the user to work comfortably with most equipment and in most situations. Indeed the serious technologically based musician will be able to predict and desire the next steps forward. Many even help create them.

Composition

If we are going to compose, we need somewhere to write the music. Many composers now use a computer. But computers are no good without something in them to make them do the job you want. This is called software. Software is specifically written for composing music in computers and one such program is called a sequencer. There are several types of these, made by different companies. Apple makes one sequencer called Logic Audio, often shortened to just Logic. Other popular sequencers include Cubase made by Steinberg, and Digital Performer. The computer has the ability to intake material and alter it through various functions. This is how we can use it to compose. Think of it as similar to writing an essay in a word-processing program in your computer. Another feature of a sequencer is that because it is specifically built for music, instead of typing material in like in word-processing, we can play music straight in. This means we can have a piano keyboard connected to the computer. So a sequencer can be thought of as manuscript paper and the keyboard as a pencil. Once set to record mode, the computer will capture what has been played. On the computer screen the music that has been captured can be manipulated and edited, and this is where the composing takes place: editing phrases, deleting notes, transposing and rearranging, much like on paper. In traditional composition, there is no possibility of a performance of the piece until it is played, but the computer can play whatever you have written immediately. To do this it needs sounds. These are often stored as samples on sound modules or samplers. Of course, we also need to be able to hear what we have done so we need some **speakers**. A small amount of equipment for composing is normally called a workstation.

Composing using MIDI

But how are workstations able to record and play back music? The answer is that one piece of equipment, say the computer, must be able to communicate with other pieces of equipment, like the keyboard or a sampler. To enable this communication, a protocol called MIDI (Musical Instrument Digital Interface) was invented. This protocol or language, which is **digital**, means that electronic musical instruments (computers, samplers, sound modules, and so on) can be plugged into one another and "talk" to each other.

For example, if we play a note on a keyboard linked to a computer with sequencing software, the note will be analyzed according to several parameters, its pitch, length, and velocity (how hard the key was struck) being the main ones. This information will then be translated into MIDI and sent to the computer. Computers can also be thought of as a type of tape recorder. The computer is not recording sound to tape though: it is recording MIDI. Computers are digital and are therefore compatible with MIDI, and able to "capture" it. Sequencing software enables them to do this. Furthermore, the computer can store the performance on its hard disk. Again to use the tape recorder analogy, in addition to recording, the computer can also play the MIDI information that it has stored. If we press play on the sequencer the computer will output or play the MIDI information. This information can be sent wherever we want it to go. It is most likely that we will want to hear something though, so usually the MIDI will be sent to sound modules or samplers.

It is important to understand that MIDI is not sound. It is a code that represents the original musical object, in our case the note struck on the keyboard. This material can then be stored and sent out of the computer. It is only when the code arrives at a piece of equipment that makes sound – a sound generator, like a sound module or sampler – that it can be used to generate a sound. Think of this in the same way that a musician will see notes on paper and then play according to those instructions. Similarly, a sound-generating device will see MIDI and then react to those instructions. The sound module will then play a sound which can be sent to a mixing desk or console for alteration or mixing, or sent to a speaker so we can hear it.

Another important feature of MIDI is its use of channels. Channels enable composers using technology to write polyphonic music. This means having more than just one line. For example, if we play a note on the keyboard again we can record this in the sequencer and send it out on MIDI channel 1. When it arrives at a sound module it can also see this arriving on channel 1. We can then select the sound we want the module to play on its channel 1. This could be anything, from an oboe to a drum loop. In this way MIDI enables composers to write substantial multilayered compositions, one line at a time, and hear them played back together in perfect synchronization. The idea is that information sent on, say, MIDI channel 1, will only be read and used by receiving devices on their channel 1. All other channels will ignore that signal. In other words a "master" device could communicate with a "slave" device without other devices also reacting. Think of this as like addressing a letter. Many people may see the letter over the course of its journey but only the addressee will read it and react to it.

For example, if we were writing a piece of pop music we could send the guitar part out of the sequencer on MIDI channel 1 and the piano part on MIDI channel 2. When these parts arrive at a sound-generating device, only MIDI channel 1 will react to the MIDI coming in on channel 1. Channel 2 will react to the part coming in on channel 2. A sound-generating device that is able to play two or more parts with different sounds is called multitimbral. In practice, a multitimbral sound module can contain many thousands of sounds which the composer can select and experiment with.

Again remember that MIDI is not sound. The information sent out of the computer in MIDI language is just a code for the original note. This code includes information regarding the pitch, velocity, and duration of the note in addition to other parameters. When this arrives at the sound module it will play that pitch, velocity, and duration on whichever channel we have sent it to. The sound will depend entirely on which one we have selected the sound module to play on its channel 1. We can select any sound available from the module to put on any channel. In the above example, of course, it is the guitar sound we should select from the sound module's library of sounds. We could select a different sound on the sound module which would then respond exactly to the same MIDI information. So we could select a clarinet or a cello or a voice. The MIDI information coming in would have exactly the same note parameters but the type of sound would change. Think of this like a conductor giving a part written for violin to a flute player. The notes are the same but the sound is different. Changing sounds in this way is part of the creative process for composers in studios.

Sound modules themselves usually come with pre-existing sounds already in them which have been preset during manufacture and are therefore known as presets. A sampler, on the other hand, enables the composer to record in their own sound material, alter it and use it as their own personal sound for composition. This combination of MIDI channels, samplers, and multitimbral sound modules gives composers enormous possibilities. Imagine having a multilayered composition and being able to send each part to a choice of potentially thousands of different sounds. In addition, by using daisy-chaining and MIDI Thru boxes we can use lots of electronic musical equipment at the same time, giving composers almost limitless possibilities of sound combinations.

An important principle of technology is always to understand which form information is being transmitted in. We have just looked at MIDI which translates the various parameters of a musical entity into a digital language which can then be read by other equipment compatible with the MIDI format. As we have already learned, MIDI is a digital language, meaning it comprises computer binary code representing musical sounds but is not the music itself. In any workstation or system of music equipment there will also usually be an analog component. **Analog** is a system of coding events, in our case music, using a continuously changing electrical voltage. In a MIDI workstation all the information flowing around is digital. That is, except for the sound modules and samplers which are outputting analog information. This means that the sound modules and sampler are receiving MIDI, which is telling them to output particular notes via the appropriate channels. They are responding to these requests, and in a MIDI studio are sending out sound in analog form. Both analog and digital systems are used extensively in music technology, and much equipment can use both formats, but the important thing to remember is that both are just representations of sounds and not the original musical sounds in themselves. In fact, there is no sound present in the above system. It is only when a signal is received at the speaker, and the speaker then pushes its cone back and forth creating variations in sound pressure, that our brains decode those variations and we recognize them as music.

The composing itself takes place largely in the sequencer. Sequencers are designed so that MIDI data is presented in clear ways to composers so that they can edit and manipulate it and thus create music. In practice, this means graphic representations of MIDI data. The most widely used of these is usually the main page of the sequencer or the "arrange page" as it is generally called.

In the arrange page MIDI data is represented as graphic blocks. Other editors common to most sequencers include a matrix editor, which shows each note represented against a vertical piano keyboard to illustrate its pitch and a horizontal scale to show its place in time. Sequencers normally contain other information about the parameters of a note: for example, in the matrix editor of Logic Audio, the velocity of a note is illustrated by the block representing the note being color-coded. For example, red is for maximum velocity. Sequencers will also contain other graphic editors, like the "score editor," which produces a graphic of the MIDI in standard Western notation. To make these editor pages useful, sequencers contain a large number of tools which can be used for the manipulation and editing of MIDI inside them. This is where the composing takes place. It is here that the notes can be totally manipulated and altered by various parameters. Some of the tools are sophisticated and reasonably complex and take some time to master, while new tools are continuously being introduced. But many of the tools presented for the manipulation of MIDI and composing are easy and intuitive. In fact, many are not dissimilar to word-processing. For example, a group of notes can be selected and deleted, or if you hold on to them with the mouse, made longer in duration. This can be an extremely liberating experience for composers used to manuscript paper, especially as the results can be heard immediately.

The important thing here is to realize that because the material is digital, it can be altered and subjected to many different processes for the purpose of creating music. More software may come on the market, some of the present software and working methods may disappear, but sequencers and computers enable composers to manipulate material, save versions of it, edit it and hear it back instantly.

Digital audio

So far, the composing I have been talking about has been entirely to do with the manipulation of MIDI. Computers and sequencers, though, can also deal with "digital audio." If we record someone singing using a microphone and a tape recorder this would be an analog recording. In other words, the microphone **transduces** the sound waves made by the vocalist and converts them into an electrical signal that is then stored on magnetic tape. However, we have seen that computers are digital machines. So we can get our singer to sing again into a microphone which then generates the same electrical signal. This signal, instead of being sent directly to tape, can be converted into digital code. In music studios a piece of equipment called an "analog to digital converter" is used to do this. The actual process of conversion is mathematically complex, but as far as musicians are concerned, this opens up another world of possibilities. The digitized **audio file**, within the computer, can be subjected to various processes. Remember, a digital file is composed of binary code, a series of numbers representing something, in our case sound. We can therefore edit the numbers that represent the sound and when played back we will hear the results of the digital editing. For example, a whole recording can be raised or lowered in pitch or stretched in time. There is a substantial amount of software for the editing of digital audio on the market, but some comes self-contained within sequencing packages like the Audio Factory in Logic Audio. So by understanding the various types of ways of capturing and representing sound, and the control over the various parameters that we have to edit music, it is easily possible to see how and why composers write music in studios and what the various possibilities for musicians are.

Recording

Recording is another main area that comes under the broad heading of music technology. Whereas composers use technology to manipulate material – MIDI or audio – into musical structures and hope primarily to display their musical ideas, the recording part of technology is largely to do with the accurate capture, representation, and storage of the performance of a composition. Composers usually use workstations, as we have seen above, but the home of the sound recordist is the control room. Although a whole building that has technological facilities for composers and the recording of music is typically called a studio, more correctly, and definitely in the professional world, the area where the musicians play is the studio, sometimes also called the live or performance area. The rooms where the sound recordist and the equipment are located are called the control room and machine room respectively. The mixing desk and monitors will be in the control room and the tape recorders and computers in the machine room.

The field of sound engineering can appear, and indeed be, somewhat scientific in its approach. The basis for this is that the sound engineer is primarily capturing someone else's idea in sound. Therefore the sound recordist or sound engineer, as they are also known, should have a training that is mainly concerned with the physics of sound and the equipment used to capture it. The nature of sound and hearing is usually studied along with such subjects as valve technology, electronic synthesis, amplification, and sampling theory and conversion. Two areas that are fundamental to sound engineering, though, are microphone use and mixing.

Both microphone use and mixing are wide subjects. If you are interested in these fields you would be well advised to look at books in the list of further reading at the end of this chapter. Again, these areas both contain large amounts of technical information that needs to be learned, but after that, practical experience of actually using the equipment for recording and mixing of music is vital. As with composing, once you have some control over the equipment the creative part can begin. Although the basic principles can be learned, the sound engineer has to interpret things like how the composer or conductor wishes to hear the music. In fact, the role of the sound engineer is even greater, in that often it is the engineer who decides on the overall "sound" of the recording. There can be as much difference between the "sounds" of different engineers as there is between the voices of two different composers. One sound engineer may have a particular liking for recording in a particular studio or using a particular type of **microphone placement**, all of which make the music sound different. For example, because of the material the walls are made from, the height of the ceiling, and so on, some recording studios can emphasize particular parts of a musical performance, making the music sound richer or thinner.

The number of variables in recording a piece of music is enormous, many of which the sound engineer has varying degrees of control over. It is the artistic choices which the sound engineer makes in this area that determine the over-all "quality of the sound" of the recording. It may have become apparent while reading the above that there are many areas between sound recording and composing that are similar and to some extent overlap. For example, compo-sers can record a musical performance, place it into a sequencer and edit it into a composition. A composer can equally "**rip**" an already existing record-ing from a CD and use that in his own composition. It is really only when the composer has his music performed by acoustic musicians from a traditional score on paper and recorded in a recording studio that there is any totally marked delineation in the role. In the professional world people tend to specialize in one or the other, but largely because of digital technology, there are many areas that overlap and most of these are also in the area known as production.

Composition and production

Production is the area of music technology concerned with the overall "feel" of a piece of music or a recording. Digital technology has meant that composers now have access to software that replicates extremely expensive production hardware only previously available to professional recording studios. In pop music the "feel" and "sound" of the recording is in some cases as important as, or more important than the composed elements of harmony and melody. Even the recording of an orchestral performance will be produced – the sound altered according to the **producer**'s requirements and tastes.

The areas of composition and production also overlap, as many composers use techniques borrowed from production. Once we have captured a sound we can do things to it. We can process it. All the techniques we are about to look at therefore come under the broad heading of "signal processing." Many proces-sing applications were devised for purely technical needs. For example, if there is extraneous noise in a recording, say a rumble from traffic noise or air conditioning, it can be located and reduced by the use of EQ. EQ is short for equalization, which is a technique used to boost or reduce a selected part of an audio spectrum. Many of these sorts of processing applications, though, are also used creatively and have been since they were invented. For example, we could record a perfectly good note on a flute, we could EQ the bottom range of the recording and the flute will sound quite different with the bottom range reduced. This, of course, may be exactly the sound we want to compose with or the sound we want on our final recording. Therefore, we process music with such effects. Once a sound is captured we can really process it in two types of ways. We can alter the way in which it plays back either by altering something to do with the way the original plays back in time, "time-based effects," or altering something to do with the volume: "dynamic effects." Dynamic effects include compression, limiting and gateing; while time-based effects include reverberation, echo, flanging, phasing, and chorusing, just to name some of the more important.

I am going to take one of these – reverberation or reverb, as it is usually referred to – to explore production further. All sound when we hear it naturally comes to us with some reverb. Reverb is the ambience that we hear as part of sound caused by multiple reflections from surrounding surfaces. It also gives use an impression of size and distance. For example, imagine the sound of an orchestra playing in a cathedral and then the sound of an orchestra playing in the open air. The two have quite different sounds and this is largely to do with reverb. Composers and sound engineers have software that will replicate many different types of reverb. We can place our material so that it sounds like it is in a cathedral or the open air. Such software will also allow us control over particular parameters such as room size and material of construction. Reverb was originally used so that engineers could create the sound of a particular space or environment on music recorded in studios. This is because music studios are kept deliberately low in natural reverb: although reverb can be added to a recording to create the right feel, it cannot be taken off a source recording. Reverb, though, along with most other effects has been used and is still used extensively in music production. Also, because such equipment for all sorts of effects is able to control different parameters at the same time, we can make some quite unnatural sounds, taking us into the worlds of "sound design" and creating "special effects."

Composing with sound

The use of effects and processing is not just a part of the production of the overall finished sound of a complete recording. Composers who use sequencers can apply effects themselves. They can then compose with this processed sound, or in other words, compose with an altered sound rather than with a straight "acoustic" sound that is later processed. For example, a composer could be writing with a piano sound in the sequencer and from the outset process this sound. He or she could give it an extremely long reverb, say six seconds, and also another effect, delay for example, which makes the note repeat itself, and compose with that processed sound. This new sound, of the piano with the reverb and delay, is quite different to an unprocessed piano and will provide new sonic material which requires different approaches to composition. The new sound may well in itself provide inspiration to the composer. Composers also frequently work with samples that they have stored on the hard disk of their computers. Such sounds can be edited and personalized by the composer and stored in that form for use at a later date. The software to do this is called a **virtual instrument**. Another way of working with samples is to stream them directly from a computer hard drive, as with Tascam's GigaStudio. In addition, much equipment, both hardware and software, is automated, and furthermore, hardware and software can control each other. Automation of many functions, direct recall of past equipment settings, and unlimited "undoing" of editing means composers can produce music to a professional level which would previously have involved several people and been extremely expensive.

Technology allows direct access and control over sound. The ability to alter a composition and hear it back immediately, to alter existing sounds in real time, and to make new sounds, are some of the more important aspects of music technology. For composers, the possibility of instant playback of their ideas without having to wait for musicians to interpret their music can be significant. Not having to translate sounds to and from musical notation can in itself provide new ways of thinking and new sources of inspiration. For some, the possibility of having a world of sound at the fingertips can be as overwhelming as others find it liberating, but it is as well to be aware that technology opens up new possibilities in creative thinking. In much of rock and pop there is usually no reference to notation anyway. Indeed, the manipulation of musical ideas through technology can provide much of the inspiration. In fact, most commercial music would not even exist without technology and many of the developments in pop music are inextricably linked to advances in technology. For example, in live performance, it would be impossible to hear someone singing softly over a drum kit, but by using equipment such non-traditional arrangements have become standard and really allowed pop music to take the form that it has for some decades now. It was in the world of pop music that technology had another revolutionary effect: live performance (see chapters 11 and 16). A pop band of four musicians would be restricted to a relatively small palette of color (voice, percussion, guitar and piano) but by using electronic instruments with access to libraries of sounds, a small group of performers could use an enormous range of timbre. Currently, in experimental art music, technology is allowing composers to interact with performers, and so-called "live electronics" is very much part of compositional research carried out in academic institutions.

At first, technology for musicians can appear overwhelming because much of the equipment is designed to be useful in as many applications as possible. Most electronic musical equipment will be usable in all the areas previously outlined – composing, recording, production, and live music – but of course there will be items of equipment that will become redundant when being used in only one application. For example, a mixing desk for composers at a workstation might be used very little at all: in some cases it is used primarily as a mechanism to connect the outputs of machinery together, but not for balancing or sound modification which could be carried out in the workstation's software. The very flexibility and functionality of technological music equipment means that it is also compatible with other systems and this has been the trend for the last few years and looks set to continue. Until quite recently, for example, film and TV music composers have synchronized video of film with their equipment through the use of "time code." This means that the film and the music equipment would run in complete synchronization with each other by having machinery "locked" together at the same time. Very useful for writing music directly to the picture. Now, though, composers often digitize their film into a video file. Because the film is digitized and computers are digital devices, the film can be input into the computer. This means that the film and the music run together on the computer screen in the sequencer. Benefits of this include easier synchronization of music with the exact frames in the films, and also practical things like not having to wait for a video player to rewind. There is no denying that music technology has had a massive impact on the way in which music is composed and produced, but it has also thoroughly revolutionized the way in which it is distributed and consumed: just think of iPods, minidisks, and Napster. Indeed, the impact of technology has now become a subject of study in itself, and its applications and various manifestations are of growing interest to musicologists in terms of how music is received, read, and understood (see particularly chapter 16).

Making music in home studios

Composers can now master and distribute their own music by themselves. The "mastering" process is the term given to making a final production master of a recording which is then cloned or copied. In large commercial recordings this can take the form of expensive tape being digitized into a master copy, an optical disk or glass master of this being made, and then duplicated onto tens of thousands of CDs for distribution by a record company. Sequencer software enables composers to do exactly the same process in their own workstations by "bouncing" their music onto the computer hard disk. Editing software and laptop computers are easily good enough for the creation of master copies of music that will be commercially released. The music can then be placed into software for burning onto a CD and within minutes, a composer can have his music on a professional format ready for distribution.

Multimedia, film, the Web

Digitization has meant that music is in consonant format with other media. The most practical result of this for musicians is the easy interface with other media – like the film composer mentioned above, putting film and music together in the same sequencer. But from the distribution point of view, this also means that audio files are easily placed on the World Wide Web. Anyone can create a piece of music and have a potentially worldwide audience. This seamless progression from original musical idea to worldwide distribution is having quite profound effects on the economics, business, and legal aspects of music as well as at the more creative end of things, where most musicians' interests lie. Musicologists are interested in the impact of technology in these fields and the manifold impacts of technology on music are featuring more and more in academic articles (see chapters 11 and 12). The practical application of technology in academic music research is also increasing. Experiments in performance studies and the psychology of music use software and hardware for analyzing musical thinking, performance, and creative processes, while in ethnomusicology, performances are recorded and examined (see chapters 4, 6, and 13). Although not directly music technology, technology in a broader sense is being used to clean up previously indecipherable medieval manuscripts and also to make historical recordings clearly audible. Music technology as a term can be broadly defined in the academic arena and can also include areas such as developments in instrument engineering.

Careers

Because many of the principles of music technology are similar, to varying degrees, to those used in other media, the number of jobs open to those with a training and interest in the field is large. As well as the more traditional composer, sound engineer, and producer, all sorts of organizations from post-production houses to music publishers, record companies, and Web designers, are interested in those with knowledge of the discipline. Post-production is a broad term, involving a range of companies that undertake the final stage of mixing audio and visual content in ways that are appropriate for various broadcasting standards, including media from films, TV, radio programs, and advertisements. Most of the work they carry out is in digital formats and uses equipment and software similar to those used exclusively in music. Film editing, sound effects, dubbing, and mixing all have a sizable number of people from musical backgrounds working in them. Directly within music itself, technology has given rise to a number of new jobs such as music programmers who program samples into compositions and **pro-tools** engineers, while many other musical professions have changed as a result of technology. It is rare to find a copyist working in the commercial environment who produces handwritten parts, instead of using a music-notation software program like Sibelius or Finale. In education, music technology is a firm part of the curriculum and the need for teachers to be competent in the discipline is increasing. For performers, a knowledge of recording processes is helpful in the professional world. For students, the ability to be able to put printed musical examples in essays and complete theory exercises in software notation programs is a distinct advantage and in many institutions a minimum requirement.

Courses

Music technology is found to varying degrees and in various guises in universities and music colleges. It is possible to study for a degree specifically in music technology covering many of the parts of the discipline from composing with computers and sound synthesis, through to music on the Web and computer programming. The subject is so large, though, that all parts of it will only rarely be covered. More often, degrees are offered in one particular branch of it, say sound recording, and offer in-depth study of all the various sub-branches – in this case, orchestral recording, pop recording, acoustics, digital audio, studio design, and so on. For those with less interest in the musical and creative side of things but more in the technology itself, with some musical applications, a study of electronics may be more useful. Often though, music technology will be found associated in one way or another with composition, either as an integrated part of a "composition course" or as an offshoot such as sequencing or computer music. In many ways, though, studying music technology is similar to performance. To be good at music technology you need to gain mastery and technique over hardware and software – in effect, your instrument – just like a pianist practices for years to gain control and technique at the piano. If treated in this way the manifold possibilities and developments of this exciting and evolving subject will be open to you.

Chapter summary

- Music technology as a term covers an enormous range of material, approaches, and ideas. However, people often specialize in just one branch of it like composition or production.
- Even though developments in technology are continuous there are some basic concepts that underpin the subject, and once these have been mastered, even new developments are easily understandable.
- Music technology sometimes has a reputation for being very technical and scientific, yet it is really like any other musical field. It is highly creative and practice makes perfect!

Discussion topics

1. Does music technology influence the way that composers compose as much as a pen and paper?
2. Listen to two different CDs of the same piece of music. How much difference do the varying recording and production techniques make to the overall "sound" and "feel" of the music ? Do you prefer one of the recordings to the other, and if so why?
3. If access to music technology becomes even more widespread and cheaper, and if it becomes more and more "user friendly," what do you think could be some of the implications for music and musicians as a whole?

Further reading

Bennett, Stephen (2002), *Making Music with Logic Pro*, 2nd edn (Thetford, Norfolk: PC Publishing).
    A clear introduction to using this sequencing package effectively from the start. Contains many useful user tips.
Brice, Richard (2001), *Music Engineering*, 2nd edn (Oxford: Newnes).
    An excellent, thorough and comprehensive guide to all aspects of sound engineering, including good chapters on the development of electric instruments, digital audio and recording consoles.
Brown, Roger and Griese, Martin (2000), *Electronica Dance Music Programming Secrets* (Hemel Hempstead: Prentice Hall).
    Useful introduction to programming all sorts of commercial music including trance, house and techno for beginners.
Rona, Jeff (2000), *The Reel World: Scoring for Pictures* (San Francisco and Milwaukee, WI: Miller Freeman Books).
    A book about the practicalities of composing for films and TV with useful chapters on setting up a studio, writing the score and recording film and TV music.
Sinclair, Ian Robertson (2002), *Electronics Made Simple* (Oxford: Made Simple).
    An excellent book describing and explaining in detail the basic electronics behind lots of different types of equipment. Useful chapters on digital signals, CD systems, and computers.

Two informative monthly magazines are also worth reading. *Music Tech Magazine* published by Anthem Publishing Ltd, Bath, is possibly the best magazine of its type with lots of practical information, tutorials and useful articles on how to get the best from equipment. *Sound on Sound* published by SOS Publications is better for those who are not complete beginners and contains informative reviews of new equipment and useful tutorials in both the music production and sound recording areas.

Glossary

Sampler	A piece of equipment into which a sound can be recorded, manipulated, and stored. There are hardware samplers made by companies like Akai and software versions like Emagic's EX24.
Sound Modules	Equipment that can store many thousands of sounds. The sounds are already in the unit and can be used in that state or they can be altered and saved back into the unit. Sound Modules normally have a mixture of acoustic and more

	synthesized type sounds. Sound Modules come under the broad heading of sound-generators and are always MIDI compatible. Common sound modules include Roland's Proteus and EMU's Virtuoso series.
Mixing	The art of balancing the various parts of a musical composition into a whole.
Speakers	These are more normally called in monitors in studio situations. Different speakers are used for different reasons. For example, near-field speakers are used for detailed listening. The term monitor is used a lot in studio situations and can also refer to computer displays and television screens.
Digital	A system that represents data using binary code.
Analog	Electrical circuitry that represents a signal by using changing voltage levels. The signal and changing voltage levels are analogous to each other, hence the name.
Transducer	A device for transforming energy from one form to another. Many examples of transducers can be found in music but one of the more common is a microphone. Sound waves go into the microphone and are then converted i.e., transduced into electrical signal.
Audio file	The generic name given to various types of digital storage for audio. Examples include mp3, WAV and AIFF.
Microphone placement	How and where microphones are placed in a recording studio in relation to performers. For example, a soloist could be recorded from in front or above, and from close or far away or any other combination. This obviously affects the "sound" of a recording quite dramatically.
Ripping	The process of taking a pre-existing recording and converting to it to an audio file for use in another composition. All sorts of moral and legal problems surround "ripping" if the original material is under copyright.
Producer	A person who takes overall artistic and/or business control of a recording.
Virtual Instrument	Software versions of samplers and synthesizers.
Pro-tools	A high-end professional audio editing system.

16 The economics and business of music

Chapter preview

All music is shaped by economic circumstances, even the "pure" music of the Western classical tradition. This chapter traces the economic development of Western music since around 1800, including the successive transformations of the music business: on the one hand, from the production of commodities to the management of rights, and on the other, from sheet-music publication to the recording industry to part of the global communications and media industry. Aspects covered include the development and chronic problems of the music profession, copyright and the performing and mechanical rights that arise from it, and the impact of technology on both the social and business practices of music. The chapter concludes with an analysis of the current state of the music business and its prospects for the future.

Key issues

- The relationship between music and economic context.
- The impact of changing technology on music employment.
- The role of copyright in the music business.
- The transition of music publishing from selling commodities to managing rights.
- The future of the record industry in the digital age.

Snapshot of 1825: Beethoven's Ninth and the music business

The Symphony raised frantic enthusiasm. Many wept. Beethoven fainted with emotion after the concert; he was taken to Schindler's house, where he remained asleep all the night and the following morning, fully dressed, neither eating nor drinking. The triumph was only fleeting, however, and the concert brought in nothing for Beethoven. His material circumstances of life were not changed by it. He found himself poor, ill, alone but a conqueror: conqueror of the mediocrity of mankind, conqueror of his destiny, conqueror of his suffering. "Sacrifice, always sacrifice the trifles of life to art! God is over all!"

(Rolland 1919: 46–7)

This description of the aftermath of the first performance of Beethoven's Ninth Symphony (Vienna, 7 May 1825) was penned almost a century later by Romain Rolland, the French writer whose books did more than anything to spread the cult of Beethoven across the world. For Rolland, as for other writers of his time, art transcends material circumstances, and so Beethoven's poverty becomes a sign of his authenticity as an artist. This is an approach that writes the marketplace out of music and its history, but of course music has always existed in the marketplace, and you cannot understand it as the human practice it is unless you factor in its economic context. So this chapter begins by setting music of the nineteenth- and twentieth-century Western "art" tradition into its economic and business contexts, before going on to explore the developing relationship between the music business and technology, its foundations in copyright law, its current state, and its prospects.

Fig. 16.1 Title page of Beethoven's Three Piano Trios, Op. 1 (1795). Though it was published in Vienna, the title page is in French because that was the accepted language of the cultured classes across much of Europe; if it had been in German, sales would have been lower.

To start with a concrete question: what is the significance of Prince Lichnowsky's name on the title page of Beethoven's Op. 1?

During Beethoven's lifetime serious music – what we now call "art" or "classical" music – was still primarily an aristocratic pursuit, or at any rate, it was primarily paid for by the aristocracy. However the traditional relationship between composers and their aristocratic patrons was changing. If you were a successful composer of the generation before Beethoven, you aspired to become a *Kapellmeister*, directing the music at an aristocratic or royal palace – like Haydn, who was in charge of music for the Esterházy family in what is now Hungary, and who formally counted as a servant, though one whose distinction as a composer was prized by the family and recognized throughout and beyond the Austro-Hungarian empire. Beethoven's own early employment with the Elector Maximilian Franz at Bonn followed a similar pattern, but after he moved to Vienna in 1792, at the age of twenty-one, he never again occupied such a post: equipped with letters of introduction from Bonn, he entered the houses of the aristocracy as a guest, rapidly gaining a reputation as a brilliant improviser.

Aristocrats interested in the arts, or wishing to be seen as guardians of Vienna's musical heritage, were eager to be associated with the fashionable and charismatic young composer, and it is in this context that Prince Lichnowsky paid for the publication of Beethoven's Op. 1 – and in return had the work dedicated to him. His support of Beethoven went further: in 1800 he gave Beethoven an annuity of six hundred florins a year – not enough to live comfortably on (in 1804 it was reckoned that a middle-class bachelor needed twice that [Cooper (ed.) 1991: 69]), but enough to provide considerable security. The arrangement ended after the two men fell out in 1806, but in 1808 Beethoven was invited to become *Kapellmeister* at the royal court in Westphalia, and in order to keep him in Vienna a group of aristocrats offered him the much more substantial sum of four thousand florins a year for life: their aim, the contract said, was to put Beethoven "in a position where the necessaries of life shall not cause him embarrassment or clog his powerful genius."

Of course this arrangement, which provided the basis of Beethoven's finances for the rest of his life, was quite exceptional. However, its value was considerably diminished as a result of persistent inflation during the period of the Napoleonic wars, and so Beethoven had to supplement his earnings in much the same way as more ordinary composers did. There were basically three main sources of income: teaching, selling music for publication, and putting on concerts. Beethoven did all three, and in these terms the most successful period of his career was 1813–16, as a result of the popularity of the works he wrote to celebrate the victories against Napoleon and the subsequent Congress of Vienna (such as *Wellingtons Sieg* and *Der glorreiche Augenblick* – works that Beethoven scholars have seen as an embarrassment, but that's another story). This enabled Beethoven, in 1816, to make a bank deposit of ten thousand florins, on which he earned 8 percent interest.

By the time of the Ninth Symphony, however, Beethoven's deafness had become profound, so that it was more or less impossible for him to perform or teach: this made it important for him to maximize his income from compositions, anticipating the pattern of later full-time composers (full-time in that they did not teach or perform). Beethoven completed the score in February 1824, and in the same month wrote to offer it to several publishers (Schlesinger in Paris, Probst in Leipzig, and Schott in Mainz), in each case quoting a price of six hundred gulden (the equivalent of 1,500 florins). It was sold to Schott on 3 July, but Beethoven was not above having second thoughts, writing back to Probst on 28 August:

> In regard to the symphony, which is the grandest I have written so far and for which even foreign artists [i.e., publishers] have already made offers to me, it might be possible to arrange for you to have it. But, if so, you must make up your mind with all speed. For I have already received a portion of the fee for this symphony. At the same time I could give this man other works for the money he has paid me. Although God has specially blessed me …, and although I am never at a loss for publishers, yet you are well aware that I like simple honesty in business dealings … Do not abuse my confidence; and do not make any use of this offer of mine in conversations with other people. My fee is 1000 gulden A.C. … I find money matters very tiresome.
>
> (letter 1305 in Anderson 1961)

Beethoven's business ethics may have been questionable, but selling a work for the highest possible price was important because, once sold, it generated no further income for the composer (unlike nowadays, as explained below). However publication took time (the symphony appeared in 1826 – from Schott, as nothing came of the late approach to Probst), and the intervening period offered the opportunity to put on performances from which the composer kept the profits: these concerts were called *Akadamien* and are often referred to as "benefit concerts" (the benefit in question being the composer's). There were at that time no dedicated concert halls in Vienna, so such events were housed in theaters or ballrooms: for the Ninth Symphony Beethoven hired the Kärtnerthor Theater, which normally housed Italian opera. The basic fee, including the theater orchestra (which Beethoven supplemented) and lighting, was a relatively modest four hundred florins, but there were additional heavy expenses including the construction of platforms for the performance. Nevertheless Anton Schindler, Beethoven's amanuensis, calculated that ticket sales should bring in four thousand florins, so that even after allowing a thousand for copying the parts there should be a profit of at least two thousand.

In the event Schindler's calculation proved too optimistic. There were problems with publicity, the concert was late in the season, the royal box was empty: while expenses were more or less as anticipated, the gross receipts were only 2,200 florins, leaving a modest profit after expenses of 420 florins.

And here we come back to Rolland, whose romanticized account is evidently based on Schindler's own:

> The government official Joseph Hüttenbrenner, who still lives in Vienna, helped me bring home the exhausted master. I then handed Beethoven the box-office report. When he saw it, he collapsed. We picked him up and laid him on the sofa. We stayed at his side until late that night; he refused both food and drink, then said no more. Finally, when we noticed that Morpheus had gently closed his eyes, we withdrew. The next morning his servants found him sleeping as we left him, still dressed in the suit he had worn in the concert-hall.
>
> (Schindler 1966: 280)

If what the admittedly unreliable Schindler says is true – and in this case there is little reason to believe otherwise – then Beethoven did indeed faint with emotion, just as Rolland says, but the emotion was not the one that Rolland implies: as so often in the history of music, what was at issue was money, or the lack of it.

The rise and fall of the music profession

In Beethoven's day the Italian opera which the Kärntnerthor Theater normally housed was much more of a middle-class, commercial proposition than the aristocratic tradition of serious instrumental music. As a form of entertainment it occupied a role not so different from film and TV today, in a way that classical symphonies never did (and the rhetoric of "serious" versus "light" or "entertainment" music largely goes back to the uneasy relationship between Beethoven and Rossini: see chapter 1). In the decades after Beethoven's death, however, a new middle-class market for symphonic music developed across the capitals of Europe, and many present-day musical institutions date from this period. An example is the Vienna Philharmonic Society, which was founded in 1842 as a musicians' cooperative based on the Kärntnerthor Theater orchestra; the famous subscription concerts began in 1860.

In London, which even then was a trailblazer for the market economy, such developments took place a generation earlier, with the Philharmonic Society of London being founded as early as 1813: this is also part of the story of the Ninth Symphony, for the Society actually commissioned it for a fee of £50, in return for which they received a presentation score, the first British performance, and a right to exclusive use of the symphony for a limited period (there was disagreement between Beethoven and the Society about how long that period should be). Although this may look like another example of sharp practice, given Beethoven's promotion of the symphony in Vienna, England was traditionally treated for publication purposes as a separate market from Continental Europe, and the directors of the Society do not seem to have resented it: they sent Beethoven a gift of a hundred pounds in the last weeks of his life in the mistaken belief that he was destitute – an act that George Bernard Shaw, with perhaps just a hint of exaggeration, described as "by far the most creditable incident in English history" (Ehrlich 1995a: 33–6; Reith 1949: 163).

The English premiere of the Ninth Symphony was something close to a disaster, as a result of what had already become an antiquated system by which only one rehearsal was allowed per concert; it was almost thirty years (1852) before the first properly rehearsed London performance was given – by the pointedly named New Philharmonic Society, which brought in Berlioz to conduct it. As the name indicates, it was competition that raised performance standards, and it was new audiences and larger venues that made competition possible (the New Philharmonic Orchestra performed in the Exeter Hall, which had a capacity of two thousand). The Ninth Symphony was also brought, in a suitably doctored form, to lower-middle-class audiences that had never before encountered such music: the flamboyant Louis Antoine Jullien ("the long-haired, the dark-eyed, the graceful-actioned M Jullien," as a *Musical World* critic put it) took over the "Promenade" concerts at the Drury Lane Theatre in 1841, which offered a diet of overtures, waltzes, and quadrilles – the instrumental version of light music – and in the first season scheduled a performance of the finale of the Ninth Symphony, with the singers replaced by brass instruments. There was an element of showmanship in this; before conducting Beethoven, Jullien would put on a pair of white gloves brought to him on a silver salver. But it was the dissemination of classical music among an increasingly broad, ticket-buying, middle-class public that created the context against which the development of the music profession and the music business needs to be understood, not only in Britain (on which I shall focus), but in Continental Europe and North America too.

It is important to realize that the expansion of concerts was merely part of a wider phenomenon that embraced domestic as well as public spaces. The piano was the focus of a middle-class cultivation of performance that ranged from parlor ballads to sonatas, and somehow combined the functions of vehicle for self-improvement and home entertainment center. By the end of the nineteenth century the main elements of the music business consequently consisted of the manufacture of pianos, a gigantic industry on both sides of the Atlantic, and the publication of huge quantities of sheet music to satisfy the resulting demand. This also meant that teaching – basically the piano, but including general musicianship – became the mainstay of the music profession: musicians were often called "professors," meaning teachers.

It is possible to identify a number of economic models in operation here. Piano manufacture involved a degree of mechanization, particularly in North America, but the need for expensive material and human resources meant that there were only limited opportunities for reducing unit costs through economies of scale. By contrast, sheet music was a classic example of capitalist mass production: there were significant set-up costs (such as the cost of engraving, plus of course the lump sum to the composer), but printing costs were extremely low, meaning that once the initial investment had been recouped, the price was essentially unrelated to production costs. That could translate into big profits when, as sometimes happened, you could sell two hundred thousand copies, but of course you frequently couldn't – and the result was a business that worked the same way as Hollywood cinema does today, with a relatively small proportion of blockbusters making up for the flops. Another result was that there was a great deal of pirating (the pirates had the advantage of not wasting money on flops).

It was the professional musicians who were at the sharp edge of the market economy. Throughout the nineteenth century and into the twentieth there was a chronic surplus of capacity over demand in the music profession: too many trained performers and teachers chasing too little work, giving rise to low wages in the orchestra pit and shabby gentility for teachers. From around 1920, however, new technologies in the form of the radio and the gramophone began to have a major influence on patterns of musical employment – an influence that was initially benign, but rapidly became catastrophic. Whereas the old technology of the piano had encouraged participation in performance, the new technologies encouraged different forms of participation: listening and dancing. And in order to listen or dance you didn't need the same sort of skills you did to perform. The result was, in time, nothing short of a wholesale transformation of the social role of music, and hence of musical culture in general.

It didn't seem that way at first. Optimistic commentators of the 1920s saw the new technologies of reproduction as a means by which dissemination of existing musical culture would become even more widespread, both socially and geographically; the newly founded BBC (British Broadcasting Company, later Corporation) not only for the first time brought professionally performed classical music to a mass audience but also attempted to inculcate the knowledge and attitudes necessary to understand it (this was the heyday of Percy Scholes and the "music appreciation" movement). But for working musicians, the most important new technology was not radio or the gramophone, but film. Audiences for silent movies expanded prodigiously in the 1920s, with even the smallest town acquiring at least one cinema. And the silent movies were in reality anything but silent: music was an integral part of them, and music was the one area of film technology that had not been mechanized. Small cinemas had a pianist, large ones had orchestras. Employment opportunities for musicians rose to unprecedented levels. Small wonder then that in 1928 the critic Edwin Evans described the cinema as "the most important musical institution in the country" (Ehrlich 1995b: 47).

The date is poignant, for it was only months before the sudden and complete collapse of this employment market that occurred with the introduction of talkies in 1929 (further accentuated by the stock-market crash of the same year, which triggered a global economic depression effectively lasting until after World War II). As eventually became evident, the technologies of reproduction of which the talkies represented the cutting edge simultaneously chopped off all three legs of the pre-war economy of music: a musical culture in which participation meant listening or dancing slashed the demand for pianos, for sheet music to play on them, and for teaching of the skills required to do so. For teachers there was no easy answer, and in Cyril Ehrlich's words they "experienced not dole queues but genteel underemployment" (Ehrlich 1995b: 47). For piano manufacturers there was also no easy answer, but in terms of the industry as a whole the decline in instrument manufacture was compensated by the spectacular growth of reproduction technology. For music publishers there was an answer, but it would involve a fundamental transformation of the music business.

Giving music its due

In order to understand this we need to briefly consider the legal basis of the music business, in other words copyright law. The basic purpose of copyright, which originated with books but also covered music, was to protect the investment of the publisher by banning unauthorized copies, and as we saw with Beethoven the practice was for the composer to sell the work outright to the publisher. But ownership of intellectual property is not quite the same as ownership of other kinds of property. For one thing, it became standard as early as the eighteenth century for the publisher's rights to revert to the composer after a set period, rather as if the publisher had a lease on the work rather than owning it outright. And during the nineteenth century the expectation developed that the publisher would share the profits with the composer by paying royalties: this means it perhaps makes more sense to think of the composer retaining ownership but letting out specific rights in the work to the publisher, whose job becomes to manage them. Having said that, there continued to be notorious cases where composers were unwise enough to sell their works outright: one, dating from the turn of the century, was Samuel Coleridge-Taylor's sale to Novello of *Hiawatha* (Ehrlich 1989: 4), which generated huge revenues through sales to choral societies from which neither the composer nor his widow benefited. (In the second half of the century the same kind of sharp practice was widespread in the record business, with inexperienced bands being signed on terms that gave them little or no investment in their future success.)

What became the crucial extension of music copyright, however, was performing right, the principle incorporated into the Berne Convention of 1886 (but not into UK law until 1911) that buying a piece of sheet music doesn't confer the right to perform it in public. That right remains with the composer and/or publisher, depending on the contract between them, and generates a separate income stream which, for reasons that will become clear later, is administered through a dedicated collection society, such as the PRS

(Performing Right Society). This was founded three years after the 1911 Act, partly as a consequence of the Coleridge-Taylor scandal, and operates under the motto "Giving music its due." (Equivalent organizations include SACEM in France – founded as long ago as 1850 – and ASCAP and BMI in America.) But while it was a group of publishers that set up the PRS, the majority of publishers at this time had little interest in performing right: their central business was selling sheet music, and they saw performances as of value primarily as a means of generating publicity and hence sales. In fact sheet music often bore a statement "This song may be sung in public without fee or license," and the publishers would sometimes pay a popular singer to perform it, printing "as sung by …" on the cover (Ehrlich 1989: 6).

But this all changed with the collapse of the sheet-music market after 1929: one publisher saw annual sales plummet from £71,000 in 1921 to £14,000 in 1935 (Ehrlich 1989: 66). It is important to realize that this did not represent a collapse in the consumption of music: it was rather a

---

Box 16.1 Collection societies acronym buster

ASCAP	American Society of Composers, Authors and Publishers
BMI	Broadcast Music Incorporated
HFA	Harry Fox Agency
MCPS	Mechanical Copyright Protection Society
PPL	Phonographic Performance Limited
PRS	Performing Right Society
SACEM	Société des auteurs, compositeurs et éditeurs de musique

---

Box 16.2 What rights are there in music?

- copyright on the words and music lasts for seventy years after the composer's/author's/songwriter's death
- in the case of sheet music there is also copyright on the typography, which lasts twenty-five years
- in the case of recordings, there is also copyright on the recording, which lasts fifty years
- payments are triggered when
  - music is performed or broadcast live (performing right)
  - recordings are manufactured or distributed (mechanical right)
  - recordings are played in public or broadcast (performing and airplay rights).

Other royalties (e.g., on sales of sheet music) depend on the contract between artist and publisher. The copyright terms shown above are standardized across the EU, but vary in other parts of the world.

---

relocation of consumption from the reading of notes on the page to listening to music in live or, increasingly, recorded performance. The result was that performing right became more and more central to the music business, especially after a ruling in 1933 that it applied to broadcast as well as live music (Ehrlich 1989: 69). Equally important was the principle that copyright law applied to recordings, which created additional income streams: mechanical royalties, generated when a record was manufactured, public performance royalties when it was played in public, and airplay royalties when it was broadcast. (Again these are administered by dedicated societies: the first by the MCPS in the UK and HFA in the US, the others by PPL in the UK and SoundExchange in the US – the latter only since 1995, as prior to then US law did not provide for public performance or airplay royalties.) All this means that, for the publishers, the long-term answer to the catastrophe of 1929 lay in remodelling their core business from the selling of sheet music to the administration of rights.

These developments were also linked with changes in the music itself. Throughout the nineteenth and the first half of the twentieth centuries there was a wide spectrum of music from the concert hall to the music hall, from symphonic music to light music, but there was a stylistic continuum between them. All relied on essentially the same set of basic musical skills (whether in terms of instrumental or vocal performance, knowledge of harmony, or musical literacy): this created the sense that there was a common musical culture, with the teacher as the transmitter of skills at its heart, and encouraged a degree of professional mobility among musicians. The same can be said of the early stages in the development and dissemination – first to Europe, ultimately across the globe – of American popular culture: of the popular-song style associated with Tin Pan Alley (the music publishers' district in New York), of Hollywood film scores (many of which were composed by émigrés from pre-war Europe), and of the enormously popular output of the crooners, such as Bing Crosby and Frank Sinatra, who took advantage of sound-amplification technology to create a new, more intimate vocal style. Elements of the blues and jazz, with their fundamentally different skill set, found their way into these genres of popular music, but only as translated into the dominant, "common-practice" style.

But the rhythm and blues, rock 'n' roll, and soul styles that developed rapidly in North America and Britain from the 1950s were quite different, with their much more direct relationship to the blues (and later jazz), their orientation to the guitar rather than the keyboard, and their association with a "youth generation" for whom they became an emblem of difference from adult culture (popular as well as classical). While in social terms the growing up of the rock generation relocated the popular music tradition emanating from the 1960s (Jimmy Carter was the last US President to have an interest in classical music), a basic distinction remained in place between a classical tradition oriented towards written music, and a popular tradition oriented towards live or recorded performance. Combined with the explosion of activity in the popular music sector, however that is measured, the result was that the music business developed from one centered on the dissemination of printed music to one centered on the dissemination of musical sound through recording technology.

While "music publishers became primarily concerned with the negotiation of property rights" (Ehrlich 1995b: 40), then, the role of the recording industry developed to the extent that for a long time the terms "music business" and "record company" seemed virtually interchangeable. For the latter part of the century, the industry was dominated by the "big six" multinationals: Universal, Polygram, CBS (acquired in the 1980s by Sony), RCA (acquired in the 1980s by BMG), Warner, and EMI; in rock a measure of this dominance has been the coining of the term "indie" for music associated with the smaller, independent labels, which are generally seen as contributing disproportio- nately to the development of new trends only later taken up by the majors. Since 2000 the number of majors has been reduced to five, as a result of a merger between Universal and Polygram, and then four, with the merger of Sony and BMG. (In 2000 there also was an attempt to merge Warner and EMI, which was blocked by regulators; EMI was instead taken over in 2007 by the private equity firm Terra Firma.) The activities of these firms encompass much more than the term "record company" implies: the recording process is a relatively minor element in a spectrum of activity that includes not just the manufacture, marketing, and promotion of product but also – for example – talent-spotting and artist development. (It also involves, of course, the work of the lawyers and accountants who are widely seen as the real decision-makers in the music business.) And given the extent to which the multinationals employ freelancers, it is hard to draw a clear line between their activities and those of the independent sound engineers and producers who work with them, not to mention booking agents (who arrange live concerts and tours) or band managers. Even the parallel industry of equipment manufacture (including recording and playback equipment as well as instrument manufac- ture, and increasingly integrated with the computing and media appliances markets) is structurally linked with the recording industry, as demonstrated by the conspicuous role Sony plays in both.

As in book publishing, so with recording contracts: a small number of high-profile deals, with seven-figure advances against royalties, grab the head- lines. But there are also routine mechanisms by which working musicians generate income from the global business built on musical property rights. For example, one important part of the jigsaw is registering your work with the collection societies described earlier in this chapter. Let's suppose you're a songwriter. Royalties are generated whenever your music is performed in public, whether live, broadcast, or recorded – including in shops, restaurants, or airports, which may generate a lot more income than performances in more conventionally musical environments. But there is no way you could monitor such use yourself, and that is where the collection societies come in. If you live in the UK then you or your publisher needs to register your work with the PRS/ MCPS (the two societies operate a joint registration scheme) and with the PPL; this is done electronically, and Fig 16.2 shows Robbie Williams's page from the PPL database. The collection societies all work in broadly the same way: they collect revenues from users (such as live music venues, broadcasters, or shops) and distribute them to their members. For instance, the PRS has a team of inspectors to make sure that everyone who needs a licence buys one; then, in order to work out how they should distribute the income from the licences, they analyze returns from selected venues as well as broadcasters' program listings, and audit a sample of them to make sure they are accurate. Finally the income is distributed to PRS members, minus a commission. There is also a system of international agreements by which different performing right

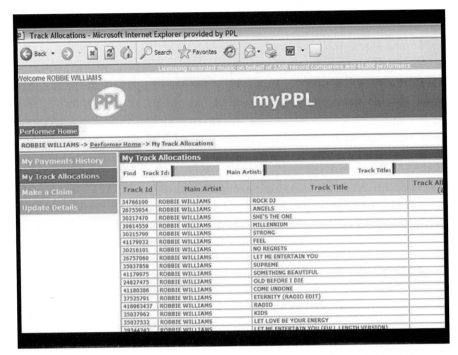

Fig 16.2 Robbie Williams's PPL page (source: PPL AGM presentation 2007, http://www.
ppluk.com/ppl/ppl_cd.nsf/agm-presentation/$file/PPL%20AGM%20Presentation%
202007.pdf)

societies in different countries cooperate, so that collection takes place on an
international basis.

Classical music in the marketplace

So how does all this fit with the economic models I described earlier?
In general the recording industry fits the same mold as the publication
of printed music, only more so: again there are high fixed costs and low
marginal costs, and a pattern by which a few highly profitable ventures
compensate for a large number of unprofitable ones. The most significant
difference between the music publication and recording industries is probably one of scale, for the "Gutenberg effect" – the creation of a whole new
market as a result of drastic reductions in marginal costs, as with the invention of movable type – really only reached music with recording technology;
up to then the potential market was always constrained by the specialized
skills, and the leisure to acquire them, that the consumption of printed music
entailed.

It is important, however, to understand how cultural industries like the music business differ from classical economic models based on commodities, in which price is a function of supply on the one hand and demand on the other. The price of oil is rising as I write because global demand is increasing (particularly in China) while supply is relatively fixed: the market is nervous about political instability in the Middle East, which could drastically reduce supply and send prices rocketing. If the same logic applied to the music business, you might expect CDs of Beethoven to sell at higher prices than CDs of Boccherini (for which there is much less demand), but of course, that is not the case. The basic reason for this is that supply is elastic: if a particular CD sells out, then more can be produced at minimal cost. Rather than raising the price, then, the most effective way of maximizing revenue is to increase demand. So it makes sense to see the core activity of the recording industry as the creation of demand, which it achieves primarily through various kinds of planned obsolescence.

One of these is the charts. High-profile shows like the BBC's *Top of the Pops* were originally based on sales of 45 rpm singles, but nowadays listings are maintained (by the Official UK Charts Company) for a large number of differ- ent market segments. These reflect consumption, being based on sales through mainstream retailers (which means that they underestimate music that depends on other outlets, such as Asian music sold through corner shops), but more importantly they also generate consumption through contributing to an accelerated cycle of obsolescence in a highly fashion-conscious market.

Another and more obvious form of planned obsolescence is the succession of recording and playback technologies whose improving standards of reproduc- tion during the course of the twentieth century led consumers to repeatedly replace and expand their collections: since the 1920s, when mechanically recorded 78s gave way to the technically superior electric 78s and so created the first mass market for records, there have been LPs, stereo LPs, tape casset- tes, and CDs, in addition to other technologies that never generated a mass market for delivery of recorded music (such as quadrophonic records or mini- disks). As Box 16.3 shows, new technologies offering better sound have gen- erally succeeded one another quite regularly – until the introduction, well over twenty years ago, of the CD. This is important. The CD combines sound quality good enough to satisfy anybody who is prepared to be satisfied, on the one hand, with near-indestructibility (at least as compared to its vulnerable shellac and vinyl predecessors) on the other, which means that this particular cycle of planned obsolescence seems to have come to an end. To be sure, since 2000 a whole new market has developed for mp3 downloads and players, such as the Apple iPod (and more recently iPhone), but they do not offer better sound quality than CDs, indeed quite the reverse: consumers are not replacing their CDs with downloads, in the ways they replaced their vinyls with CDs. This is one of the reasons for the malaise that is currently affecting the recording industry.

Box 16.3 Main media for the delivery of recorded music	
From	
1900s	78 rpm shellac disks (acoustic)
1920s	78 rpm shellac disks (electrical)
c.1950	45 rpm vinyl disks (EPs), 33 rpm vinyl disks (LPs)
1958	stereo LPs
1960s	also cassette tapes
1980s	compact disks
2000s	also mp3 downloads

I shall come back to this malaise at the end of the chapter, but first I want to emphasize the perhaps obvious point that the music business and music as a social practice are by no means the same thing, because it is not just professionals who create music. There is a widespread conservative critique of contemporary musical culture, which is that the once participatory tradition of music-making based on the piano has been replaced by the passive couch-potato culture of recorded music and television. But anybody who is or can remember being a teenager knows different: participatory musical culture has developed to an unprecedented level in contemporary Britain, only most of the music in question is rock and pop rather than classical. People involved in this local, amateur, or semi-professional music-making buy instruments, mp3s, and concert tickets, but they are not employed as musicians and consequently they are not part of the wage economy. Incidentally, this might be considered the contemporary version of the chronic over-supply of musicians that I previously referred to, now taking the relatively benign form of bands whose members aspire to giving up their day jobs, but never do.

It might also be said that classical music has increasingly little to do with the music business, especially as represented by the "big four" (this is an area of the market in which smaller labels play a particularly significant role). In part this is because of the general position of classical music in contemporary society, which is a rather paradoxical one. Classical music remains a high-status culture, but one whose proportion of the overall market has diminished both in Europe (though less so in parts of Continental Europe than in Britain) and, more dramatically, in North America, where high-quality recordings of individual works generally sell between three hundred and two thousand copies (Botstein 2004: 58); curiously, at the beginning of the twenty-first century the music of the European "art" tradition seems most deeply embedded not in Europe or America, but in Asia (particularly Israel, Taiwan, Korea, and Japan). In some critical circles a sense of crisis or failure has become pervasive. Lawrence Kramer (1995: 3–4) describes audiences for classical music as "shrinking, graying, and overly pale-faced," and the figures bear at least some of this out: in the United States "the median age of listeners to classical radio has persistently remained in the range of 52–60" (Botstein 2004: 41), from which its incipient demise is frequently predicted – though of course, if the median age remains the same, that might simply mean that people acquire a taste for such music, or find the time to listen to it, in middle age.

Yet in many ways the story of classical music over the past half century, at least in the UK, has been one of outstanding success. London became a major center of recording after World War II (Walter Legge's Philharmonia Orchestra was set up in 1945 specifically to make recordings, as a rival to the major Continental orchestras); recording both necessitated and, through the income it generated, made possible rehearsal schedules that would previously have been quite unaffordable. At the same time the combination of recordings and the BBC spread expectations of high performance standards, and the result was a virtuous circle linking demand and supply. All sectors of music education were reformed, and it was perhaps because of this that large numbers of British performers began to forge international careers in a way that had never happened before.

Towards the end of the century there were major changes in the dissemination of classical music, too. The critically reviled Classic FM, a commercial radio station oriented towards easy-listening classics and generally excerpting individual movements, opened up a new audience in the 1990s, taking listeners not so much from Radio 3, the BBC's classical-music station, but rather from its light-music and talk channels. New markets were also created through the adoption of pop-based methods of promotion and image management; as an example, the top-selling artist in the 2003 BPI (British Phonographic Institute) sales chart, with an astonishing 10.6% of the total classical market, was the sixteen-year-old New Zealand soprano Hayley Westenra, whose album *Pure* took less than three months to go double platinum. And the following year, English National Opera staged an hour-long extract from the third act of Wagner's *Die Walküre* to an audience of fifty thousand at the Glastonbury Festival. Though I can't produce the figures to prove it, there can be little doubt that total audiences for classical music – whether in the concert hall or at home – are higher today than ever before. Why then the persistent sense of crisis and failure?

There is not just one reason for this. For some people, the domination of the sales charts by figures like Westenra represents a sell-out of classical values to popular culture. (But then there is Scottish violinist Nicola Benedetti, born in the same year as Westenra, who signed a million-pound contract with Deutsche Grammophon in 2004; she may look like a pop star, but she plays core repertory by Mozart, Mendelssohn, and Macmillan.) There is also the dominance of repertory now one or two centuries old at the expense of contemporary compositions – though to put this in perspective, in rock and pop too it is increasingly the backlists, not the new acts, that create the lion's share of recording-industry profits (more about this shortly). In fact classical music, again mainly because of the backlists, is itself a profitable sector of the recording industry, though the scale is relatively small and the profits may be on the back of less well-known musicians who have to subsidize their own recordings. Its success is therefore that of a niche market – and maybe that is a kind of failure, by comparison with the long-gone days when "music" meant classical music.

Another reason lies in changing patterns of musical consumption. In the interwar period – the heyday of the music-appreciation movement – there was widespread belief that radio and the gramophone would reinforce the culture of concert attendance by increasing audiences for classical music. To some extent that happened; as a result of government subsidy in Europe and tax regimes in the US, there was a significant expansion in the number of orchestras in the post-war period, and the pessimism of commentators like Kramer needs to be set into this context of audience expansion. Conservatories, too, expanded during this period. Yet the great change, boosted in the last decades of the century with the establishment of Classic FM and other commercially oriented classical radio, was the development of a quite new audience for recorded music, not only in Europe and America but across the world, and hence a change in the balance between listening in the concert hall and listening at home (or, in the case of personal and in-car stereo, on the move). The net result is that at the beginning of the twenty-first century the chronic problems of the music profession still remain: too many orchestras chasing too few listeners, and the production of more instrumentalists and singers than there are jobs.

In some ways the most vulnerable element within the classical-music economy is the concert. In a classic study of the economics of the performing arts, William J. Baumol and William G. Bowen (1966) drew a distinction between two types of industrial production. On the one hand there is the kind of industrial production applicable to sheet music and recordings (and also to washing machines, televisions, and computers), where innovation, competition, and the rationalization of production have resulted in long-term falls in prices. On the other hand there is craft production, which is related directly to the costs of human and material resources, and therefore not susceptible to the same kind of efficiency gains. And a conspicuous example of the second type is the performing arts, which as a result have become steadily more expensive relative to the prices of other everyday goods, including recorded music: as Botstein (2004: 57) says, "Even for those interested in classical music, going to concerts and keeping orchestras and opera companies alive can seem an irrational extravagance when one can buy a single recording of a Sibelius symphony and conclude that no further recording or live performance is required."

This doesn't apply to pop concerts, where powerful amplification makes it possible to play to huge audiences, and by the beginning of the twenty-first century live performance had become a highly profitable sector of the pop economy. (The biggest profits, however, come from the management of rights, that is publishing.) And while acoustic music, as played in concert halls, does not allow the same economies of scale as pop concerts, there is another way of escaping Baumol and Bowen's problem: when classical concerts are given by amateurs, motivated by the sheer pleasure of playing, as in the still substantial British traditions of youth orchestras or amateur choruses. It is, then, only when applied to the professional classical concert, and also to professional opera, that Baumol and Bowen's analysis is really compelling. But of course, these are key elements of classical musical culture as it has developed since the early nineteenth century.

The moral may be that free-market models cannot be straightforwardly applied to the arts, as politicians have attempted since the days of Reagan and Thatcher. Even in the heady days around 1900, when classical music was the basis of genuinely profitable industries such as sheet-music publication and piano manufacture, it depended on continuing levels of public or private philanthropy (Botstein 2004: 60); as we have seen, this is a pattern that goes back to (and beyond) the days of Beethoven. Viewed this way, the explicit subsidizing of classical music by quasi-governmental organizations like Arts Council England, and the less obvious but actually more substantial subsidy that comes from the BBC, represent the continuation of a long tradition. And that is before you factor in the effects of industrial development charted by Baumol and Bowen. In short, the sense of classical music's failure may derive from expectations that were never reasonable in the first place (Botstein 2004: 66).

The music business between past and future

What then of the future? All business goes in cycles; just as the musical bull market of the 1920s crashed in 1929, so the long run of post-war prosperity culminated in the 1980s before running out of steam in the 1990s. The CD had encouraged thirty-something and older consumers in all segments of the market to renew their collections on an unprecedented scale; this is when record companies discovered the value of their backlists, particularly as regards what now became known as "classic" rock. But this process was in the nature of things a finite one, and as sales tailed off in 1990s, so a newly defensive, even embattled mood settled on the industry.

CD saturation may have been the underlying problem, but industry malaise took the form of recurrent neuroses concerning copying technologies. Just as the industry had once campaigned for levies on cassette recorders or blank cassettes, so it now attempted to restrict certain products to certain markets (as in the farce of allowing the import of only "professional" DAT recorders), invested in technologies for copy protection (regardless of the convenience of users who found their CDs would not play on their computers), and took out lawsuits against digital sampling and internet download sites, such as the peer-to-peer (i.e., file-sharing) site Napster. The story is not creditable to the music industry, which failed to keep abreast of technological developments, and as a result found itself outflanked by the illegal download sites in much the same way that the BBC had found itself outflanked by the offshore radio stations of the 1960s, or before that, the sheet-music publishers had found themselves outflanked by the rise of recording technology. In particular the industry failed to grasp the opportunities new technology was creating; it is hard to disagree with the widely disseminated opinion of Guy Hands, the chief executive of EMI's new owners Terra Firma, that it "stuck its head in the sand." Instead of exploiting the new opportunities afforded by the internet, the major record companies resorted to litigation in order to maintain the status quo, and at the time of writing they had filed more than twenty-six thousand lawsuits against downloaders in US courts. It would be reasonable to suspect any industry that sues vast numbers of its own customers of working to the wrong business model. And in the UK, the same might be said of the vigorous (and, in its conflation of copyright in works and in recordings, misleading) campaign spearheaded by the BPI during 2006–7 to extend the fifty-year copyright term on recordings: prompted by the prospect of losing control over much of their backlists in the next few years – *Please Please Me* will be fifty years old in 2013 – the majors pressed to secure further payback over the coming decades on expenditure they had made back in the 1960s, claiming in defiance of logic that this would stimulate investment in new acts, and disregarding the evidence that long copyright terms (such as have existed in the US since 1998) have the effect of making the vast majority of the recorded heritage inaccessible to the public (Brooks 2005). At the time of writing the battleground has shifted to the EU Commission, but regardless of the outcome there is a widely held view that the music industry is fighting yesterday's battles, not tomorrow's.

Some postmodernist musicians and commentators have celebrated the advent of downloading and sampling technologies as instruments of freedom: in the early 1990s, Thomas Porcello spoke of rap samplers "directly challenging … legal definitions of intellectual property, at times aiming polemically to explode the concentrations of power and ownership in the industry" (1991: 70). And there are indications that, at that time, the more progressive elements of the industry were looking to a future in which copyright enforcement would largely break down and consumers would be swamped by the mass of available material: in such a situation, the most valuable service would be helping consumers find what they wanted, and accordingly substantial funds were invested in researching ways of delivering music customized to individual consumers' tastes. (A favorite metaphor is the creation of a personalized radio station, playing just the music you want to hear.)

How large a market this may open up is not clear at the time of writing. But in any case, it is not obvious that copyright is going to break down as completely as Porcello or the music-industry pessimists anticipated: intellectual property rights have shown considerable resilience in a rapidly changing market. Napster lost a high-profile case in the US courts and was forced into bankruptcy, being relaunched as a legal subscription site in 2003. Mobile mp3 players, which the US record companies had tried to have banned in 1998, opened up a new market, with Apple's iPod achieving world sales of a million in 2004 (when an iPod dock became available as a factory option in the BMW 3 Series and Z4 Roadster); by the time Apple's iTunes download library launched in the UK, in June 2004, the PRS had negotiated a licensing agreement with Apple and the BPI had announced an Official Download Chart. In February 2006 a Michigan teenager made the billionth iTunes download, while in April 2007 Apple announced that it had sold one hundred million iPods worldwide. Illegal downloading may still be widespread, but the music business has in this way harnessed new technology to the established structures of ownership with some success, though at the cost of bringing a new player – Apple – into the market. Yet the situation is far from clear. Its ambivalence is best illustrated by the Arctic Monkeys, who shot to fame after their recordings were distributed for free on MySpace in 2005, and whose subsequent concerts were sell-outs: this was widely interpreted as the death-knell of the old system. It is worth remembering, however, that later that year they signed to the independent Domino label, while a month later Rupert Murdoch bought MySpace for $580m.

The music business in the twenty-first century, then, presents a strange mixture of the old and the new. On the one hand, it continues to pursue its traditional aim of creating demand through planned obsolescence. A new audio format introduced in 2000, SACD (Super Audio CD), was merchandized on the back of home cinema technology, and offered two enormous advantages for the industry: incompatibility with existing CD players (except in the case of so called hybrid disks), and unprecedented levels of copy protection. Perhaps it is for these very reasons that it has so far failed to achieve significant market penetration, and in 2007 the first signs emerged of an industry reaction against over-zealous copy protection. On the other hand, quite unforeseen markets continue to emerge: back in 2001, when the first ringtone was sold in Finland, who would have predicted that within two years the UK ringtones market would be worth £70m, more than the market for CD singles (£63m)? Needless to say, the MEF (Mobile Entertainment Forum) promptly announced the UK Ringtones Top Twenty Chart.

But perhaps the most telling sign for the future came at the very start of the century: the merger in 2000 of Time Warner, the Warner parent company, with the internet services provider AOL (America Online), creating

> **Box 16.4 Where are music sales going?**
>
> Here is a selection of news stories from the first few days of October 2007:
>
> 1 October: the Britpop band The Charlatans announce that they will place their new single on the Xfm radio website for free downloading, hoping to boost ticket sales for their concerts.
> 2 October: after over 1m people register to buy tickets on-line, the Spice Girls' London reunion concert sells out in thirty-eight seconds.
> 3 October: Radiohead's website crashes after the band announce that fans can download their new single for whatever price they want to pay.
> 4 October: the Recording Industry Association of America wins its case against a thirty-year-old Minnesota woman, who is ordered to pay $222,000 for illegally downloading 24 songs ($9,250 per song).

what brands itself "the world's first fully integrated communications and media company." Although there was a partial spinoff of the record division in 2004, the pattern was set: in 2006 (the year after Rupert Murdoch acquired MySpace), Universal became a wholly owned subsidiary of the French conglomerate Vivendi SA, whose activities encompass interactive games, television, film, and telecommunications as well as music. All this can be interpreted as part of a larger historical process. I have explained how publishers, who in Beethoven's day were simply printers and disseminators of sheet music, turned themselves into managers of property rights. In a rather similar way, record companies, whose main business was at one time the production of shellac, vinyl, or laser disks, have become part of a global media business increasingly oriented towards the selling of information; it is entirely in line with these larger trends that in the case of download libraries, which look set to become the foundation of the music business for years to come, there is no physical product. But the point is a broader one. In the musical economy of the twenty-first century, the prime importance of the recording may not be in terms of direct sales, but as a tool for marketing the intellectual property that is music, and so opening up the revenue streams that really matter, such as live performance, soundtrack licensing, and secondary merchandizing.

It wouldn't be quite fair to say that the "music" has gone out of the music business, but there has certainly been a blurring of margins: the fact that the main competition to the music download market comes from computer games and other internet-based services shows how far music has become part of the world of communications and media in general. What is beyond doubt, however, is that the "business" side is still firmly in place, and looks set to remain so for the foreseeable future. But then, just how far the future is foreseeable is anyone's guess.

Chapter summary

This chapter has shown that
- music has always been shaped by economic circumstances, as illustrated by the example of Beethoven.
- classical music has always depended on patronage, whether by individuals or the state.
- music employment goes in cycles, but generally suffers from overprovision.
- music publishers developed from the sale of commodities to the management of property rights.
- record companies have increasingly become part of the global media business, but are struggling to adapt to the digital revolution.

Discussion topics

1. Classical music has always been subsidized, but is that an argument for it being subsidized in the future?
2. Does today's music industry give its customers what they want, and if not, why not?
3. Is it possible to imagine a musical culture without copyright?

Further reading

Books

Blake, Andrew (1992), *The Music Business* (London: Batsford).
    Balanced and approachable introduction by a cultural theorist, though now showing its age.

Botstein, Leon (2004), "Music of a century: museum culture and the politics of subsidy," in Nicholas Cook and Anthony Pople (eds.), *The Cambridge History of Twentieth-Century Music* (Cambridge: Cambridge University Press), 40–68.
    Wide-ranging if pessimistic survey of twentieth-century "art" music in its economic context.

Burnett, Robert (1996), *The Global Jukebox: The International Music Industry* (London: Routledge).
    Remarkably prescient overview of the global music business and technology.

Ehrlich, Cyril (1995b), "The marketplace," in Stephen Banfield (ed.), *The Blackwell History of Music in Britain: The Twentieth Century* (Oxford: Blackwell), 39–53.
    Concise social and economic history of British music-making in the twentieth century.

Eliot, Marc (1993), *Rockonomics: The Money behind the Music*, rev. edn (Secaucus, NJ: Carol Publishing Corporation).
    Highly readable account of the American rock music industry.

Harrison, Ann (2003), *Music: The Business – The Essential Guide to the Law and the Deals*, 2nd edn (London: Virgin Books).
    Practical introduction to the UK industry, aimed at the working musician.

Kusek, Dave and Leonhard, Gerd (2005), *The Future of Music: Manifesto for the Digital Music Revolution* (Boston: Berklee Press).
    Depicts a possible future beyond the music business as we know it today.

Negus, Keith (1993), *Producing Pop: Culture and Conflict in the Popular Music Industry* (London: Hodder Arnold) and (1999) *Music Genres and Corporate Cultures* (London and New York: Routledge).
    Sociological studies of the inner workings of the music industry, based on interviews and case studies.

Passman, Donald (2004), *All you Need to Know about the Music Business*, 4th edn (Harmondsworth: Penguin).
    Another practical introduction for the working musician, but with a US emphasis.

Websites

Radio 1 "How to ..." guides: www.bbc.co.uk/radio1/onemusic/howto/
Approachable beginners' guides to the industry with a pop orientation.
"Collection societies: MCPS, PRS and PPL": www.bemuso.com/musicbiz/collectionsocieties.html

Informative page on collection societies, part of Rob Cumberland's "Bemuso" site
mi2n (Music Industry News Network): www.mi2n.com/
Music industry news service, including newsletters by subscription.
"The Commercial World of Music" (William and Gayle Cook Music Library, Indiana
    University): www.music.indiana.edu/music_resources/industry.html
    Comprehensive links pages

A great deal of information about the music business (including most of the
unattributed facts and figures in this chapter) may also be found in Wikipedia (http://
wikipedia.org/) or on the web pages of such organizations as record companies, the
BPI (www.bpi.co.uk/), PRS/MCPS (www.mcps-prs-alliance.co.uk/), PPL (www.ppluk.
com/), RIAA (www.riaa.com/), BMI (www.bmi.com/), ASCAP (www.ascap.com/), HFA
(www.harryfox.com/), and SoundExchange (www.soundexchange.com/), as well as
the UK and US Music Publishers Associations (www.mpaonline.org.uk/), (www.mpa.
org/). In some cases membership or payment is necessary to access the full
information available. URLs were accurate as of July 2008.

References

Anderson, Emily (ed. and transl.) (1961), *The Letters of Beethoven*, 3 vols. (London:
    Macmillan).
Baumol, William and William Bowen (1966), *Performing Arts: The Economic Dilemma*
    (New York: The Twentieth Century Fund).
Blake, Andrew (1992), *The Music Business* (London: Batsford).
Botstein, Leon (2004), "Music of a century: museum culture and the politics of
    subsidy," in Nicholas Cook and Anthony Pople (eds.), *The Cambridge History of
    Twentieth-Century Music* (Cambridge: Cambridge University Press), 40–68.
Brooks, Tim (2005), *Survey of Reissues of U.S. Recordings* (Washington, DC: Council on
    Library and Information Resources and the Library of Congress) (www.clir.
    org/PUBS/reports/pub133/contents.html).
Burnett, Robert (1996), *The Global Jukebox: The International Music Industry* (London: Routledge).
Cooper, Barry (1991) (ed.), *The Beethoven Compendium: A Guide to Beethoven's Life and Music*
    (London: Thames and Hudson).
Ehrlich, Cyril (1989), *Harmonious Alliance: A History of the Performing Right Society* (Oxford:
    Oxford University Press).
Ehrlich, Cyril (1995a), *First Philharmonic: A History of the Royal Philharmonic Society*
    (Oxford: Clarendon Press).
Ehrlich, Cyril (1995b), "The marketplace," in Stephen Banfield (ed.), *The Blackwell
    History of Music in Britain: The Twentieth Century* (Oxford: Blackwell), 39–53.
Eliot, Marc (1993), *Rockonomics: The Money behind the Music*, rev. edn (Secaucus, NJ: Carol
    Publishing Corporation).
Harrison, Ann (2003), *Music: The Business – The Essential Guide to the Law and the Deals*, 2nd
    edn (London: Virgin Books).

Kramer, Lawrence (1995), *Classical Music and Postmodern Knowledge* (Berkeley: University of California Press).

Kusek, Dave and Leonhard, Gerd (2005), *The Future of Music: Manifesto for the Digital Music Revolution* (Boston: Berklee Press).

Negus, Keith (1993), *Producing Pop: Culture and Conflict in the Popular Music Industry* (London: Hodder Arnold).

Negus, Keith (1999), *Music Genres and Corporate Cultures* (London: Routledge).

Passman, Donald (2004), *All you Need to Know about the Music Business*, 4th edn (Harmondsworth: Penguin).

Porcello, Thomas (1991), "The ethics of digital audio-sampling: engineers" Discourse," *Popular Music*, 10, 69–84.

Reith, John (1949), *Into the Wind* (London: Hodder & Stoughton).

Rolland, Romain (1919), *Beethoven* (London: Kegan Paul).

Schindler, Anton (1966), *Beethoven I Knew Him*, ed. Donald MacArdle, transl. Constance Jolly (London: Faber).

Index

absolute music 85–6
Absurd, Theater of the 145
acousmatic music 213
Adams, John 146
Adler, Guido 19, 61
Adorno, Theodor 45, 88–9, 90, 137, 190,
    194–5, 209
aesthetics *see also* absolute music; work,
    concept of; autonomy, musical;
    formalism
  and judgment 83–5
  and social practice 82, 88, 89
Africa, music of 100, 107, 114,
    226, 231
analog 255, 256, 266
analysis *see also* performance, and analysis
  acoustic 38–9
  and composers' theories 28
  and interpretation 36
  and popular music 196
  and psychology 30
  and the compositional process 27–8,
    237, 242
  and the listener 29–31, 37
  of jazz 181
  post-tonal 33–6
  Schenkerian 29, 33, 37
  semiotic 30, 32, 41
    in film-music studies 210
    in opera studies 148–9
  style 36
Andes, music of the 105, 107, 109,
    112–13, 115
appropriation 47, 58 *see also* authenticity;
    bebop
Arabic music 102
Ars Nova 10, 24
"art" music 26, 195, 214, 246, 280–3 *see also*
    India, music of
  and jazz 178
  and popular music 188–9

atonality *see* tonality, in modern music;
    serialism
Auden, W. H. 147
audio, digital 256
audio-vision *see* Chion, Michel
authenticity 108–9, 184
autonomy, musical 87 *see also* work,
    concept of

Babbitt, Milton 247
Bach, C. P. E. 26
Balkans 20
ballade *see formes fixes*
ballet music 168
Baumgarten, Alexander 83
BBC (British Broadcasting Corporation)
    171, 273
bebop 177–8, 181
Becker, Howard 51
Beethoven, Ludwig van 50–1, 162, 267–71
  Piano Concerto No. 4 164
  Piano Concerto No. 5 160
  String Quartets 165
  Symphony No. 3, "Eroica" 8–9
  Symphony No. 6, "Pastoral" 162
  Symphony No. 9 89, 162, 267, 270–2
  Violin Concerto 155
Berg, Alban 144
Berlioz, Hector 163, 272
Birtwistle, Harrison 145
Blade Runner 201–3
Blume, Friedrich 17
Boulez, Pierre 137
Bourdieu, Pierre 53
Brahms, Johannes
  piano concertos 164
Brazil, music of 106, 107
Brecht, Bertolt 144
Brendel, Franz 16, 18
broadcasting 171–2, 275 *see also* BBC
  radio 50, 189